URBANIZATION IN THE WORLD-ECONOMY

STUDIES IN SOCIAL DISCONTINUITY

Under the Consulting Editorship of:

CHARLES TILLY
New School for Social Research

EDWARD SHORTER
University of Toronto

Published

Michael Timberlake (Ed.). Urbanization in the World-Economy

David Levine (Ed.). Proletarianization and Family History

Susan Walsh Sanderson. Land Reform in Mexico: 1910–1980

Manuel Gottlieb. A Theory of Economic Systems

Robert Max Jackson. The Formation of Craft Labor Markets

Michael B. Katz. Poverty and Policy in American History

Arthur L. Stinchcombe. Economic Sociology

Jill S. Quadagno. Aging in Early Industrial Society: Work, Family, and Social Policy in Nineteenth-Century England

J. Dennis Willigan and Katherine A. Lynch. Sources and Methods of Historical Demography

Dietrich Gerhard. Old Europe: A Study of Continuity, 1000–1800

Charles Tilly. As Sociology Meets History.

Maris A. Vinovskis. Fertility in Massachusetts from the Revolution to the Civil War

Juan G. Espinosa and Andrew S. Zimbalist. Economic Democracy: Workers' Participation in Chilean Industry 1970–1973: Updated Student Edition

Alejandro Portes and John Walton. Labor, Class, and the International System

James H. Mittelman. Underdevelopment and the Transition to Socialism: Mozambique and Tanzania

John R. Gillis. Youth and History: Tradition and Change in European Age Relations, 1770–Present: Expanded Student Edition

Samuel Kline Cohn, Jr. The Laboring Classes in Renaissance Florence

Richard C. Trexler. Public Life in Renaissance Florence

Paul Oquist. Violence, Conflict, and Politics in Colombia

Fred Weinstein. The Dynamics of Nazism: Leadership, Ideology, and the Holocaust

John R. Hanson II. Trade in Transition: Exports from the Third World, 1840–1900

The list of titles in this series continues at the end of this volume.

URBANIZATION IN THE WORLD-ECONOMY

Edited by

Michael Timberlake

Department of Sociology and Social Work
Memphis State University
Memphis, Tennessee

1985

ACADEMIC PRESS, INC.

(Harcourt Brace Jovanovich, Publishers)

Orlando   San Diego   New York   London
Toronto   Montreal   Sydney   Tokyo

ACADEMIC PRESS, INC.
Orlando, Florida 32887

United Kingdom Edition published by
ACADEMIC PRESS INC. (LONDON) LTD.
24–28 Oval Road, London NW1 7DX

LIBRARY OF CONGRESS CATALOGING IN PUBLICATION DATA

Main entry under title:

Urbanization in the world-economy.

(Studies in social discontinuity)
Includes index.
1. Urbanization—Addresses, essays, lectures.
2. Urban economics—Addresses, essays, lectures.
3. International economic relations—Addresses, essays,
lectures.   I. Timberlake, Michael.   II. Series.
HT321.U34   1985   307.7'6   84-12511
ISBN 0-12-691290-4 (alk. paper)

PRINTED IN THE UNITED STATES OF AMERICA

85 86 87 88   9 8 7 6 5 4 3 2 1

CONTENTS

3

Logic, Space, and Time: The Boundaries of the Capitalist World-Economy
JOAN SOKOLOVSKY

4

The Informal Sector and the World-Economy: Notes on the Structure of Subsidized Labor
ALEJANDRO PORTES

5

Systems of Cities and Urban Primacy: Problems of Definition and Measurement
PAMELA BARNHOUSE WALTERS

6

Theories and Measures of Urban Primacy: A Critique
CAROL A. SMITH

PART III   Regional Implications

7

Class Relations and Urbanization in Guatemala: Toward an Alternative Theory of Urban Primacy

CAROL A. SMITH

8

Urban Primacy and Incorporation into the World-Economy: The Case of Australia, 1850–1900

ROGER CLARK

9

The Political Economy of Contrasting Urban Hierarchies in South Korea and the Philippines

ROGER J. NEMETH and DAVID A. SMITH

CONTRIBUTORS

Numbers in parentheses indicate the pages on which the authors' contributions begin.

CHRISTOPHER K. CHASE-DUNN (269), Department of Sociology, The Johns Hopkins University, Baltimore, Maryland 21218

ROGER CLARK (169), Department of Sociology, Rhode Island College, Providence, Rhode Island 02908

GLENN FIREBAUGH (293), Department of Sociology, Vanderbilt University, Nashville, Tennessee 37235

JEFFREY KENTOR (25), Department of Sociology, The Johns Hopkins University, Baltimore, Maryland 21218

BRUCE LONDON (207), Department of Sociology and Social Psychology, Florida Atlantic University, Boca Raton, Florida 33431

JAMES LUNDAY (325), Department of Sociology, The Johns Hopkins University, Baltimore, Maryland 21218

ROGER J. NEMETH (183), Department of Sociology, Hope College, Holland, Michigan 49423

ALEJANDRO PORTES (53), Department of Sociology, The Johns Hopkins University, Baltimore, Maryland 21218

SASKIA SASSEN-KOOB (231), Graduate School, City University of New York–Queens, New York, New York 11367

CAROL A. SMITH (87, 121), Department of Anthropology, Duke University, Durham, North Carolina 27706

DAVID A. SMITH (183), School of Social Sciences, University of California, Irvine, California 92717

JOAN SOKOLOVSKY (41), Department of Sociology, The Johns Hopkins University, Baltimore, Maryland 21218

MICHAEL TIMBERLAKE (3, 325), Department of Sociology and Social Work, Memphis State University, Memphis, Tennessee 38152

PAMELA BARNHOUSE WALTERS (63), Department of Sociology, Indiana University, Bloomington, Indiana 47405

KATHRYN B. WARD (305), Department of Sociology, Southern Illinois University, Carbondale, Illinois 62901

PREFACE

The processes of urbanization have long been regarded as integral to socioeconomic development. However, scholarly opinion about global urban patterns is divided, ranging from claims that the growth of urban population in a given region is an inevitable concomitant of modernization to assertions that too-rapid urban growth, especially in a region's largest city, may actually impede balanced development. Despite this diversity of opinion, observers agree that there is tremendous global unevenness in patterns of urbanization.

Our understanding of uneven development has been transformed in recent years by the emergence of the world-system perspective, which, however, has until now illuminated aspects of dependency and development other than urbanization. The purpose of this book is to use the world-system paradigm to systematically interpret processes of urbanization. The book is directed toward students of urbanization and development who may approach their subject from a variety of academic disciplines, including anthropology, political economy, geography, history, political science, and sociology.

The general contribution of the world-system approach is that it allows us to see how some urban processes at the local or regional level are shaped, in part, by global structures and processes. For example, the growth and decline of particular cities is influenced by their involvement in, and function for, this worldwide social system. The changing character of the urban labor force of particular cities is similarly influenced by global processes: Changes in the world-economy have an impact on core cities, such as New York City, and on peripheral cities, such as Manila. We also interpret differences among countries in levels and rates of urbanization, degrees of urban primacy, and characteristics of the urban labor force in terms of the structural features of the encompassing world-system. In so doing, the authors of chapters in this book do not abandon traditional concerns of scholars of urbanization. Rather, these traditional concerns are approached in a new light, one that has shone on other aspects of social change but that has not yet been cast directly on urbanization.

Because of its systematic approach to urbanization from the world-system perspective, this book is much more than a collection of loosely related essays. It addresses several conceptual and theoretical issues that are pertinent to our task and then presents several examples of concrete research on urbanization from the world-system perspective. The book contains the work of members of a network of scholars who, to varying degrees, have communicated with one another about their research as it has developed. The idea for the book was conceived at The Johns Hopkins University by participants in the research project on urbanization in the world-system, headed by Christopher Chase-Dunn in the Department of Sociology. As a postdoctoral fellow in the department, I had the good fortune to participate informally in this project. Several of the chapters in the book are contributed by people who have worked directly with this project. These include the chapters by Kentor, Sokolovsky, Walters, Chase-Dunn, and myself and Lunday. Earlier versions of several of the other chapters were presented as papers at sessions organized by Chase-Dunn at an annual meeting of the American Political Science Association (Portes, London, and Firebaugh) or organized by me at an annual meeting of the American Sociological Association (Nemeth and David A. Smith, Sassen-Koob, and Ward). Carol Smith presented work related to her chapter in a colloquium sponsored by the Department of Anthropology at Johns Hopkins. Finally, I had been in contact with Clark since our graduate school years at Brown University, where our interests in urbanization and development had been kindled by Sidney Goldstein, Robert Marsh, Dietrich Rueschmeyer, and Basil Zimmer, and where Peter Evans sparked our concern with the world-system and dependency approaches to development.

Although this is an edited collection, it has not been an easy project. I have benefited from the help of many people along the way, none of whom, of course, are responsible for any of the book's shortcomings. Participants in Chase-Dunn's project were very helpful in the early stages. In addition to those who contributed chapters, I appreciate the support, criticism, and inspiration of Patricia Arregui, Doris Cadigan, Carin Celebuski, and Vicki Walker. I thank Charles Tilly, editor of this series, for recognizing the book's promise and helping to make it better than it otherwise would have been.

For their help in typing parts of the manuscript and for other efforts related to the manuscript's eventual publication, I am grateful to Pam Skalski and Shirley Sult in Baltimore and to Janice Barnes and Elise Flowers in Memphis. Much of my time in preparing the book was supported by a 1980–1982 postdoctoral traineeship in the Department of Sociology at Johns Hopkins from the National Institute of Mental Health (Grant #5 T32 MH14587-06), and I am thankful for the support of Edward McDill and

James Fennessey, who were primarily responsible for this training grant. For her remarkable ability to creatively administer grants so as to obtain more supplies, pages of photocopying, minutes of long-distance phone calls, and miles of professional travel per grant dollar than "possible," I thank Binnie Bailey. Of course, I am very grateful to Chris Chase-Dunn for welcoming and encouraging my participation in his urbanization research project, and we both appreciated the project's support by the National Science Foundation (Grant #SES 7825071). Finally, for their support and patience, I thank my wife Andrea and sons Matthew and Benjamin. At last there is evidence that I really was working on a book and not sneaking off to the Cross Street Market for another soft-shell crab sandwich and National Premium Lager.

PART I

INTRODUCTION

1

THE WORLD-SYSTEM PERSPECTIVE AND URBANIZATION

Michael Timberlake

INTRODUCTION

Urbanization processes have typically been studied by social scientists as if they were isolated in time and explicable only in terms of other processes and structures of rather narrow scope, limited to the boundaries of such areas as nations or regions within nations. However, within the past 15 years, the study of large-scale social change has been transformed by the emergence of the world-system theoretical perspective. World-system scholars have adumbrated properties of the modern world-economy that allow us to view it as a coherent whole. Much of the research pursued from the point of view of this perspecitve has been historical, and it has dealt with either the system as a whole or how local social formations (e.g., class relations, social movements, states) are transformed as regions of the world are first incorporated into the structure of the sytem, and then become subject to processes that reproduce it (cf. collections edited by Bergesen, 1980; Goldfrank, 1979; Rubinson, 1981). The claim is not that world-system processes determine everything. Rather, the fundamental lesson is that social scientists can no longer study macrolevel social change without taking into account world-system processes. Specifically, processes such as urbanization can be more fully understood by beginning to examine the many ways in which they articulate with the broader currents of the world-economy that penetrate spatial barriers, transcend limited time boundaries, and influence social relations at many different levels.

Urbanization has been one of the most frequently studied features of the modern world. Since the dramatic growth and spread of urban agglomerations beginning in the nineteenth century, scholars have concerned themselves with documenting, for different countries and regions of the world,

URBANIZATION IN THE WORLD-ECONOMY   3

such aspects of urbanization as the size and growth of the largest cities, the relative size of urban populations, and changes in urban hierarchies (e.g., Weber, 1967; Davis, 1972; Berry, 1973; Goldstein and Sly, 1977). These phenomena have then been related to other developmental processes, such as level of economic development and differentiation (e.g., Davis and Golden, 1954; Gibbs and Martin, 1962; Hill, 1974) or political change (e.g., Pye, 1969). With few exceptions, there have not yet been attempts to interpret patterns of urbanization in light of a world-system perspective. The aim of this book is systematically to apply elements of this broad perspective to certain macrolevel dimensions of the urbanization process. We attempt to specify theoretically and examine empirically some of the ways in which urbanization patterns articulate with the morphology and dynamics of the world-economy.

THE STUDY OF URBANIZATION

Within North American social science the process of urbanization has conventionally been viewed as an evolutionary outcome of, first, the elaboration of trade relations among relatively isolated localities, and then of industrial development within regions or nations. As in other fields of sociological interpretation, the organic analogy and functionalism have been brought to bear on interpretations of the process of urbanization. The conventional understanding of the growth of ancient cities, for example, stresses as fundamental such general processes as growing specialization and the evolutionary nature of technological change that induces specialization and, thus, promotes some degree of urban concentration. The importance of trade, especially long-distance trade, in giving rise to towns and diffusing technology is emphasized. Such approaches are particularly useful in identifying limitations on urban growth (e.g., limitations placed on the food supply by the level of technical development in agriculture). This general approach has been applied intensively to analyzing the connection between urbanization and industrialization.

Written at the turn of the century, Weber's (1967) seminal statistical study of nineteenth-century urbanization employed an explicitly Spencerian interpretation of city growth. The growing concentration of the population in cities is viewed as a "natural" outcome of economic growth and differentiation (Weber, 1967:154–229), having to do with factors such as the application of machine power for agricultural production (in the United States) and the attendant job-displacing effects that "encourage" migration to cities, as displaced farm workers seek employment. Market forces (even those of the world market) are taken into account, but more or less as natural forces would be:

economic development, or the integration of isolated social and economic groups, demands the concentration of a portion of the population in commercial cities. Similarly . . . the enlargement of the market, which is one aspect of the process of growth of industrial society from the village economy to the world economy, has brought about centralization in the manufacturing industries and enforced the concentration of another portion of the population in industrial or . . . commercial cities. (Weber, 1967:185)

Cities are the reflections in space of the division of labor brought about by industrialization.

The approach taken by Weber turned out to be far from barren. His study itself is highly useful in documenting the rise and spread of urban agglomerations around the world in the nineteenth century. Research on urbanization spawned by both early and more recent "Chicago School" sociologists and human ecologists has also used an evolutionary–organic framework and has yielded a wealth of descriptive and theoretical material on the spread of urbanization over time and space (e.g., Davis, 1972; Hauser and Schnore, 1965; Hawley, 1981), the relationship between urbanization and other aspects of the industrial division of labor (Hawley, 1981; Gibbs and Martin, 1962), urbanization and regional development (McKenzie, 1933), and regional development and the elaboration of city systems (McKenzie, 1929; Bogue, 1949; and Duncan *et al.,* 1960).

From this general perspective urbanization, or expansion of the local community, and integrated regional development result from ecological processes.[1] Regionally, urban growth is seen as a process of centripetal movement, but from the point of view of each urban center growth is viewed as centrifugal expansion. Cities expand by growth away from centers. It is

---

[1]Human ecologists define their task as one of studying the human population as a system with emergent properties. The "ecological complex" is composed of the four main referential concepts of human ecology: population, organization, environment, and technology (Duncan and Schnore, 1959). Furthermore, the unit parts studied are "patterns of activity" that, when ordered as a system, emerge as "organizations of activities" (Duncan and Schnore, 1959:136). Human ecology is macrosociological, avoiding the reductionism inherent in social psychology and "psychological sociology" (Schnore, 1961). Hawley describes the field as the "study of territorially based systems, of which the urban community is a prime example" (1981:9). Human populations "develop" by organizing in response to environmental changes. *Environment* is used in its broadest sense, and includes other organizations. *Organization* is also used very broadly; "it refers to the entire system of interdependencies among the members of a population which enables the latter to sustain itself as a unit. The parts of such a system— families, clubs, shops, industries, for example—cannot be self sustaining; they can only survive in a network of supporting relationships" (Hawley, 1981:9). Processes that human ecologists have studied include the changes communities undergo as interdependencies are elaborated; "the ways in which the developing community is affected by the size, composition, and rate of growth or decline of the population"; the significance of migration to community change and stability; and changes in the nature and structure of the functions performed in communities (Hawley, 1944:404–405).

the patterns of outward movement that are described by human ecologists such as Hurd (1903), Burgess (1925), and Hoyt (1939). The central motivating factors behind centrifugal expansion posited by scholars such as these are reviewed by Hawley (1981). They include (1) sheer population pressure; (2) increasing specialization of, and competition among, functions at the center, driving out less dominant functions; (3) obsolescence of physical structures; and (4) the revolution of short-distance transportation.

McKenzie (1929) focused on urbanization at the regional level early in this century, and his work has influenced later interpretations of the urbanization process. Changes in medium- and long-distance transportation technology and territorial specialization are posited as the motors behind integration across urban centers within regions. Dominant centers emerge, toward which the activities of other urban centers in a region become directed. Hence, systems of towns and cities emerge. Other ecologists developed classifications of cities in terms of the degree of dominance-subdominance within a region (e.g., Bogue, 1949). The human ecologists had been influenced, of course, by the work of geographers such as Christaller (1966), Lösch (1954), and Gras (1922). Recent advances in the ecological approach to urbanization and regional development have been made primarily by urban geographers (cf. Berry and Horton, 1970; Berry 1971, 1973; Bourne and Simmons, 1978; Friedman and Alonso, 1964).

Against this approach stand Marxian interpretations of urbanization. Writers in this tradition have taken less for granted about the nature of urbanization—at least they have not taken the same things for granted. More attention is paid to the fundamental ways in which urbanization processes are embedded in specific historical modes of production. One can overemphasize differences between the evolutionary ecological approach to urbanization and a Marxist approach.[2] Perhaps differences are due to divergent emphases. For example, both acknowledge the importance of many of the same factors—long-distance trade, military and naval power, and slavery—in explaining the development of the ancient cities. However, a Marxian analysis of the rise of the cities in both classical Greece and the Roman Empire stresses the requirements of the slave mode of production. For example, Anderson (1974b:35–39) regards the "introduction on a massive scale of chattel slavery" as the "decisive innovation" of this era.[3]

Hopkins (1978) stresses the importance of military conquest by the empire in his discussion of Roman urbanization: "Conquest materially . . . fed this growth of towns by stimulating migration from the countryside,

---

[2]See Hawley's (1984) article on the relation of human ecology theory to Marxian theory.

[3]Anderson, with typical irony, points out that this "generalized and captive surplus labour was necessary, to emancipate their ruling stratum for the construction of a new civic and intellectual world" (1974b:35).

and by providing a replacement agricultural labor force of slaves'' (1978:61). Slaves also populated the towns and displaced free men there, thus encouraging migration and urban growth in the colonies. The slave mode of production and the social relations entailed in it are given explicit attention. Moreover, these considerations are seen as fundamental to the emergence of particular urban formations.

The reemergence of cities in medieval Europe should also be analyzed in terms of the class relations that characterized the period. Pirenne's history (1952) of the medieval cities centers attention on the importance of the revival of long-distance trade and the reemergence of a settled, free, burgher class that later expanded into a broader middle class in the towns. The later rise of the absolutist state went hand in hand with the consolidation of the power of this class (cf. Anderson, 1974a). Thus was ensured the continued ascendance of towns because the political changes that occurred involved the institutionalization of the economic relations (i.e., merchant capitalism) of which the towns were the spatial reflection.

The pattern was different in Eastern Europe because ''there was no urban bourgeoisie to inflect the character of the Absolutist State'' (Anderson, 1974a:218). Hence urban growth was stiffled. Wallerstein (1974) goes beyond this, arguing that the development of Poland and Bohemia was constrained by its peripheral position vis-à-vis Western Europe.[4] Economic relations that transcended national boundaries (i.e., relations operating at the level of the emerging capitalist world-system) helped to shape the particular urban pattern that emerged here. Wheat production for export to Western Europe flourished in the East, thus strengthening the position of the aristocratic landowners at the expense of urban interests. Hence, in comparison to the West, urbanization in Poland was retarded.

Similarly, when scholars in this tradition focus their attention on the relationship between industrialization and urbanization, there is a commitment to analyze the structural conditions that give rise to both. Dobb's analysis of the industrial revolution and its bearing on urban growth provides an illustrative contrast to the earlier quotation from Weber:

> With starvation as a relentless goad to employment and with labour unorganized, many of the factors to which comment is so often directed today as retarding mobility had no place. . . . [W]ith the coincidence of enclosures and the ruin of village handicrafts to cause extensive rural over-population, England was exceptionally well placed in the possession of that favourable condition of the urban labour market which industrial Capitalism required. (Dobb, 1963:272–274)

---

[4]More on the general world-system perspective on peripheralization appears in the chapters immediately following.

Dobb typifies Marxian approaches to the analysis of social structure in that the processes of capital accumulation and class struggle are given central importance.

More recently, Marxian scholars have specifically directed their efforts toward understanding the nature of urbanization. In this endeavor writers have often explicitly confronted some of the assumptions of conventional urban social science. Harvey (1973, 1982), Castells (1977), Pickvance (1978), and Gordon (1978) are prominent among those who, using Marxian concepts, have begun to build a compelling framework with which to analyze the social and physical structure of urban life.[5]

From this perspective urbanization cannot be understood apart from the mode of production under which it exists. It is assumed that the process of urbanization is different in important respects under capitalism than under other modes of production. Under capitalism there is a unique logic that has an important bearing on urban growth and decline. Investments in the built environment are made to facilitate profit-making through commodity production and exchange, and labor exploitation. Again, behind earlier, pre-capitalist urbanization was the logic of surplus extraction through tribute, conquest, and subsequent use of slave labor. For example, in contrast to urbanization under capitalism, towns in the Roman Empire were primarily "consumer towns" in which lived the owners of large amounts of land, supported by income from these estates. "The arena for strictly urban economic development was thus very limited. There was no urban institution which rivalled tenancy as a medium of exploitation" (Hopkins, 1978:79). Capitalist cities are, on the other hand, organized more around market trade and commodity production, and less around political redistribution and warfare. Thus it is crucial to view the nature of urbanization in terms of processes endemic to capitalism.[6]

Cities emerge, grow, become interdependent, and decline in response to the logic and contradictions of capitalism—a mode of production with identifiable space requirements. Edel argues that urban phenomena can best be interpreted in light of specific "aspects of the accumulation process" (1981:87). These include the conditions under which labor is employed in creating value and surplus value, the way in which labor is reproduced, and the way in which surplus value is circulated and reinvested. Housing problems, urban renewal, urban disinvestment, community political organiza-

[5]In this category we include many of those who have worked to develop what has become known as "the new urban sociology" (Walton, 1981). Also see Pickvance (1983) for a discussion of what is "new" about the new urban sociology.

[6]These processes are given different emphases by Marxian scholars of urbanization. Edel (1981) emphasizes accumulation but argues that competition and class struggle are the fundamental motors behind the process.

tion, and many other "urban" issues can be understood within a framework that explicitly acknowledges these factors.

Similarly, Harvey (1982:373–412) turns our attention to some of the space requirements of capitalism that produce many changes in the physical and social structure of urban areas.[7] The circulation of capital in different forms has implications for urban structure. Harvey points out that two ways in which capitalists seek to obtain competitive advantage are by adapting new technologies and making use of new locations for production and distribution facilities. Either of these efforts to gain advantage over competitors (and thereby to garner relative surplus value) by individual capitalists may have important urbanization consequences. For example, to the extent that labor is an object of capital—by necessity responsive to changes in the location of investments—shifts in the location of capital investments will be reflected in shifts in the location of population, the decline of some population centers, the increasing significance of others, the decline of particular neighborhoods within cities, and so on. Certainly urbanization has accompanied industrialization, but not because "industrialization" per se has dominated, but because urbanization "was the expression of the capitalist logic that lay at the base of industrialization" (Castells, 1977:14).

The recognition that urbanization must be analyzed as a component process of the capitalist mode of production has been elaborated by hypotheses connecting patterns of urban development in less developed countries with mechanisms that link, in various ways, the economies, social classes, polities, and other institutions of these peripheral countries with those of the more developed countries of the capitalist core. *Dependence* is a term used to describe, in a general way, these asymmetrical economic, political, and cultural relations that characterize interaction between the core and periphery (see, for example, Frank, 1966; Castells, 1977:44; Galtung, 1971). The acknowledgment by many scholars of and in the Third World that dependence is a crucial aspect of capitalist accumulation at the world level has led, in turn, to a fruitful body of research and theory linking dependence to variation in patterns of development across countries. Included is a small but growing body of work on dependence and urbanization (cf. Quijano, 1975; Castells, 1975:39–63; Portes and Walton, 1981; Kentor, 1981; Perlman, 1976). These research efforts have included quantitative cross-national studies, historical studies of countries, local institutions, social movements, social classes, and in-depth case studies of "marginal" classes in Third World cities.

---

[7]"The production of spatial configuration can then be treated as an 'active moment' within the overall temporal dynamic of accumulation and social reproduction" (Harvey, 1982, Chapter 12).

The impact of the Marxian and dependency critiques has been to move the study of Third World urbanization beyond the stage at which passing mention of the importance of taking into account the colonial history of the countries in question constituted sufficient discussion of world-economic forces. Proponents of these perspectives have argued persuasively that urbanization must be studied holistically—part of the logic of a larger process of socioeconomic development that encompasses it, and that entails systematic unevenness across regions of the world. The dependence relation is an important theoretical concept used to pry into the ways in which the processes embodied in the world-system produce various manifestations of this unevenness, including divergent patterns of urbanization (cf. Quijano, 1975:122–135; Walton, 1976; Portes, 1976:7–69).

The world-system perspective, as developed and elaborated by Wallerstein (1979) and others is discussed in a general manner in Chapters 2 and 3 (this volume), and I will avoid repeating what is presented there. I will, however, point out that this perspective is in agreement with the Marxian and dependency positions on many issues. "Developmental problems" in different world regions are, in part, outcomes of processes of the capitalist world-system and must be understood in terms of the system as a whole. However, whereas dependency theory applies mainly to the postcolonial Third World, the world-system perspective allows one to focus upon any level of the system (core, semiperiphery, or periphery) since the emergence of capitalism as the dominant mode of production in Europe in the sixteenth century. The world-system is dynamic, changing as capital adapts to contradictions and crises. Hence, it is not sufficient to identify the structure of the world-economy in any simplistic way. Yet there is an internal logic to the system that is understandable in terms of its processes, among the most important of which is the "peripheralization" of regions of the world-economy that accompanies accumulation, and the subsequent expansion of the system. Further, the perspective entails the argument that there are relatively stable, identifiable, structural expressions of these processes. Thus urbanization patterns, along with other developmental patterns, are expected to be shaped, in part, by the operation of the world-economy (e.g., Chase-Dunn, 1983b). It is this hypothesis that guides the work presented in this volume.

While the world-system perspective is tremendously indebted to both dependency theory and Marxian theories of social change, it differs from them in several important respects. It diverges from the first in focusing on the system as a whole, rather than conceiving of dependency as an internal-external relationship from the point of view of the dependent country. In contrast to more orthodox Marxian interpretations of capitalism, the world-system perspective tends not to delineate distinct stages of capitalism, which begin with the stage of competitive capitalism in the nineteenth century. Rather, Wallerstein describes the emergence of a capitalist world-economy in Europe in the "long 16th century." Its changes are then interpreted in terms of "cycles of world-system development" (Chase-Dunn, 1980–1981). It differs further from orthodox Marxian theory not because accumulation and class struggle are less central to the theory, but because regional uneveness, the importance of the interstate system, cultural diversity, and the structure of the world-economy are given central importance as well. In contrast, many Marxian scholars maintain that unequal development across regions is transitional (e.g., Szymanski, 1981). These scholars acknowledge that, due to the genesis of capitalism in northwestern Europe, a gap in the level of development emerged between the early capitalist countries and others. But the orthodox position assumes that this gap will be closed as capitalist relations of production become evenly spread over all global regions. In fact there are a growing number of discussions by Marxists of the "new international division of labor" that they see emerging in the world today. This, it is maintained, will serve to further reduce differences among countries in the extent to which capitalist relations of production have become reproduced more or less evenly (e.g., Cohen, 1981; Warren, 1980).

Wallerstein sees the articulation that is exhibited among economic, political, and cultural realms and across the hierarchical regions (e.g., core–periphery) of the world-economy as an integral aspect of the operation of the capitalist world-system. In contrast, other Marxian analysts are likely to view these features of the system as exogenous to capitalism. Harvey (1973), for example, interprets nonmarket relations, such as the influence of a large corporate conglomerate on the state (or vice versa), as a mode of integration that, while important to the capitalist mode of production, is nevertheless external to it. Differences such as these between the world-system perspective and orthodox Marxian orientations are delineated elsewhere (e.g., Chase-Dunn, 1980–1981, 1983a). No attempt is made to resolve them here. Suffice it to point out that most of the contributions in this volume work from the assumptions of the world-system perspective, and these assumptions are sufficiently different from orthodox Marxian positions that a significantly different interpretation of urbanization patterns and processes emerges.

For example, world-system scholars are much less likely to see the recent increase in informal labor sector activities in the core countries as constituting "peripheralization" of core labor. Rather, they would point out that the degree of exploitation in the core fluctuates over time (with cycles in the world-economy) but that fundamental differences persist between the conditions under which core and periphery workers are employed and reproduce. World-system theorists emphasize the apparent fact that labor in the periphery tends to be much more highly exploited than does labor in the core; wages are lower for given levels of productivity, and efforts to organize labor are subject to much more overt and harsher repression than in the core. Even if core workers do not themselves directly benefit from this arrangement, they benefit indirectly by being able to take advantage of the "postindustrial" labor force structure in the core. The occupational structure in the core provides jobs that are safer, cleaner, more interesting, and more remunerative than those in the periphery.

MACROLEVEL PATTERNS OF URBANIZATION

The urbanization topics covered in this book are limited to the analysis of levels and rates of urbanization across the world-system over time, urban primacy, systems of cities within and across countries, overurbanization, and patterns of labor force composition. Each of these macropatterns has held a central place in urbanization research, both as phenomena worthy of attention in themselves, and as important factors conditioning economic growth and other features of development.

The level of urbanization, as indicated by the proportion of the population living in urban areas, has long been understood as an important correlate of economic and social development. This simple statement has, of course, been criticized for failing to acknowledge the numerous examples in which growth within nations of the urban proportion has not been accompanied by economic growth. This criticism has led to the concept of overurbanization. Although it is a concept with several definitions, *overurbanization* seems originally to have represented the notion of urbanization without industrialization. This apparent paradoxical situation—a paradox because it has been assumed that the existence of cities is dependent upon an occupational structure with a significant proportion of industrial occupations—is thought to be both a result of economic stagnation and an obstacle to future development efforts. The concept is usually discussed as a matter of labor force distribution. Even in the absence of detailed labor force data for large numbers of countries, we are able to observe striking differences among them. The distribution of the labor force into agricultural, manufacturing, and service occupations shows tremendous variation over just the past 30 years, and equally impressive differences among different regions of the world are also evident. One of the most striking regional differences concerns variation that exists with respect to the balance of secondary, or manufacturing, employment relative to tertiary, or service, employment. In Chapters 4, 11, 14, and 15 (this volume), some of the salient features of labor force structure are described and linked to the structure of the world-economy.

Another aspect of the urbanization process emphasized in this collection is the phenomenon of urban primacy. Emerging from urban ecological theories of dominance within systems of cities and the bearing of this on regional development, primacy has been one of the most useful concepts relating macropatterns of urbanization to other aspects of socioeconomic transformation. On the one hand, some degree of hierarchical ordering of cities within a system of cities, usually in terms of population size, has been perceived as a sign of a healthy and growing socioeconomic system. On the other hand, extreme dominance by one primate city (e.g., the existence of one large city in a region or country in the absence of other large- and medium-size cities) has been cited as an important factor contributing to economic stagnation, regional inequality, and weak political integration. Several of the chapters in this book focus specifically on urban primacy. Chapter 12 (this volume), for example, shows that when changes in the size relationships among cities in the world-system as a whole are examined, shifts in patterns of economic and political dominance across regions over time are reflected.

The following two chapters (2 and 3) in this book provide an overview of the world-system perspective, and each of the remaining chapters represents an application of the general perspective to one of several aspects of the urbanization process. Urbanization topics covered are limited to examination of levels of urbanization per se across zones of the world-economy, overurbanization and urban labor force composition, and urban primacy. Before proceeding, a few preliminary comments are in order regarding the nature of a world-system perspective on urbanization.

A World-System Perspective on Urbanization

As we have seen, orthodox Marxists have indeed interpreted urban phenomena as part of the capitalist mode of production. For example, Edel (1981) has specified several "conditions of existence" of the capitalist mode of production in relation to which urban patterns should be understood. Capitalism is by its nature expansive, and reproduction of this mode of production involves accumulation. Hence urban phenomena must be related to aspects of the accumulation process, such as the way in which labor is employed, the way in which labor power is reproduced, and the way in which surplus value materializes in the circulation of commodities (Edel, 1981:22–35).

Such analyses need, further, to account for distortions caused by class conflict. It is essential to realize that capital's requirements are not satisfied without struggle, including struggle centered around the state. Analysis of urban housing policies, levels and rates of urbanization across regions, and urban ecological structure—such as patterns of racial and ethnic segregation, metropolitan expansion, and central city decay—all could be usefully approached in terms of these requirements of the capitalist mode of production.[8] Carol Smith's contributions in Chapters 6 and 7 (this volume) are perhaps more akin to the orthodox Marxian position than any of the other chapters in the book. Her analysis of the city-size hierarchy in Guatemala's urban development in the nineteenth and twentieth centuries is critical of theories that emphasize colonialism, export dependency, and rural collapse to the exclusion of class relations.

From the point of view of approaches such as these, the link between industrialization and urbanization in evolutionary ecological approaches is rather superficial, since the nature of industrialization itself is part of the accumulation process. Marxian interpretations also suggest the importance of the role played by intracapitalist competition at the national level. The "anarchy of the market" dictates that individual capitalists must, in order to survive, struggle to capture relative surplus value. They may employ new technologies or make locational changes in production or marketing functions in seeking to gain competitive advantage over other producers (Harvey, 1982:Chapter 12).

Factors that the conventional Marxian approaches to urbanization rarely stress, but which the world-system perspective would emphasize, include the impetus for expansion of the system provided by the availability of cheap raw materials in the peripheral areas, more highly coerced labor in these areas, and political–military rivalry among competing core powers. These themes run through neo-Marxian theories of imperialism, but world-system theorists understand them in terms of institutional features basic to the functioning of capitalism. Kentor, in Chapter 2, provides a useful introduction to the world-system perspective. He examines the concept of a hierarchical division of labor in the world-economy and the consequences of this for economic development. The characteristics of the core, semiperiphery, and periphery are discussed with an emphasis on how the interaction of economic and political dynamics generates an international hierarchy of production and exchange. His discussion also focuses on the processes that reproduce the core–periphery hierarchy and the resulting implications for mobility within the system, and the necessity of this type of stratification for the perpetuation of the capitalist world-economy.

A crucial theoretical issue for the world-system perspective centers upon the criteria for establishing the outer boundaries of the system over time. Sokolovsky, in Chapter 3, begins by pointing out that this task is an obvious

---

[8]See Procter (1982) for an interesting beginning attempt to synthesize Marxian perspectives on urbanization.

prerequisite to any long-term study that assumes that exchanges between systems are fundamentally different from exchanges within the system. This is extremely important for the study of urbanization. Long-run changes in the urban patterns of regions are expected to be contingent upon the region's position in the world-system, and the prior question of whether it is in the system or not at a given point in time.

Wallerstein has not presented a formal theoretical model. His work is historically contingent, but it has led others to sketch the beginnings of something like a formal theory. The chapters by Kentor and Sokolovsky contribute to this task, as have earlier efforts by Chase-Dunn and Rubinson (1977, 1979) and Chase-Dunn (1978). The latter have identified structures and processes that characterize capitalism as a world-system. I draw heavily on this work in the following introduction to the remaining chapters of this book. In this way I hope both to show the utility of applying the perspective to the specific processes of urbanization and to introduce the contents of this book in a concise manner.

According to the framework sketched by Chase-Dunn and Rubinson (1979), the capitalist mode of production is constituted as a world-system, embodying several "institutional constants" throughout each of its four historical epochs. The core–periphery division of labor and labor control, and the interstate system are the two institutional constants in this schema. The interstate system fragments the class struggle, confining it within the various nation-states of the system, which are themselves unequal in terms of military, political, and economic strength. Core states are relatively stronger and labor is relatively free in contrast to peripheral labor, which is often subject to coercion over and above that typical of the wage labor system within the core. Surplus product is appropriated from the periphery to the core by a number of market and nonmarket mechanisms within the context of the interstate system. Underdevelopment is reproduced within the system, in the sense that the development gap between the core and the periphery remains even though both "develop." It is sometimes argued that labor in the core benefits from the unequal exchange between zones of the world-economy, and, to the extent that this is true, there are objective reasons for the tremendous differences among nations and across zones in the intensity of the class struggle and in the conditions under which labor is employed.

We can expect the macrolevel urban patterns that are the focus of this book to reflect the basic institutional features of the system in several ways. In Chapter 13, Firebaugh shows that levels of urbanization and rates of urbanization for countries vary according to structural position in the world-system. Likewise, differences in the occupational structure and the distribution of the labor force within nations and among the hierarchical zones themselves (core, periphery, semiperiphery) are interpretable in light of these institutional constants (see Timberlake and Lunday, Chapter 15, this volume). There are also reasons to suspect that peripheral regions will have city systems that are internally less well integrated than those in core areas. Portes's argument in Chapter 4 concerning the functional importance to capitalist accumulation of the informal sector in peripheral areas hinges on core–periphery differences in the prices of labor, which emerge from the unequal distribution of production and power in the world-system. Over-urbanization in the periphery, then, reflects more than poor planning and rapid population growth; it is a reflection, as well, of the reproduction requirements of the capitalist world-economy as a whole. Furthermore, Sassen-Koob (Chapter 11) indicates that the changing nature of these requirements is restructuring the labor force in core areas as well. Her research indicates that the growth of the "high tech" sector in several key core cities is exacerbating class differences.

The world-system is also characterized by three types of "cycles which occur in each of the four epochs" (Chase-Dunn and Rubinson, 1979:279). First are the long waves of increasing capital accumulation and increasing velocity of exchange followed by slow-down and stagnation. There are several studies that examine relatively local patterns of urban change in terms of cycles of accumulation and stagnation (e.g., Mollenkopf, 1981), but very little work has been done on macro-urban processes in the world-economy. At this broader level, several research questions come to mind. Do rates and levels of urbanization vary in such a way as to reflect these cycles? How is this complicated by the core–periphery division of labor? Do city systems at the world level or national level become more integrated and hierarchical during upswings in the cycle?

Another cyclical feature of the world-system involves core competition. "This refers to a cycle of uncentricity vs. multicentricity in the distribution of power and competitive advantage among core states" (Chase-Dunn and Rubinson, 1979:279). In Chapter 12, Chase-Dunn explores the hypothesis that the population size hierarchy of the world city-system mirrors changes from periods of single-state hegemony in the world-system to periods of decentratralization, or multicentricity.[9]

A third world-system cycle is "the structure of core–periphery trade and control," which exhibits cyclical fluctuations between relatively free-market exchange and exchange that is highly controlled politically; for example,

---

[9]This line of research could reasonably be pursued further by examining the possible correspondence between cycles of unicentricity versus multicentricity and the degree of integration of national or regional city-systems within the periphery or core.

trade that is organized rigidly "within colonial empires."[10] It is quite possible that this cycle, too, would have consequences for macro-urban patterns. This dimension of the world-system is obviously affected by the other dimensions, especially by the cycle of core competition, and it is unrealistic to discuss one cycle in isolation. Nevertheless a few highly speculative hypotheses can be advanced that relate this cycle to macro-urban issues. For example it is quite possible that peripheral economies will be somewhat freer to develop more differentiated economies during periods of free-market exchange.[11] If this is true, this general economic differentiation, in turn, should be reflected in more occupational heterogeneity in the urban labor force of the periphery as a whole, and especially in the more developed peripheral countries with stronger states that are able to exert relatively more resistance to the coercion of the interstate system.

If we pursue this further, we may find evidence that highly specialized peripheral cities and city systems become somewhat more internally differentiated during periods of free-market relations than they are during periods of rigid colonial rule, when virtually all the trade of a given peripheral country is with one core country. In addition, we may find that changes in the city-size distribution in peripheral areas may not have a one-to-one correspondence with these cycles, but may, afterall, reflect the specific production functions of each peripheral area. Clark, in Chapter 8, shows that variation in the degree of primacy in the colonies of nineteenth-century Australia can be understood in terms of the different space-requirements involved in the production of different commodities. The production of some commodities involves relatively more centralization of facilities, workers, complementary services, and so forth than others, and to the extent that a country's economy is highly specialized, a shift in what is being produced may have significant effects on the city-size distribution. There may be some uniformity in the space requirements of peripheral production, but this remains an issue for future research. In fact, Clark's work indicates that, within one peripheral area, regional differences in production were linked to different patterns of urbanization. Nemeth and Smith (Chapter 9) also indicate that production requirements are likely to contribute to city-system

---

[10]Berry and Kasarda (1977:386–400) relate primacy at the national level in less developed countries to the colonial history of the country. They propose that the cities within given colonial empires be considered as single systems.

[11]It is during these relatively free-market moments that nations in the periphery that contain a favorable mix of industrial infrastructure, access to raw materials, and a center coalition dominated by an industrial bourgeoisie are likely to manage to diversify trade relations, both in terms of different commodities and in terms of different trade partners.

integration in their comparison of urban hierarchies in the Philippines and South Korea.

In addition, there are four secular trends that have characterized the world-system since its inception. Two of these trends are "the integration of new populations and territories" into the world-economy and the "intensification and deepening of commodity relations" (Chase-Dunn and Rubinson, 1979). The history of the capitalist world-system has been—until it recently reached its limits in this respect—the history of expansion into new territories, and the incorporation and peripheralization of them. As the system has expanded, precapitalist cities have been incorporated, and they have often been quite large. As Chase-Dunn shows in Chapter 12, this has some effects on the changing city-size distribution of the world-system as a whole.

Even though all major world regions are now incorporated, there seems to be plenty of room to deepen and intensify commodity relations in many peripheral areas in which large segments of the populations continue to rely on subsistence subeconomies (see Sokolovsky, Chapter 3).[12] The secular increase in world urbanization can be viewed in terms of integration into the capitalist mode of production, and the functional role of cities at different hierarchical levels of the system can be analyzed in terms of the relations to the reproduction and expansion of the system.[13] Urbanization, of course, would be expected to increase also because of the spatial requirements of industrial production as more and more areas and people are drawn into social relations governed by the production and exchange of commodities and as productivity in agriculture increases.

The importance Portes (Chapter 4) attributes to the "informal sector" in less developed countries leads one to speculate about a possible impending crisis in some peripheral areas, brought about by the contradictions between the functions this sector performs for the world-system and the tendency in capitalism to progressively include more areas in "fully" capitalist exchange relations. According to analyses presented in this volume (Portes, Chapter 4; Timberlake and Lunday, Chapter 15) there is much evidence that market relations have not yet uniformly penetrated regions within the world-economy, especially insofar as such uniformity in this sphere is reflected in similar occupational structures.

One still finds huge differences between the core and periphery in the balance of jobs in manufacturing, services, and agriculture, even when the comparison is made between the periphery today and the core areas of a

---

[12]As is pointed out below this deepening of commodity relations is likely to present itself as a threat to the core–periphery division of labor.

[13]See Cohen (1981) for a discussion of the functional roles fulfilled by organizations in the large cities of the modern core.

much earlier period. Equally striking is the gap between wages in the core versus those in the periphery. If Portes's analysis is correct, then, to the extent that the periphery succumbs to the tendency in capitalism for market relations to spread uniformly, one of the cornerstones of unequal exchange—the informal sector, and the reproductive function it serves with respect to the world-system—will erode. Wallerstein has argued that when all labor is free we shall have socialism, and it is true that, under capitalism, labor has become increasingly free with abolition of serfdom and of slavery. But it is also true that important differences remain in the degree to which labor is coerced across the zones of the world-economy. There is more coercion of labor in the periphery than in the core, wages are lower in the former, and political power is used more to exploit labor there. In Chapter 14, Ward reminds us that it is undoubtedly the women of the Third World who disproportionately perform the less remunerative reproductive tasks that characterize the informal sector. Although women are superexploited almost everywhere, Ward shows that there are substantial differences across regions of the world in the extent to which they engage in wage labor.

Finally, the world-system has been characterized by two other secular trends: increasing power of states over their populations, and increasing size of economic enterprises in terms of the amount of capital and the number of workers controlled by single firms. While it is quite hypothetical, it is nevertheless plausible that these two trends, when considered with other features of the world-system, especially the core–periphery division of labor, will yield important insights into the urbanization process. In the periphery, for example, the increasing scope of governmental power has often been limited by, among other things, the weak integration across social, political, and economic spheres within the territory of the nation-state. The state grows, to be sure, but its bureaucratic apparatus is spatially confined to the region in which the primate city is located, thus acting to crystallize a primate city-size distribution. London's description of the situation in Thailand (Chapter 10) illustrates some of the implications of political centralization in the face of weak political and economic integration in that peripheral country.

Furthermore, in the absence of economic growth, the increase in the size of government within the periphery has, in all likelihood, contributed to the disproportionate size of the service sector in comparison to the industrial sector. Large firms may also exacerbate primacy and overurbanization in the periphery. Even when manufacturing firms are locally owned, they often rely on technology imported from the core—technology that was developed in response to much higher wages and that will therefore do little to absorb workers from the hypertrophied tertiary sector. At the same time, the technology is likely to be of a massive scale relative to the small home markets in the periphery, thus contributing to monopoly control at the national level (cf. Merhav, 1969) and the further disproportionate concentration in one or two large cities of the nonagricultural populations. In the meantime, the core displays a different kind of overurbanization—the post-industrial labor force structure characterized by a growing tertiary-to-secondary ratio. But in the core the tertiary is much more likely to include high-technology research and development functions and financial and managerial control functions that serve the world-economy as a whole. These central control and production functions are largely absent from the periphery.

The discussion immediately above is meant as a list of implicit hypotheses, many of which are investigated in the chapters below, relating world-system theory to the macrolevel urban phenomena introduced in the preceding section. For purposes of explicating the basic features of the system, I have considered in isolation processes and structures that ideally must be considered together. The secular trends of the world-system, for example, are operating in the context of its cyclical processes, and the manifestations of the former will undoubtedly be masked or exaggerated, depending upon which moment in which cycle is under consideration.

One last caveat should be submitted before outlining the organization of the book. Urbanization processes are, in a direct sense, population processes. The secular increase in the proportion of the world's population that is urban reflects rural-to-urban migration, increasing levels of fertility or decreases in mortality rates in cities relative to rural areas, the emergence of cities from what had been small rural villages, and the expansion of existing urban areas. There is a vast literature on urbanization as a demographic process (e.g., Goldstein and Sly, 1977), and there will no doubt be efforts in the future to link these demographic dimensions of the urbanization process to world-system theory. However, aside from Firebaugh's discussion in Chapter 13, this book leaves such efforts to future work.

ORGANIZATION OF THIS BOOK

The remainder of this book is organized into three broad sections. Part II includes chapters that deal primarily with theoretical and conceptual considerations in relating the study of urbanization to the world-system. The chapter by Jeffrey Kentor serves to introduce the reader to the world-system perspective in general, and Chapter 3, by Joan Sokolvsky, discusses problems in specifying the boundaries of the world-system in different periods. Taken together these two chapters provide a general orientation to the perspective.

The remaining chapters in Part II deal in a conceptual manner with some of the basic urbanization patterns that are the focus of the entire volume. The chapter by Alejandro Portes discusses the informal labor sector within peripheral areas and its importance to the reproduction of core–periphery relations at the global level. Pamela Walters's contribution in Chapter 5 introduces the concept of urban primacy, relates it to world-system processes, and discusses problems of measuring the phenomenon. She concludes by introducing a new measure of primacy that overcomes many of the problems inherent in earlier attempts.

Carol Smith, in Chapter 6, provides a critique of several of the theories of urban primacy as well as several proposed measures. She divides conventional primacy explanations into three groups: colonialism caused urban primacy, dependence on export production caused primacy, and primacy was caused by collapse of agricultural production for export. She dismisses each of these explanations and, in anticipation of her subsequent chapter, suggests that closer attention to class structure and class relations is likely to provide a more fruitful approach to explaining urban forms.

Regional implications are the theme of Part III. The five chapters in this section attempt to interpret urbanization patterns in specific regions (Central America, Australia, South Korea, the Philippines, Thailand, and the United States) in light of some of the theoretical considerations developed in Part II. In Chapter 7, Carol Smith develops her class analysis of urban patterns suggested in the preceding chapter. She presents the results of field work in Guatemala by examining the class-based nature of urban patterns there. Roger Clark (Chapter 8) examines urban primacy in each of the provinces of late nineteenth-century Australia. He finds that, more than simple "dependence" on the larger world-economy, the specific requirements of different production activities help to explain variation in levels of urban concentration.

Roger Nemeth and David Smith, in Chapter 9, compare the urban systems of South Korea and the Philippines. They are able to explain many of the differences they find in light of world-system considerations, such as the time of incorporation into the system, the function each region serves in the world-economy, and the role of international politics. But, like Carol Smith, they are sensitive to the importance of local class relations in determining local urban patterns. Finally, they suggest that, aside from its overly mechanistic language, human ecology theory still provides a useful perspective on urban systems development that may complement a Marxian world-system approach. Bruce London, in Chapter 10, discusses urban primacy in Thailand in terms of political centralization and patterns of elite dominance within that country.

Finally, Saskia Sassen-Koob's contribution (Chapter 11) focuses on the effects on cities in the United States of the mobility of capital and labor. She examines the consequences of the demands for centralized "control capability" that are generated by the international reorganization of production. These consequences have included changes in the composition and destinations of labor migrants to U.S. cities and changes in class composition and class relations in certain core cities.

The contributions in Part IV represent efforts to describe various global patterns of urbanization and to interpret these patterns in terms of the theoretical considerations developed in Part II. Chase-Dunn, in Chapter 12, presents data on city-size hierarchy at the world level for the past 1000 years. He finds that changes in the world city-size distribution correspond to cycles in the world-system. Glen Firebaugh (Chapter 13) analyzes levels of urbanization across two zones of the world-system, the core and periphery. He finds that significant differences exist in the correlates of urbanization at each level.

Kathryn Ward's chapter (Chapter 14) shows that patterns of labor exploitation in the world-economy are not gender neutral. There is good evidence that women disproportionately comprise subsectors of the labor force that are superexploited, but there are significant regional differences in the extent to which this exploitation takes place in the arena of urban wage labor. Finally, James Lunday and I examine recent patterns of labor force structure in the world-economy (Chapter 15). Using the very broad occupational categories that are available, we find important differences between the labor force composition across the three-tiered zones of the world-system. Furthermore, the differences are interpretable in light of the world-system perspective.

For the most part, both the regional studies and the global analyses support interpreting urbanization patterns in light of world-system processes. Having stated this, it should quickly be added that the contributions indicate that any such interpretation must be made with care. The temptation to apply world-system theory mechanistically to urban processes should be avoided. Thus many of the chapters point to the importance of considering the manner and extent to which world-system processes articulate with "local" social formations and relations, such as class relations. Furthermore, the contributions presented here also illustrate gaps between current theory and reality—gaps that the authors whose work is presented here, along with others working in the area of urban political economy, will undoubtedly address in future work.

PART II

THEORETICAL AND CONCEPTUAL CONSIDERATIONS

2

ECONOMIC DEVELOPMENT AND THE WORLD DIVISION OF LABOR

Jeffrey Kentor

The goal of this chapter is to introduce the reader to the growing body of literature referred to as the world-system perspective. This theoretical approach argues that there exists a politicoeconomic structure at the global level that in part determines the relations of production and exchange within and among nation-states. Within this world-system is a hierarchical division of labor among what Wallerstein (1974, 1977, 1979, 1980) refers to as the core, semiperiphery, and periphery. It is argued by world-system theorists that this hierarchical structure—and the relations of production and exchange it represents—functions to maintain and reproduce the present capitalist world-economy.

Through the 1960s, economic development was understood within a "modernization" framework (see Hoselitz, 1960). A country's economic advancement was seen as a function of primarily intranational qualities. Underdeveloped countries were considered "premodern" inasmuch as their populace had not acquired a modern (i.e., capitalist) mentality (Inkeles and Smith, 1974). Often, these countries were characterized as having a dual economy: a small modern sector and a larger, precapitalist sector. From a modernization vantage, the path toward economic growth was twofold. First, the population must be educated and encouraged to adopt a modern work ethic; second, the developed countries must invest the necessary capital with which the underdeveloped countries could industrialize. The social and economic problems endured by these countries as they developed were considered to be "normal" growing pains that all countries experience on the path to industrialization. It is important to note that from this perspective there is no a priori systemic constraint on a country's economic

25

development. It was at least conceivable that all countries could eventually become modern.

Beginning in the 1960s, however, a growing number of scholars argued that modernization theory could not explain economic development. In his classic article on the "development of underdevelopment," Andre Gunder Frank (1966) argued that economic growth in underdeveloped countries was actually inhibited by contact with the developed world, pointing out that, historically, underdeveloped countries grew most rapidly during periods of least contact with the modern world. He argued that penetration by the developed economies caused a "de-industrialization" of peripheral economies as the productive infrastructure was reoriented toward the raw material needs of the developed world. This process of underdevelopment is deepened as cheap imports from the developed countries drive the manufactures of the indigenous producers out of business. Further, this process rendered the underdeveloped economies dependent upon the core economies of the world-system both for markets for their exports and for provisioning their domestic needs. Of importance here is that, in Frank's view, economic development is a function of the international relationship between the developed and underdeveloped countries. Peripheral countries become dependent upon the developed countries for capital, technology, and markets. They are not able to determine their own economic development, which becomes determined by the needs of the larger world-economy.

In 1974, Immanuel Wallerstein outlined what has become known as the world-systems perspective, itself an outgrowth of dependency theory. Wallerstein argued that a country's economic development occurred within the context of the larger world-economy. The present capitalist world-system (originating in the sixteenth century) is characterized by a relational process of unequal development that generates and reproduces a hierarchical world division of labor. Within Wallerstein's framework (at least relative) underdevelopment is a functional necessity of the capitalist world-economy, allowing for maximum accumulation of capital in the developed core of the world-system.

Wallerstein posits a three-tiered division of labor in the world-economy: core, semiperiphery, and periphery. I preface the discussion of this formulation with three points. First, this hierarchical division of labor is not simply a quantitative continuum: there are qualitative differences as well. Second, the system of the world-economy is a dynamic one. That is, the processes that characterize this division of labor may change over time. Third, while countries may exhibit mobility within this hierarchy (i.e., a country may move from the core to the semiperiphery), the division of labor within the capitalist world-economy is reproduced. From a world-system perspective, this division of labor is necessary for the maintenance of the world-economy.

Two essential features characterize the world division of labor. The first is the predominant type of production in which a country is engaged: high-technology, capital-intensive production in the core and labor-intensive production in the periphery. The second feature is wage levels, with core labor receiving relatively higher wages than labor in the periphery, holding constant the level of productivity. The emphasis in these distinctions concerns the method rather than the product of production. The United States and India both produce wheat. In India, however, wheat production is a (relatively) low-wage, labor-intensive process, while in the United States it is a high-wage, capital-intensive process.

While core and periphery are intuitively meaningful concepts, it is more difficult to conceptualize the notion of the semiperiphery. For Wallerstein (1974, 1977, 1980) the semiperiphery is a qualitatively distinct category that acts as a stabilizing force in the world division of labor, obscuring the gross inequalities between the core and the periphery and providing the illusion of a continuum of economic development. But the semiperiphery is not a homogeneous category, as is the case with the core and the periphery. It includes qualitatively heterogeneous groups of relatively (upwardly or downwardly) mobile countries between the core and the periphery of the world-economy.

Although these countries within the semiperiphery may be descriptively heterogeneous, there are commonalities among them that make this a meaningful category. Within the semiperiphery there is a mixture of core (capital-intensive) and peripheral (labor-intensive) production, or, more correctly, there is less of an imbalance of productive types than in the periphery. This leads to relatively higher levels of class conflict in semiperipheral states as competing interests vie for control of the state apparatus.[1] In this type of situation, the state cannot act in a mercantile manner to the benefit of the diverse capitalist interests. Further, this internal conflict induces a structural weakness in the state itself, that is, the absence of what Moore (1966) refers to as a "center coalition."

Second, semiperipheral states are often used by core powers competing among themselves during periods of economic downturns in the world-

---

[1]Examples of this are eighteenth-century France and pre-Civil War America. In both instances there was conflict between agrarian and industrial capitalists over state policies toward international trade: industrial capitalists pursued tariff protection from foreign manufactures, while agrarian capitalists pressed for tariff relief from agricultural imports.

economy. They may perform subimperialist functions such as extracting surplus from the peripheral areas, or may themselves become the site for such extraction.[2]

While the semiperiphery is, by definition, being exploited by the core, it is itself able to exploit the periphery. Just as several underdeveloped countries will trade with only one or two core countries and not among each other (Galtung's (1971) structural model of imperialism)—to the advantage of the core powers—so too will semiperipheral countries have a nexus of peripheral countries from which to extract favorable trade relationships.

Finally, if the semiperiphery may be distinguished from the periphery by the existence of some capital-intensive (core) production, it may be distinguished from the core by the locus of ownership of this industrial production. While the semiperiphery does in fact exhibit an increased level of industrialism relative to the periphery, ownership of these industries (both direct and portfolio) and resulting accumulation of surplus capital remains under the control of core interests. Further, this relationship appears to be a historically constant (if relative) process in the capitalist world-economy, as pointed out in Wallerstein's (1980) discussion of "putting out" industries in the seventeenth century and Evan's (1979) remarks concerning Brazil and other semiperipheral states in the twentieth century.

As labor costs escalate in the core, production is transferred to the semiperiphery. This has resulted historically in the growth of a labor-intensive informal sector and more recently in capital-intensive production. In both instances, ownership remains in the hands of the core capitalists.

Countries within this world division of labor exhibit both vertical (across levels) and horizontal (within level) exchange and production relationships. What characterizes vertical, interlevel hierarchy is a net outflow of surplus capital from the periphery to the core and semiperiphery, and from the semiperiphery to the core. Further, moving vertically in the world-system, the amount of exchange and the number of exchange partners increases (Galtung, 1971). Finally, two clusters of exchange *orbits* may be identified: several underdeveloped countries exchanging with one or two core states (but not among themselves) and several peripheral countries exchanging with one or two semiperipheral states.

A similar relationship exists within the core and, to a lesser extent, the semiperiphery. For a given core country to be hegemonic, for example, it is necessary for it to obtain a net inflow of surplus capital within as well as across levels of the world-economy. Relative disadvantage within levels may be offset by favorable surplus exchange across levels.

---

[2]Such was the case with eighteenth-century Portugal, which was coerced by Spain, a downwardly mobile core power, to yield market and capital concessions in Spain's unsuccessful attempt to retain core status.

It should be noted that these relationships are embedded within the long-term historical context of the evolving world-system. The development of this capitalist world-economy has not been linear. Rather, it has exhibited cyclical patterns at various levels. First, there are systemic cycles. That is, the system as a whole exhibits a cyclical pattern of economic growth and contraction (Chase-Dunn and Rubinson, 1979). Second, there are cycles within levels of the world-economy. Of particular importance are those within the core: periods of relatively high ("multicentric" core) and low ("unicentric" core) levels of competition (Bousquet, 1980). Finally, there are interlevel fluctuations. The relationships among core, semiperiphery, and periphery are not constant. Instead, there appear to be periods of relatively formal and informal ties between the core and the semiperiphery (Bergeson and Schoenberg, 1978). This refers to periods of relatively strong and weak colonial ties, respectively, and the ensuing trade relationships across levels of the world-economy.

Production and Exchange

I first discuss the production and exchange relationships in the world division of labor on an economic basis and then examine the interaction of these dynamics with political processes.

As stated above, the world-economy represents an unequal hierarchical exchange among economic regions. But what constitutes such a region? There are two (compatible) ways of understanding this concept. The first uses the notion of urban agglomerations. An *urban agglomeration* is generally defined as the area within which a majority of the population is oriented toward a given urban area (a city), usually in terms of work but also in terms of food distribution or some other measure of orientation. This results in a flow of people toward a specific urban area. At the point where the predominant population flow is toward another urban area, a new urban agglomeration is defined. An *economic region* may be similarly defined as that area within which some majority of commodity production and exchange is centered. This is a more difficult concept to operationalize than that of urban agglomeration, due to the overlapping and hierarchical nature of economic regions. Further, the structure of these regions is not necessarily uniform across the world division of labor. Core regions may be national (as suggested by the existence of a strong political boundary), whereas peripheral regions may be local or even continental.

One should note that the primary interest is not in exchange per se, but in the unequal production relationships these exchanges represent. This is not to argue that exchange is not necessary for the perpetuation and growth of the world division of labor. As Marx (1971:88–89) points out in the

Grundrisse, production, circulation, distribution, and consumption are different moments of the same general process of socioeconomic life. This suggests a complementary notion of an economic region: an economic region is the smallest unit that contains a core–periphery division of labor. The concepts of core and periphery become relative terms existing at various levels of the world-economy (local, national, continental, etc.). This allows us to discuss situations in which a particular production process is peripheral relative to the world division of labor, but central relative to the local or national division of labor (e.g., textile manufacturing in a peripheral country). Combining these two notions of economic regions enables us to examine the multilevel interactions of production and exchange relations and the relative nature of the division of labor as a system of stratified nested and overlapping hierarchies.

As was argued earlier, however, the world-economy is not simply a reflection of economic processes, but the interaction of economic and political processes. Here world-system theory differs from that of Marx. Marx (e.g., 1971) understood direct political coercion (primitive accumulation) to be the initial force that generated the relations of production necessary for the capitalist mode of production. Once these relations were in place, according to Marx, primitive accumulation would no longer be necessary, because the capitalist system would reproduce these relations on an essentially economic basis. Marx's discussion, however, is based upon an intranational analysis of capitalism. Frank (1980), using the term *primary accumulation,* argues that direct political force is continually necessary to maintain the world division of labor upon which capitalism is based. From this international analysis of capitalism, any given economic region may not exhibit a capitalist mode of production (i.e., may have nonwage labor) while still playing a functional role in the international world-economy by providing for the extraction of surplus accumulated by the core (see Sokolovsky, Chapter 3, this volume).

It is likely, in fact, that the state performs a critical role in affecting position of mobility within the system. The extent to which an economic region can be penetrated and its economy restructured to the benefit of the world-economy is dependent upon the nature of the political boundaries that surround it. The analogy of a selectively permeable membrane may be useful. It suggests that to the extent that the political boundary or "membrane" can selectively control the extent and the nature of the interaction with the external arena, it can better control its internal development.

Similarly, a strong state can provide the necessary impetus for mobility with the world-economy. As in the cases of the Soviet Union and China, a strong state provided protection from foreign penetration, allowing indigenous industry to develop by extracting surplus from the domestic population. However, while the state is necessary for stability and mobility within the system, it is not sufficient. It is a mechanism that facilitates indigenous industrial development.

Figure 2.1 is a diagram representing the production–exchange network of the world-system as conceptualized above. There are four conceptual levels in this hierarchy: zones, nations, regions, and cities. Each interaction (indicated by each rectangle in the diagram) represents a twofold input relationship. By examining the relationships suggested by this chart, both cross-sectionally and longitudinally, it may be possible to understand the structure and evolution of the world division of labor. The nature of this exchange network is further discussed below.

MECHANISMS OF REPRODUCTION

I turn now to a discussion of the mechanisms by which this world division of labor is reproduced. There are three dimensions across which these

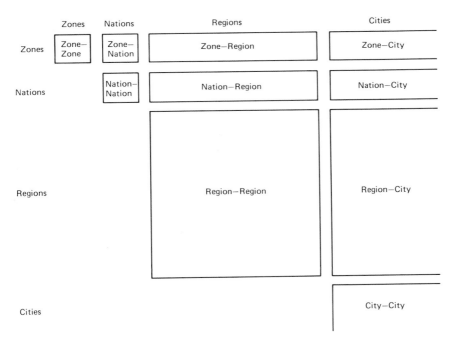

FIGURE 2.1   A diagram of the hierarchical and overlapping exchanges possible at various levels of the world-economy.

boundaries are maintained. The first of these is direct organizational control over economic processes: the extent to which an organizational actor (broadly speaking) is able to exert its will and resist others' to obtain favorable outcomes. This direct control is both economic and political. Economically, variables such as investment and trade dependence directly affect what is produced within a country, where it is marketed, and the price obtained. There are also indirect ramifications of investment and trade dependence. By modifying the composition and extent of trade in the world-economy and by controlling the flow of profits, external actors are able to affect the long-term productive infrastructure discussed below. The political aspects of this dimension include colonial status, military strength, and political treaties: the mechanisms of primary accumulation.

The second dimension is that of indirect determinants of position in the world-economy: the productive infrastructure and resources available to compete in the world market. This is represented by a country's level of development, including per capita income, composition of the labor force, and communications and transportation networks. Additionally, it includes the natural and human resources necessary for economic development. Politically, this dimension includes the absolute size of the state. This will determine the extent of the domestic market (i.e., effective demand) and, hence, how attractive it will be to foreign investors.

The third dimension across which the boundaries of the world-economy are maintained is that of a status system, a cultural hierarchy that attempts to impose a prevailing consciousness throughout the world-system. This social psychological component includes variables such as media exchange (television and radio production and exchange, book publications and translations) and export of educational technology. It is the export of an ideology that structures the realms of perception of individuals to legitimate the inherent inequalities of the modern world-economy.

But how is this hierarchy maintained? That is, what are the mechanisms by which capital is extracted from the periphery and accumulated by the core and, to a lesser extent, the semiperiphery? There are four theories of prominence that attempt to explain this flow of surplus across the world-economy.

1. *Class interests.* Aspects of this argument are put forth by Galtung (1971), Amin (1976), and Wallerstein (1974). Generally, this position argues that core interests generate a small elite in the host country whose interests are allied with those of the core capitalists, rather than with those of their own country. This international class allegiance causes the peripheral elite to reorient state policy to the benefit of the foreign interests.

2. *Unequal exchange.* This concept is derived from a labor theory of value. The exchange of capital intensive commodities produced in the pe-

riphery results in a net outflow of value, due to the equalization of the rates of profits. Emmanuel (1972) and Amin (1976) have urged that it is the unequal exchange due to wage differentials that causes part of the net outflow of capital, regardless of the level of capital intensiveness in the production process. Wage levels in the periphery are kept artificially low by core interests, so trade of ostensibly equal value, as indicated by world market prices, actually results in an unequal exchange. From Emmanuel's perspective, the changing nature of foreign penetration (transnational investment in manufacturing for the host market) should have little impact on this unequal exchange—so long as wage levels remain unequal (holding constant the level of productivity). The reorientation of peripheral economies toward production for the world-economy drains surplus in another manner: commodity exchanges are carried by core transport.[3] The more a peripheral state finds it necessary to participate in the world-economy, the more it must utilize core shipping. This transport monopoly enables the core to extract artificially high fees for peripheral exports, thereby increasing the level of unequal exchange (Frank, 1979).[4]

　　3. *Structural blockages.* This position has been most recently put forth by Ragin and Delacroix (1979; Delacroix and Ragin, 1980). They suggest that specialization of peripheral economies inhibits the development of backward internal linkages, the productive infrastructure supporting the export economy. A natural division of labor (in a Durkheimian sense) does not occur, and the indigenous economy does not develop.

　　4. *Decapitalization.* This is the argument advanced by Chase-Dunn (1975), Bornschier and Ballmer-Cao (1979), and Bornschier (1980). It focuses on the effects of penetration by transnational corporations. Initial foreign investment (flows) increases the monetized segment of the host country's economy due to net positive inflows of capital, and causes an initial increase in indicators of economic growth. These inflows also, however, begin a process of uneven development within the host country, both in terms of productive sectors (modern vs. traditional), with the foreign investment sector enjoying a technological advantage over the indigenous producers, and in terms of regions, locales of foreign penetration receiving higher wages and more varied consumer goods. The high profits generated by the multinational corporations are not reinvested in the host country

---

[3]Frank calculates that in 1928, nearly two-thirds of the world shipping fleets were owned by Western European countries, and that the United States accounted for the other third. He concludes that presently underdeveloped countries derived almost no profit from shipping.

[4]Frank (1979) calculates that shipping charges incurred by underdeveloped countries in 1928 amounted to $U.S.1.32 billion. Frank also finds that transport charges for peripheral exports were higher than those charged to core exports to the periphery, and cites Saul's (1960) assertion that it was the transport revenues that allowed the British to increase foreign investments from £10 million in 1816 to £700 million in 1870.

because of high risks, specialization of the multinational, and underconsumption (especially when the foreign investment is oriented toward domestic consumption). These profits are instead invested outside the host country, which results in a net outflow of capital. This process, combined with the negative effects of uneven development, culminates in a long-term negative effect on economic growth in the penetrated peripheral economy.

ASSOCIATED-DEPENDENT DEVELOPMENT

The historical character of the core–periphery relationship has recently come under discussion, as expressed in the works of Cardoso and Faletto (1979), Amin (1976), and Evans (1979). They argue, basically, that the old dependence relationship of raw material exports from the periphery in exchange for core manufactures has been supplanted (at least in the semi-periphery) by what Dos Santos refers to as the "new dependency": core investment in manufactures either for export (assembly plant production) or for consumption in the host country. It is argued that this production for the local market has resulted in the increased levels of dependence and development, what has been termed *associated-dependent development* (Cardoso and Faletto, 1979). This is especially evident in underdeveloped countries with large domestic markets, where increased levels of consumption are particularly attractive.[5] This increasing level of industrialization effects a growth in backward internal linkages, with industry and services facilitating such growth. This "internalization of the domestic market" (Cardoso, 1972) or "internalization of imperialism" (Evans, 1979) is brought about by the alliance of the transnational corporation, the local bourgeoisie, and the state.

But to what extent does this apparent alteration in the historical core–periphery relationship actually represent a fundamental change in the stabilizing functions of dependency in the world division of labor? As Evans (1979) points out, increased industrialization in the "advanced periphery" of the world-economy is not a sufficient indicator of associated-dependent development. For this shift in dependency relations to generate a qualitative change in the world hierarchy there must be a shift in the locus of surplus accumulation of capital.

There are two questions here: To what extent does associated-dependent development result in upward mobility for a given state? and, To what extent does it affect structural mobility; that is, does it alter the structural

---

[5]Transnational corporations have a vested interest in perpetuating high levels of income inequality, which allow for domestic consumption of the luxury commodities produced in the peripheral economy.

relationships among levels of the world-economy? While Evans (1979) argues that associated-dependent development is generating upward mobility for Brazil, it is questionable whether this has any structural impact on the system as a whole. First, the low wage "comparative advantage" of underdeveloped countries perpetuates a low standard of living among their working classes. Second, local production allows the multinationals to avoid tariff barriers erected to protect the indigenous industry. The high-technology production enables them to undercut local manufacturers, resulting in a monopoly for the transnational. As indigenous competition is stifled, the multinationals are able to obtain artificially high prices for their goods. Finally, the transnationals retain control over both the exported technology (including royalties) and the industrial base itself.

This suggests that associated-dependent development actually describes a qualitative process of "semiperipheralization." It is not simply a quantitative upward push; it is the restructuring of the peripheral economy into that of the semiperipheral economy.

BOUNDARIES OF THE SYSTEM

The reader should be aware of two issues central to the world-system paradigm. The first concerns the external boundary of the world-system. How are we to understand the composition of the current capitalist world-economy across both time and space? Joan Sokolovsky discusses these questions in Chapter 3.

The second question concerns the internal boundaries of the system. On what theoretical and/or empirical bases are we to classify those countries within this capitalist world-economy as core, semiperipheral, or peripheral? This is the final topic of this chapter.

There have been numerous attempts to define empirically positions in the world-economy. The most common method has been to rank countries by level of development: per capita income, size of the domestic market, or energy consumption (see, among others, Chase-Dunn, 1975; Bornschier and Ballmer-Cao, 1979; Dolan and Tomlin, 1980; Gobalet and Diamond, 1979; Kentor, 1981).

There have been a few attempts to describe this hierarchical division of labor multidimensionally. Snyder and Kick (1979) used a block model design to group countries across the four dimensions of trade flows, military interventions, diplomatic exchanges, and conjoint treaty memberships. Their analysis generated 10 block structures that Snyder and Kick argued could be grouped into core, semiperiphery, and periphery.

Gidengil (1978) used Wishart's mode analysis, a type of cluster analysis, in a test of Galtung's center–periphery formulation. The dimensions considered in this study were level of development, degree of import and export processing (vertical trade), export partner and commodity concentrations (feudal trade), and degree of inequality (disharmony of interests). This analysis generated five clusters. Gidengil identified one cluster as core, one as periphery and three intermediate (semiperipheral) groups.

While both analyses identify levels of core, semiperiphery, and periphery, the countries that comprise these levels differ, especially for the semiperiphery. Table 2.1 compares the countries categorized by Snyder and Kick and by Gidengil. Of the countries used in both analyses, there is a strong agreement as to those countries belonging to the core (89%), a modest agreement for the periphery (75%), and little agreement as to the composition of the semiperiphery (38%). Clearly the dimensions included in the analyses have a substantial impact of the composition of these levels. This difference is not an artifact of method. It is the result of an insufficient theoretical specification of the semiperiphery. The implicit assumption in both articles seems to be that the semiperiphery is simply those countries between the core and the periphery. This inability to locate accurately the semiperiphery is of crucial importance in empirical analyses, as various interaction effects have been postulated and described concerning the relationship between the dependence and position in the world-economy (Bornschier, 1980; Delacroix and Ragin, 1980; Dolan and Tomlin, 1980; Gobalet and Diamond, 1979).

A third approach is to examine the outcome of those processes thought to generate the world division of labor. Amsden (1976) charts the trade in manufactures between developing countries and finds that a small number of developing countries (referred to as *semiindustrialized*) are responsible for 60% of the exports of manufactures within developing countries. (Thirty percent of all manufactured exports of developing countries were sold to other developing nations). One argument put forth in Amsden's paper is that these semiindustrial countries may depend on peripheral markets for exports of their manufactures. This is similar to Wallerstein's (1977) argument that one mechanism of mobility for semiperipheral countries is exploitation of peripheral markets.

Maizels (1963) takes a similar approach to that of Amsden. He locates countries hierarchically in a two-dimensional space of per capita manufactures and finished manufactures as a percentage of total exports. Maizels argues that the export sector becomes increasingly industrialized as a consequence of industrial growth. Maizels distinguishes intermediate products from finished goods, asserting that a low level of processing (smelted metals or chemicals exported for further refining) is often representative of a narrow (one or two product) export sector, and is only a slight elaboration of

TABLE 2.1
A Comparison of Two Attempts to Define Position in the World-Economy in 1970[a]

Country	Position		Country	Position	
	Synder & Kick (1979)	Gidengil (1978)		Snyder & Kick (1979)	Gidengil (1978)
United States	C	C	Peru	SP	SP
United Kingdom	C	C	Argentina	SP	SP
Netherlands	C	C	Turkey	SP	SP
Belgium	C	C	Israel	SP	C
Luxembourg	C	C	Finland	SP	C
France	C	C	India	SP	C
Australia	C	C	Pakistan	SP	C
Spain	C	C	Burma	SP	P
Portugal	C	C	Ecuador	P	P
West Germany	C	C	Brazil	P	SP
Austria	C	C	Paraguay	P	P
Canada	C	C	Chile	P	SP
Italy	C	C	Dominican Republic	P	P
Japan	C	SP	Guatemala	P	P
Greece	C	C	Honduras	P	P
Sweden	C	C	El Salvador	P	P
Norway	C	C	Nicaragua	P	P
Denmark	C	C	Costa Rica	P	P
South Africa	C	SP	Jamaica	P	P
			Indonesia	P	SP

[a] C, core; P, periphery; SP, semiperiphery.

an agricultural or mining economy. Finished goods (those not subject to further processing) represent those economies that are truly industrialized, with capital-intensive, high-wage production. (Unfortunately it is not possible to compare Maizel's structure with the others' as his ranking is for 1955).

As may be evident, part of the problem in determining position in the world-economy results from failing to distinguish between the process (how a country attains its position in the world-economy) and the outcome (the current position). If we can separate these dimensions, it is possible to causally model the system (recognizing of course that the system is non-recursive).

A second problem in any determination of position in the world-economy concerns the availability of comparable data both across countries and over time. Williams (1981) has recently developed measures of the primary conceptual indicators of position in the world system: wage levels (holding levels of productivity constant) and relative level of capital intensiveness. These data, however, are only available for selected countries between 1960 and 1975. For earlier periods (and for other countries) the only data available are trade statistics, estimations of national income, and labor force composition. In order to obtain consistency—and, one hopes, accuracy—in determining position, it is necessary to construct a series of indicator scales beginning at each time point when new data become available and to compare them with more accurate scales at hand for the present period. For example, one could construct an indicator of position using trade data as far back as 1800. The world structure indicated by this scale could be compared over time with structures derived from more accurate scales available at later points in time.

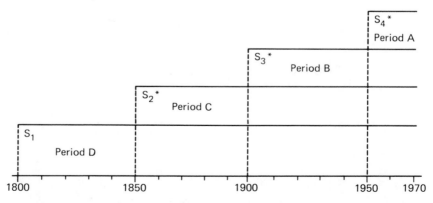

FIGURE 2.2   A model of reference-based serial cluster analysis. An asterisk represents the reference indicator.

A model of this method, which might be termed *reference-based serial cluster analysis,* is presented in Figure 2.2. In this hypothetical example there are four different indicators (or groups of indicators) S_1–S_4 available at various time points. Zone clusters of countries representing core, semi-periphery, and periphery are derived from each indicator at equal intervals, depending on data availability. Clusters are compared across indicator levels to determine the accuracy of the earlier measures, relative to the most recent indicator.

In closing, I would like to emphasize that the goal of this chapter has been to familiarize the reader with the major concepts of the world-system paradigm, which are used throughout this text. The reader should be aware, however, that there is current debate surrounding many of the topics covered. This will become evident in the following chapters.

3

LOGIC, SPACE, AND TIME: THE BOUNDARIES OF THE CAPITALIST WORLD–ECONOMY

Joan Sokolovsky

Introduction

In contrast to traditional cross-national comparative studies, research undertaken from the standpoint of the world-system perspective must contend with a unit of analysis whose spatial dimensions, never formally specified, change across time. Although there is a growing literature on the compatability of quantitative research methods with the world-system approach (for example, see, Bach, 1980; Chase-Dunn, 1979a; Hopkins, 1978), less attention has been given to the problem of mapping the outer boundaries of the system as they expand over time. Yet this task is an obvious prerequisite to any long-term study that is predicated on the assumption that relations between elements of the system are qualitatively different from exchanges with areas external to the capitalist world-economy (Wallerstein, 1974).

In part this problem has been overlooked because most work utilizing a world-system paradigm has either been devoted to historical analysis of particular situations or to contemporary comparative studies where it is assumed that all areas have been incorporated within the capitalist world-economy. The result is a lack of long-term quantitative empirical research using the system as the unit of analysis.[1] This article explores the possibility of applying a theory of the logic of capitalist development to the historical record in order to delimit the changing boundaries of the system. Such a theory must be broad enough to encompass both the core and the periphery

---

[1] The articles in Bergeson's *Studies of the Modern World System* (1980) are a notable exception in this respect.

of the system across time, yet explicit enough to distinguish the incorporation of areas within the European world-economy from significant interactions between systems.

MEASURING INCORPORATION: THE PROBLEM

The outer boundaries of the capitalist world-economy define the area in which a hierarchically ordered division of labor based upon maximization of capital accumulation reproduces itself by means of an interaction between economic networks and power relations. The incorporation of external areas into this system, defined by Wallerstein and Martin (1979:193) as the integration of "production processes into the interdependent network of production processes that constitutes the world market," can be conceptualized both spatially and by degree of penetration. It not only involves changes in a multitude of socioeconomic and political dimensions, but the arena in which these changes occur varies from a household, regional, state, and system-wide level. Generally, changes in production relations, property laws, and household organization are required so that labor power can be directed toward those activities that will net the most profit in the world market. Politically, the area must be brought within the state system so that external pressures can be brought to bear upon production at the local level.

Nowhere is this process complete. Even in contemporary western societies not all activities are governed by market imperatives. Similarly commodity relations have existed in social systems in the past that would not be characterized as capitalist. Nor does the process of incorporation follow any regular temporal sequence. In China, significant economic integration occurred before any state-to-state political or military exchanges were institutionalized, while in Japan a military "opening" came first.

In the absence of a universal pattern, every researcher is free to focus on particular aspects of the incorporation process. Choice of criteria results in divergent time frames. Additionally, segments of larger entities like the Chinese and Ottoman empires felt the impact of capitalist penetration at different times and at varying rates. Thus Wallerstein *et al.* (1979) note that scholars have fixed on dates as far apart as 1600 to 1908 as the time when the Ottoman Empire came within the framework of the capitalist world-economy.

THE INCORPORATION OF THE CHINESE EMPIRE: AN ILLUSTRATION

There is even less consensus as to the nature of the historical interactions between Europe and the Chinese Empire. A closer examination of the literature on Chinese–European relations serves to illustrate how prolonged the process of incorporation can be. Conventionally, the Opium War and the Treaty of Nanking (1840–1842) are seen as the demarcation line for the opening of China to a century of Western exploitation (Compilation Group, 1976:110). The Treaty of Nanking and the Supplementary Treaty of the Bogue, along with two French and American agreements, marked the end of the Chinese imperial government's ability to resist peripheralization. Among its provisions, Hong Kong was ceded to the British and five treaty ports were opened to western trade. The administered trade monopoly system used by the Chinese to control foreign trade was abolished. Tariffs were lowered and inland transit duties limited. Western diplomats achieved access to and equal status with Chinese officials.

Yet data can be pieced together to show a pattern of increasing integration of the Chinese production process in the world-economy from the sixteenth century. China engaged in a trade of luxuries with the west from Roman times. By the sixteenth century the Chinese exchanged tea, silk, and porcelains mainly for Mexican silver. McDonald (1979:539) argues that silver linked China to the west from this time, encouraging monetization of the labor tax during the sixteenth century and provoking a recession in those areas most affected by the seventeenth-century decline in foreign trade.

A similar pattern is found for the eighteenth century. The population of the empire more than doubled at this time, rising from around 150 million to over 300 million (Jones and Kuhn, 1978:109). The area of cultivated land greatly expanded, as did commercialization of agriculture and the market system. But as internal frontiers diminished, unemployment resulted. Both landless peasants and overeducated gentry sought work in a bloated bureaucracy. In consequence, the tax load on the peasantry increased constantly. While Western silver flowed into China the tax burden was lessened by a steady inflation. Cheaper silver helped subsidize rising grain prices, which tripled during the eighteenth century. The system encouraged increased cash-cropping, especially of tea.

The tea trade is of primary importance in assessing China's impact on the European economy. By the end of the eighteenth century, the British East India Company's conquest of India served to turn this trade into a necessity for Great Britain. Operations in India were financed by government loans, which totaled £28 million by 1800. At about the same time, tea became an item of mass consumption in England. The East India Company's monopoly of the tea trade enabled it to pay its debts in London, and the 12½% duty on tea imposed by the government provided about one-tenth of the total British revenue (Greenberg, 1951:3). Moulder (1977) emphasizes the growth of this staple trade as the key to China's inclusion within the world-economy.

In exchange for tea, the British shipped silver and Indian cotton to China. As North Chinese cotton was substituted for the Indian variety, the British balance of trade worsened. After some experimentation, the English merchants discovered in opium a product that the Chinese would buy in great quantity. By 1830 the trade balance had shifted against the Chinese. When the opium trade caused silver to flow out of China, the value of silver increased. China had a bimetallic monetary system. Peasants paid their taxes in copper but tax quotas were assessed in terms of silver. Thus more copper was needed to fill the same silver tax quota. Widespread tax-resistance movements resulted, leading occasionally to revolt.

The Chinese effort to deal with the growing problem of opium addiction and the silver drain, and British resistance to that effort, served as the ostensible cause of the Opium War. In a broader sense, we can say that the war was fought to determine the terms of China's entry into the world-system and to ensure its peripheralization. Basu (1979:171), for example, views it as "culminating the first phase of a peripheralization process that had been long in the making."

However, another school of thought contends that even military defeat failed to ensure China's integration within the world-economy. Murphy (1974) notes that western impact on Imperial China never really penetrated to the countryside where land tenure, social relations, and technology remained relatively unchanged until 1949. Similarly, Lippit in his analysis of the relevance of the concept of the "development of underdevelopment" in China contends that capitalist pressure had only limited impact:

> China became an underdeveloped country in the late imperial era because the interest of the gentry class was in preserving the status quo, because the economic and social changes associated with economic development would have undermined the social order that provided everything it wanted. And China remained an underdeveloped country in the first half of the twentieth century because the class structure and relations of production remained largely unchanged. (1978:322)

All of these interpretations hinge upon different dimensions of Chinese–European interaction. There is no completely satisfactory way to reconcile the prolonged process of capitalist penetration with the necessity of mapping the system as it changes over time, but clarification of the nature of the boundaries of the world-economy should help to provide a general framework applicable to a range of societies.

THEORETICAL FRAMEWORK

The process of incorporation can best be understood within the context of the capitalist world-system in which production for exchange dominates over production for use. Focusing upon the extraction of surplus within the labor process, theorists working in the Marxist tradition have proposed a model for analysis of the interconnection between production processes in the world-economy. Within the division of labor, commodity prices interact according to their values as expressed in terms of the socially necessary labor time needed to produce them (Luxemburg, 1968:102). The quantity of abstract human labor needed to reproduce the labor power required in a commodity's production fluctuates with world market conditions as expressed not only by the development of the forces of production but also with the definition of the minimal subsistence needs of the workers (Marx, 1977:275).

Although human biological needs mark a bottom limit for the price of labor power, minimum subsistence has a social content that varies according to the power of competing class interests. The segmentation of the working class by national boundaries means that the definition of human needs will vary from Chad to the United States. As the prices of commodities will reflect supply and demand as well as the respective powers of the forces involved in production and exchange, the distribution of surplus value will result from class struggles objectively located at the level of the whole system (see especially Amin, 1980:149–173; Bukharin, 1973:106).

Therefore the incorporation of an area within the capitalist world-economy must involve a way to ensure the interaction of the price of its commodities, including labor power, with the demands of the world market, and a mechanism whereby relations of political and military power can be transformed into rates of exploitation. In *nonperipheral* incorporation this will mean the strengthening of local capitalists vis-à-vis workers, peasants, and traditional elites. In this manner, system-wide pressures and opportunities contributed to a restructuring of the socioeconomic and political relations within the Russia of Peter the Great and Japan at the time of the Meiji Restoration, resulting in a mobilization of surplus that enabled these states to enter the system as part of the semi-periphery. *Peripheral* incorporation signifies the ability of metropolitan capitalists to exert pressure on local production relations to ensure maximum capital accumulation at the core. Here the international state system serves the dual purpose of fueling the expansion of the world-economy through competition among core powers and providing the structure within which external pressures can be brought to bear upon local production processes.

State System and World–Economy

Although the state system is an integral part of the process of incorporation, the inclusion of an area within it is not synonymous with the incorporation of that area in the world economy. For example, the Ottoman Empire played a crucial role in the European balance of power long before its economic integration within the system. While the operation of the interstate system is interdependent with the world-economy, state policy makers have interests apart from the economic demands of national elites. Foremost among these is the preservation of the state itself and, secondarily, its political regime. State survival is mediated by factors such as military strength and administrative efficiency. These elements reflect not only the overall economic strength of the state but especially its ability to mobilize and deploy the resources available to it.

The impact of class struggle on the state at the system level ultimately determines the success or failure of particular actors. Thus Wallerstein (1980) shows how in eighteenth-century Prussia the existence of a politically powerful but economically weak aristocracy interacted with the need of major European powers to neutralize the military strength of Austria to produce a bureaucratically centralized, militarily strong state with the potential for transformation into a core power.

The interrelationship between the state system and the world-economy, analytically separable but both dependent upon the structure of global class alliances, determines the pattern and timing of the expansion of the system. The interaction between these two dynamics helps to explain why the incorporation of an area cannot be modeled in any particular sequential pattern. European imperialism in the late nineteenth century testifies to the spiraling nature of this process. Thus, the use of state machineries by competing groups of national capitalists in their struggle for markets, resources, and investment opportunities helps set in motion a military competition for division of the earth. Particular conquests might have brought no economic benefit to national elites but may have been motivated by strategic considerations, the need to preserve the balance of power, pressure from increasingly strong domestic military interests, or for reasons of national pride. There was often a gap of many years before the territory was exploited economically in any systematic way.

From this perspective it is less important to determine the economic benefit derived from any one conquest than to understand the process at a global level. However, to chart capitalist penetration of any specific region, we must analyze the way in which economic and political factors resulted in a situation where alternatives to integration within the system were eliminated.

EXCHANGES BETWEEN SYSTEMS

The expansion of the capitalist world-economy from its European base occurred in a world already divided between other world-systems, world empires, and minisystems. Relationships existed on multiple levels between systems. Often trade networks linked them but contact could also come in the form of military encroachment, alliances, and cultural exchange. The complex nature of these interactions is obscured by a Eurocentric analysis that focuses too exclusively upon the European impact on individual societies.

Thus the study of Chinese–European interaction, for example, must take into account the intricate cultural, political, and economic ties that linked China, India, the Ottoman Empire, and Southeast Asia for many centuries. Within the trading network, the range of goods varied from luxuries such as Chinese silks and porcelains, through widely distributed Indian cotton textiles and Indonesian pepper, to the short-distance trade in foodstuffs that fulfilled the subsistence requirements of the trading ports of Malaysia and shifted needed rice from South India and Burma to Ceylon and Bengal or from Vietnam to China (Simkin, 1968:254–256).

The economic relationship between different systems has been defined as an exchange of unequals (Frank, 1978a:8) or preciosities. Such a conceptualization postulates an exchange of surpluses without consequences for the internal dynamic of each society. In its ideal form this relationship would involve a "trade between A-B in which the producers of A think that they are giving B something utterly worthless; the producers of B think they are giving A something worthless; however each thinks they are receiving something marvelous" (Wallerstein, 1978:230–231). This type of exchange is contrasted with a trade of necessities ordered around a single division of labor.

Historically, the boundary between the two types of exchanges is much harder to delineate. Schneider (1977:20–29) speculates that an exchange of low-bulk, high-value luxuries may have profound consequences for the trading partners. She posits the existence of a precapitalist world-system in which a Chinese and Indian core mobilized energy for its development partially through the export of textiles in return for silver and gold from the peripheral areas of Europe, Southeast Asia, and West Africa. In that these metals were valued rewards used in the construction of a political hierarchy and military machine, treasure diverted from peripheral areas lessened the ability of rulers in those areas to mobilize resources within their territory and increased the power of core entities correspondingly. Indeed, Elvin (1973:204) links the fourteenth-century decline in the Chinese economy, in part, to a silver shortage caused by the decline in foreign trade. In this sense, trade involving bullion can be considered "a disguised transfer of essential goods" (Schneider, 1977:27).

Further, there are no clearcut distinctions between a trade in preciosities and a staple trade. At one level, trade of necessities may be the result of technological advances, particularly in shipping, which make long-distance exchange of goods profitable between societies. As the arena in which profitable trading can take place expands, the price of commodities may become interactive across a range of systems. Thus as the Portuguese competed with Chinese merchants for access to pepper and spices in the East Indies, both were forced to pay increasingly higher prices. Increased demand for a product is likely to lead to increased production, especially when the political authority in a region has the power to change production patterns. This may be done directly, as when the sixteenth-century rulers of islands in the East Indies established new pepper estates to meet the rising world demand (Meilink-Roelofsz, 1962:241), or indirectly through a tax structure that favors the production of cash crops. As a consequence, an increasing percentage of the people will be tied to the export trade network, both as direct producers and in support of those producing for the world market. Finally, a state may become dependent on the revenues derived from contact with the larger system.

Europe participated in the Indian Ocean trade indirectly from Roman times but became more directly involved during the sixteenth century. Its inclusion in this trade network must be distinguished from the expansion of the capitalist world-economy. Superior naval power enabled the Portuguese to dominate the spice trade and extract surplus in the form of plunder, but this occurred within the context of the traditional trade. The response of Asian societies varied with their economic and political power. A number of Indian Hindu princes allied with the Europeans to counteract Moslem power, which was perceived as the greater threat. Some producers of desired commodities benefited from increased world demand. In other areas, when the Portuguese attempted to force producers to sell their cash crops at lowered prices, production to meet subsistence needs was reemphasized. Japan insulated itself from the disruptive effects of European contact by withdrawal from the trading network. China attempted to incorporate Europe within its system of international relations by restricting trade to one tightly controlled port.

In each of these societies, the actions taken were determined by struggles between competing interests within the state. Such conflicts occurred within the context of the rewards and threats represented by the expanding capitalist system but were clearly divisible from it. Most notable in this regard was the rapid reversal of policy on overseas exchange by the Ming Dynasty in China. As Elvin (1973) notes, between 1405 and 1433 the Chinese navy under the eunuch Cheng Ho carried out trading expeditions to points as far away as the east coast of Africa. However as the internal traffic in grains shifted to the reconstructed inland Grand Canal, the importance of an overseas naval capability to the Chinese state declined. The foreign-trade-oriented faction in the imperial court lost influence to an elite with interests centered around the land who resented the expense involved in naval up-keep. By 1433, Chinese overseas trade was officially prohibited by the state. Thus, during the sixteenth century when European trade in the Indian Ocean was expanding, the Chinese Empire was attempting to insulate itself from contact with the outside world.

Portugal's domination of the spice trade resulted in a fragile tie between the East Indies and the capitalist world-economy. It depended on naval superiority and alliances with regional powers. Arrighi (1979:161) defines this political linkage in which capital accumulation by core powers requires the constant use or threat of force as nominal incorporation. The meaning of this concept varies when considered from the perspective of the system or the area incorporated within it. For the metropolitan bourgeoisie, surplus in the form of plunder derived from this type of "primitive accumulation" may be crucial for capitalist development, although such a linkage would be expensive to maintain and, in the long run, likely to result in the destruction of the peripheral society's ability to reproduce itself. Conversely, a society whose production processes have been unaffected by nominal incorporation would be better able to sever its connection with the world-economy in the event of a change in power relations.

Clearly the use of power to extract surplus is not unique to the capitalist mode of production. Amin (1980:50–55) sees it as an essential characteristic of the tributary mode of production and locates the impetus for the expansion of empires in the need of the ruling class to maintain or increase its share of surplus product. Within this social formation, further research may show that some of the trade between societies involved elements of capitalist relations as, for example, the expansion of the porcelain industry in China to meet foreign demand. However, in such cases exchange relations whether in the form of trade or tribute were dominated by the dynamic of production for use.

Effective Incorporation

It follows that while power relations are a vital aspect of the system, by itself plunder does not constitute effective incorporation. The secular trends of the capitalist mode of production are toward lifetime proletarianization of labor, industrialization, and integration of the labor process through price-fixing markets. But these characteristics cannot delimit the boundaries of the system because nowhere are they complete. Further, too great an emphasis on these elements obscures the extent to which the expansion of the system since the sixteenth century has depended on coerced labor and state involvement in the market system.

Incorporation does require a reorganization of the production process such that alternatives to production for exchange are increasingly eliminated. Arrighi (1979:163) notes that peripheral incorporation is marked by the extent to which the density and connectedness of internal economic networks are weakened but this holds equally true for political and economic relations that link different systems. Indeed incorporation is marked by the progressive channeling of all forms of human interaction through the capitalist division of labor. With the alienation of resources like forests and common lands, the household becomes less self-sufficient and more dependent on production for the market to fulfill its subsistence requirements, while more and more individuals are left with nothing but their labor power to sell. Local trading networks are restructured to meet the extraction needs of the larger system. In this manner, the destruction of intersocietal trading networks, as between China and Southeast Asia in the early nineteenth century, was a prerequisite for the maximization of capital accumulation by core powers. Thus the existence of Sino–Siamese trade would adversely affect the terms of trade for Europeans in both places.

We can say that any area has been peripheralized when a structure exists so that political and economic mechanisms can be employed to adapt production processes to metropolitan demand. The area must be integrated within the state system and surplus must be extracted through regular networks that tend to reproduce themselves. This does not mean that the majority of the population of an area incorporated within the world-economy cannot be engaged in what appears to be subsistence agriculture. Capitalist penetration occurs progressively and peasant farming is in many ways functional to the operation of the system. It acts as a labor reserve for an expanding system and is a means of maintaining a labor force when the economy is in contraction. It provides cheap food and part-time employment for an underemployed urban work force. Additionally, the urban worker who spends his youth and old age in a rural village need only be paid wages sufficient to fulfill his immediate requirements. Hence we can say that an area is incorporated within the system when the structure of economic networks and power relations can be used to manipulate subsistence agriculture in response to global imperatives. Anthropological literature from Mexico (Migdal, 1974), Vietnam (Scott, 1976) and China (Yang, 1954; Skinner, 1971) is filled with examples of the way in which system-wide pressures contribute to changing emphases on cash-cropping or subsistence agriculture. Finally, as Portes demonstrates in this volume (Chapter 4), adaptation of subsistence techniques to the urban environment through the informal sector continues to be a significant means by which surplus is extracted from the periphery to the core of the world-economy.

CONCLUSION: THE BOUNDARY PROBLEM

The meaning of incorporation is further complicated by the difficulty in determining the unit that is said to be incorporated. In larger entities like the Chinese and Ottoman empires, different regions may enter the system at different points in time as part of the process of destroying the traditional economic and political links within a system. Regions must be delineated to include those areas that supply the subsistence needs of regions where workers specialize in production for the world market. To add to the complexity of the problem, interdependent aspects of incorporation may be expressed on different levels. For example, changes in production relations on a regional level may be facilitated by alterations in land tenure or tax structures expressed on the level of the state. One way of handling this problem would be to resolve that if regional incorporation resulted in the creation of new political units, like the states of Eastern Europe and North Africa that arose out of the dissolution of the Ottoman Empire, each region would be treated individually. However if the national unit was ultimately maintained despite uneven penetration by the world-economy, as was the case with China, then the state would be treated as the unit of incorporation.

An alternative way of viewing this problem is to treat cities as units of incorporation because the urban area acts "as a generative centre around which an effective space is created out of which growing quantities of surplus product are extracted" (Harvey, 1973:249). Here the city is conceptualized as a "growth pole" with the economic and political capacity to attract surplus from a surrounding hinterland and to redirect surplus flow through a hierarchically ordered system of cities extending to the level of the global economy. In this way class coalitions between regional elites and core capitalists find spatial expression in the urban hierarchy.

This method of conceptualization is only possible if city systems can be demarcated to include those areas that supply the food needs of the regions where exchange with the core is more prevalent. The definition of the city system has important consequences for the measurement of the effects of the world-economy on the division of labor. Once again the Chinese case illustrates this point. Skinner (1977) describes eight rather self-contained regional city systems within late Imperial China. Yet, while the Chinese government was able to restrict foreign trade to Canton, that city performed certain economic central-place functions for the whole empire. Its importance in this respect is indicated by the fact that in 1843 Canton, along with Peking, the imperial capital, was the only city to be described as primate within its regional context.

The percentage of overall Chinese production for the international market was very small in relation to the total domestic market. However if only South China, where most such production took place, is treated as the Canton hinterland, the percentage increases accordingly. When Canton is analyzed in its local regional context, the importance of foreign trade is still greater. Without losing sight of the unevenness of capitalist penetration, the Canton region must also be analyzed in terms of its political relationships. The area was always linked to the outer world through the central state apparatus that had control of its tax structure, legal property relations, and military defenses. Further, the terms of its entry within the system were determined by a power struggle involving all of the empire. Thus incorporation may be considered in terms of city systems only if the political relationships that link cities are not omitted from a study of exchange networks.

The aim of this essay has been to demonstrate the need for a means of delimiting the boundaries of the system that is comparable across time and space. It has raised more problems than it has answers for. However, by measuring the expansion of the system in terms of an interaction between economic networks and power relations, researchers should be able to define criteria for the inclusion of areas at specific points in time without denying the long-term nature of the process of incorporation. Examination of the changing structure of these relationships should enable us to chart the penetration of a region by the capitalist world-economy from relations of plunder through effective incorporation. It should also be possible to use this framework to test theories about the nature of the development of city systems at different stages during the process of incorporation.

4

THE INFORMAL SECTOR AND THE WORLD-ECONOMY: NOTES ON THE STRUCTURE OF SUBSIDIZED LABOR*

Alejandro Portes

INTRODUCTION

The study of urbanization, together with that of migration, has placed its practitioners at the crossroads of two major strands of "developmental" thought. One concerns the anthropological and sociological literature exploring how the poor survive under the constraints of underdeveloped capitalist economies. The other is the historical and economic literature on state policies, unequal exchange, and the systemic insertion of countries within world-capitalism. The line of reasoning I wish to explore in this essay offers some promise of articulating both levels in a manner that goes beyond the perennial recognition that "micro" and "macro" structural phenomena are somehow related.

The relevance of this issue to the new emphasis placed by international agencies on "basic needs" as an approach to development lies in clarifying the way such needs have been taken care of so far in many underdeveloped countries and, more important, the way such strategies for survival articulate with requirements of the capitalist economy.

My problem here is the *informal economy* or *informal sector*. My argument can, in part, be interpreted as a defense of the concept against accusations of irrelevance or academic voguism. On the contrary, I suggest

*This essay originally appeared in the *Institute of Development Studies Bulletin,* volume 9, number 4 (June) 1978; Institute of Development Studies, University of Sussex. The Institute has kindly given permission for it to be reprinted here.

that the *informal economy* represents a fundamental concept for understanding the operations of capitalism as a world phenomenon and constitutes a missing element in contemporary world-system formulations of relationships between core and periphery. The data on which this proposition is based come, primarily, from a series of recent field studies conducted in different countries of Latin America. Important examples of these studies include Roberts (1976), Mangin (1967), Uzzell (1974), Peattie (1968), the Leeds (1969), and Lomnitz (1977a, 1977b).

Earlier formulations defined the informal economy as the way the marginal poor took care of themselves in the city. Squatter settlements, which served as loci for much informal economic activity, lost the stigma of the past since they did not represent problems, but "solutions to the problem." Later studies observed, however, that the informal sector was more than an exercise at self-preservation. The "marginals" turned out to be profoundly integrated in the production, distribution, and consumption structures of the city. Studies in Ciudad Guyana, Rio de Janeiro, and Mexico City, among others, showed how closely interdependent shantytown economies and those of the broader city were in fact.

These studies went on to note the profound dependence of informal economic activities on decisions, events, and resources in the formal sector. This assertion is correct, when seen from the point of view of the individual shanty-town worker or petty entrepreneur. From the point of view of the dominant economic system, the opposite is, however, more accurate. The organization of "formal" capitalism in peripheral underdeveloped countries appears profoundly dependent on the informal sector and this dependence extends beyond the way workers in that sector take care of their own needs. Further, the hypothesis can be advanced that functional effects of informal economies reach, through a series of interlinked mechanisms, to the very centers of capitalist accumulation.

WAGE LEVELS IN CENTER AND PERIPHERY

It is generally accepted that the percentage of the labor force of advanced industrial countries that is fully *proletarianized*—that is, fully dependent for its reproduction as labor on monetary wages—is higher than that in peripheral countries. It is also generally agreed that real wage-levels in the core capitalist countries are higher, on the average, than those in the periphery for exactly the same type and amount of work.

Reasons why labor in core economies is more fully dependent on wages and why those wages are higher come down, in the ultimate analysis, to the same thing. Though the argument can be made in many forms, the formulation by Alain de Janvry (1976–1977) is the most useful for present purposes. Profits to capital depend on maintenance of wages paid to workers at a minimum relative to productivity. Actualization of money profits depends, however, on the sale of the product. The process of capital accumulation entails a constant growth in productive capacity, a trend that constantly outstrips demand. The market for core capitalist production is also, by and large, a "core" market. Expanding that market to avert or attenuate crises of over-production means putting more money in the hands of the mass of consumers. Pressures to expand the internal market thus lead to incorporation of remaining "subsistence redoubts" into the money economy and to higher wages. It is this organic integration of profits and wages in core economies that, in part, counteracts the downward pressure on wages. Surplus obtained by exploiting workers cannot be actualized without selling the product to other workers.

This "organic" nexus disappears under peripheral capitalism. The fundamental reason is that the hegemonic sector in these economies produces for export. Profits, in other words, are actualized by sale in markets abroad, rather than in the country. While domestic enterprises and branches of multinational enterprises also produce for a restricted internal market, their existence and functioning are ultimately dependent on export earnings. Nor is the situation limited to countries exporting agricultural products and materials; the more industrialized peripheral countries have also become increasingly dependent on manufactured exports to sustain their internal economies.[1]

Under these conditions, downward pressure on wages is not counteracted by pressures to expand the internal market. The logic of peripheral capitalism is one where profits are maximized by keeping labor costs at a minimum. Cheap labor is indeed what gives many peripheral countries a "competitive edge" in the international market. The pressure on wages is reflected in two aspects: first, actual restrictions in the consumption levels of workers and, second, a continuous attempt to cheapen their consumption, that is to transfer part of the costs of their reproduction to other economic units.

LABOR COSTS

Asking why wage levels in central and peripheral capitalist economies must differ is not identical to asking how peripheral labor costs are kept low. Strategies suggested by the existing literature amount to two: the first is the use of a reserve army of labor. This strategy tends to inhibit wage revindications, thus keeping consumption levels low. The second consists of subsidizing wages paid by capitalist enterprises through use of workers

---

[1]Evidence of this for Brazil can be found in Bacha (1976) and Baer (1975). For Mexico see Blair (1974) and Rhodes (1973).

from the rural subsistence sector. Workers reared in villages, under subsistence conditions, come to work for wages in mines, plantations, and urban plants. Wages paid amount to the reproduction of the worker while employed. Collectively, however, capitalist enterprises save the costs of supporting workers during their early unproductive years (cf. Meillassoux, 1972).

This "subsidy" of subsistence to capitalist economies is compounded when the worker ceases to be useful and is forced to return to the village. By shifting replacement and welfare costs into the subsistence sector, capitalist enterprises in the periphery save a significant part of the real wage bill. A way of saying the same thing is that coexistence of subsistence and capitalist modes of production enables capitalist enterprises to exploit not only the labor of the worker, but of his kin in the village, as the latter are forced to provide for his needs during periods of idleness and old age.

The reserve army and subsistence-transfer strategies do not suffice, however, to explain fully the situation in many peripheral societies. Latin American countries, in particular, present a situation where subsistence economies have a diminishing and, in some cases, vestigial importance. For most Latin American countries, it would be risky indeed to affirm that villages producing for subsistence provide the bulk of labor for enterprises in the capitalist sector or that they fully subsidize its welfare costs. As to the reserve army argument, it should be remembered that a considerable proportion of employed labor in the formal capitalist sector consists of skilled workers. More important, workers in the formal sector are those to which protective legislation most directly applies and those most capable of deriving support from existing labor organizations.

Despite the restricted effectiveness of the above mechanisms in many peripheral countries, wages continue to be comparatively low, even those going to skilled labor. Cases such as Brazil, documented in Table 4.1, provide a compelling illustration of the disparity.

An additional mechanism must exist. Though political repression of working class demands has certainly proved effective in the short run, a more stable and less overt mode of controlling labor costs is needed to ensure stability. Means to sustain effective downward pressures on labor costs can not find their sole locus in an economic sector of decreasing relative importance, such as subsistence agriculture, but in one whose growth accompanies that of capitalism itself.

CLASS STRUCTURE AND THE INFORMAL ECONOMY

For purposes of the argument, the class structure of a peripheral society can be crudely divided in four groups:

TABLE 4.1

Comparative Wage Scales[a]

	Brazil	Japan	Germany	Belgium	United Kingdom	Italy	United States
Unskilled labor	0.24	0.74	1.27	1.34	0.96	0.67	3.00
Light assembly	0.32	0.65	1.40	1.42	0.82	0.72	2.89
Machine operator	0.68	0.68	1.50	1.64	1.01	0.86	3.24
Maintenance mechanic	0.65	0.78	1.60	1.83	1.42	0.92	3.29
Toolmaker	0.81	0.79	1.73	1.87	1.61	1.02	5.03

[a] U.S. dollars per hour, 1975. Source: Brown and Ford (1975, p. 124).

Class I: Owners, managers, and top-level state administrators;
Class II: Nonmanual workers—clerks, technicians, and salaried professionals;
Class III: Manual workers in public and private enterprises; and
Class IV: Informal sector workers.

The first three classes comprise the formal sector. Interests of the first class are, however, structurally contrary to those of the other two. Class I members are dependent, directly or indirectly, on the rate of profit. While, for some, this may be tied to expansion of the internal market, the structure of peripheral capitalism leads to dominance of export-oriented enterprises and interests. This means an unmitigated downward pressure on the portion of the product going, as salaries and wages, to Classes II and III. The increase in the share of the product of formal capitalist enterprises going, as profits, to Class I can thus be managed in two ways: decreasing the consumption levels of Classes II and III or decreasing the costs of inputs consumed by these classes.

Individual actors and enterprises in the informal sector have been defined according to a number of characteristics. Bryan Roberts (1976) observes, however, the two characteristics that most significantly identify these activities. First, they are labor intensive; second, they avoid formal state supervision and regulation. The two characteristics combine to reduce substantially the "input" costs of whatever goods or services are produced, thereby cheapening the price of the outputs. Long and strenuous hours are contributed by the individual himself, by unpaid kin, and by others in his informal network of friends and acquaintances. Absence of state supervision means, first of all, greater ease in avoiding taxation; it also means avoiding the rigidities of labor legislation. Informal sector workers are seldom paid the official minimum wage, nor do they have access to health insurance, unemployment compensation, old-age pensions, or other indirect benefits. Hiring and laying off in informal enterprises is done on a much more casual basis, entirely dependent on need.

The "competitive edge" of the informal sector in relation to the formal one in peripheral countries parallels the "edge" that the periphery as a whole has in relation to the capitalist core in the international economy. In both cases, it is based on access to cheaper sources of labor.

Depending on the specific situation, the relationship between the classes above may be defined as one in which Class I—the owners—use Class IV—the informal sector—against the intermediate classes or as one in which Class I allows Classes II and III to exploit Class IV, thereby cheapening their costs of consumption and reducing upward pressure on wages. In whatever version, the fundamental point is that the informal sector subsidizes part of the costs of formal capitalist enterprises in peripheral countries, enabling them to enforce comparatively low wages on its own labor. Basic needs of formal sector workers are partially met by goods and services produced using unpaid or more cheaply paid informal labor. Paralleling the mechanism of subsistence-transfer, but in a far more diversified and complex manner, the capitalist sector is thus able to exploit not only the work-energy of the worker but that of his kin, neighbors, and friends as well.

Uses of Informal Labor

Let us consider the hypothetical case of a worker employed in a soft drink plant in a large Latin American city. He lives in a fairly good house in one of the local shantytowns. He probably could afford rented rooms or even a small house in the city, but he would get less comfortable quarters for a high price. In the shantytown, he pays no rent. He probably bought the lot through informal contract and built the house with materials purchased locally over a period of time. Let us assume he has a wife, three children, an unemployed sister, and an aging mother. The children go to public school. To supplement the family income, the women set up a little business. It might be a front-room store in the house or a cheap-food stand somewhere in the city. The initial small investment comes from the man's wages. The family also raises a pig or two and a few chickens.

Food is seldom bought in the supermarket, but locally from petty merchants who give credit. Eggs, milk, and other products may be bought from individual neighbors. Vegetables and meat come, at times, from the village. Clothing is usually secondhand, bought cheap or gotten free from families in the city and refitted by the women or the shantytown tailor. The house has electricity, a radio, and television. Electricity is either bought legally, purchased from a neighbor, or tapped illegally. Appliances and other items of furniture might have been bought in long-term installments from a store in town; most likely, however, they were gotten secondhand through informal contacts and repaired locally. Appliance repairs and all similar services are always done in small shops in the shantytown or linked through social contacts with it.

Wage-workers in the private and state sectors in peripheral countries live lives conditioned, at every step, by their relationships with the informal economy. Though those workers are also consumers of formal-sector goods, a substantial proportion of their needs are satisfied by informal sources. This is especially true of services but also extends to goods, such as food and refurbished durables. The relative cheapness of these goods and services is what enables the worker to meet his basic needs and even save within the constraints of a meager wage. His savings may, in turn, initiate other family-based informal enterprises.

The shantytown or squatter settlement is the most common living environment of the class of informal sector workers. Its very size has forced everywhere a rupture in the rules of conventional urban land speculation, reducing housing costs for *both* informal and formal sector workers.[2] Shantytown housing represents a major indirect subsidy to wages, passed on and ultimately benefiting owners in the formal sector.

This subsidy, like most others provided by the informal economy, depends on physical contiguity of formal and informal sector workers. In the shantytown, both groups are indistinguishable, with the same individuals frequently alternating between periods of formal and informal employment or simultaneously holding jobs in both sectors. At first glance, this symbiotic relationship appears as evidence of the dependence of informal activities on money wages. The opposite is, however, more accurate, as the consumption "yield" of wages are multiplied by informal sources of supply.

This subsidy-to-consumption is not limited to Class III workers. The same applies, albeit less directly, to clerks, technicians, and professionals. Though there is less empirical evidence on this point, Class II workers appear to make use, in a vast number of ways, of informal sector goods and services. Cheap and abundant domestic labor is but the most visible evidence of the subsidy to middle-class consumption provided by the informal economy. While available studies concentrate on the political symbiosis between middle-classes and the shantytown, anyone familiar with Latin American

[2]Among others, Lomnitz (1976, 1977a, 1977b), Collier (1976), Turner (1968) and Mangin (1967) have documented the importance of the shantytown to the reproduction of labor in the periphery.

cities knows that access and consumption of goods and services outside the formal economy is an everyday practice in middle-class households.

The "cheapness of labor" for formal capitalist enterprises is thus partly a consequence of the "cheapness of life," in turn based on everyday transactions with the informal economy. This subsidy-to-consumption is probably the most important, but not the only role played by informal sector workers.

Not surprisingly, Class I owners and managers have reached down to the informal economy in order to bypass costs of expanding employment of Class III workers. The revival of the "put-out" system or *maquila* in peripheral shantytowns of Mexico City is a case in point. As described by Lomnitz (1977b), production is farmed out, usually via an intermediary, to shantytown workers receiving less than the minimum wage and no indirect compensation. In one variant, clothing materials are distributed to women working at home and paid a piece-rate for finished apparel. In another, construction workers are recruited by an informal contractor and organized to perform a particular job. In a third, firms recruit and organize children and women to market brand-name products in the streets.

Conclusion: Marginality and the World-Economy

The rapid progress of social research on the "urban poor," the "marginals," the "shantytown," and finally the "informal sector" in Latin America has helped develop, during a period of a few years, a major body of knowledge about a previously ignored population. At the local level, the picture appears essentially complete, at least in the present conjuncture. However, the articulation of this working-class population within an international economic order remains problematic.

Recent advances in the literature owe much to social scientists working close to the field. Researchers repeatedly found that "marginals" did not form an inert mass, but were in fact quite adept at turning their restricted opportunities to advantage. The rationality of the urban poor was highlighted and the mythologies of the past—radical anger and the "culture of poverty"—effectively discredited.

The next step was the discovery that economic activities of the "marginal" population were not conducted in isolation, but were in fact profoundly articulated with those of the dominant economy. At this point, the concept of *informal sector* gained increasing acceptance. Earlier formulations defined the informal sector as interstitial: it operated in the gaps of economic opportunity left by formal enterprises. The theory was that the informal economy owed its dynamism to the still incomplete and imperfect penetration of capitalism in the periphery. A corollary was that the informal economy represented a transitional phenomenon, since the growing consolidation of capitalism would eventually deny its raison d'être.

Later years have brought no evidence of the weakening of the informal sector and have, in fact, produced new findings indicating that its role in the economy is far more central than originally thought. While convincingly denying the interstitial character of the informal economy, recent studies still insist that its existence and dynamism are dependent on the formal sector. This argument stands the situation on its head: though there exists a symbiotic relationship between the two, from the standpoint of basic structural arrangements, the opposite is the case.

Recent analyses from the world-system perspective have shown with great clarity reasons for the sustained peripheral expansion of central capitalist economies (Magdoff, 1969; Wallerstein, 1977; Wallerstein and Hopkins, 1977). The argument complements that of de Janvry, summarized above: the need to prevent and attenuate downward turns in core economies leads to sustained pressures for market expansion. This, in turn, means increased proletarianization of the labor force. A labor force that is proletarianized—that is, fully dependent on money wages—is one that, sooner or later, gives rise to strong organizations for demand-making. Thus, to the upward pressure on wages created by the economic needs of capital accumulation, there are added those created by the political need for social stability.

Co-opting workers in the core economies can only be achieved through transferring costs. According to the theory, capitalism as a world-system has been able to achieve market expansion and social peace in the centers by constantly expanding its activities in the periphery. High consumption of some workers has thus been subsidized by sustained exploitation of others.

The theory draws a blank, however, when it comes to explaining how disparities between core and peripheral wages can be indefinitely maintained. It argues, at most, that this depends on use of a semiproletarianized labor force whose reproduction is partially subsidized by subsistence enclaves. As seen above, this mechanism is inadequate to explain conditions in Latin America and, probably, in the more industrialized peripheral economies elsewhere.

It is from this perspective that the literature on the dynamics of informal economies acquires its full meaning. The informal sector—a vast network of activities articulated with, but not limited to remaining subsistence enclaves—has implications that go beyond the peripheral countries. Direct subsidies to consumption provided by informal to formal sector workers within a particular peripheral country are also indirect subsidies to core-nation workers and, hence, means to maintain the rate of profit. Thus, through a series of mechanisms, well-hidden from public view, the apparently isolated labor of shantytown workers can be registered as gain in the financial houses of New York and London.

The concrete forms that this transfer takes range from low-price raw materials and foodstuffs to an increasing flow of cheap manufactures. Meeting basic and perhaps not-so-basic needs of workers in the fully monetized capitalist sectors is a process partially dependent on the labor of workers whose basic needs are either not met or met outside the money economy. It is this situation that raises doubts about naive policies designed to "increase the standard of living" of the poorest (informal) sector workers in underdeveloped countries or incorporate them fully into the money economy.

5

SYSTEMS OF CITIES AND URBAN PRIMACY: PROBLEMS OF DEFINITION AND MEASUREMENT

Pamela Barnhouse Walters

INTRODUCTION

Social scientists have long studied the size distribution of cities within urban systems. In particular, urban systems in which the largest city is disproportionately large, or *primate*, have received a great deal of attention, typically in conjunction with the study of underdevelopment in the periphery or semiperiphery of the world economy. That is, urban primacy and underdevelopment are thought to be related processes. Aside from the question of what economic, social, or political processes cause or follow from urban primacy, however, many studies of primacy have paid insufficient attention to two issues that must be addressed, implicitly or explicitly, prior to any analysis of primacy: what constitutes a *system* of cities, and how to measure the size distribution of cities in a way that captures the theoretically relevant variation. This chapter raises the definitional and measurement issues that are logically prior to the study of urban hierarchies or the size distribution of cities. The nation-specific or world-system causes or consequences of particular types of city-size distributions (e.g., primate city-size distribution) are not considered in any detail in this chapter. Other chapters in this volume review some of the prior research on city-size distributions (see Smith, Chapter 6; Clark, Chapter 8), present the results of new studies of the causes and consequences of urban primacy in different nation-states (see Smith, Chapter 7; Clark, Chapter 8; Nemeth and Smith, Chapter 9; London, Chapter 10), or describe the changing size distribution of the largest cities in the world-economy (Chase-Dunn, Chapter 12).

Many studies of primacy or other characteristics of city systems take the nation-state as the unit of analysis, on the assumption that states and urban systems are coterminous. The argument in this chapter is that although city systems can often be defined by national boundaries, there are many cases in which one city system encompasses multiple states, and other cases in which a single state contains multiple city systems. To develop arguments concerning the bounds of city systems, however, the first section considers what constitutes a system of cities, particularly the type of linkages that exist among cities within an urban system. The definition of city-system boundaries is addressed in the subsequent section. A brief review is then offered of the role that city systems have been expected to play in economic growth for purposes of identifying the range of theoretically important characteristics of city systems for which measures should be available. The final section discusses the limitations of the measures of urban hierarchies that have been used in prior studies and proposes a set of new measures that are capable of capturing the theoretically important variations in city-size distributions.

INTRASYSTEM LINKAGES AMONG CITIES

Cities are the basic units of urban systems. Our definition of what constitutes an urban system, then, depends in part on our view of the nature and functioning of individual cities.

Cities would not exist apart from specialization and differentiation of economic activities, either between a city and its hinterland or among different cities. This analysis is more concerned with the consequences of specialization and differentiation among cities for purposes of our discussion of city systems. One of the reasons that has been advanced for the existence of cities is that cities are "central places" that perform retail and service functions for an area that may be larger than that served by cities' production functions. In addition to economic specialization, however, the existence of cities is a form of spatial differentiation. Lösch (1965), for example, explains this differentiation in terms of specialization of economic functions within some defined geographic area. Starting with an assumption of a fairly uniform population distribution across a defined geographic area, he argues that the development of individual cities is a form of spatial differentiation that occurs if and only if production for exchange occurs. That is, the existence of individual cities indicates that specialization of production, exchange, and a division of labor exist within some defined geographic region.

The concepts of specialization and differentiation have been invoked to explain relationships among *groups* of cities as well as the existence of individual cities. Cities are often centers of commodity production, specializing in the manufacture of different products. Consequently, trade can be thought of as the fundamental relationship among cities, and as a direct outgrowth and indicator of production specialization. That is, because of the cost of transport, trade between cities would be uneconomical in the absence of specialization and its corresponding production efficiency. Transportation considerations are thought to constitute such an important feature of trade and production specialization that Alonso (1965) has argued that the cost of transport is a major explanation of the pattern of spatial distribution and concentration of cities. This argument evolves from theories of the most efficient location of firms.

Lösch (1965) also defines the interactions among cities in terms of trade between different centers of commodity production. Each center of production is surrounded by a market area, the size of which is determined by the range of the good(s) produced. A system of cities, according to this argument, is defined as a "systematic arrangement of the nets of market areas of the various commodities" (p. 111), the nodes of which are cities. His discussion, then, explicitly recognizes that cities exchange both with their individual hinterlands (market areas) and with other cities.

Of course, cities are not only centers of specialized commodity production. The routine service activities that support commodity production are also centered in cities. In addition, some cities, generally large cities, perform critical activities other than commodity production and its requisite support services that are central to the economic and political functioning of a large area. These *central place* functions, as they are called, include finance, communications, transport, and government. The leading cities of a system, then, perform certain highly specialized functions for the system as a whole, and thus generally have interactions with a large proportion of the other cities in the system.

We have seen that patterns of interaction, in the form of trade or exchange, among cities are generally thought of as consequences of production and other central place function specialization among cities. The specialized functions that are performed by individual cities, however, are not equally important for the functioning of the entire economic and political system. Most obviously, a hierarchy of central places exists based on the specific functions performed by those cities (see, e.g., Berry, 1965). The same concepts apply to the more locally based cities in a system, however. Friedmann (1964:347), for example, argues that "Within a given area, cities may be systematically arranged in hierarchies according to the functions they perform." Furthermore, he suggests that it is the specialization of functions that determines the characteristic relations of cities to each other, implying that patterns of interactions between pairs of cities are not constant across pairs and are influenced by the pair's respective places in the total urban hierarchy.

Friedmann (1965:349) additionally suggests that the existence of a hierarchy of urban places is functional for the system as a whole: it "represents the ultimate means for organizing a geographic area into its component social, political-administrative and economic spaces" (in italics in original). Berry and Kasarda (1977:391) make essentially the same point when they argue that the urban hierarchy is "the instrument whereby society, polity, and economy are integrated over space." A system of cities performs these integrative functions because cities are centers of economic activity, nodes of transport and communications networks, and centers of regional economies. An important function of urban hierarchies, according to theorists such as Friedmann and Berry, is the diffusion of economic change throughout the country. The urban hierarchy, then, has been understood to be the means by which the economy is spatially integrated.

A final important characteristic of city systems that must be considered is whether the exchange that occurs among the urban places in the hierarchy is fundamentally equal or unequal in nature. The existence of a hierarchy of city functions could imply complementary and mutually beneficial exchanges among the cities (analogous to Hawley's [1981] argument concerning the reciprocal nature of exchange between a city and its hinterland) or exchanges that disproportionately benefit some cities at the expense of others (analogous to Harvey's [1973] analysis of the unequal relationship between city and hinterland). Harvey argues that the appropriation and redistribution of surplus value is a fundamental characteristic of city systems. Moreover, Harvey extends the argument that the urban hierarchy integrates the space economy to suggest that "The flow of goods and services throughout this space economy are a tangible expression of that process which circulates surplus value in order to concentrate more of it" (pp. 237–238). Trade between cities is not necessarily mutually beneficial, and the development and functioning of city systems cannot be adequately analyzed apart from an understanding of "an urbanized space economy as a surplus-creating, -extracting and -concentrating device" (p. 238). Much of the research on urban primacy has adopted the latter definition of the nature of intercity exchange, on the assumption that large cities, particularly primate cities, appropriate a disporportionate share of the system's surplus value.

Our understanding of what constitutes a system of cities is based on the previous discussion of the functioning of and relationships among individual cities. The units of urban systems, cities, are both centers of production and/or ancillary services *and* nodes of exchange networks, and these functions are, in part, determinative of the interactions among cities. A *system* of cities is a productive division of labor, which implies not only economic specialization among the cities of a system (performance of differential functions) but also a hierarchical relationship with power differentially distributed across the units. Exchange is an important activity in and of itself but it is also an indicator of production specialization and the interdependence among cities. Through a variety of economic and political means (including, but not limited to, economic production), cities extract surplus from their hinterlands and exchange it with other cities. The process of surplus exchange among cities is not reciprocal in nature either. A defining feature of city systems, then, is their function for the redistribution of surplus value. In this manner, cities constitute exchange nodes, since they often mediate the economic transactions among smaller units in the system. Given that interdependence among cities is manifested by transactions and exchanges, and that exchange reflects production specialization and differential functions, I have chosen to focus on the exchanges among cities as I analyze the nature of city systems.

What, then, flows among cities? Clearly, exchange of goods and services indicates a productive division of labor, because exchange without specialization would be inefficient. Two of the factors of productive activity— labor and capital—also flow (are exchanged) among cities. Since capital is liquid, it can be relatively easily transferred between cities, but labor (in the form of population) is more resistant to movement. Population flows, along with differential fertility and mortality rates, are the factors that produce changes in the size distribution of a city system, however. Power—economic, political, and military—does not in itself flow among cities but, rather, determines the flows of goods, services, labor, and capital.

THE BOUNDS OF CITY SYSTEMS

Before discussing some of the specific characteristics of urban hierarchies, the logically prior issue of the area within which a closed system of cities can be understood to exist must be addressed. Most discussions of city systems assume that they exist within a relatively self-sufficient economic region, generally understood to be a national economy. National borders, then, are often assumed to constitute the bounds of city systems. The problem of defining the boundaries of systems of cities consequently rests on the determination of what constitutes relatively closed, self-sufficient economic regions (given that city systems have been defined in terms of production, related economic activities, and trade).

Before considering the bounds of regional city systems, however, consider that a *world* system of cities may provide the best context within which to understand the functioning of smaller city systems that are bounded by regional economies. Specialization and exchange among cities takes place not only on a national or regional level but also at the level of the world-economy as a whole. Although it is not particularly useful to suggest that there is a *single* world-level city system, the largest cities within different urban systems are obviously tightly interconnected and constitute central places or centers of economic and political control for the entire world-economy (see Chase-Dunn, this volume, Chapter 12; Friedmann and Wolff, 1982). These same cities are often the primary points of connection between regional city systems and the world-economy. At a minimum, this concept of a world-level system of leading cities suggests the importance of studying the relationships among different urban systems and/or the relationship between an urban system and the world-economy for understanding the characteristics of a particular urban system.

The role of large cities, or *world cities* as Hall (1966) first called them, as places that perform functions extending far beyond their national borders has long been recognized. It should be noted that although world cities are invariably large cities, their far-reaching economic and political roles determine their size, not vice versa. The concept of world cities, however, has generally been applied only to the large cities of the core. For example, such core cities as London, New York, and Tokyo perform central place functions for the world-economy as a whole, including political, military, and economic functions, and are engaged in a complex set of interactions with each other. However, the roles of leading peripheral cities in the world-economy have been recognized by dependency theorists, although more in terms of their dysfunction for peripheral economies than for their potential function for the world-economy as a whole. Large cities in the periphery probably play a role in the world-economy that is as important for the functioning of the world-economy as a whole as the role of cities in the core. Most fundamentally, peripheral cities may serve as points of surplus accumulation from peripheral regions for distribution to core cities, and they tend to be less strongly connected with each other than with core cities.

The concept of a world-system of cities is useful for comparative or case studies of smaller city systems and is an interesting topic of research in and of itself. Core and peripheral cities perform different functions in the world-economy (related to the different production functions of core and peripheral areas within the worldwide division of labor), and world cities are connected with each other in a variety of complex ways. Urbanization patterns of any one city, and change in these patterns over time, need to be analyzed in light of the city's position, or change in its position, in this network of world cities.

The units that usually are discussed as city systems (distributions of cities within smaller economic regions, usually nations) are nested within the world-system of cities. These subsystems of cities, or urban hierarchies, can be understood, in part, in the context of the role that their principal city plays in the world-system of cities. This concept has sometimes been applied to the analysis of urban hierarchies in the periphery—it is recognized, for example, that the city system of Argentina cannot be understood apart from the role that Buenos Aires plays in connecting the Argentinian economy to the core. This concept should be extended to other production areas to argue, for example, that neither can the urban hierarchy of England be understood apart from London's role in the world-economy and its connections with other world cities.

Having established a conception of a world network of cities that contains within it multiple, smaller city systems, we can move to a consideration of what comprises and bounds these smaller city systems. A city system exists within a more or less well-defined region, which could be thought of as the collective hinterland of the city network. Economic regions have been defined in a variety of ways. In an attempt to delineate economic regions independently of state boundaries, Lösch (1965) argued that the bounds had to be analyzed in terms of commodity production and corresponding trade areas. Market areas for a given commodity combine to form a network of areas for the commodity, and finally the networks of market areas for the various commodities form a systematic arrangement. By this mapping strategy, one can determine the bounds of "the ideal economic region" in terms of a "self-sufficient system of market areas" (p. 111). Of course, trade exists between distinct city systems, so the concept of closure is relative rather than absolute. Lösch's definition of a relatively closed economic region is based on patterns of exchange of commodities and services, as well as lines of communication.

Other researchers also identify patterns of trade or other forms of interaction among cities as the means of determining the scope of a relatively closed city system. Skinner (1977:216) argues that an urban system is a "cluster of cities within which interurban transactions [are] concentrated and whose rural–urban transactions [are] largely confined within the region." Transport networks are especially important in determining the patterns of these interurban transactions. Other commonly used indicators of linkages among cities include communication flows, trading and market areas, flows of labor (commuting and migration patterns), and capital flows such as investments (Arregui, 1981). Bourne and Simmons (1978:11) argue that the existence of a relatively closed system is implied by "the presence of strong interactions among a set of elements (cities) in a bounded area (nation) and the existence of feedback effects which regulate growth and exchange." The defining feature in their definition is the strong intrasystem interactions, at least relative to the intersystem interaction patterns.

As defined here, the bounds of city systems rest on a consideration of the patterns of connections among cities in the same system and in different systems. The concept of a system suggests that flows within a system are more dense than flows between systems. That is, the existence of a *system* of which the elements are cities implies a degree of integration among the units, or a network of connections or transactions. As previously argued, the major connections among cities consists of the exchange of goods and services, communications flows, and flows of labor and capital.

The existence of multiple city systems within the world-economy implies systems of relatively closed networks, such that the connections between cities in the same city system are greater (more frequent, more dense) than the connections between cities in different city systems. The pattern of flows is influenced by spatial distribution (distance between nodes), and by a variety of barriers to flows. Political borders are usually understood to constitute the most effective barrier to linkages between cities, and closed city systems have usually been understood to exist within national boundaries. Geographic boundaries of various types—rivers, mountain ranges, oceans, and so forth—have also effectively limited flows among cities, even within the same political unit. Economic, communication, and transportation systems (and dysjunctures in them) often determine flows, but are also often themselves influenced by political borders. When several different types of barriers overlap, the demarcation between economic regions and/or city systems is the clearest. National political borders usually represent this most dense barrier to flows, because of political restrictions themselves, the fact that political boundaries often follow geographic divisions, and the influence of political boundaries on economic production and exchange as well as on communication and transportation systems. This may represent a departure from the determinants of the bounds of city systems in previous centuries, when natural geographic boundaries (irrespective of political borders) constituted a far more effective barrier to the flow of goods, services, people, and capital than they do now due to the introduction of modern communications and transportation technology.

In general, national political boundaries are the most meaningful barrier to flows between cities and therefore the most useful device for determining the bounds of city systems. There are some instances, however, when the boundaries of city systems (thought of in terms of relatively dense flows or connections) may not be coterminous with national borders. These situations usually occur when a nation is geographically extensive, and may contain more than one city system within it, and when the country is geographically quite small and its collective hinterland clearly extends beyond its national boundaries. Skinner (1977), for example, has argued that traditional China contained more than one fairly autonomous city system;

Berry (1971) makes the same point concerning India. Analyses that aggregate these distinct city systems into an artifical national system yield misleading results. The most obvious examples of countries whose cities are
clearly part of a city system extending beyond national boundaries are the
city-states of Singapore and Hong Kong. In some cases, groups of small
nations may collectively constitute a city system—this possibility should be
considered in the cases of, for example, Belgium, the Netherlands and Luxembourg, or the countries of Central America.

CITY SYSTEMS AND ECONOMIC GROWTH

The entire city system, or urban hierarchy, has often been understood to
play an important role in regional economic development. Berry (1965) and
Friedmann (1965), for example, both argue that the network of urban places
is an important mechanism for integrating the space-economy. Cities, especially large cities, are sometimes thought to be *growth poles,* acting as
centers from which economic activities disperse throughout the rest of the
economy. More specifically, economic innovations are thought to originate
in the larger urban centers, and from there are expected to "trickle down"
to progressively smaller cities in the urban hierarchy. The most efficient
diffusion of economic innovations and activities, then, is facilitated by a
balance of cities of various sizes that are regularly geographically dispersed
throughout the economic region. The theory of trickle-down effects leads
to the assumption that an optimal urban hierarchy is characterized by a
regular distribution of city sizes and a fairly even geographic distribution
of cities of each size class. An important exception to this theoretical principle is that not all large cities act as growth poles. Some cities use the
surplus they extract for consumption purposes, and some reinvest it for
purposes of enlarging productive capability. Hoselitz (1955) distinguishes
between these two ideal-types of urban places by referring to them as *parasitic* and *generative* cities, respectively. Obviously, theories referring to the
trickle-down effects and the effects of growth poles assume that the large
cities are generative in nature.

For the purposes of our discussion of urban hierarchies, the important
aspect of theories of city systems and economic growth is the assumption
that a regular distribution of city sizes is "normal" and facilitates even,
balanced economic growth. This concept has been so widely accepted that
it has taken the form of a law, or rule—the rank–size rule. In a city system
that conforms to the rank–size rule, the second largest city is one-half the
size of the largest, the third largest city is one-third the size of the largest,
and so on. When this ideal rank–size distribution is graphed on double-

logarithmic paper, it forms a straight line, hence it has also been called a log-normal distribution. Again, a rank–size or log-normal distribution of city sizes is hypothesized as the optimal urban hierarchy for purposes of economic growth and development. Conversely, a city system that is not characterized by a log-normal size distribution is thought to constitute an impediment to growth and diffusion in the economic region, perhaps because of the proportionately larger gaps in the urban hierarchy that may act as breaks in the diffusion process. Some social geographers, notably Christaller (1966), argue the converse relationship, suggesting that a rank–size city system follows from (rather than produces) an integrated space economy.

There are two basic reasons for the assumption that a log-normal city size distribution is "normal." First, many researchers have argued that most "mature, healthy" economies are characterized by log-normal city-size distributions, and thus have concluded that this particular size distribution best facilitates economic development. The second reason derives from the mathematical log-normal distribution. The theoretical, mathematical log-normal distribution, which is approximated by many observed city-size distributions, is a "steady-state distribution of [a] simple stochastic process" (Berry, 1965:118). This correspondence leads to the question of whether observed rank–size distributions of cities could be viewed as the steady-state outcome of a simple stochastic process. Berry summarizes this argument as follows: If one assumes a fairly even spatial distribution of cities at some arbitrary starting point, and the existence of a closed system, and if growth is the result of "many factors operating in many ways," then the distribution of city sizes will conform to the rank–size rule once the steady state of the stochastic process has been achieved. In other words, a log-normal city-size distribution has been thought of as the expected, "normal" outcome of the long-term operation of a healthy market economy, given a fairly large geographic area and the simultaneous effect of a variety of cross-cutting influences, because this process roughly corresponds to the mathematical process from which the theoretical log-normal distribution is derived. Berry (1965:119–120) justifies these assumptions as follows: "For all large, complex systems of cities which exist in the world, however, aggregate growth patterns do conform to such a stochastic process, so that one macroscopic feature of these systems is a rank–size regularity of city sizes. The regularity may, in turn, be 'explained' by the stochastic process." Aberrations from the rank–size rule, once manifested, are assumed to inhibit subsequent economic development because they represent a dysjuncture in the integrative mechanism of the urban hierarchy.

The most studied aberration from the rank–size rule is the primate city-size distribution, in which the largest city in the urban hierarchy is many times larger than the next largest city. This phenomenon is considered to represent a particularly difficult obstacle to economic growth throughout the region, and primate city-size distributions are usually considered to be a characteristic of underdeveloped economies. Primacy, itself a result of lower levels of economic development, may in turn inhibit subsequent development since it implies a lack of a balanced network for the diffusion of economic change throughout the country (see, e.g., Berry and Kasarda, 1977). Primate cities, in that they indicate an overconcentration of urban resources, are viewed as parasitic in relation to the rest of the national economy (Hoselitz, 1955), which contrasts with the generative role presumably played by the largest cities in log-normal city-size distributions. Breese (1969) specifies that one of the dysfunctions of a primate city is that it consumes a disproportionate amount of the underdeveloped country's wealth without a compensating disproportionately large contribution to national productivity.

Researchers have not always hypothesized that primacy is dysfunctional for economic development. The earliest observer of primacy, Mark Jefferson (1939), introduced the concept with the observation that the largest cities in the "leading countries" of the world were primate cities. Jefferson, then, considered that primacy was positively associated with national development, as expressed in his law of primacy: "A country's leading city is always disproportionately large and exceptionally expressive of national capacity and feeling" (p. 231).

Research on the relationship between primacy and national development has yielded, at best, inconclusive evidence. Neither Berry (1961) nor Mehta (1969) found any relationship between primacy and level of economic develoment. El-Shakhs (1972), however, argued that the relationship between primacy and development is curvilinear: that nonprimate city systems are associated with low and high levels of development, while primate city systems are found in countries in "transitional" developmental periods. (See Clark [Chapter 8, this volume] for a more thorough review of studies concerning primacy and economic growth.) In terms of other correlates of primacy, Berry (1961) found that it was unrelated to national urbanization levels. Linsky (1965), however, found an interaction between primacy and country size. In large countries, primacy is seldom found, but in smaller countries, primacy is associated with low national income, an export economy, ex-colonial status, and high population growth—in short, an underdeveloped economy. Neither these studies nor others consider the correlates of *changes* in levels of primacy over time; nor do they indicate either the causes or consequences of primacy.

CHARACTERISTICS OF CITY SYSTEMS

Results of studies concerning the causes, consequences, or correlates of certain types of city-size distributions are, of course, heavily dependent on the analysts' definitions of important characteristics of city systems and on the chosen measures of such characteristics. In prior analyses of city-size distributions, most researchers have focused on one of two distinct characteristics of city systems: the dominance of the largest city in the system (the question of urban primacy), or the overall shape of the entire distribution of city sizes. Both of these characteristics are functions of the relative sizes of cities within the same urban system, usually measured in terms of population. There are, however, other important characteristics of city systems that are not considered in an analysis that focuses on the distribution of city sizes. For example, the role that city systems are expected to play in the integration of a space-economy depends on the geographic distribution of cities of various size classes (see, e.g., Berry, 1965; Friedmann, 1965). Similarly, distance between cities and the "range" of goods and services produced by individual cities are considered to be important determinants of the size distribution of cities (Lösch, 1965). Analyses of city-size distributions do not account for variation in such locational parameters. Furthermore, theories concerning urban hierarchies consider not only the size distribution but also the hierarchy of functional specialization of individual cities to be important characteristics of urban systems. Although it is often assumed that the largest city in an urban system is the dominant city in terms of the performance of economic activity or central place functions, there is not necessarily a direct relationship between city sizes and functional complexity throughout the entire urban system. Population size may be a limiting condition for specialization or the performance of certain central place functions; yet it cannot be assumed that size dominance is directly related to functional complexity or functional dominance of cities (Smith, Chapter 7, this volume, demonstrates the divergence between city size and functional complexity for the case of Guatemala).

This is not to argue that the distribution of city sizes is a meaningless characteristic of urban systems. Size relationships, in and of themselves, are important indicators of structural and spatial inequalities in an economic region. The overwhelming size dominance of the largest city (primacy) is studied, in part, because of the obvious social problems in primate cities of many urban systems, particularly those in which the growth rate of the largest city is far in excess of the growth rate of intermediate and smaller cities. These problems include high rates of under- and unemployment, inadequate housing, proliferation of squatter settlements, the lack of a diversified industrial structure, and so on—problems that have come to be associated with the more general phenomenon of "overurbanization". Finally, most theories of the role of city systems in economic growth consider that a "regular" distribution of cities of various size classes is critical for economic integration and for the diffusion of economic innovation throughout the relevant region. The important point, however, is that size distributions are not the only important characteristic of urban systems and, furthermore, that variation in locational parameters and/or functional complexity among urban systems may be important determinants and/or outcomes of variation in city-size distributions.

As previously stated, two concerns have been dominant in prior research on city-size distributions: the size of the largest city in relation to other cities in the system, and the shape of the total city-size distribution. The measurement of characteristics of city-size distributions obviously depends on the researchers' focus and on the particular questions that are posed concerning urban hierarchies. Furthermore, it is difficult to describe both of these characteristics of city systems with the same measurement technique. The following discussion briefly outlines the primary research questions and measures that have been used in previous studies of city-size distributions.

Researchers interested in the primacy, or dominance, of the largest city in an urban system have generally used a ratio measure of the size of the largest city to the size of other cities or total urban population in the city system. The Davis index (or the Ginsberg index), which has perhaps been most widely used (see Davis, 1976), is the ratio of the population of the largest city over the sum of the populations of the four largest cities. It is, therefore, a measure of the share of the population of the four largest cities that is accounted for by the first city. A higher number signifies greater primacy, or size dominance, of the largest city. This and similar ratio measures ignore variation in the sizes of the second, third, and fourth largest cities; furthermore, changes in the ratio may result from size fluctuations in any of the four largest cities. Because of this feature, such a ratio measure cannot distinguish, for example, a distribution with two very large cities (two-city primacy) from a more even city-size distribution. There are, therefore, problems with using this type of ratio to measure the size dominance of the largest city. Moreover, the relative size of the largest city is not the only characteristic of urban hierarchies of theoretical interest, although many studies of city systems have focused exclusively on it.

Empirically and theoretically, the relative size of the largest city and the shape of the size distribution of the rest of the cities may be the result of two different processes. Vapñarsky (1969) first made this argument with respect to Argentina's city system but it pertains to other urban systems as well. The relative size of the largest city may be a function of its role as a link between the economic region and the larger world economy. More specifically, Vapñarsky and others have argued that primate cities are the result of a country's economic dependence in the world economy. The size distribution of the remaining cities, however, particularly in peripheral regions in which the largest city is the almost exclusive point of connection between the regional economy and the world economy, may be the result of the degree of internal integration or interdependence in the regional space-economy. Social geographers who refer to the role of urban hierarchies for integrating a space-economy are less concerned with the size dominance of the largest city per se than with the size distribution of the entire city system or all cities but the largest one.

Empirically, the size dominance of the largest city and the size distribution of the remaining cities have been found to be somewhat independent phenomena. In regions with primate first cities, for example, the size distribution of the remaining cities may be fairly flat (even) or may be close to lognormal. Vapñarsky (1969) pointed out that the former pattern characterized Argentina until the end of the nineteenth century and the latter pattern characterizes Argentina at the present. In regions in which the largest city conforms to the log-normal rule, the remaining cities may also follow the log-normal rule (as in the case of the United States), or may form a fairly flat city-size distribution. The latter pattern, according to Vapñarsky, is a characteristic of a region that is fairly independent from the rest of the world-economy and that has a low level of internal integration; a situation that is uncommon in the contemporary world but that may have occurred more frequently in earlier historical periods in regions that had not yet been incorporated into the capitalist world-economy and that were not part of other world-economies or world-empires (see Sokolovsky, Chapter 3, this volume). In her historical analysis of regional city systems in Guatemala, Smith (Chapter 9, this volume) also demonstrates that largest-city dominance and the size distribution of the remaining cities are distinct processes. She characterizes the largest city as primate or nonprimate, and the size distribution of the other cities as log-normal or "immature" (of relatively equal size), and relates this pair of characteristics of urban hierarchies to urban class relations. Although neither Smith nor Vapñarsky made this distinction, nonprimate cities may either be of the size expected according to the rank–size rule or smaller than expected. Furthermore, the size distribution of the remaining cities may be primate for areas in which the two largest cities are considerably larger than the remaining cities (two-city primacy).

Single-country historical studies of change in the size distribution of all of the cities, the largest several cities, or all but the largest city have generally been based on visual inspections of plots of city sizes by rank. This type of strategy is inappropriate, however, for comparative and/or historical research that involves a large number of cases. Several researchers have, therefore, developed summary measures of the shape of city-size distributions. A variety of means have been used to describe the overall city-size distribution (although the same measures could also be used to describe the shape of the distribution of all but the largest city), and much discussion has centered around the question of which statistical distribution best fits the distribution of observed urban hierarchies. In a review of commonly used statistical models, Richardson (1978) indicates that the rank–size rule, the log-normal distribution, and the Pareto distribution all yield similar results, although the log-normal distribution has been most commonly used. Carroll (1979) clarifies that, although these three distributions are unique, they yield similar results in the "upper tail," corresponding to the size distribution of the largest cities in an urban system. The question of which statistical model most accurately describes the largest number of observed cases (city-size distributions), however, is not useful for purposes of assessing variation in city-size distributions. Furthermore, it is not clear why a single statistical model was expected to fit most cases. (For example, Richardson [1973a] shows that none of the models satisfactorily fits primate distributions.)

A few researchers have used either the rank–size rule or the log-normal distribution as a point of reference from which a statistical summary measure of deviation was developed. McGreevey (1971), for example, introduced a summary measure of city-size distributions that is sensitive to variation along the entire range of city sizes. He computed a chi-square measure of the deviation of the observed distribution of cities from the distribution that would be expected based on the rank–size rule. Smaller values of chi square indicate greater conformance to log-normality. While this procedure has many advantages over ratio measures, McGreevey's chi-square statistic does not indicate whether the observed deviations were in the direction of primacy or in the direction of more equally sized cities. Again, it should be noted that any measure of an observed city-size distribution's overall fit to some reference distribution may be insensitive to important variations in the sizes of individual cities. A measure of the shape of the total city-size distribution might not detect important variations in largest-city primacy, for example.

A single summary measure of city-size distributions, therefore, cannot capture all of the theoretically important variation in both the shape of the city-size distribution and the dominance of the largest city or cities. Many studies have confused these two general characteristics of city-size distributions by relying on a single summary measure of primacy or the shape of the overall distribution. It is important to measure these two characteristics separately, particularly for purposes of large-scale empirical comparisons that cannot rely on visual inspection of graphs of city-size distributions. For some purposes, it may also be useful to describe the shape of the total city-size distribution and to be able to discriminate between cases that have two dominant cities and those with a more even distribution of city sizes. The measures of city-size distributions that are described in the following section were developed with these purposes in mind.

PROPOSED MEASURES OF CITY-SIZE DISTRIBUTIONS

The first and most general measure that we propose describes the overall shape of the city-size distribution. Following McGreevey (1971), I find a chi-square measure of deviation from the rank–size rule to be a useful summary measure, except that I propose to sign such a measure to indicate the overall direction of the deviations to be able to distinguish, for example, primate city-size distributions from distributions with more equal city populations. Note that the rank–size rule is used as a statistical point of reference from which to measure deviation; it is not considered a normative guide. The measure is a summary of the deviations of the observed city sizes from the sizes that are expected on the basis of the rank–size rule, divided by its degrees of freedom to allow comparisons between distributions that may include different numbers of cities.

This measure uses the largest city as the starting point for computing expected city sizes. The expected size of the largest city always, by definition, equals its observed size. Visually, a plot of the observed and expected city sizes by rank would always show the two lines converging at the largest city. This approach differs from other strategies in which the expected city-size distribution was chosen as the best-fitting line with a slope of -1 (Vapñarsky, 1975) or was plotted from the bottom rather than the top of the city-size distribution (Smith, Chapter 7, this volume). The important point, however, is to use a consistent strategy for calculating the expected distribution. Because we want to be able to compare the size distribution of city systems with different total numbers of cities, the largest city is the preferred starting point. The expected and observed sizes of the second through the nth largest cities are computed as proportions of the size of the largest city.

The direction of the deviations are signed such that a positive number indicates that the observed city-size distribution is more primate than lognormal. That is, the second through nth cities tend to be smaller than expected, so there is a positive difference between their expected minus observed sizes. A negative number indicates that the observed city sizes tend to be larger than expected, yielding a negative difference between their expected minus observed sizes. This type of city-size distribution is relatively flat, since the cities are more equal in size than the rank–size rule predicts. This is a *multicentric* city-size distribution. The summary measure of the overall city-size distribution, the *Standardized Primacy Index 1* (SPI1), is calculated as follows:

$$\text{SPI1} = S \times \left[\sum_{1}^{n} \frac{(1/i - O_i/O_1)^2}{(1/i)} \right] / (n - 1)$$

where

$$S = \begin{cases} 1 & \text{if } \sum_{1}^{n} (1/i - O_i/O_1) \geq 0 \\ -1 & \text{otherwise} \end{cases}$$

and

i is the city's rank, O_i the observed size of the ith city, n the number of cities used to calculate index.

This index controls for variation in the absolute sizes of the cities between two different city-size distributions. If, for example, two different city-size distributions had the same shape but different populations of their largest city, their SPI1 values would nonetheless be equivalent. That is, variation in the SPI1 index reflects variation only in *relative* city sizes.[1]

Let us illustrate the range of variation captured by the SPI1 measure by comparing graphs of city-size distributions with the computed index values for the same city systems. The city-size distributioon for the 10 largest cities

---

[1]For some research purposes, it may not be desirable to control for differences in absolute city sizes. In that case, a similar strategy may be used to calculate an alternative index, which we call the Absolute Primacy Index 1 (API1). Returning to the previous example of two city-size distributions with equivalent shapes but different sizes of the largest city, we would find that the API1 would have a larger absolute value for the distribution with the larger first city. The alternative index is calculated as follows:

$$\text{API1} = S \times \left[\sum_{1}^{n} \frac{(O_1/i - O_i)^2}{(O_1/i)} \right] / (n - 1)$$

where

$$S = \begin{cases} 1 & \text{if } \sum_{1}^{n} (O_1/i - O_i) \geq 0 \\ -1 & \text{otherwise} \end{cases}$$

in Mexico is shown in Figure 5.1.[2] Mexico City is clearly dominant in size, and all of the other cities are considerably smaller than expected on the basis of the rank–size rule. As such, the SPI1 value is positive and fairly large. Israel, however, has a more multicentric city-size distribution (see Figure 5.2). The second through eighth largest cities are larger than expected, and the SPI1 value is negative and fairly large. A simple chi-square measure of deviation from the rank–size rule would not distinguish adequately between these two types of city-size distributions. The city-size distribution of the 10 largest cities in the United States, often cited as the classic case of log-normality, is shown in Figure 5.3. The size distribution of the city proper population data is very close to log-normal, and its SPI1 value is fairly small. The size distribution of the urban agglomerations, however, looks more multicentric (New York is a little too small for the rest of the cities), and its SPI1 value is negative although small.

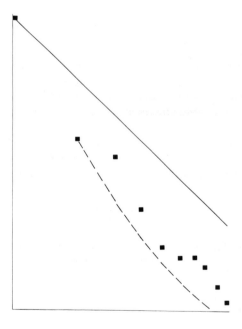

FIGURE 5.1 City-size distribution for Mexico, 1977. ———, expected distribution starting from first city; — — —, expected distribution starting from second city; ■, city proper; ●, urban agglomeration. SPI1 = .056; SPI2 = −.061; SR = 3.973.

[2]In this and in all of the following figures and sample index computations, the data are taken from the United Nations *Demographic Yearbook 1980*. Data are for the most recent year available. When available, the population figures for urban agglomerations are used, but otherwise the data are for the city proper.

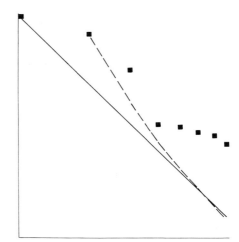

FIGURE 5.2   City-size distribution for Israel, 1979. SPI1 = −.135; SPI2 = −.116; SR = .256. See Figure 5.1 for key.

As previously argued, it is often useful to describe the shape of the distribution of city sizes *excluding* the largest city. Such a measure would be required for studies that investigate whether first-city dominance and the shape of the rest of the city-size distribution are different phenomena. Based on the same logic used to compute the SPI1, but substituting the second-largest city as the basis for calculating expected city sizes, a similar summary

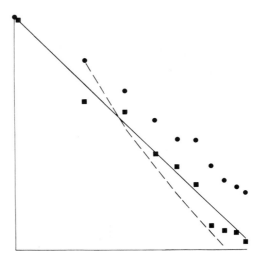

FIGURE 5.3   City-size distribution for the United States, 1977. City proper: SPI1 = .003; SPI2 = −.184; SR = 4.841. Urban agglomeration: SPI1 = −.039; SPI2 = −.161; SR = .798. See Figure 5.1 for key.

measure of the shape of the distribution of all but the largest city, referred to as the SPI2, can be calculated as follows:[3]

$$\text{SPI2} = S \times \sum_{2}^{n} \left[\frac{(1/(i-1) - O_i/O_2)^2}{1/(i-1)} \right] /(n-2)$$

where

$$S = \begin{cases} 1 & \text{if } \sum_{2}^{n} (1/(i-1) - O_i/O_2) \geq 0 \\ -1 & \text{otherwise.} \end{cases}$$

Again, let us illustrate the type of variation in city-size distributions captured by this index by comparing plots of city-size distributions with their index values. The city-size distribution for Argentina, the classic case of primacy, is shown in Figure 5.4. Although the second through tenth cities are smaller than expected when one starts with Buenos Aires, and the SPI1 has a large, positive value, the distribution of the cities excluding Buenos Aires is fairly multicentric, and the SPI2 is negative. Returning to Figures 5.2 and 5.3, we see that for urban agglomerations in Israel and the United States, respectively, the distributions of the cities excluding the largest are multicentric, as are the total city-size distributions (the SPI1 and SPI2 values are both negative). The city-size distribution for Canada (Figure 5.5) provides an interesting example of two-city primacy. The SPI1 is negative, indicating that all of the other cities are larger than expected and suggesting a multicentric distribution. The first two cities (Toronto and Montreal), however, are almost equivalent in size, and when the distribution starts from the second rather than the first city, the next three cities are all smaller than expected. The SPI2 value is, correspondingly, positive. It is clear that the SPI1 and SPI2 measures capture different sources of variation in city-size distributions.

---

[3]Again, a similar measure of the shape of the distribution starting with the second largest city but based on absolute rather than relative city sizes may be computed as follows:

$$\text{API2} = S \times \sum_{2}^{n} \left[\frac{(O_2/(i-1) - O_i)^2}{O_2/(i-1)} \right] /(n-2)$$

where

$$S = \begin{cases} 1 & \text{if } \sum_{2}^{n} (O_2/(i-1) - O_i) \geq 0 \\ -1 & \text{otherwise.} \end{cases}$$

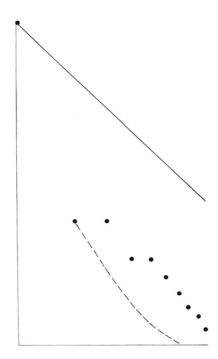

FIGURE 5.4   City-size distribution for Argentina, circa 1975. SPI1 = .136; SPI2 = −2.65; SR = 72.790. See Figure 5.1 for key.

Neither of these measures of the shape of the city-size distribution, however, directly assesses the relative dominance of the largest city or cities in the city system. Such a measure of relative size dominance can be obtained by comparing the sizes of the largest three cities in the distribution. Instead

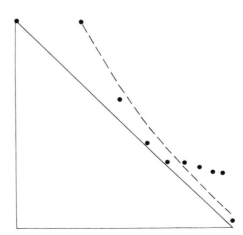

FIGURE 5.5   City-size distribution for Canada, 1979. SPI1 = −.066; SPI2 = .011; SR = .011. See Figure 5.1 for key.

of using a ratio measure of the size of the largest city relative to the three largest cities, which only provides a measure of first-city dominance (primacy), a measure of the ratio of the slopes between the first and second, and second and third cities can be used. If the observed distribution fits the rank–size rule, all three of the largest cities lie along a line with a slope of -1. If the first city is dominant (that is, if the second and third cities are smaller than the rank–size rule predicts), then the slope between the first and second cities is steeper than the slope between the second and third cities, and a ratio of the two slopes yields a number greater than one. If, however, the first two cities are dominant (that is, if the second city is larger than the rank–size rule predicts, but the third city is smaller than predicted), the slope between the second and third cities is steeper than the slope between the first and second, and the ratio of the slopes is a figure less than one but greater than zero. The Slope Ratio (SR) may be calculated as follows:

$$SR = \frac{(\ln O_1 - \ln O_2)/(\ln 1 - \ln 2)}{(\ln O_2 - \ln O_3)/(\ln 2 - \ln 3)}$$

$$= \frac{\ln(O_1/O_2)}{\ln(O_2/O_3)} \times \frac{\ln(2/3)}{\ln(1/2)}$$

$$= .58 \times [\ln(O_1/O_2)]/[\ln(O_2/O_3)].$$

The meaning of particular ranges of values of the SR follows:

If $SR > 1$, the first city is dominant (primate). Larger numbers indicate greater primacy.

If $0 < SR < 1$, the first two cities are dominant (two-city primacy). Smaller numbers indicate greater two-city primacy.

If $SR = 1$, all three cities lie on the same line (although not necessarily a line with a slope of -1).

The SR, then, varies from zero to positive infinity and is an indicator of the relative dominance of the largest city and the largest two cities in the city-size distribution. The slope ratio for Canada, for example, is close to zero, indicating two-city primacy; the slope ratio for Argentina is quite large, indicating first-city primacy; and the slope ratio for urban agglomerations in the United States is close to one, indicating a more log-normal distribution among the largest cities. These examples, of course, do not exhaust all possible variations in city-size distributions.

Under one very limited set of conditions, the signing procedure for the SPI1 measure poses a problem of which readers should be aware. For city systems that exhibit two-city primacy *and* in which the third through nth largest cities are smaller than expected, the sign of the SPI1 measure is determined by whether the sum of the positive deviations is larger than the sum of the negative deviations. If the absolute value of the sum of all of the deviations is small, slight variations in the relative sizes of the cities may cause a reversal in the sign of the index. Since the chi-square value of the index tends to be large under these conditions (all of the cities deviate from their expected sizes), this may cause the SPI1 value to change from a large negative to a large positive number, or vice versa. In this case, trends in the SPI1 measure are misleading and it should not be used as a measure of the city-size distribution. To reiterate, this problem is not necessarily apparent in all cases of two-city primacy but only in cases in which not only is the second city much larger than expected but the rest of the cities are much smaller than expected. For example, the SPI1 value would be unlikely to change signs due to small variations in the size of Canadian cities even though Canada's city-size distribution is two-city primate (see Figure 5.5) because all of the deviations are in the same direction.

There are a couple of different strategies that could be used to resolve this problem when it becomes apparent. After cases of two-city primacy are identified (the slope ratio is close to zero), one could decide that two-city primacy should be considered to be a case of primacy and, as such, any negative SPI1 values could be switched to positive values. If one is studying trends in a single region over time and the sign-switch problem is apparent because of two-city primacy, one could disregard the SPI1 measure and instead rely on the SPI2 and slope-ratio indices as measures of the city-size distributions.

This group of measures of distinct characteristics of city-size distributions is particularly suitable for purposes of large-scale comparative research that cannot rely on visual inspection of graphs. As interval measures, they do not incorporate a priori cutoff points for classification of city systems as, for example, primate or nonprimate. Instead, they allow for an ordering of city systems along the dimension of interest. Use of this group of measures allows for the assessment of variation in city-size distributions along a number of important and theoretically distinct dimensions. One of the possible reasons for the equivocal nature of past research on, for example, primacy is that much of past research relied on single measures of the shape of city-size distributions. We expect that measurement of these theoretically distinct characteristics of city-size distributions, and analysis of the correlates of change along these distinct dimensions in longitudinal comparative research, will advance our understanding of the social, economic, and political causes and consequences of certain types of city-size distributions.

6

THEORIES AND MEASURES OF URBAN PRIMACY: A CRITIQUE

Carol A. Smith

INTRODUCTION

Of all scholarly work dealing with urbanization, that focused on urban primacy has been most influenced by world-system theory, especially in its earlier guise as dependency theory. It is not difficult to understand why. The primate city, more than any other urban phenomenon, has been closely identified with the structured economic imbalances and social inequities characteristic of Third World countries, countries we now refer to as the peripheral parts of an all-encompassing world-economy. Theories of both economic dependency and urban primacy grew up with the Latin American experience in mind. In Latin America, economic domination by the colonial and post-colonial powers of the world-economic core was obvious to most observers and urban primacy was overwhelmingly in evidence.[1] The main popularizer of dependency theory, Andre Gunder Frank, paid special attention to urban primacy in his description of the mechanisms promoting the underdevelopment of Latin America. He did not refer to the specific literature on primate cities developed by geographers, but he clearly depicted the over-large national and provincial centers, so characteristic of

[1]Alejandro Portes (1976) found urban primacy in 18 of the 20 Latin American countries on which there were data. He observed that the growth of these overlarge cities appeared to follow directly upon the development of strong ties to the world market. Portes identified primacy wherever the first-ranking city had a larger population than the combined populations of the next three cities in rank. I show below that this index of primacy is inadequate; several of the cases identified by Portes as primate cases are in fact log-normal or rank–size. Nonetheless, an impressive number of extremely primate cities exists in modern Latin America.

modern Latin America, in his metropole–satellite model (Frank, 1969:3–17).[2] After Frank, other students of underdevelopment in the Third World elaborated upon that model with theories of direct relevance to urban primacy per se (e.g., Johnson, 1970; Portes, 1976; Roberts, 1978). Urban primacy became an explanation for economic dependency and economic dependency became an explanation for urban primacy.

The close connection between theories of urban primacy and theories of economic dependency can be observed even among scholars who otherwise cling to traditional modernization theory. Brian Berry, for example, found it necessary to propose a compromise model to deal with primate cities (see Berry, 1971), even though most of his work on urbanization has been oriented by a modernization perspective (see, e.g., Berry and Horton, 1970). This does not show the overwhelming power of dependency theory when it comes to explaining urban primacy. For, in fact, modernization and dependency theorists do not differ all that much in how they explain overlarge cities; they differ mainly in how they evaluate the consequences of overlarge cities. Of the three main theories of urban primacy (reviewed below), two are as easily espoused by modernization theorists as by dependency theorists. The third theory is not so much a competitive theory as an extension of the two classic theories, which tries to take into account newer, postcolonial forms of dependency. Even this theory could be subsumed under a modernization perspective.

My critique of the three dominant explanations for urban primacy, all inspired by dependency theory, centers around this very issue. The main objection dependency theory levels against modernization theory is that it posits a unilinear trend toward the development of capitalism, assuming that all countries will follow, sooner or later, faster or slower, the same path to development. The alternative dependency theory proposes is that countries drawn into the orbit of the world-economy as part of the periphery (i.e., as producers of primary goods) might very well remain in a *permanent* state of underdevelopment. They would do so through the development of distorted political and economic institutions (such as urban primacy) that prevented them from following the path blazed by the first "modernizers." Yet dependency theory itself posits a unilinear trend in capitalist development, one that is only more monolithic, in that "distorted" as well as "normal" developments are considered part of the same process feeding the needs of capitalist growth. Scholars in the two camps differ

[2]Frank's metropole–satellite model has metropoles extracting surplus from satellites at four different levels of the system: world, national, regional, and local. Frank is somewhat vague in his definition of metropole, but his empirical descriptions suggest a pattern wherein city-based commercial groups exploit the populations of their hinterlands.

mainly in how critical they are of capitalism per se. Where modernization theorists admit to growing pains in the transitional period, dependency theorists emphasize the inequities created by capitalism at all stages, and they note the uneven distribution of these inequities in the world-economy.

Scholars in both camps also agree about the basic nature of urban primacy: that it is ugly, that it is linked to the development of capitalist relations of production, and that it is disproportionately located in the peripheral countries of the world-economy. They debate other, less dramatic, points. How permanent is the state of primacy likely to be? Is regional primacy the same thing as national primacy, and caused by the same forces? What are the precise mechanisms by which urban primacy develops? What are the particular economic and political consequences of urban primacy? How can one redirect the urban growth in peripheral economies so that primacy does not occur? These less dramatic questions originally motivated me to examine the pattern of urban development in Guatemala during this century. But in trying to answer these questions I discovered that the several widely accepted explanations for urban primacy as a general phenomenon—which I too originally accepted—did not fit the case at hand very well. The problem lies in the assumption that a uniform force, capitalism, will produce a uniform result wherever it meets certain general economic conditions. None of the particular theories of urban primacy pays any attention to how variations in the local substrate, such as variations in local class structure, condition the pattern of urban development. (And two equally underdeveloped economies can be otherwise quite different.) Thus none of the theories can explain, for example, why Guatemala developed a primate city before 1970, but El Salvador did not. The only theory that can explain the divergent patterns in these two countries is one that takes variations in local, historical conditions into account.

Another problem I found in extant theory was a certain lack of rigor in the ways people define urban primacy, and considerable vagueness in what people mean by underdevelopment. Everyone agrees that urban primacy is associated with a low level of economic development. Yet the statistical association between development and primacy turns out to be quite weak. I discuss this problem at some length in the following section because the measures and definitions of urban primacy and of underdevelopment have obscured the real nature of the two phenomena. Urban primacy is not merely the existence of a city that is much larger than any other. It is a city that is too large in relation to a *system* of cities, whose sizes must be described in specific terms—whether in terms of population, economic infrastructure, or bureaucratic institutions. And underdevelopment is not simply the existence of a low level of GNP. It is a particular condition of inequality that generates poverty, brought about by the development of specific economic and political institutions that reproduce that inequality.

My critique of extant theory, then, has several objectives. One is to clarify what urban primacy is as a *social* phenomenon and to suggest more rigorous measures that scholars should take to it. Another aim is to raise questions about widely accepted theories of urban primacy, as a prologue to an alternative theory I propose in this book (Smith, Chapter 7, this volume). My third and most ambitious goal is to critique certain fundamental propositions in world-system and dependency theory. My alternative theory of urban primacy is one that explains the growth of a single dominating city not through the operation of some general universalizing force, but rather through the ways in which people respond, usually in their class interests, to the actions of other people, also operating in their class interests. In other words, I propose a class-relational theory as an alternative to the dependency theories of urban primacy. I suggest that modifications of world-system and dependency theory must be done along these lines to explain *any* particular institution in the modern world-economy.

DEFINITIONS AND MEASURES OF URBAN PRIMACY

Urban primacy is usually defined as a situation in which the largest city (or several cities) within an urban system is "overlarge"; that is, much larger than lower-ranking cities. The question then becomes by how much must the largest city exceed the size of the second city before one considers it overlarge. The rule of thumb is that it must be significantly more than twice the size of the second-ranking center (Mehta 1969:296). In Chapter 5 of this volume, Walters describes some previous attempts to measure urban primacy. As she points out, one of the most often used measures is the Ginsberg Index (or Davis Index), which is the proportion of the population in the top four cities held by the largest one. Urban systems that score well above .5 would have primate cities by this measure. When used to describe Guatemala's urban system in 1883, the Ginsberg method produces an index of .66 (Guatemala City is four times the size of Quezaltenango), indicating considerable primacy.

Walters also discusses log-normal or rank–size definitions of primacy.[3] Yet by this definition, Guatemala City was *not* overlarge in 1893 (see Figure 6.1(A)). According to the rank–size rule, Guatemala City should have had

---

[3]Zipf (1949) identified the log-normal system some 30 years ago, finding that many urban systems (if properly defined) statistically approximated this (Pareto-type) distribution. He considered log-normalcy a sign of system integration and its absence a sign of immaturity.

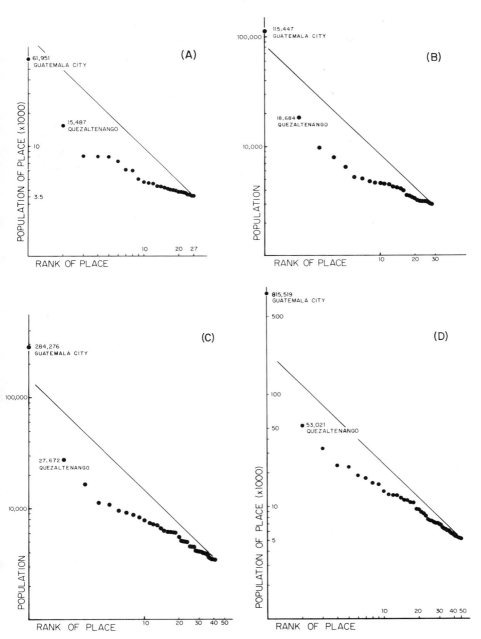

FIGURE 6.1   City-size distributions in Guatemala: A, 1893; B, 1921; C, 1950; D, 1973.

a population of 94,500 rather than the 62,000 it did have. Although four times larger than Quezaltenango, it was only two-thirds the size one would predict for it considering the number of towns in Guatemala whose populations exceeded a certain urban threshold (in this case the 27 towns with populations exceeding 3500).[4]

All definitions of urban primacy are based, ultimately, on the rank–size distribution of urban centers assumed to be normal for well-integrated, developed economies. Since the Ginsberg definition derives from the rank–size definition and yet rests on fewer observations, it must be considered a less-adequate definition or measure of the phenomenon—no more than a quick estimate of the normalcy of the rank–size distribution. Thus, in the Guatemalan case considered here, we must conclude that the urban system was *not* primate in 1893. Secondary cities in Guatemala were simply less developed than the primate city. That is, all of Guatemala's major cities were "too small" in relation to the standard set by the average or smallest urban centers.[5]

Figure 6.1 shows city-size distributions for four different points in Guatemala's recent history. From these data we see that Guatemala's urban system became primate not in the decades preceding 1893, but rather in those preceding 1950. It seems clear from this example that any explanation for urban primacy based on *when* it occurs—its association with certain

---

[4]In most current empirical research (e.g., Berry and Horton, 1970), one assesses the fit of a distribution of cities to the rank–size (log-normal) distribution by drawing a regression line of rank on population and measuring its slope. Vapñarski and El Shakhs have proposed refinements of this procedure, but both of them accept the basic notion that one should "average" the errors. Harris (1970) and Skinner (1977), by contrast, do not use regression for determining the slope of the log-normal line, but rather determine a lower population threshold for the definition of *urban* (2000 for Skinner; 10,000 for Harris) and draw a line sloped at 45° (-1) from that point. The method used by Harris and Skinner is legitimate in its assumptions about log-normalcy and is much simpler to use than the regression method; it is, however, fraught with the problem of picking an odd-size place at the lower limit. The usual convention, on the other hand, allows odd-size *large* cities, which are much more common than odd-size small cities, to have more weight and to overdetermine the slope of the log-normal line. It also fails on occasion to distinguish the situation in which secondary cities are too small vis-à-vis smaller cities as opposed to the situation in which the primate city is simply too large. The Harris–Skinner convention, therefore, seems preferable, especially if one has adequate rationale for the city size used for the lower limit in the study and the analysis is longitudinal rather than cross-sectional.

[5]I should acknowledge that in some uses of the term (e.g., Jefferson, 1939) *urban primacy* means simply that the first-ranking city in a country or region is large or important vis-à-vis other cities, but not necessarily overlarge. In rating any first-ranking city more than twice the size of the second-ranking city as *overlarge*, however, the Ginsberg Index and other indexes like it (based on the rank–size distribution) imply a normative judgment of urban primacy.

economic events such as the rise or decline of an export economy—should be tested with data comparing actual city-size distributions rather than indexes that roughly approximate them. Yet, as I show below, virtually all comparative studies linking urban primacy to various economic developments rest on inadequate measures of urban primacy—some even less precise than the Ginsberg Index.

By 1973 Guatemala's secondary cities had inched closer to a rank-size distribution even as Guatemala's primate city was growing well beyond that distribution (Figure 6.1(D)). In other words, Guatemala's national urban system headed toward greater log-normalcy at the same time it was developing greater primacy. If we define the rank–size distribution as normal, and if we assume that primacy is deviation from the rank–size distribution, we would have to conclude that Guatemala's urban system was becoming more normal at the same time it was becoming more deviant through primacy. Vapñarski (1975), who found the same pattern for Argentina's cities that I describe for Guatemala, proposed a solution to this paradox. If we agree that primacy does not constitute the only possible deviation from log-normalcy (in 1893 Guatemala's city-size distribution was neither primate nor log-normal; Figure 6.1(A)), and if we concede that primacy and log-normalcy are not mutually exclusive (in 1973 Guatemala's city-size distribution was both more primate and closer to log-normal; Figure 6.1(D)), the paradox dissolves.

Vapñarski theorized that the obverse of log-normalcy—that distribution in which most cities fall below the log-normal line—is immaturity rather than primacy.[6] Immature systems may or may not be associated with primacy, just as log-normal systems may or may not be associated with primacy. As a causal explanation, Vapñarski suggested that immature systems lack the strong commercial linkages between local cities (internal integration) characteristic of log-normal systems, whereas primate systems show openness to outside control and influence (external dependency) not found among self-sustaining nonprimate systems. If we concurred with Vapñarski about causality, we would conclude that Guatemala's urban system became more mature and well integrated at the same time it became more dependent. We do not have to accept Vapñarski's causal explanation (examined more fully below), but we should take seriously his view that the causes of primacy can be independent of the causes of log-normalcy. And we must

---

[6]Vapñarski's term for the concave as opposed to linear distribution of city sizes derives from his theory that as urban systems become better integrated through commercial interchange (i.e., more mature), they will evolve from concave (immature) distributions to linear (log-normal) distributions. (See also Johnson [1980] for a discussion of this general class of city-size distributions.)

accept the demonstration (for Argentina as well as Guatemala) that deviations from log-normalcy other than primacy exist. In other words, we cannot assume that a nonprimate distribution is log-normal.

Can we assume that log-normal systems are mature, functionally integrated, and related in some way to economic development? Virtually everyone does so, on the grounds that most developed countries have log-normal urban systems. But no widely accepted theory explaining this association exists (Richardson, 1973), and even the empirical evidence showing the association is contradictory.[7] Cross-sectional studies consistently show a poor correlation between level of urbanization or level of economic development on the one hand with log-normalcy on the other (Berry, 1961; Mehta, 1969). Longitudinal studies, by contrast, almost always show urban systems tending toward log-normalcy as they mature or become more functionally integrated. Vapñarski's study of Argentina is but one of several case studies described in Berry and Horton (1970:74–93) showing such a tendency. In addition, those few case studies that have shown the urban system in question actually to be properly bounded,[8] mature, and functionally integrated (independent of the city-size distribution itself) almost always report log-normal systems (see Skinner, 1977; Marshall, 1969, Harris 1970).[9]

---

[7]Richardson discusses some eight or nine theories and finds each of them capable of generating the distribution, but all of them either vague or limited as explanations. He concludes, "there are so many influences interacting to mold the relative size of cities that it would be too difficult to include them all within a single model" (1973:249). That many influences interact to mold the relative sizes of cities is, of course, Berry's theory of the rank–size distribution (Berry and Horton, 1970:73). Berry argues that when many forces affect the urban pattern in many ways such that the only systematic influence upon size is the expectation that all cities will grow at the same rate, log-normalcy results; but when only a few special forces cause urbanization, primacy results. Although Richardson (and I) find this vague, it is probably the most widely accepted theory of the rank–size distribution of city sizes.

[8]National boundaries are used to define most urban systems (cf. El Shakhs, 1972), although it seems clear that this criterion would produce interconnected urban systems in only some cases. Skinner (1977:211–213) and Appleby (1978:16) rely on ecological criteria. Using major watershed divides seems a reasonable way to divide up traditional China, where data on commercial movements must be limited; but using similar criteria leads Appleby to leave the major wool entrepôt city of Arequipa out of Puno's wool-exporting urban system. Defining urban systems by explicit commercial criteria seems pereferable, using either Marshall's shopping-linkage method (1969:72–79) or Berry's commodity-flow method (1966:157). Certainly if one's theory of city-size distribution is economic, economic criteria should be used, whereas if it is cultural, political, or something else, another criterion may be reasonable. To use achievement of log-normalcy to bound an urban system (cf. Vapñarski, Harris), however, seems clearly improper.

[9]Skinner's work is especially important because it provides evidence independent of the city-size distribution itself that the immature urban systems were poorly integrated ones. Neither Skinner nor Harris discusses generic theories of primacy; nor do they distinguish between primacy in mature versus primacy in immature systems. Their empirical work demonstrates, however, that many systems considered log-normal in the literature—invariably China (cf.

I find the case studies more convincing than the cross-sectional studies for three reasons. First, cross-sectional studies invariably take the national urban system as the unit of analysis, even though lower-level or higher-level systems may be more salient. India's urban system, for example, lacks national unity, being fragmented into four macroregional commercial systems, each of which is primate (as Berry 1971:122–123 carefully demonstrates); when the four primate systems are grouped into a national "system," they become log-normal—Harris (1970:130–132) explains why—and thus log-normalcy rather than primacy is improperly assigned to India in cross-sectional studies.[10] Skinner (1977) shows the same to be true for traditional China, and Harris (1970) illustrates the pattern for modern Russia. Second, virtually all correlational studies have defined log-normalcy as the absence of primacy; yet a good many nonprimate systems are simply immature (see above) and thus quite unlikely to have the same relationship to development or urbanization as log-normal systems, which are also nonprimate. Finally, cross-sectional studies almost always assume the relationship between primacy and development to be linear, an assumption for which there is no good evidence (see below). None of these objections obtains against the majority of case studies, whether longitudinal or not, that also have finer (and more credible) measures of maturity or functional integration than level of urbanization or GNP, the usual measures in the cross-sectional studies. On these grounds, then, I too assume that log-normalcy is associated with urban maturity and functional integration—but not necessarily with economic development in its modern sense.[11]

El Shakhs, 1972)—are merely nonprimate. Their work also supports the widely accepted notion that log-normalcy will be found in mature, well-integrated urban systems, while illustrating the obvious point that national urban systems are not necessarily the relevant or the well-integrated urban systems.

[10]Harris points out that if one groups several log-normal systems together one would find a layered or "immature" distribution when graphed (1970:130–132). Skinner shows that properly specified urban systems in China (macroregional) tend to the rank–size distribution, while improperly specified ones (national) appear immature or layered (1977:236–249). Marshall, on the other hand, shows that properly specified systems in Ontario, Canada (at the small, local level), appear layered, while improperly grouped ones appear log-normal (1969:152). Berry notes that India is log-normal (nonprimate, anyway) at a national level, even though primate at the macroregional level, and shows the latter to be the relevant urban-system level (1971:122–123). Each of these cases illustrates how important it is to specify properly the urban system to be described (i.e., to provide independent evidence, other than mere proximity, that urban centers form a system.) This particular measurement problem is not a petty one, since some theories of city-size distributions suggest that one finds primacy only because the relevant urban system has not been specified properly.

[11]In Smith (1982) I discuss log-normal systems at greater length, treating the question of city-size distributions in modern and premodern economies and defining modern economies as those that utilize free wage labor.

In accepting that log-normalcy is desirable, one does not necessarily agree that primacy is pernicious. Most scholars do, but then most scholars consider primacy the obverse of log-normalcy. El Shakhs (1972), however, suggests that primacy assists the transition to development and thus is actually beneficial; at the same time he agrees that log-normalcy is the urban system found in fully mature (developed) economies. I consider El Shakhs's study in some detail here, not only because it is influential, but also because it is based on certain assumptions about urban systems and economic development that are widely shared in the social science community and that I consider to be false.

El Shakhs's study suggests an explanation for the poor linear correlation between primacy and level of economic development. He solved the puzzle (a puzzle because everyone assumes that *some* relationship should exist between the economy and the shape of the urban system) by showing that the relationship is curvilinear rather than linear. Urban primacy develops during the early or "take-off" stages of economic development, when centralization and concentration of nonagrarian functions are necessary to reorganize the traditional economy. Once the economy is developed (with *development* defined as achievement of high mass consumption), "spread effects" lead to decentralization and a decline in urban primacy. Primacy, then, is transitional in this model, being preceded and followed by a rank–size distribution. Moreover, primacy is seen not as a hindrance but as a necessary stage of development, a stage to be fostered rather than throttled. Brian Berry, who finds this evolutionary model an improvement over his own earlier (1961) suggestion that primate systems are immature, provides a rationale, lacking in El Shakhs's treatment, for the active role of primacy in the transition to development: "primate cities provide the . . . greatest gains in systematic order through organization . . . as the system is moved from one level of organization to another" (1971:138).

El Shakhs finds rather good cross-sectional support for this theory, using a sample of 75 national cases, measuring city-size distributions for level or degree of primacy, and measuring level of economic development by 1950 GNP figures.[12] The Latin American cases, most of them strongly primate, work well inasmuch as most of them have intermediate-level GNPs. Guatemala, for example, ranks 4 (high) in primacy and 42 (midway) in economic development. Studies by Wrigley (1978) and Robson (1973) lend some

---

[12]El Shakhs's measure of primacy considers the entire city-size distribution down to an urban cut-off point (usually population 10,000) rather than the top few cities. It is thus a sturdier measure than the Ginsberg Index, for example, but it continues to classify as log-normal those systems that are not primate—regardless of the actual relationship between smaller and larger cities.

historical support to the thesis, as does historical work by El Shakhs himself, who shows both the United States and the United Kingdom to have had urban systems less primate after development than before.[13]

What El Shakhs has done, without realizing it, is to separate immature urban systems from log-normal systems. He uses the usual measure of log-normalcy (nonprimacy), which does not distinguish between the two non-primate distributions. But in his test immature systems fall in one group (the least developed) while log-normal systems fall in another group (most developed), leading to a curvilinear pattern for nonprimacy. In this case, then, it matters little that China's national system is coded as log-normal when it really is immature (Skinner 1977:131). Countries like India, which appear to have log-normal urban systems but which are actually primate (see above), remain improperly characterized, but apparently few such cases exist in the sample because they do not swamp the overall pattern. We must conclude, then, that El Shakhs's study provides strong evidence linking immature urban patterns to low levels of GNP, primate urban patterns to intermediate levels of GNP, and log-normalcy to high levels of GNP.

But it is a mighty conceptual leap to assume that countries with intermediate-level GNPs are developing. Many countries that measure intermediate in GNP (most Latin American countries, for example) have done so ever since such measures have been taken (Cardoso and Faletto, 1971). In that case, how "transitional" can such intermediate cases be? In addition, a good number of countries (Argentina, for example) have measured primate for some 200 years, suggesting that even if primacy is the first step toward economic development, it cannot be a very powerful first step. Finally, most people who see primacy as pernicious would grant that countries with primate urban systems are likely to have GNPs higher than countries with undeveloped or immature urban systems. They are unwilling, however, to agree that these intermediate countries are developing. Rather, Browning (1958), Cornelius (1975), Walton (1976), and Portes (1976) link urban primacy directly to *under*development, arguing that it is both a sign and result of the economic dependency that is causing underdevelopment. They see no contradiction between underdevelopment and moderate levels of GNP because they define underdevelopment as increasing regional and income inequality, worsening rural–urban terms of trade, and deepening immiserization of the poor, rather than as a certain level of commercial growth.

A study that is basically correlational cannot establish causality—cannot show whether primacy is cause, consequence, or side effect of moderate

---

[13]Since many urban systems in now-developed countries that are log-normal did *not* go through a primate stage (see Russell, 1972), the historical evidence cannot be considered strong, much less decisive.

levels of GNP. Thus El Shakhs's argument that primacy promotes development runs into trouble if a case can be made for a competing explanation for his data, such as the one just cited. The dependency interpretation is no more plausible on the strength of evidence, but whereas the modernization view fails to explain *why* urban primacy causes development, E. A. J. Johnson (1970) has provided a persuasive explanation for why it might promote *under*development. He notes that primate urban systems, by definition, lack enough small cities to service the rural population and enough medium cities to connect regional systems to the national economy. As a result, economic linkage between places becomes dendritic and monopolistic rather than intelocking and competitive.[14] The primate city, as the headlink of the dendritic system, monopolizes its hinterland and grows at the hinterland's expense, becoming a control center rather than a service center. Finally, rural areas and smaller towns suffer from lack of access to urban functions in proportion to their distance from the primate city. In this way primacy causes regional inequities as well as greater rural–urban inequities.

Berry (1971:142–143) concedes these points to Johnson, although he remains persuaded by El Shakhs. He observes that there is little question that certain systems (e.g., most of Latin America) tend toward urban primacy as well as certain related economic distortions; the issue boils down to whether one considers such places to be "developing" or "under-developing." Given the fundamental disagreement on this point, it would be foolhardy to promote urban primacy in the Third World on the evidence now in hand. We cannot be sure that primacy is absolutely damaging to economic development, but we are fairly sure that few developed countries have primate urban systems—a correlation confirmed even by El Shakhs's study.

This section concludes by reaffirming several widely accepted notions about urban primacy, even though it shows that this acceptance is poorly grounded in data or theory. Several of the points developed here will be helpful in assessing whether or not any of the standard theories of the causes (rather than consequences) of urban primacy explain its development in Guatemala.

Three explanations for modern urban primacy have been proffered in the literature: colonialism, export dependency, and rural economic collapse. In the following sections I show that none of them explains why Guatemala

---

[14]Johnson introduced the term *dendritic,* by which he meant a central-place system in which centers become smaller with distance from the first-ranking or primate center rather than spacing themselves in an interlocking network that has smaller centers locating between larger ones. Smith (1976:34–36) explains how dendritic systems create monopoly.

developed primacy when it did, even though Guatemala's pattern of urban development closely resembles that of most other Latin American countries. I develop the negative evidence at some length because my novel explanation for primacy in Guatemala, developed in Chapter 7 (this volume), gains credibility as an explanation for primacy in other parts of the Third World to the extent that standard explanations are shown wanting.

EXPLANATIONS FOR URBAN PRIMACY: COLONIALISM

Berry (1961) was one of the first to suggest that colonialism caused urban primacy, observing that not only colonized but also metropolitan countries (Spain, Portugal) tended to have overlarge administrative cities. Berry has given two explanations for this, which suggest yet a third one. His first explanation was that empires are controlled by key cities in both metropolitan and colonized countries; these cities become the foci of imperial interchange—part of a single, empire-wide, urban system—and thus operate at a different and higher level than local or indigenous cities. This account, which suggests that colonial cities become primate because they serve as control centers rather than service centers, is espoused by E. A. J. Johnson. Berry's second explanation is more amenable to El Shakhs's view of urban primacy. In a review of the nature of urbanization in Asia (1971), Berry argues that colonial cities often helped traditional economies modernize. They failed to do so mainly when high rates of urbanization, induced by colonial destruction of the traditional economy, "outstripped rates of economic growth and confounded the trickle-down process" (1971:139).

In both accounts Berry subscribes to the dualization thesis, wherein the major cities of colonial or excolonial states are the loci of "modern" influences, while other places are "traditional and backward." Poor articulation between the two systems can sometimes abort the normal urban growth process (or the trickle-down effect) and sustain the primacy of modern cities over traditional ones, but there is no inherent problem in colonial urban monopoly. The problem, if there is one, is not that primate cities wield too much influence, but rather that they do not wield enough. Implicit in theories positing dual economies is the idea that if one properly defined the relevant urban systems—which under colonial regimes would never correspond to a national system—the primacy apparent in both colonial and metropolitan urban systems might disappear. Primacy becomes, in effect, improper specification of the urban system. The appeal of this idea is that it provides a generic theory of primacy; the problem with it is that it is tautological unless it is made very specific, predicting primacy only in the administrative seats of colonial regimes. That is, if one explains primacy in every urban system (local as well as national) with the argument that the primate center alone belongs to a higher-level system without independent evidence that this is so, one only reaffirms that a primate center is primate—different from, or more important than, other places in its system.

We can quickly dispose of the theory that primacy is linked to *formal* colonial rule with the Latin American data. Guatemala City, administrative center for all of colonial Central America, has been Central America's largest and most important city since shortly after the conquest (Floyd, 1961).[15] But Guatemala City was *not* primate during the colonial era, even in its local or Guatemalan urban system. We cannot examine the entire array of city sizes for Guatemala until 1893, some 70 years after the end of formal colonial rule. But we know that Guatemala City was not significantly larger than Quezaltenango before 1893, and was not primate by the rank–size rule even then (Figure 6.1). Nor is Guatemala anomalous in Latin America. Richard Morse and several of his students examined the urban systems of eight Latin American countries and showed that seven lacked primacy in the latter part of the colonial period, although all had developed primacy by the early twentieth century (Morse, 1971, 1974).

Turning to the metaphorical extensions of the colonialism theory, can we explain the absence of primate centers in most South and Central American countries under colonialism as the failure of administrative cities in the colonies to establish themselves as control centers for their hinterlands or as sources of metropolitan influence? Morse and others argue strongly to the contrary, stating that, from the beginning, Latin American cities were situated specifically to control hinterlands and to organize the exploitation of natural resources desired by the metropolitan powers. Frank (1966) and Stavenhagen (1969) point out that colonial cities were the specific means by which the metropolitan bureaucracy extended its control throughout the system—from the metropolitan centers, through national capitals, to the smallest village. Provincial towns appropriating small agricultural surpluses were simply the smallest elements in an overarching metropole–satellite pattern that channeled profits upward to the national and international systems. Frank, in particular, argues that through this mechanism, Latin American economies were modernized, in the sense that traditional (indigenous) patterns were destroyed and supplanted by the colonial economy, based on capitalist market relations. Not all Latin Americanists agree with

[15]The first capital of the Audiencia of Guatemala was located in what is now Antigua. After disastrous earthquakes and floods in 1773, the capital was moved to its present location. Whatever its location, however, Guatemala's colonial capital always took first place in its administrative region, which included most of present-day Central America as well as the Department of Chiapas, Mexico.

Frank's entire argument, but few dispute his specific claim that colonial cities in Latin America completely controlled (and transformed) indigenous economies (see Portes, 1976).

The situation in Guatemala is no less clear-cut. Guatemala City, even though relatively small in population, totally dominated other Guatemalan towns in commercial as well as political functions during the colonial era (Woodward, 1966). All major towns in Guatemala were situated to exploit the resources most important to the metropolitan country, their locations relative to one another following the central-place design for administrative monopoly rather than commercial competition (Smith, 1975). The resource most consistently important to colonial Guatemala was its indigenous population (Maya Indians). This population was densest and most productive in the western highlands, where Quezaltenango and most of Guatemala's other major towns were located during the colonial period. Guatemala City itself was located more or less centrally vis-à-vis its administrative territory, which included all of Central America, if one measures centrality by population rather than area.

The Spanish and mixed (ladino) population lived in the towns, the indigenous population in rural hamlets. The Spanish bureaucracy, which controlled commerce as well as administration, allowed few if any commercial establishments (e.g., marketplaces or other kinds of urban functions) outside the adminstrative cities (Smith, 1973). Through this means colonial towns maintained a monopoly over the commercial life of the colony—a control pattern commonplace throughout Latin America (Appleby, 1978; Bromley and Bromley, 1975; Kaplan, 1965; Siverts, 1969). Even today the administrative towns founded by the colonial bureaucracy continue to control much public transportation and the distribution of most imports (Smith, 1972, 1975).

When the first Guatemalan census was completed in 1893, before the colonial urban system had been dismantled by liberal politics and a plantation-based economy, the western highlands held eight of Guatemala's 10 largest towns. By 1950, when export production rather than tribute collection dominated Guatemala's economy, only 1 of Guatemala's 10 largest towns was located in the western highlands. Four were located in the plantation area, which had no major towns in the colonial period. Although the western highlands remained the most densely populated part of Guatemala, it was now least rather than most urbanized. Thus even today Guatemala's towns are located to exploit economic resources rather than to serve its rural population.

In sum, the colonialism theory, which appears to work well in Asia (Berry, 1971; Hay, 1977), simply does not account for the Latin American pattern. It can be salvaged only if respecified to state that urban primacy develops when colonial rule is imposed on already urbanized societies. The problem with the original theory for Latin America is that virtually *all* its cities were colonial cities, imposed by the metropolitan bureaucracy. Hence there could be no disjunction between the city appropriated by the colonizers to administer the colony and indigenous ("traditional") cities.

EXPLANATIONS FOR URBAN PRIMACY: EXPORT DEPENDENCY

The respecified colonialism theory of urban primacy can accommodate the negative evidence, but still cannot explain the positive evidence—why primacy developed in Latin America when it did. One alternative theory appears to explain both: export dependency. This theory also accounts for the fact that primacy was induced by colonialism in Asia. Formal colonialism began in much of Asia and Africa in the first quarter of the nineteenth century, roughly the same time it ended in Latin America. Plantation economies dominated most countries in both Latin America and Asia, colonial and noncolonial alike, by the last quarter of the nineteenth century. Indeed, production of agricultural exports for the world market encompassed the entire periphery of world capitalism. With this trend arose urban primacy, first in Latin America, then in Asia, later in Africa (Hay, 1977). New patterns of demand in the now heavily urbanized and industrialized core areas of world capitalism, as well as changes in transport, technology, and finance, were responsible for this development (Wallerstein, 1980). The condition of the world market in the late nineteenth century not only overrode the political conditions extant in peripheral countries when it came to export production, it largely determined them. Where the British created formal colonies in Asia and Africa, they assisted "independence"—that is, their own access to its produce—in Latin America.

The export dependency theory of urban primacy, first fashioned to explain the Latin American urban pattern (Browning, 1958; Hardoy, 1975; Walton, 1979), is now the dominant explanation for urban primacy in other parts of the Third World also (Hay, 1977; Johnson, 1970; McGee, 1977). Urban primacy has, in turn, become a key element in dependency theory (Chilcote, 1974; Frank, 1969; Sunkel, 1973), a model emphasizing distortions in local economies caused by dependence upon external consumer and capital markets. The view that export-oriented production of primary goods promotes primacy is not, however, unacceptable to modernization theorists like Berry (1971) and El Shakhs (1972), who see development potential in both phenomena.

What, in either view, links urban primacy to export dependency? E. A. J.

Johnson (1970:152–157) provides one view. He observes that export commerce requires only one major outlet from the producing region to its external markets. Small, local centers are superfluous for shipping out as opposed to redistributing goods, the more so when a small elite living in a primate center constitutes the only population requiring nonlocal consumption goods. In addition, new forms of transportation associated with the rise of export production allow large cities to dominate remote hinterlands—one or two cities to control an entire country. Especially important are railroads, which tend to funnel commercial activity toward a single major entrepôt along dendritic transport routes (Appleby, 1976). Yet another element is the destruction of local industry through free trade with more developed countries, which undermines the economic base of provincial cities in the periphery. What attacks the commercial sustenance of provincial cities enhances the commercial importance of primate centers, through which most imports flow (Johnson, 1970:210–211). Finally, foreign investment in the infrastructure necessary for export development tends to strengthen one city above all others, usually the national capital or a port. And once a primate city emerges, "the process of agglomeration tends to become cumulative since other places are starved of the resources to follow suit" (Roberts, 1978:48).

Is the evidence strong enough to warrant the near-universal acceptance of the idea that export dependency causes urban primacy? The most frequently cited evidence for Latin America is the study carried out by Morse and his students on the urban systems of eight major Latin American countries. McGreevey (1971) found that for seven of the eight, the *level* of export production correlated with *degree* of primacy. It should be noted, however, that two of the supporting cases were fully primate by 1800, long before the major shift in their economies took place.[16] It should also be noted that the measure of primacy used in this test was the Ginsberg Index, a measure that we have seen is not adequate for dating the onset of actual primacy. The McGreevey study, then, is far from definitive.

Let us now consider briefly the way Guatemala's urban system evolved by looking back (Figure 6.1) at its city-size distribution at the four points for which we have usable national census information (1893, 1921, 1950, and 1973)[17] and comparing these data to the history of export production. Table 6.1 gives the volume of coffee production in Guatemala from 1870 through 1970 at 10-year intervals, showing that by the time Gua-

[16]Santiago, Chile, and Havana, Cuba, were the exceptional cases, primate from the first censuses of 1758 and 1792, respectively.

[17]There are only five usable national censuses for Guatemala (1893, 1921, 1950, 1964, and 1973). I omit the statistics from 1964 here in order to keep the interval between measures roughly the same (some 25 years).

TABLE 6.1

Coffee Export Production, Guatemala, 1870–1970[a]

Decade	Metric tons
1870	6,970
1880	13,800
1890	24,300
1900	35,200
1910	32,100
1920	45,200
1930	43,700
1940	47,400
1950	45,200
1960	79,900
1970	95,900

[a] The figure for each decade is given as the average of the 3 years up to and including the decade year. Sources: 1870–1930 (Jones, 1940); 1940–1970 (FAO Production Yearbook, 1971). Jones's figures, given orginally in *Quintales de oro*, were converted into metric tons.

temala's first national census was completed in 1893 the coffee economy was fully established. (Coffee alone is considered here because it earned more than 75% of Guatemala's foreign exchange between 1880 and 1950.) In the next census year, 1921, coffee was in its heyday, having reached a level of production and a position of importance in the economy it was not to exceed until much later. There was little change in the level of coffee production between 1921 and 1950, when the next reliable census was taken, but other agricultural exports, chiefly cotton and sugar, had gained some importance in Guatemala's overall export picture. By 1973, when the last national census was taken, the volume and value of exported manufactured goods exceeded that of exported agricultural goods (World Bank, 1978:15), but little employment had been shifted out of coffee (or agriculture generally).[18]

[18]Coffee earned 66% of Guatemala's foreign exchange in 1966, but only 26% in 1975; cotton rose to more than 20% before settling down to around 12% in 1975, about the same level as sugar. Income from the export of manufactures grow from less than 5% in 1960 to more than 30% in 1975 (World Bank 1978:29). Before 1960, however, the only serious competition in the export arena to coffee came from bananas, produced in a small foreign enclave by the United Fruit Company between 1936 and 1964. Even in those few years, however, bananas and United Fruit never played the dominant role in Guatemala's economy they played in other Central American republics (Winson, 1978).

Comparing Figure 6.1 to Table 6.1 gives mixed support to the export-dependency theory. On the one hand, the trend is clearly toward increasing primacy with each census period, as export production generally expands. Thus it would be difficult to refute the claim that export production pushed Guatemala's urban system in the direction of primacy. On the other hand, the timing seems off. The volume and value of coffee production had reached "modern" levels by 1900. From the response to export production recorded by McGreevey (1971) for other Latin American countries, we would expect full-fledged primacy in Guatemala by 1921; we do not find it until 1973. The jump in primacy between 1950 and 1973 is the most pronounced, even though we would expect the trend toward the production and export of manufactured goods to have dampened it. There is little to suggest that any diminution in primacy would take place even if Guatemala's dependence on the export of unprocessed agricultural goods were much reduced. Nonetheless, when coupled with the cases examined by McGreevey, the Guatemalan data support the notion that most export-dependent economies develop primacy sooner or later; but all these cases also show that it might be quite a bit sooner or quite a bit later than the establishment of a plantation economy. Thus the crucial linking mechanism remains to be identified.

The export-dependency theory is further damaged when tested on cases other than the ones on which it originally was based. If we were to correlate degree of export dependency with degree of urban primacy in the five Central American countries today—all of them heavily dependent upon the export of classic agricultural staples (coffee, cotton, bananas)—we would find a very poor correlation. Four of the five countries had reached per capita levels of export dependency as high as Guatemala's or higher by 1925 (Torres Rivas, 1971:295), but only two of them (Guatemala being one) now have significantly primate urban systems. The most export-dependent country of all, El Salvador, is least primate, even though its plantation system was organized in the same way and at the same time as the country that is most primate, Guatemala.

Noting that the gross association between export dependency and urban primacy takes into account neither the vast differences possible in export economies nor the significant differences possible in primate urban forms, and following the general trend in dependency theory of stressing divergent as well as convergent patterns of dependent growth, Bryan Roberts suggests a refined model (1978:49–60). He links the two different types of urban primacy described by Vapñarski (1975) to two very different paths to export dependency described by Cardoso and Faletto (1971). One path to dependency has export production controlled by foreigners, creating an encapsulated plantation enclave in the local economy. As a single city grows, provincial centers stagnate or even decline and internal commercial relations contract, leading to a national urban system that remains immature while becoming primate. According to Roberts, Peru provides a good example. The situation differs where indigenous capitalists control export production. Again a single major city grows more than any other, but provincial centers become better articulated at the same time because they serve a broader-based export development. The result is a national urban system that is both log-normal and primate. Argentina, as described by Vapñarski, exemplifies this pattern.

Though much more elegant than its predecessor, Roberts's refined export theory does not explain the Central American cases any better. Guatemala and El Salvador have the most similar export economies in all respects specified by Roberts, yet they developed the most different urban systems: Guatemala's relatively immature and extremely primate, El Salvador's relatively mature and nonprimate. (The three other countries, all characterized by well-developed export production in foreign enclaves, are equally diverse.) Nonetheless, it seems worthwhile to pursue this line of inquiry, if only to discover why two apparently similar countries with similar economic systems have such different urban forms. Any adequate explanation for Guatemala's primacy must also account for El Salvador's lack of primacy.[19] To this end I look briefly at the social and political features of export production in Guatemala and El Salvador, seeking differences that may be relevant to an explanation.

The republican state was responsible for promoting the production of export crops in every conceivable way throughout Central America. But initially the state had a much harder time of it in Guatemala and El Salvador than in the other countries. Both these countries were densely populated by an indigenous peasantry that provided considerable revenue to commercial, ecclesiastical, and governmental groups in the post-colonial as well as the colonial period (Torres Rivas, 1971). Hence powerful interests stood to lose from the "liberal" policies necessary to entrain coffee production: expropriating Church property, ending tariffs and local market monopolies, reforming land and labor laws. Affected interest groups, including Indians, resisted strongly (Cardoso, 1975; Ingersoll, 1972), and a major legislative reform was required to pave the way for coffee production. The reform took place in Guatemala in 1871 and in El Salvador in 1885, some 30 years after Costa Rica had begun coffee production on a

---

[19]It is frequently asserted that primacy follows from size of country more than any other single factor. Mehta (1969), for example, argues that small countries are more likely to be primate than large ones. Yet El Salvador, the smallest country in continental Latin America, also has an urban system most closely approximating log-normal.

major scale with much less fanfare and little disruption of preexisting social institutions.[20] The struggle over the expansion of commercial export-crop production in El Salvador and Guatemala was such that a very small national bourgeoisie emerged to profit from it. When put in place, the coffee plantations of both countries were large, unlike those in the rest of Central America, and required considerable amounts of hired or coerced labor.

In Guatemala, Germans were the important coffee middlemen, controlling 64% of the export trade in 1935–1936, the only season for which such data are available (Jones, 1940:208). When Germans were later expropriated, North Americans filled the breach. In El Salvador, by contrast, nationals largely controlled coffee processing and marketing. Foreigners owned more plantations in Guatemala than in El Salvador, though production of coffee remained largely in the hands of nationals in both countries. What really differentiated El Salvador and Guatemala, however, was neither plantation ownership nor market control, but rather the way plantations acquired labor.

In El Salvador most land put into coffee production had earlier been held by peasants. Thus the very process of creating plantation holdings created a plantation workforce; that is, the expropriated peasantry became a landless proletariat seeking full-time work for wages. In Guatemala most land appropriated for plantations was owned by the Church if it was owned at all; few peasants were directly disenfranchised (Cardoso, 1975).[21] Hence the workforce for Guatemala had to be created through other means, mainly coercive. Systems of labor recruitment strongly reminiscent of colonial practices were used against the corporate Indian villages of the highland area adjacent to the plantation zone from 1871 through 1944 (Carmack, 1979; Jones, 1940), obtaining labor that was unwilling, seasonal, and very poorly paid. Peasant communities and forms of livelihood were totally transformed in the process, but it is important to note that a peasant economy nonetheless persisted. This was not the case in El Salvador, where coffee so completely engulfed the national economy that no other economic systems retained significance.

By 1900 El Salvador had become one vast, very densely populated plan-

---

[20]According to Cardoso (1973), the "liberal" reform preceding the introduction of coffee in Costa Rica cannot be equated with the same reform and struggles that took place in Guatemala and El Salvador. The introduction of coffee was much less disruptive in Costa Rica and the classes created by coffee less clearly defined as bourgeoisie and proletariat.

[21]Carmack (1979) agrees with Cardoso, though he notes that much of the "unclaimed" land was communal land held by Indian communities that typically stretched from highland to lowland; though the expropriation of the lowland portion of an Indian community did not disenfranchise an Indian peasantry completely, it did make it much more vulnerable to proleterianization.

tation area; preexisting rather than new towns grew in response to improved transport and commercial stimulus, with the urban system approximated a rank–size distribution by 1920. In the same era, plantations were established in a "new" area of Guatemala, the western two-thirds of the Pacific lowlands. This part of Guatemala was relatively remote from the national capital, around which all earlier forms of export production had developed; in fact, the area that was to be the most heavily exploited in the modern era was thinly populated and economically depressed in the colonial era (MacLeod, 1973). Thus coffee production involved a major redistribution of population that stimulated the development of many new towns and created several new administrative districts (Paull, 1976). Having moved into a relative vacuum, coffee created its own urban and cultural landscape rather than modifying a preexisting one. The task was completed by a railroad that connected all the major lowland towns to one another, to Guatemala City and the Atlantic port, and briefly to Quezeltenango. The railroad was completed in 1912; by 1921 the population of the plantation zone stabilized at its present 15% of Guatemala's population.[22]

United Fruit established banana plantations in all the Central American republics with Atlantic ports around the turn of the century. They never took hold in El Salvador and were significantly reduced in importance in Guatemala in the 1940s by revolution and disease. Although this classic form of foreign-enclave production for export played a more important role in the three remaining countries of the region, its urban impact was small. The company established a single major city in each country with which it dealt, to which it funneled supplies, and from which it took the fruit. The enclave city did little to disturb relationships between other cities with respect to internal or other external commerce. Nor has the recent rise of cotton production greatly affected the shape of Central American urban systems; cotton is now important throughout the area, where log-normal as well as primate urban systems are found.

We can conclude that nothing in the degree of export development, type of export staple, or national interests of export-enterprise ownership accounts for either the distribution or the timing of urban primacy in Central America. Differences in the sociopolitical as opposed to the strictly economic features of export dependency seem a more promising avenue to explore. Guatemala, for example, retained an enclave peasantry, whereas El Salvador did not. And Guatemala developed two physically separate urban systems, each serving a different class (the lowland plantation owners as

[22]In 1893 less than 20% of *western* Guatemala's population was located in the Pacific lowlands of the region, where most coffee plantations are located; by 1921 that area held approximately one-third the region's population, the same proportion held today.

opposed to the highland administrative elite), while El Salvador did not. I will take up and develop these differences in Chapter 7 after treating the third and last theory of urban primacy, which provides yet another element useful for developing my case.

EXPLANATIONS FOR URBAN PRIMACY: RURAL COLLAPSE

The most recent theory of primacy is associated with new developments in both urban primacy and economic relations between the core and the periphery of world capitalism. Friedmann and Sullivan (1974) note that urban primacy deepened even as some Latin American countries turned from exporting raw materials to greater manufacturing activity. Quijano (1974) observes that primacy is especially pronounced in those countries undergoing import-substitution industrialization, which puts greater emphasis on urban rather than rural production for export.[23] This new economic thrust is linked to the economic decline, even collapse, of the rural peripheries once engaged in plantation production for export. A certain amount of industrialization based on imported capital (dependent development) is taking place everywhere in Latin America, but is most fully developed in countries such as Chile, Uruguay, Mexico, and Argentina (Soares, 1977), which are also characterized by extreme urban primacy. Whether this is a continuation of the old agricultural-export dependency pattern (and old urban primacy pattern) or is a new development remains a matter of debate.

Most scholars who espouse the rural collapse explanation for the recent surge in urban primacy (Portes, 1976; Quijano, 1974; Roberts, 1978; Soares, 1977) stress the continuity of early and late economic dependency, and early and late urban primacy. What links early and late primacy for them is the continued importance of national capitals that remain open to and influenced by larger, more dominant, urban systems. What distinguishes late from early primacy is only the decline of many secondary (provincial) centers and the rise of high unemployment or informal employment in primate centers, changes they explain as follows.

In early dependency, provincial centers play a major role in controlling the rural countryside and extracting a surplus from it. Such towns are, in fact, the local manifestation of an overarching metropole–satellite pattern, which channels profits upward to the national and international systems

---

[23]The "dependent development" argument, in a nutshell, is that import-substitution industrialization in the Third World has the effect of lessening the industrializing country's dependence on the importation of consumer goods but merely shifts this dependence to the importation of capital goods. Continued dependence requires continued growth of primary-goods exportation to obtain foreign exchange and to service the foreign debt.

through ever-higher-level urban centers. Provincial centers can still be dwarfed by the national capital, which has ties not only to them but also to external metropolitan centers, yet their role is complementary to that of the national capital and their populations usually grow as fast. But as the dynamic of economic dependency shifts from control over markets to reorganization of production—mainly through plantation agriculture—traditional urban centers in the provinces begin to play a marginal role. Plantation requirements for wage labor, which must be fed with increasing quantities of commodities, threaten the traditional monopolies of provincial urban elites and push provincial towns toward gradual obsolescence. The primary urban function of such towns becomes passive rather than active as they are transformed from commercial extractors of rural surplus to commercial outlets for the sale of imported manufactured goods (Roberts, 1976:104).

In later dependency, national capitals develop belts of highly capitalized agriculture around them at the same time that labor-intensive export-crop production declines. More economic opportunity concentrates in the few major cities of the country, and many people from both rural areas and provincial centers migrate directly to the major cities, inflating primate city growth even further. Increasing rationalization of the new capitalist modes of production undermines the rural basis of the economy and a general collapse of the provincial economies occurs. The long-term outcome is the redundance of many in the rural labor force, whose response is direct migration to the new economic growth centers of the country—the primate centers. But in the large (primate) cities, there is a corresponding shortage of work for the incoming migrants because the industrialization taking place is capital intensive rather than labor intensive. Thus an increasingly marginalized urban labor force (the informal sector) complements an increasingly marginalized rural population.

It is difficult to refute the logic of the continuation argument—that the urban primate pattern in both early and late manifestations is basically caused by the continuing economic dependency of the world periphery on the world core, a relationship mediated by overlarge national capitals in the periphery. Yet it is important to note that the rural collapse theory is quite different from the export dependency theory in its causal elements or mechanisms. In export dependency theory, as in the formal colonialism theory from which it grew, primacy develops from the concentration of urban infrastructure in a single center, usually the national capital. (Export dependency theory emphasizes commercial concentration, formal colonialism theory emphasizes administrative, military, and religious concentration.) It is assumed that the concentration of urban functions leads to a concentration of urban people, the latter being what is actually measured in urban analyses.[24] Those who espouse the rural collapse theory of urban primacy, however, point to the massive migration of people to one or a few cities; most make no assumptions at all about urban infrastructure, and some stress the *lack* of urban infrastructure in the primate city.

Not only does the proximate cause of urban primacy change with shifts in the nature of economic dependence, but so do some of the immediate consequences. The concentration in primate cities of administrative and commercial functions is likely to reinforce particular political and economic monopolies, whereas concentration in primate cities of recent migrants (or even of foreign industry) might very well challenge those monopolies. Thus it seems that insistence upon showing the continuities rather than the discontinuities of the dependency pattern may obscure as much as it clarifies.

Appleby (1978), who studied urban evolution in a local rather than national urban system (Puno, Peru), may be unique in offering the rural collapse theory as an alternative to rather than an extension of export dependency theory. He discovered that primacy developed in Puno's urban system *after* rather than *during* the big wool-export boom of the late nineteenth and early twentieth centuries—a sequence rather similar to Guatemala's. In examining the impact of wool export and its aftermath on the shape of Puno's urban system, Appleby observed that the export economy did not undermine the small colonial towns of the region, as he was prepared to expect by Johnson (1970) and others; it merely changed their urban functions and favored certain towns (those located near modern transport) over others. Whereas formerly small administrative towns extracted tribute from peasants, now small market towns purchased wool from small-scale commodity producers. But the economic foundation of urbanism remained roughly the same in the region and supported the same kind of city-size distribution: immature but nonprimate.

According to Appleby, *collapse* of the wool-export market rather than its development caused urban primacy in Puno. For as peasants' means of livelihood declined, the economic basis of small-scale urbanism in the region also dried up, and Puno's rural population had no alternative but to

---

[24]Many theories of primacy assume that certain cities are over-large in commercial or administrative functions rather than in population—that population is simply an easy measure of commercial or administrative concentration (Berry and Horton, 1970; Johnson, 1970). Marshall (1969:168) is one of the very few scholars to have tested the assumption that population figures accurately reflect urban centrality; the North American systems he examines do show a fairly good, though far from perfect, correlation—but his sample includes only five small urban systems. I know of no other tests of the fit between population and function of urban centers.

flood the region's major cities. Thus, collapse of the rural economy, which in this instance coincided with collapse of the export economy, caused primacy. One can see that Appleby's explanation for primacy in Puno can be extended to situations where the export economy itself causes primacy. If peasant holdings produce for the export market, small towns and cities are preserved and with them a nonprimate urban distribution; quite the opposite occurs if enormous plantations utilizing a small or mobile labor force replaces a peasant economy. In Appleby's description, then, lies a potentially generic theory of urban primacy that may account for its variable occurrence with export economies. The organization of rural production rather than the location of the consumer market is the crucial variable (see also Appleby, 1976).

Yet if we emphasize the technical *forces* of production, as Appleby does, we cannot find in this thesis the key differences between Guatemala and El Salvador, which share the same basic type of export economy. Both are at the very earliest stage of import-substitution industrialization; both rely heavily on export production of the same basic crops produced by very similar enterprises; and both have closer commercial ties to North America and Europe than to each other. But if we consider the differences in *relations* of production between the two countries, we move closer to the answer. Whereas El Salvador absorbed its peasantry into its export economy and has developed a unified urban system based on exports, no part of which is declining, Guatemala maintained its peasantry in a relatively isolated part of the country and developed a new urban system to service the export economy. Economists argue that incomes have declined precipitously in the western highlands of Guatemala as demand for seasonal peasant labor has leveled off while population has continued to grow. Fletcher *et al.* (1970:23) observe that annual per capita income in the area has fallen from U.S. $97 in 1959 to U.S. $51 in 1966. Many would agree that the subsistence base of that zone was collapsing—much as the peasant economy of Puno, Peru did—and with it the old colonial towns of western Guatemala. That is, it appears that Guatemala is at present unable to maintain its rural poor—especially its Indian poor from densely populated western Guatemala—and that these people are swelling the population of Guatemala City.

This variant of the rural collapse theory not only selects that feature of Guatemala that differentiates it from El Salvador, it also fits the timing of Guatemala City's explosive growth better than the other two theories. The main problem with this theory for Guatemala is that information about urban migrants to Guatemala City simply does not support it. Guatemala's rural poor, especially its rural Indians from the western highlands, are *not* the people pouring into Guatemala City (Bataillon and Lebot, 1976), as the most recent theory of urban primacy would predict.[25] Roberts (1973) found recent migrants to Guatemala City to have the following characteristics. Most come from eastern rather than western Guatemala; most come from larger rather than smaller provincial towns; most are ladino rather than Indian; and most are competitive with city-born people with respect to occupational characteristics (education, skills, and so forth). A good many migrants are of middle-class origin: children of professionals, established merchants, large landowners. In short, the characteristics of migrants resemble those of the receiving community (Guatemala City) more than those of the sending communities, and migrants appear to be pulled rather than pushed to the city. Roberts notes in a later publication (1978) that this is not unusual for Latin America. But it means that we must search for a more complex explanation for Guatemala's primate urban system than the theory of rural collapse.

Looking at the relationship between different levels of the overall urban system, a neglected element in Appleby's study, may help us here. It is important to recall that Peru's capital, Lima, was primate in colonial times and showed no signs of abating before, during, or after Puno's wool-export boom. Moreover, Arequipa, Puno's major wool entrepôt city (though outside the department Appleby picked for study), was quite clearly primate to its wool-producing hinterland, which included Puno *during* the wool-export heyday. Certainly one cannot blame a collapsing rural economy for the primacy of either Lima or Arequipa. It is arguable, in fact, that the later growth of primacy in Puno was simultaneously the diminution of primacy in the higher-level urban system headed by Arequipa.[26] The point here is that urban primacy involves more than the growth of a single city; it involves a set of relationships between cities at different levels of an urban system. In the case of Guatemala, therefore, we must concern ourselves not only with the rise of Guatemala City, but also the relative decline of Quezaltenango—conditioned, perhaps, by changes in the development pattern of the smaller, local cities articulating Guatemala's provincial economy.

[25]Bataillon and Lebot (1976) find that in Guatemala most urban migrants are from urban centers, whereas most rural migrants (such as seasonal plantation workers) are from rural areas.

[26]Appleby's otherwise exemplary study is flawed by its assumption that a particular "regional" urban system is somehow more relevant to Puno throughout its history than any other; it seems more reasonable to assume that different urban systems coalesce around particular commodities or types of exchange in different historical periods. The Department of Puno may bound the relevant local system of today, but it is certainly open to question that this was true during the heyday of wool export, when Arequipa was the major railhead and shipping point for most British factors of Puno wool.

Let us begin with the rural economy since the pattern of urban migration alerts us to the possibility that the rural economy of the western highlands may not be collapsing after all. Direct measures of rural incomes I have made show that, if anything, the opposite is true.[27] Rural incomes appear to be declining only because they are measured in per capita agricultural output of subsistence crops; but since the decline in subsistence-goods production has been more than matched by growth in artisanry, commerce, and specialized agriculture, measures of subsistence output are irrelevant. I do not attempt to document here the commercial transformation of the rural economy of the western highlands in response to the development of plantation agriculture in the adjacent lowlands, since I have done so elsewhere (see especially Smith, 1978). I simply outline the nature of the changes and their impact on the provincial cities of the area, especially in western Guatemala, which is Quezaltenango's hinterland.[28]

When coffee plantations were installed in the lowland portion of western Guatemala in the second half of the nineteenth century, they required labor and commodities that would at least seasonally maintain their highland labor force. And because a plantation bourgeoisie rather than a mercantile elite dominated Guatemalan politics after 1871 (Cardoso, 1975, Winson, 1978), administrative measures no longer blocked the development of industry and market centers in the peasant areas of western Guatemala—rural production and exchange systems that were increasingly to compete with the traditional urban systems of the region. As early as 1893, over half the *rural* population in two departments of the western highlands (Quezaltenango and Tononicapan) were engaged in artisanry or commerce rather than agriculture, occupations that during the colonial era had been monopolized by urban dwellers. By 1921 major wholesale marketplaces had grown up in rural townships that previously held no urban functions, taking over the distribution of domestic goods in the region, a function previously exercised exclusively by the region's colonial administrative centers. And by 1950 a

---

[27]I have direct measures of income on some 100 highland communities (hamlets) in western Guatemala over the past 50 years. These data indicate major increases in cash incomes (adjusted for inflation), major differentiation in occupation, and much higher standards of overall consumption at the end of this period than at the beginning.

[28]I cannot argue that provincial cities in eastern Guatemala have had the same functions and histories as those of western Guatemala. Roberts (1976), who discusses provincial towns in eastern Guatemala, finds them much less dynamic than provincial towns in highland Peru or than what I claim for the provincial towns of western Guatemala. But I assume that understanding the dynamic of provincial towns in western Guatemala is more crucial for understanding the general urbanization process in Guatemala, not only because these towns are larger and more numerous than their counterparts in eastern Guatemala but because they have always played more important roles in the export economy of the country.

full-fledged rural marketing system was in place in what was now a regional urban system that articulated the two physically separated but economically joined elements of export production: the highland peasant zone, which provided plantations with food and labor, and the lowland plantation zone, where actual production took place. This marketing system was hierarchically organized, functionally integrated, and quite efficient (Smith, 1972). Its integument, however, was rural rather than urban, for in many respects domestic commerce in western Guatemala was now manned by the rural peasantry rather than by the urban mercantile elite (see Smith, 1972).

Thus by 1950 the traditional colonial (merchantile) cities of western Guatemala—especially Quezaltenango and other department capitals in the highlands—were in serious decline, at least with respect to population size and some traditional urban functions. Growth of lowland cities kept the western region from losing urban population altogether.[29] But the net urbanization of western Guatemala between 1921 and 1973 was a mere 1%. In fact, Guatemala's 10% urban increase between 1921 and 1973 can be accounted for entirely by the growth of Guatemala City. The cause of this stagnation of decline in Guatemala's provincial centers, however, was not rural collapse, but rural development. Moreover, since the stagnation of old secondary cities in the provincial periphery of Guatemala was matched by the increasing strength of new urban centers (the small local market towns, which barely merit the term *urban* if we consider only their size but which clearly merit the term if we consider their function), one could argue that the decline of colonial administrative centers in western Guatemala presages the growth of a stronger and better organized regional *urban* system as well as a stronger and better organized *rural* economy. That is, the provincial urban system may not be declining or stagnating; it may simply be changing.

If I were to press this interpretation forward to generate a theory of urban primacy, I would be forced to argue that rural development rather than rural collapse caused urban primacy in Guatemala. Even if this were the whole story for Guatemala, it would hardly explain the development of urban primacy throughout modern Latin America, much less its appearance in earlier periods. The peculiarities of Guatemala, however, do point to another kind of explanation for urban primacy, one that stresses class composition and relations in different cities at different levels of an urban system. This explanation focuses attention on the forces repelling rural migrants from some urban magnets and drawing them to others. In other

---

[29]In 1921 the lowland portion of western Guatemala was 6.8% urban, the highland portion about 15% urban; by 1973 the urban level in both zones was virtually the same: 17%. (In these comparisons I count all centers above 2000 population as urban.)

words, it explains the *selectivity* of urban migration—why people migrate to Guatemala City rather than to Quezaltenango—rather than assuming, like the rural-collapse theory, that a displaced rural population will automatically select one city, the primate city, over all others. In Appleby's account, for example, it is never clear why rural people migrated to Puno at a certain point rather than to Arequipa or Lima; the collapse of a rural economy per se might explain an increase in urbanization, but it does not explain *primacy* or why a local rather than regional system becomes primate. Other rural collapse accounts suffer the same limitation.

CONCLUSION

In Chapter 7 of this volume, I describe an alternative theory of urban primacy, one that emphasizes class structure and class relations. This theory accounts for the economic conditions associated with primacy in present-day Guatemala, fits the timing of primacy in Guatemala, and accounts for the differences in urbanization between Guatemala and El Salvador. I also apply this theory to other cases of urban primacy in Latin America, and show that two other features of the class-relations theory make it more compelling than any of the theories presently accepted by most scholars. First, it can provide a general explanation for primacy (e.g., the same explanation for the primacy of Lima in the colonial era, Arequipa in the wool-export era, and Puno in the postexport era), and at the same time it allows the nature of urban primacy (class composition and relations in the primate cities) to vary and the character of the primate city (e.g., Lima, Arequipa, Puno) to be quite different. Second, it can account for the latest pattern of urban development in Latin America—the rapid growth of selected *secondary* cities—better than any other theory.

I should note that my alternative theory does not deny importance to the economic forces identified in the other theories; that is, to colonial exploitation, export dependency, or rural employment. Each of these has operated to produce the conditions that create urban primacy at one time or another. But economic forces do not directly produce social phenomena. They act as forces through the influence they wield over the behavior of people whose interests and behavior are also influenced by those of others. Thus, when one deals with a social phenomenon such as urban primacy, one must deal directly with the social groups producing the phenomenon. Otherwise one's theory will never explain apparently anomalous cases, such as the ones discussed above. By considering the way in which certain general economic forces affect the behavior of people, moreover, we can understand why all three of the theories I have critiqued have some value, though none is complete on its own. Obviously colonialism affects class structure and interests, as does the development of export agriculture, and the later development of industry based on capital imports. But they do not do so in the absence of other influences, nor do they overwhelm people and events without meeting certain resistance that can change or transform their effects. This is not a minor point, or a reduction of grand theory to smaller-scale processes. For the policy implications of a class analysis of urban primacy are quite different from those suggested by the dependency theories of urban primacy. The political implications of a class-based analysis are quite different as well. I discuss some of the policy and political implications of a class-based theory in the following chapter.

PART III

REGIONAL IMPLICATIONS

7

CLASS RELATIONS AND URBANIZATION IN GUATEMALA: TOWARD AN ALTERNATIVE THEORY OF URBAN PRIMACY

Carol A. Smith

INTRODUCTION

Social scientists interested in development and underdevelopment in the Third World now pay considerable attention to urbanization—for three good reasons. First, most developmental theories contain the assumption, either implicit or explicit, that a particular type of urban growth played a crucial role in the rise of capitalism, especially in the capitalist economies that were to industrialize first. Second, even the most superficial examination of urban statistics on underdeveloped capitalist countries show them to have urban systems very different from those of developed countries. Not only do their first-ranked cities tend to be overlarge, but the occupational composition of those cities is unusual, with a large proportion of their workers being either unemployed or employed in the informal sector. Third, it appears that development experts can be most helpful in the area of urban growth either by channeling it where most appropriate or by developing infrastructure in such a way that growth induces the preferred type of urban hierarchy. Urban planning is especially attractive because one assumes that urban growth will take place anyway and that any kind of urban growth will disrupt the "traditional" social order: hence, planners can play with the form or direction that urbanization takes without being accused of stifling non-Western values or interfering in local politics.[1]

---

[1]E. A. J. Johnson (1970) epitomizes the optimism of the urban planner who identifies urban primacy as the common problem of the Third World and advocates the "simple" solution of growth-pole centers.

This study of Guatemala's urban development in the nineteenth and twentieth centuries challenges much of the received wisdom about the pattern of urbanization in the underdeveloped world. It shows that the standard measures, assumptions, and theories of urban development, especially those pertaining to urban primacy, can seriously mislead. It demonstrates that understanding present urban patterns—a prerequisite, of course, to planned intervention—depends upon understanding local urban history and numerous sociopolitical variables rarely considered by urban planners. It suggests that the most popular urban development strategy implemented in the Third World (the so-called growth-pole strategy) is one that may have not only more negative than positive economic consequences, but grave political consequences as well. Finally, it contributes to a novel theory of urban primacy.

It goes without saying that Guatemala's history of urban growth is a particular one, and that the conclusions reached from a detailed analysis of Guatemala's development are only suggestive. Yet the pattern of Guatemala's urban development is similar enough to those of other underdeveloped countries that at least some of the findings presented here should be relevant to urban planners in other parts of the Third World. A brief comparison of Guatemala's pattern of urban growth to those of other underdeveloped countries shows how typical Guatemala's urban history is.

By Latin American standards, if not by Third World standards, Guatemala's urban population is a small percentage of its total population. Latin America as a whole was about 60% urban in 1975, a figure comparable to the developed countries in that year (Europe was 67% urban, Russia 61% urban, North America 76% urban); Asia and Africa, on the other hand, averaged well below 30% urban (Hay, 1977:90).[2] Guatemala's urban population in 1973 was 33% of its total population if one uses demographic criteria (nucleated settlements above 2000 population) and 36% if one uses administrative or "functional" criteria (nucleated settlements that serve as administrative centers).[3] The usual modern demographic definition of urban—having a population of 20,000 or more—would give Guatemala only five urban centers in 1973 and put its degree of urbanization at 18%. One city alone fits Kingsley Davis's definition of urban (having a population

---

[2]Hay counts as *urban* all places of more than 10,000 population.
[3]Guatemalan censuses sometimes use demographic criteria (centers above 2000 population) and sometimes administrative criteria (municipal centers) for defining their urban population. The earliest censuses (1880 and 1893) used criteria that are not clearly specified but seem to combine demographic and administrative elements. I have recalculated all census data into one consistent definition or another wherever I use time-series data here, though I am unable to adjust the earliest censuses.

over 100,000); that is, Guatemala City, where about 14% of Guatemala's population resides.

Anemic as Guatemala's urban development is now, it is considerably greater than its condition at the turn of the century, when no more than 15% of the population could have lived in centers of more than 2000 people, and the population in centers of over 20,000 all lived in Guatemala City and amounted to a mere 5% of the national population.[4] Since the country started out with such small urban centers and since its rural population has grown very fast in this century, Guatemala's urban population has had to grow quite a bit faster than the Latin American average just to get where it is now. Guatemala's total population grew at 1.4% per year between 1921 and 1950, and at 3.6% per year between 1950 and 1973; its *urban* population grew at 2.6% per year between 1921 and 1950, and at 4.8% between 1950 and 1973. The growth of Guatemala City has accelerated even more dramatically. It averaged 3.1% per year between 1983 and 1921; 5.0% per year between 1921 and 1950; and 8.1% per year between 1950 and 1973.[5]

The result of this pattern of growth has been extreme primacy, that is, the "overdevelopment" of a single city vis-à-vis other cities in the same system. In Latin America, Guatemala ranks second only to Uruguay in its present degree of urban primacy (Portes, 1976:30–37); it rates fourth in a recent world sample of 75 different countries (El Shakhs, 1972:34). By any of several measures, Guatemala City's primacy has increased significantly in each census period since independence. Guatemala City did not have even twice the population of Guatemala's second-ranking city, Quezaltenango, 40 years before independence. By 1893 it was four times the size of Quezaltenango, and by 1973 sixteen times.[6]

Neither the fact of Guatemala's urban primacy nor its tendency to increase in the twentieth century is unusual in Latin America. Portes (1976)

[4]The 1893 census reports more than 30% of its population living in urban centers, but it is clear from later censuses that large *aldeas* (hamlets) were counted as urban even though they had relatively few administrative functions, frequently did not exceed 500 people in population, and were rarely even nucleated. My estimate of 15% urban, then, extrapolates from a comparison of large cities in 1893 and 1921.

[5]These figures are calculated from the four Guatemalan censuses I use most frequently: 1893, the first completed census; 1921, the first census to define its units precisely; 1950, the first census considered to be quite reliable; and 1973, the most recent census. I consider all these censuses useful if proper precautions are taken in interpreting them. The 1940 census, however, is not usable (Whetten, 1961).

[6]The 1973 census reports an urban population for Guatemala City of only 815,519, some 12 times that of Quezaltenango. I have revised that figure upward to include the urban populations of Mixco, Amatitlán, Villa Nueva, and Chinautla, municipalities that most analysts agree now form part of Guatemala's urban area (Adams, 1970:131).

found a significant degree of urban primacy in all but two Latin American countries in 1970 (Brazil and Colombia), and argued that the usual measure of primacy in Brazil was confounded by the existence of two giant cities rather than one.[7] Primacy along with general urbanization has increased dramatically in virtually all Latin American countries during the twentieth century (Browning, 1958; Portes, 1976). National capitals, almost always the largest cities, have grown at the expense of provincial centers, while cities lacking administrative services have actually declined in size (Roberts, 1976). Urbanization rests on migration, and the recent pattern of urban migration in Guatemala is typical for Latin America (Zárate, 1967): migrants to the primate centers move there directly from their places of origin, rather than moving first to a regional center—in the classic European pattern known as stepwise migration (Roberts, 1978:101).

In very recent years a slight shift has occurred in the urban growth pattern for the larger and wealthier Latin American countries.[8] Major secondary cities have begun attracting migrants to the extent that they now show a slightly higher rate of urban growth than primary cities; at the same time, a relative decline in the growth of smaller cities or towns has set in (Fox, 1975:14–18), suggesting that primacy is developing at the regional level while not disappearing at the national level. This shift is not found in Guatemala, whose only large city is the primate center and whose second-ranking city, Quezaltenango, has barely kept pace with the growth of its rural hinterland. Guatemala's urban development pattern may lag behind that of Latin America's leaders only briefly, however. Recently urban planners have proposed a growth-pole strategy for Guatemala, a strategy that essentially involves beefing up the urban services offered in Quezaltenango and in the larger provincial capitals. Guatemala's recent governments seem quite taken with the idea, and plans are now afoot to implement it.[9]

The new "regional primacy" pattern in Latin America, as well as the urban growth policies fostered in Guatemala, raises a new set of questions: Is Guatemala's urban problem that its largest city has grown too big in this century—or that its secondary cities have remained too small? Should secondary-city growth be encouraged, and, if so, at the expense of which other cities? Does secondary-city growth, leading to regional rather than

---

[7]Portes uses one version of the Ginsberg Index (defined below) to calculate urban primacy in Latin America and thus identifies the city-size distribution of El Salvador, Honduras, and Nicaragua as primate even though they are barely so by the index (e.g., they are well within the range of "normal") and are clearly "immature" (see below) if graphed.

[8]These countries are Mexico, Brazil, Chile, Argentina, Peru, and Venezuela.

[9]According to the periodical *La Prensa Libre* (July 12, 1978), an Agency for International Development contract had, at that date, already been given to plan and develop the administrative and commercial services available in Quezaltenango.

national primacy, alleviate or deepen the problems associated with urban primacy? Is urban primacy the same phenomenon at all levels of the system?

Adequate answers to these questions can be given only by an adequate theory of urbanization in the modern world. We lack such a theory at present, partly because major confusions exist about what urbanization is (whether it involves the concentration of people or the concentration of economic infrastructure in particular places) and partly because most scholars of urbanization (especially those concerned with urban primacy) fail to take a systematic view of the phenomenon. Most extant theory, moreover, suffers from the ahistorical, functional bias persisting in most of sociology, and does not distinguish urbanization processes governed by capitalist as opposed to precapitalist relations of production. I have elaborated this critique of urbanization theory, especially urban primacy theory, in Chapter 6. Here I attempt to develop an alternative theory of urban primacy, which I illustrate with case material on Guatemala and several other Latin American countries. Before outlining my theory, let me briefly summarize my critique of existing theory on urban primacy and describe the measures on which I base a test of my alternative theory for the case of Guatemala.

MEASURES AND EXPLANATIONS OF URBAN PRIMACY

We have already seen (Smith, Chapter 6, this volume) that at least two kinds of primacy are possible: one is a situation in which the first-ranking or largest city deviates from an otherwise "regular" distribution of cities (rank–size or log-normal) by being overlarge; the other is a situation in which the first-ranking or largest city is much larger than any other, though the others do not conform to a regular rank–size pattern. In the second situation, secondary cities are typically "too small" in relation to the rank–size distribution; the primate city may or may not be too large in relation to that distribution.[10] I have termed the second type of distribution—where secondary cities are too small—an *immature* distribution because evidence exists linking its appearance to poorly developed urban trade (Smith, 1982). Since the forces producing an overlarge city in a mature urban system (log-normal) are different from those producing an overlarge city in an immature urban system, one must take care to distinguish the two types of urban primacy. Few scholars do so, however.

---

[10]Other irregularities are also possible. Secondary cities might be, themselves, too large in relation to the rank–size distribution, the first-ranking city might be too small, and so forth. For further discussion and illustration, see Smith (1982, Chapter 6, this volume).

Now, if we are concerned with the sizes of cities in relation to each other, we should also be very clear about what we mean by *size*. Most scholars measure urban size by urban population, under the assumption that cities have urban services in proportion to their populations. Rarely do they demonstrate that this is true. Yet secondary cities in many immature city-size distributions have far more in the way of urban infrastructure than one would guess from their populations, whereas the *primate* cities associated with such distributions have far less (Smith, 1982). If this phenomenon is widespread, as I will argue, one should not only distinguish mature primacy from immature primacy, but one should also distinguish population primacy from infrastructural primacy.

These two issues of measurement bear on theory in the following way. First, if one's theory of urban primacy has to do with the forces leading to the concentration of urban infrastructure in some places and not others, one should measure urban infrastructure rather than urban population in any tests of association, and vice versa. More important, if it can be shown that urban population and urban infrastructure do not vary directly with each other, one's theory of urban primacy should explain why urban infrastructure should concentrate in certain economies and not others *without* drawing urban population, and why urban population should concentrate in certain economies and not others *without* being drawn by urban infrastructure. Few theories of urban primacy take these possibilities into account.

There is a second sense in which the relational aspects of urban primacy are relevant to theory. We have already seen that the largeness or smallness of a city is meaningful only in relation to the sizes of other cities. We must also consider that the growth or decline in the sizes of particular cities occurs in an environment where other cities also change size. A city may become primate through the migration of people from secondary cities, from small towns, or from rural areas—which would affect the populations of these places or areas. Each particular pattern of migration suggests a particular underlying cause for migration and thus a different explanation for the growth of a primate city. An adequate theory of urban primacy, therefore, should specify the pattern of growth in other cities within the urban distribution under consideration. In other words, it should describe the growth of cities *in relation* to the growth (or decline) of other cities and population aggregates.

There is yet a third sense in which the relational aspects of urban primacy are important. Most scholars take it for granted that urban primacy is produced by population movements propelled by certain kinds of economic forces. The three prominent competing explanations of this phenomenon—colonialism, export dependency, and rural collapse (discussed in Chapter

6, this volume)—all derive from dependency theory, which is linked to the world-system theory of capitalist growth. The virtue of world-system theory is that it provides a relational perspective on urbanization in *spatial* terms. The problem with it, however, is that it fails to provide a relational perspective in human or *class* terms. A single major city grows in peripheral countries of the world-economy, in the world-system view, because this pattern of urban growth serves the interests of capital. "Capital" is sometimes represented by the bourgeoisie of the core, sometimes by the bourgeoisie of the periphery; sometimes it operates without *any* class agent. In other words, urban primacy comes into being because it meets some need of capitalism as an immanent force. Those classes that resist or struggle with capitalism, or with the dominant class that is only sometimes identified, are ignored, as are the contradictory needs of capital and of the dominant class. Yet urban primacy comes about through the patterned movement of people, usually propelled by some class interest; thus one ignores the class relations affecting people's movement into cities at great cost to theory.

If one prefers to base an account of urban growth around the issue of class relations—as I believe one should—one must make a major distinction between capitalist and precapitalist urban economies. *Precapitalist* urban economies are distinguished by having relatively immobilized labor forces, that is, systems of labor control that prevent large segments of the population from moving about freely. Most rural people (peasants) are tied either to their particular corporate communities or to large estates, unable to make a living outside those particular places. Only catastrophe or government decree moves peasants around, though a few may escape periodically to marginal areas as squatters or bandits. Rarely, however, can peasants move to cities on a regular basis and find means of supporting themselves there. In consequence, urban populations are largely self-sustaining ones, made up of elites, artisans, servants, and a relatively small casual labor force. Ties of dependency to place and patron immobilize most of the urban populace just as securely as they immobilize the rural populace. Thus urban centers in precapitalist economies are mostly small and do not grow much faster than rural populations. These circumstances typically produce "immature" urban systems, sometimes primate, more often *not* primate. (For illustrations and a discussion of the evidence on precapitalist urban economies, see Smith, 1982.)

Capitalist relations of production have very different consequences for population movement and urban growth. What defines *capitalism,* at least for Marxists, is the existence of the commodity of labor-power. And what defines *labor-power* is its divisibility and mobility. In other words, capitalist economies depend on "free" labor, which may be hired only when needed and in the quantity needed; and they depend on mobile labor, which can move about from city to city or from countryside to city with few barriers in its path. The free movement of labor in a commercially integrated urban economy produces in most cases a rank–size or log-normal urban system. As geographers put it, cities within a system of cities grow by the law of proportionate effect, such that the growth or decline of each city affects that of every other city within a system, producing in the long run a rank–size urban hierarchy.[11] Most developed capitalist economies, therefore, have log-normal urban systems. What produces the log-normal distribution is not development per se, but mobile urban populations, that is, free labor under capitalist relations of production.

What, then, produces urban primacy? I argue, like many others before me, that it most often occurs in the transition to capitalism.[12] But the social forces I consider important in the creation of urban primacy are quite different from those identified by others. I do not, for example, think that urban primacy results from the "modernization" of some sectors of the economy (such as those located in the primate city), while other sectors remain "premodern." Nor do I avoid the problem of dualism by calling the precapitalist elements of transitional economies capitalist. Rather, I assume that urban primacy is a phenomenon created by the transformation of class relations, especially labor relations, that are already contradictory, in a period that exacerbates those contradictions and in a period when precapitalist forms of labor control begin to disintegrate. Let me outline what I mean by this by first sketching the way in which class and labor relations within a transforming social formation give rise to the development of one

[11]In fact, discussion of rank–size regularity is somewhat confusing and vague. Geographers have produced good evidence showing that urban hierarchies are necessary for the efficient distribution of goods and services in an urban economy; they have also shown that "regular" or stepwise hierarchies are usually distorted by landscape irregularities and by continuous readjustments to these irregularities and others (Berry and Horton, 1970; Marshall, 1969). They argue that these two forces, in combination, produce the rank–size or log-normal form. But they have produced little direct evidence explaining the association of rank–size regularity with development or development potential. For a good discussion of the issues, see Richardson (1973).

[12]In this sense, I agree with the argument proffered by El Shakhs (1972), Berry (1971), and Wrigley (1978) that urban primacy can be transitional. But my position is quite different from theirs in several major respects. First, I distinguish two very different kinds of urban primacy, population primacy and infrastructural primacy, and argue that only one of them is transitional. The transitional form, moreover, may become a permanent form in my formulation. (This is the more likely evolutionary trajectory of Guatemala, for example, than transformation into log-normal.) Finally, I associate the development of transitional urban primacy with capitalism (free wage labor) rather than with economic "development," maintaining a distinction between core and peripheral capitalism (development and underdevelopment) that they obscure. Thus, I would argue, my formulation is free of their unwarranted assumptions about the benefits to be achieved through urban primacy.

large, dominant city within a system of otherwise small cities. I will then flesh out this schematic description with information on the real events and people of Guatemala.

What typically happens in the transitional period is that those elites of a peripheral economy tied to world commerce congregate in one city, either a national capital or a chief port. (Traditional theories of urban primacy have many explanations for this.) The concentration of elites, however, does not alone create a primate city: Latin American countries have always had elites concentrated in a few cities without those cities becoming overlarge. What does create a primate city is the concentration of free labor in one place. The national elites tied to world commerce are usually the first people in a transitional economy to realize that their class interests might be furthered by a free and mobile labor force, and they are also in a position to create and use such a labor force. In addition to dispossessing potential laborers, however, those who wish to make use of them must also weaken the hold of "traditional" (precapitalist) commercial and producing groups over labor. In other words, a national elite must crush certain opponents, primarily traditional commercial monopolists, before they can mobilize labor previously held immobilized by traditional relations of production. But national elites are not likely to fight that battle nationwide. They usually fight that battle in their own city, leaving traditional relations undisturbed elsewhere, because it is advantageous in the transitional period for them to use both types of labor: free labor in the main city and coerced labor in the provinces. Thus, at the same time that free labor is released and encourage to move to some cities, it is discouraged from entering others, especially provincial cities (the "secondary" cities of the national urban system).

Often, free labor is released from traditional forms of dependency much faster than it can be absorbed by formal employment, so it takes up positions in the informal sector. (The growth of an informal sector is also an effective way of destroying traditional monopolies in commercial and petty commodity production.) In consequence, one finds the populations of modern primate cities much larger than warranted by the existence of urban infrastructure or by employment opportunities within the formal labor sector. In provincial cities, by contrast, one often finds more urban infrastructure—commercial or petty industrial establishments—than one would guess from a count of urban populations. This is so because traditional commercial elites actively discourage the entrance of a large casual labor force, which would compete with them in commercial terms. Monopolists who use tied labor find it advantageous to keep as small a labor force as possible. Capitalists who use free labor, in contrast, prefer a large reserve.

Looking at the same phenomenon from the point of view of labor, one begins to understand why, in transitional economies, dispossessed peasants or artisans flock to an overcrowded primate city instead of moving to smaller provincial towns. In the primate city or cities they may face intense competition, but they do not face the legal and extralegal harassment they would find in provincial towns where local powers see them as threatening to their cherished monopolies. Often, in fact, migrants are actively encouraged to move to the primate city. They can find cheap places to live in squatter settlements that national (but not provincial) elites ignore; they can find more openings in both casual and formal employment for themselves and family members; and they are helped by a network of friends and relatives already "making it" in the city. Hence one finds direct rather than stepwise migration in most transitional economies, wherein secondary cities are bypassed.

With time, however, provincial elites may find it in their interests to employ free labor. (In fact, competition from the national level will ultimately force them in that direction.) Thus one often finds a pattern of regional or provincial primacy following upon national primacy. This still does not produce full labor mobility, however. The most entrenched commercial elites of precapitalist economies are those located in the smallest towns, for in these towns power domains that immobilize labor through direct, personal (often kinship) ties are much more difficult to shatter through competition. Hence urban primacy can persist for very long periods of time at both national and regional levels. And if urban primacy develops in a country (like Argentina) or period (like the present) when little rural labor is needed, it can remain in place indefinitely, even after all labor becomes free wage labor. So, even though urban primacy usually emerges because of the uneven process by which market forces direct the commodification of an economy, forcing competition among commercial groups and freeing labor to be utilized wherever needed, it can become a social phenomenon of its own, directing those parts and regions of an economy that will grow.

Given the usual spatial distribution of national elites and the constraints on their powers in most Third World countries today, one can assume that most Third World countries will go through a "stage" of urban primacy that will sometimes harden into permanence. Occasionally, however, one does find an immature urban system becoming log-normal or rank–size *without* a primate stage. One would expect this to occur, in my theory, only where an entire agrarian economy is commodified—as when a whole country (rather than one or several regions within it) switches from the production of crops with relatively immobile, coerced labor to the production of crops with mobile, wage labor. (I show below that such a transformation occurred in El Salvador, whose precapitalist economy—urban and rural— was very similar to that in the rest of Latin America, but whose "transitional'' economy was relatively unique.) The existence of such cases is important. For these cases show that urban primacy is more than a stage phenomenon; it is produced by particular types of classes and class relations in a transforming economy.

My argument, in summary, is that the growth or decline of urban centers rests ultimately on the economic interests of the politically dominant urban classes that exist at each level of the urban system, on their relationships with each other, and on their relationships with members of the working classes. Different urban class constellations, then, produce different urban forms. The four most common urban forms today seem to be produced by the following sets of urban class relations.[13]

1. *Log-normal* urban systems that are *not primate* are found where the politically dominant class is the same at each level of the urban system and that class finds its interests served by open or competitive forms of labor organization in specifically urban production or distribution enterprises. This kind of urban system tends to be associated with modern capitalist economies, not because these economies are "developed" or well integrated, but because a single class (the bourgeoisie) dominates all branches of the economy and depends upon competitive service groups and a competitive labor market at all levels of the urban system. Thus log-normalcy can exist in El Salvador as well as in the United States.

2. *Log-normal* urban systems that are *primate* are found where the politically dominant class at the highest level of the urban system is different from and has higher labor needs than the dominant classes at the lower levels of the urban system (as when provincial towns serve rural production systems while the first-ranking city houses urban industrial production), yet the dominant classes at both levels find their interests met by competitive urban service groups. In the modern world this kind of urban system seems to flag corporativism (Argentina, Costa Rica), wherein a single competitive commercial class serves at all levels of the urban economy but is required in greater numbers at the highest level of the system, where state-run or state-controlled monopolies are concentrated.

3. *Immature* urban systems that are *not primate* are found where the politically dominant class at each level of the urban system finds its interests or labor needs met by closed or noncompetitive forms of labor organization in urban service enterprises. This kind of urban system, typical throughout colonial Latin America but also found in the modern period, bespeaks a commercial economy run by guilds, state-granted monopolies, privileged

---

[13]See Smith (1982), Johnson (1980), and Kowalewski (1982) for a discussion of common city-size distributions in precapitalist society.

ethnic minorities, and the like. It appears to be the quintessential traditional (precapitalist) urban system—it was, in fact, extant in medieval Europe—but it can, nonetheless, accommodate considerable rural capitalist development (e.g., Honduras).

4. *Immature* urban systems that are *primate* are found where the politically dominant class at the highest level of the urban system is different from those at the lower levels and finds its interests served by open, competitive, urban service groups; it therefore displaces traditional, noncompetitive commercial groups from the highest-level center but not from the lower levels of the urban system (i.e., the provincial cities), where more traditional elites remain dominant and maintain opposition to competition. This kind of urban system, characteristic of much of modern Latin America including Guatemala, suggests economic dualism but is better understood as commercial class struggle. It is not that the commercial elites in secondary cities are traditional (precapitalist), while those in the primate city are modern (capitalist); it is that one group is better served by competing lower-level firms while the other is threatened by them.

Other possible urban class relations would produce slightly different urban forms.[14] But in this essay I treat only the four possibilities outlined above, the four most common in the modern world.

Urban Primacy and the Informal Sector

The case I have just made to explain the development of urban primacy in much of the periphery of the modern world rests heavily on the dynamic growth of a new urban service class, the informal sector. Let me now situate my argument within the literature dealing with that phenomenon since many writers on the informal economy have an implicit theory of urban primacy that differs somewhat from mine.

---

[14]If one reversed class interests at the two relevant levels of the urban system described under item 4 in the list, for example, one would produce log-normal regional systems within an immature national or macro-urban system, something rarely described for the modern world, though a reasonable characterization of late traditional China as described by Skinner (1977). Skinner sees commercial integration as the key and argues that commercial integration at the macroregional level in late-nineteenth-century China was relatively good, though it was poor at the national level. The explanation proffered by Skinner is mainly technological: that national-level commercial integration simply could not be accomplished in agrarian China because of its size, poor interregional transport facilities, and high transport costs. It would be foolish to discount these important elements, but I can recast these facts into the mold of my argument by asserting that labor mobility is the crux of the matter and that labor was no doubt more mobile within macroregional systems than across them, in part because of differences in regional and national needs and controls over labor mobility.

For quite some time now people have observed that the new migrants to major Third World cities appear to be unemployed, underemployed, or employed in marginal occupations for long periods of time (cf. McGee, 1973; Quijano, 1974). Keith Hart (1973), one of the first to describe fully the employment pattern in a fast-growing primate city and to find the received wisdom wrong, observed that a good deal of such "marginal" employment was relatively stable, some of it fairly profitable, and much of it of considerable importance to the operation of the city. The only marginal feature of what he termed informal employment, in fact, was its relationship to government regulation and the like. It is now rather widely accepted that most people in so-called marginal urban employment are fully if informally employed, and that the new form of employment came into existence to avoid the burden of state regulation and taxation. The more recent discussions of the informal sector, however, observe that the state often encourages rather than represses the informal sector (Bromley and Gerry, 1979; Portes, 1981; Roberts, 1978) and stress the close ties between the formal and informal economies, whose enterprises complement one another (one group competitive and labor-intensive, the other monopolistic and capital-intensive) and frequently draw on one another.

Alejandro Portes (1981, Chapter 4, this volume) who has developed the only real theory explaining the recent rise and proliferation of the informal economy in the Third World, argues convincingly that it is the dynamic element in present-day world capitalism, one that maintains the pattern of unequal exchange between world core and world periphery.[15] The informal sector supports low reproduction costs for labor in capitalist enterprise and as such represents a continuation of the pattern in which precapitalist economic systems are partially preserved in the world periphery by and for the capitalist economic system. The new feature is that the informal economy no longer represents a traditional subsistence or noncommodity economy, since people in that sector produce goods and services (commodities) to sell in markets to the formally employed proletariat. Created by capitalism, workers in the informal sector merely substitute abundant and cheap labor for capital and utilize familial modes of labor organization that maintain the low cost of their products and services. They also do a great deal of labor for the formal economy as occasional wage workers, product distributors (marketers, truckers, and the like), or raw materials procurers (see also Bromley and Gerry 1979). It is the low wages paid to people in the informal sector together with the lack of benefits, rather than the subsistence orientation of workers in that sector, that maintain their petty, undercapitalized enterprises in competition with the heavily capitalized ones.

[15]Portes rests his unequal exchange argument on the works of Arghiri Emmanuel (1972) and de Janvry and Garramon (1977).

Portes clearly links informal economy to urban primacy (1981:20–26), arguing that both hyperurbanization and informal economy are "novel structures" that are expanding in scale as subsistence enclaves in rural areas or in provincial economies decline. He takes pains, in fact, to differentiate the informal sector from petty commodity production (usually considered a rural phenomenon) on the grounds that the former is dynamic, a crucial part of world capitalism (even created by it), and its people fully engaged in market or commodity relations of production, whereas the latter is non-dynamic, partially primitive or precapitalist, and its people engaged primarily in subsistence rather than commodity production. On this point Portes differs from Bryan Roberts (1978:114), who stresses the parallels between the two phenomena and notes that petty commodity production is growing almost as fast in the rural areas of Latin America as the informal economy in its urban centers.

For Portes, the crucial distinguishing feature between the informal economy and petty commodity production appears to be location (urban versus rural), rural producers by implication being more subsistence-oriented than commodity-oriented. But commodity producers are commodity producers, whether petty or not and whether urban or not; they are not subsistence producers. Though Portes might not want to admit them into the informal sector, his definition of that sector (like that of almost everyone else) would include many of Guatemala's urban producers and distributors in the colonial era and a very large number of Guatemala's present-day rural "peasants," since neither group is subsistence-oriented. Against Portes and others, then, I argue that the distinctive feature of the modern informal sector (besides its close links to and direct maintenance of urban capital-intensive firms, a point that Portes had done much to develop) is that it is *competitive;* because it is competitive it replaces traditional urban service groups that may also have been petty commodity producers but were *noncompetitive.* This definition does not exclude many of Guatemala's present-day rural petty commodity producers (whose weaving and tailoring sweat-shops as well as low-cost distribution systems also help reproduce Guatemala City labor at very low cost); but I do not think it should. After all, these people have also robbed traditional urban service groups—those in the provincial capitals—of part of their monopoly heritage.

This brings me to my last and most important point—the difference between a class analysis and an economic analysis of urban forms, whether the latter be done in terms of the modes of production or in terms of the organization of markets and exchange. Using Portes's informal sector model, one could develop a general economic theory of urban primacy—one that could even accommodate the different urban development of Guatemala and El Salvador (as Portes's model now stands, it cannot account

for the difference). It would go something like this. Where monopoly capitalism takes over some urban industrial enterprise, but not all, and some
rural agrarian enterprise, but not all, one will find urban primacy because
free abundant labor is needed only in the few industrializing cities and the
small plantation enclaves; the movement of free labor into the former will
lead to hyperurbanization while its movement into the latter will lead to
provincial decline. But where monopoly capitalism takes over all enterprise,
urban and rural alike, one will find log-normalcy because free abundant
labor is needed everywhere in the economy. Though this theory sounds similar to the theory I developed earlier, I find it unacceptable—and a class
theory necessary—for two reasons.[16]

First, the economic theory is implicitly functionalist and teleological. It
argues that capitalism ''needs'' cheap labor and therefore gets it. This an-
imates an abstraction rather than concrete groups of people with specific
interests and reduces all of capitalism to a single, uncontradictory force.
The point is that some capitalists want cheap labor, others want a bigger
market, and still others want a larger share of the existing market. These
capitalists, or some of them at the expense of others of them, get what they
want *not* because they ''need'' it but because they have more power. Thus
I can support Portes's argument when he says that the explosive, dynamic
growth of the informal sector in the primate cities of the Third World serves
certain interests of capitalism. But I take exception to his assertion that the
phenomenon came about just for that reason—because the capitalism of
import-substitution industrialization needed it.

Second, the particular economic theory generated above to explain urban
primacy today is neither specific enough nor general enough to account for
the total phenomenon. Urban primacy existed before capitalism and may
exist after it. Certain features of modern capitalism are, of course, responsible for its spread in selected parts of the world today. But what is general
about the modern spread of urban primacy in conjunction with the modern
phase of capitalist penetration in the world periphery is that it has exacerbated certain class relations and class struggles that will generate the primate urban form. Thus again I concur with Portes that the informal sector
can help subsidize capitalist enterprises in the periphery, and that the growth
of the informal economy is as closely linked to the pattern of capitalist
penetration of the periphery as it is to the pattern of underdevelopment and
precapitalist preservation in the periphery. But I cannot agree that this is

[16]I should note that I based my critique of Portes's argument on an unpublished manuscript,
which has since been published in relatively unmodified form (see Portes 1981; Chapter 4,
this volume). Since then, however, Portes has amended his argument somewhat, making it
much less susceptible to my criticism (see Portes, 1982).

all done in the interests of capital. The informal sector develops and grows where it does because of the interests of noncapitalist as well as capitalist classes: the traditional mercantile elites, petty commodity producers in rural areas, and even the urban workers themselves.

In the following section, I illustrate my approach to explaining urban primacy by describing urban class relations in Guatemala and El Salvador, using these examples and their historical changes to define my terms more concretely. Then I develop some specific predictions based on the urban class-relations theory that other theories do not make, and test them against data I have gathered on Guatemalan cities for the modern (1970) and pre-modern (1893) periods.

Regions, Classes, and Urban Development in Guatemala

As described earlier, Guatemala's pattern of urban development has been similar to that in most of Latin America, indeed of most of the world-system periphery; it differs mainly in that it has been slower to urbanize and its urban primacy pattern is more extreme. Guatemala's second-ranking city, Quezaltenango, has never grown much faster than its rural hinterland, whereas the national capital and first-ranking city, Guatemala City, has more than doubled in the past 20 years. (see Table 7.1). Guatemala City was far from primate in the colonial period, at least with respect to population. When it came to urban services and amenities, however, Guatemala City was clearly the premier city in all of Central America, holding perhaps ten times more commercial establishments and services than any other city of the epoch. In the recent period, as I illustrate below, the national capital has gained more in the way of population than it has in urban services. Guatemala City's rapid rate of growth dates from about 1950, toward the end of the period when coffee exports dominated its economy. Today other export commodities, including a significant amount of manufactured goods, rival coffee.

Quezaltenango is the largest city in the western region of Guatemala, where most of the land and virtually all of the labor used in coffee production is located. The region divides into a lowland part, where coffee plantations dominate the countryside, and a highland part, where Mayan Indian peasants live (when not harvesting coffee), growing both subsistence and commercial crops for domestic consumption. Little urbanization has taken place in the western region in this century, though it was the most urbanized region of Guatemala in the nineteenth century and has had a well-developed export sector since 1871. More urban growth has taken place

TABLE 7.1

Population of Guatemala's Two Largest Cities over Time

	Guatemala City	Quezaltenango
1778	23,434	11,000 (17,000)[a]
1880[b]	50,522	16,634
1893[b]	61,951	15,487[c]
1921	115,447	18,684
1950	284,276	27,672
1964	572,937	45,195
1973	890,026[d]	53,021

[a] The figure of 11,000 is taken from Juarros (1823); the figure of 17,000 is quoted in Solorzano (1947); both are based on the quasi-census of 1778, reported in Cortes y Larraz (1958).

[b] The urban figures for the census periods of 1880 and 1893 are based on criteria different from those used in later censuses but the relative sizes of Guatemala City and of Quezaltenango should not be greatly affected by these differences.

[c] According to a note in the 1893 census (p. 204), the population of Quezaltenango for this year should be substantially increased because many Quezaltenango people were in the lowlands picking coffee when the census was taken.

[d] The 1973 census reports an urban population for Guatemala City of only 815,519; I have revised this figure upward in including the urban populations of Mixco, Amatitlán, Villa Nueva, and Chinautla, municipalities that most agree now form part of Guatemala's urban area (Adams, 1970:131).

in the lowland part of western Guatemala than in the highland part, bringing the once-neglected lowland area into parity with the rest of the region (see Table 7.2).

Urban class relations in modern Guatemala can be summarized as follows. There are three urban levels: national (Guatemala City), provincial (department capitals, including Quezaltenango), and local (small market towns, which I can describe only for western Guatemala). A different class is dominant at each level: a small national bourgeoisie that is oriented to export production and that controls the plantation economy as well as capital-intensive industrial enterprises in Guatemala City; a traditional mercantile elite in provincial centers; and a peasant-merchant group in the local market towns. The only urban class that finds its interests served by a highly competitive and open urban labor market is the national bourgeoisie, the dominant class in Guatemala City. Hence all urban growth in Guatemala is channeled to this single point, Guatemala City, because only there does competition produce openings for rural migrants in lower-level service firms—in this case, the informal sector. The particular relations of Guatemala's three sets of dominant urban classes to one another and to rural migrants, then, produces an urban form in which a single city dominates

TABLE 7.2

Guatemala's Urban Population as a Percentage
of Total Population by Area over Time[a]

	Guatemala[b]		Western region[c]	Western highlands[d]	Western lowlands[e]
	I	II			
1893[f]	(38.6)	(35.7)	(38.6)	(41.1)	(31.2)
1921	26.7	22.2	21.6	24.7	14.4
1950	31.0	23.2	22.0	24.1	18.6
1973	36.4	23.1	22.6	22.6	22.7

[a] Urban population is here defined as the population in all municipal *cabeceras* (lowest-level administrative centers), regardless of population size.

[b] Guatemala's urban population is given with Guatemala City's population (I) and without it (II).

[c] Guatemala's western region consists of the nine westernmost departments, which held 51% of Guatemala's population in 1893, and 40% in 1973.

[d] The western highlands consist of the departments of Huehuetenango, Quiche, Chimaltenango, Sololá, Totonicapán, and portions of Quezaltenango and San Marcos; adjustments have been made for changing boundaries in different census years.

[e] The western lowlands consist of the departments of Suchitepequez, Retalhuleu, and portions of San Marcos and Quezaltenango.

[f] The urban figures for 1893 are based on criteria different from those of other census years and thus can be used only for regional, not temporal, comparison.

all others in population if not in traditional urban functions. To see the dynamic of these relations, however, we must look at how these particular classes developed historically.

Guatemala City was not always open to rural migrants. According to Bryan Roberts (1973:99–101), a "traditional" mercantile elite dominated the city earlier, and under their suzerainty Guatemala City was a slower-paced, more tightly controlled place, where people knew one another personally and drew on information about one another's family backgrounds. This elite permitted petty (and in this sense *informal*) enterprises in its midst, but it held most lucrative positions in commerce and manufacturing in tight monopoly; in doing so, it strictly limited the growth of competitive enterprise and, with it, urban migration. The petty commercial–artisanal enterprises of this period, moreover, recruited only family labor and passed occupational skills on to family members.

The mercantile elite was itself politically dominant at all levels of the urban system in the colonial period (Woodward, 1966), but they were superseded by the new coffee bourgeoisie in 1871 (Cardoso, 1975; Winson, 1978). The new group, however, was not anxious to displace the traditional commercial groups in all of Guatemala's cities for several reasons. First, the protracted and very bitter struggle with various powerful colonial interest groups over the implementation of agrarian capitalism in the form of coffee plantations forced the new bourgeoisie to accommodate traditional groups as much as possible—as long as they did not directly interfere with commercial coffee production. Second, the plantation economy was highly localized in Guatemala; other parts of the country retained precapitalist modes of production that were better served (more fully exploited) by traditional mercantile groups. Finally, and probably most important, the new plantation economy was served by new *rural* competitive enterprise (in the highland peasant area), so that changes in urban forms of production and distribution were not required to lower the cost of reproducing the plantation labor force.

In El Salvador, by contrast, the traditional mercantile elite was itself transformed into an agrarian bourgeoisie by the coffee-export economy, and the transformation took place throughout the country, affecting the entire class structure and thus unifying the urban system while at the same time unifying the rural production system. As a result, El Salvador developed a log-normal urban system even before Guatemala developed a primate urban system.

Roberts dates Guatemala City's transformation from a traditional "colonial" city to a modern "city of strangers" at around 1950, well after the peak of the coffee-export era. Urban growth certainly accelerated at that point, so that by 1964 migrants to the city made up some 58% of the adult male population (Zárate, 1967). My hunch is that Guatemala's bourgeois revolution of 1944, together with the U.S. intervention that stifled it, were the forces that broke the mercantile monopolies in Guatemala City while threatening but not replacing them in provincial centers.[17] The traditional commercial groups could not provision the new (and mostly foreign) industrial enterprises and workforce concentrated in Guatemala City after 1944 with labor and commodities cheap enough to make the goods produced in Guatemala City competitive in the world market. Therefore, the new (postrevolutionary) urban elite of Guatemala City encouraged a dynamic, "modern" informal economy fed by fresh recruits from the hinterland, and this sector slowly replaced the "traditional" commercial groups in Guatemala City.[18] Openings in this informal economy promised and even

[17]Adams (1970) and Jonas (1974) both argue that the reformist governments of Arevalo (1945–1951) and Arbenz (1951–1954) were governments attempting to break traditional mercantile monopolies, to control large landed interests, and to free wage labor so that Guatemalan products could compete more successfully in the capitalist world market. Thus, reforms that the U.S. government regarded as leftist were simply moves to free the Guatemalan economy from U.S. market domination.

[18]I have no statistics on the rate of "traditional" business failures in Guatemala City during this era. But it was a frequent topic of conversation among people I knew in the city, many of whom turned from commercial enterprise to servicing tourists.

delivered economic payoffs to many, not just the coffee bourgeoisie, a fact that propelled the migratory trickle to flood proportions. Import-substitution industrialization developed about the same time and just as strongly in El Salvador (World Bank, 1978:15), but, because the dominant groups in all El Salvador's cities belonged to the same class, this new urban form of production developed more or less equally in all its cities rather than fueling the primacy of a single city.

It is important to observe that in both cases, Guatemala and El Salvador, the new industrialization of urban centers did not itself create a great deal of employment, since in both cases it was "heavily oriented toward capital-intensive production techniques" (World Bank, 1978:15). What it created in both places was an informal sector: a competitive labor market for employment in urban services once monopolized by small and nondynamic commercial–artisanal groups. It is also important to recognize that the informal sector must be defined quite precisely if traditional mercantile groups are to be distinguished from the modern phenomenon, and if the organization of urban services in Guatemala City is to be distinguished from that in Quezaltenango. Virtually all enterprises in provincial cities appear informal if one follows the usual definition for that sector: they are petty in scale and unprotected by state work regulations, and they utilize a good deal of unpaid or poorly paid family labor. But traditional enterprises, petty or not, are neither competitive, dynamic, nor open to rural migrants. Hence provincial cities remain small in population, though not necessarily small in urban functions, growing mainly through self-reproduction. I take up this point in more detail later.

Openings have not been available to rural migrants in most of Guatemala's cities, then, not because those cities or their hinterlands are unable to support new urban development, but rather because the dominant classes in those cities remained unchanged by agricultural-export production and by the new import-substitution industrialization and were strong enough to keep their cities closed and their commercial monopolies going.[19] I wish to

---

[19]The rapid growth of some cities (almost all of them administrative centers) in the lowland, plantation zone of western Guatemala would appear to belie this claim. But growth of lowland cities has been limited, with none of them growing at a sustained rate equal to that of Guatemala City; urbanization appears to have peaked in the coffee area, continuing mainly in the new cotton area. Furthermore, lowland urbanization consisted basically of a movement of traditional elites from the declining highland centers to the more dynamic lowland centers, rather than growth through rural migration. Urban people from the western highlands moved to the cities in the plantation area while rural people from the highlands moved to the rural part of the lowlands (Bataillon and Lebot, 1976); people residing in other parts of the country, in contrast, usually moved to the capital city. Thus the general class structure of western provincial urban centers, lowland and highland alike, was not significantly transformed in the process, nor was the commercial organization of the two sets of towns.

make clear at this point that I do not attribute the small size of Guatemala's secondary cities to their obsolete, precapitalist, or traditional character. I attribute it instead to the active struggle of the *nontraditional* mercantile elite to retain its monopoly privileges. The goals of this elite have always included money profit, calculated in terms of least cost. They are inefficient producers or distributors only because they are not competitive ones.

What maintains the traditional elite in Guatemala's secondary cities? This is easily understood at one level of analysis: the same people who hold traditional mercantile monopolies hold administrative office in the towns. And it is in the interests of these top powerholders to maintain the whole urban service system as a series of ascribed and monopolistic offices since competition at lower levels of the system is dangerous to all monopolists above them. This answer, however, begs the question of why the agrarian bourgeoisie generated by coffee and the new industrial bourgeoisie located in Guatemala City have allowed the traditional mercantile elite to hold political power in Guatemala's secondary cities. Traditional urban monopolists usually face ruin once agrarian capitalism develops because they do poorly at servicing export enterprises at low cost. In Guatemala, however, the capitalist enterprises form relatively isolated enclaves in the country, and the plantations are serviced by low-cost petty commodity producers and tradesmen located in *rural* areas. Thus urban monopolists in Guatemala's secondary cities have kept an informal sector out of their cities, but they have not kept that sector out of existence.

What evidence do I have for the notion that it is class dynamics rather than the lack of dynamic in one class (western Guatemala's traditional mercantile elite) that accounts for secondary-city stagnation there? I have three kinds of evidence. First, as I argued above, there is no lack of dynamism in the provincial economy. The urban functions of smaller centers around Guatemala's provincial capitals were completely transformed by the plantation economy, and the rural hinterland base of provincial cities developed rather than collapsed. Second, the mercantile elites of Guatemala's secondary cities were quite responsive to changes in the international economy with respect to performing their functions. They quickly dropped the less-profitable lines of local manufacture and domestic-goods distribution to take up the more-profitable lines of import–export goods distribution, labor trafficking for the plantations, interzonal trucking, and the like. They were simply unwilling to give over lucrative urban functions to small-scale competitive enterprises such as those making up the informal sector in Guatemala City. What the provincial area has in the way of an informal economy is "contained" in the rural areas. Finally, as I demonstrate below, provincial centers in Guatemala do not lack urban functions, they merely lack urban *people,* relative to Guatemala City.

The dominant class at the local level of Guatemala's urban system, the

newly enfranchised Indian merchants, performs some urban functions
(mainly the competitive ones of domestic goods redistribution and manufacture for domestic consumption), but lacks access to many important urban functions still carried out in provincial centers (the noncompetitive ones
of professional services, state services, banking, certain forms of transport,
and import–export commodity distribution). Lack of access to these urban
functions and active political and economic discrimination keeps members
of this class (Indian merchants who were formerly peasants) from entering
the already sizeable provincial towns, which have superior transport connections, and thus maintains the low population-growth rates of provincial
towns.[20]

Indian merchants in the rural market towns do not, in turn, keep rural
peasants out, so one might think that the third-level towns could simply
grow, superseding the provincial cities. Several elements in the regional pattern of class relations prevent this. For one, by maintaining certain crucial
urban monopolies, the provincial elite limits the growth potential of other
places. For another, the ethnic hierarchy effectively splits regional demand
for urban services in such a way that the numerically dominant but poorer
Indians obtain their urban services from the small Indian towns, while the
fewer but richer ladinos obtain their urban services from provincial cities;
the two urban systems are thus in shared stalemate (Smith, 1975). Finally,
Maya peasants are loath to leave their rural communities permanently for
reasons of cost and security, even though they have long given up rural
(agricultural) work for urban occupations. Peasant men pursue a wide variety of informal sector activities throughout the country on an impermanent basis, leaving wives and children to do much of the actual production
work (weaving, sewing, processing) in rural areas, where reproduction costs
are much lower.[21]

In sum, the class–ethnic division between the two lower levels of the urban system, supported by the division of urban functions, results in zero

[20]While it is *generally* true that few Indians have migrated to the major provincial towns or
taken up major commercial positions in them, a few Indian towns have grown significantly.
The most notable is that of San Pedro Sacatepequez (see Waldemar Smith, 1977), an Indian
town near a ladino administrative center (San Marcos) that now plays a very important commercial role in that particular province. In Smith (1972), I attempt to account for this anom-
aly.

[21]One could argue that in western Guatemala the equivalent of Guatemala City's informal
sector continues to reside in rural areas rather than in urban centers but that the same *economic* phenomenon is going on. In this context it is important to observe the role of ethnicity
in urbanization; economically displaced ladinos (most from eastern Guatemala) tend to join
the informal sector in major cities, whereas economically displaced Indians (most from western Guatemala) tend to join the informal sector without moving. This difference could probably be related to the different costs of reproducing an Indian as opposed to a ladino identity,
the former requiring some land and the latter requiring some education.

urban population growth throughout the entire hinterland of Guatemala City. Thus we find for Guatemala a relatively poorly integrated urban system (and immature city-size distribution) with a single major (primate) center.

One further question calling for discussion is why Guatemala's new industrial bourgeoisie displaced traditional urban service groups only in Guatemala City: Why did it make no effort to settle its enterprises elsewhere? Was it simply the strength of foreign interests in the capital city, and, if so, why only there? Was it that the traditional mercantile elite was weaker in Guatemala City than elsewhere, and if so, why? Or was it the preservation of precapitalist forms of production in the rural provinces, and, if so, what bearing did this have on urban development? My answer is essentially yes to all the above, for reasons that follow.

In the first place, foreign capital in the underdeveloped world must rely on cozy arrangements with the state—local political administrations—to protect its interests. Thus multinationals and foreign investors almost invariably prefer to locate in political capitals where the local state apparatus can more easily protect them. Once local and foreign capital are thoroughly intermixed, this pattern of concentration becomes less pronounced. Second, new forms of enterprise are much less likely to come into conflict with a traditional mercantile class in national capitals than in lower-level towns because the mercantile elite is never so closely aligned to nor identified with political groups here. Presidents and other administrators of Guatemala, for example, often have mercantile interests in other parts of the country without having them in the national capital. Mayors and other administrators in Quezaltenango, by contrast, are almost always locally based people and would find their own interests threatened by international capital or nonmercantile forms of local capital. (When urban class transformations occur, then, they almost always begin at the top and move down at a speed determined by the strength of local class interests.) Finally, the fact that Guatemala's agrarian bourgeoisie has not managed to wrest agricultural production from the control of the peasantry in the western region, as El Salvador's agrarian bourgeoisie did, means that the urban centers that serve (or exploit) that region cannot have the same functions as urban centers do where there is a free and highly mobile labor force that must sell its labor to survive.

POPULATION PRIMACY VERSUS COMMERCIAL PRIMACY

Having outlined a different theory of urban primacy and argued for its applicability to the Guatemalan case, I now propose to test the model against contemporary and historical data on Guatemala's urban system. This may reveal some aspects of Guatemala's urban structure more startling than my explanations for them. My data come mainly from western Guatemala (only 9 of Guatemala's 22 departments, but 42% of its population) because I covered only that region in my 1970 fieldwork. Although I lack detailed information on other parts of Guatemala, including Guatemala City, I am able to use some published census materials to place the national urban center, Guatemala City, in the context I produce for the regional urban system of western Guatemala. (I have data on both the lowland third of western Guatemala, the main plantation zone for all Guatemala, and the peasant highlands.) Elsewhere I have demonstrated that the two parts of western Guatemala (lowland and highland) form an integrated urban system headed by Quezaltenango, the only secondary city that provides urban services to more than two departments and articulates commerce between more than two other important towns (Smith, 1972, 1978).[22]

The predictions I propose to test are these. First, if a powerful mercantile elite has the monopoly hold on major urban functions that I propose it does, and for the reasons I suggest—their power rests on political or administrative control of the economy—we should find that all of Guatemala's important cities are important administrative centers and that administrative centers have more important urban functions than all non-administrative centers. And if, over time, mercantile monopolies are threatened by local market-town competitors, we should see greater concentration of these monopoly functions in administrative centers over time: the monopoly hold intensifying and pulling in, as it were, as it is threatened. Second, if secondary cities continue to play a crucial role in the regional economy, as I claim, yet remain closed to outsiders, we would expect them—the provincial cities or department capitals—to have more urban functions than indicated by the actual size of their populations. The divergence between population and function, moreover, should also increase over time, assuming that the monopoly hold of these places is threatened by lower-level centers. Moreover, if I am right that the lowland plantation area has essentially the same urban structure as the highland peasant area, we should find the general patterns predicted above to be equally true of both areas. Third, we would predict the opposite to be true for Guatemala City. That

---

[22]Western Guatemala divides into two economic–ecological zones: a highland, peasant zone that makes up two-thirds of the region, and a lowland, plantation zone that makes up the rest. The flow of labor, food, and income between the two zones of western Guatemala is precisely what makes it a single, integrated urban and commercial system. Most people divide western Guatemala into two regions on the basis of these economic contrasts, but this misses the defining feature of "functional" regions—interdependence and complementarity (see Smith, 1978).

is, Guatemala City should have fewer urban functions than indicated by its population size, vis-à-vis secondary cities in Guatemala, since an increasing share of its urban functions is carried out by the informal sector whose functions would be relatively invisible. The crucial point is that we should be able to document diminished formal sector employment in Guatemala City, relative to its population size, as the informal sector grows.

I begin with the data on the western region and for baseline purposes show the rank–size distribution of cities by population for that region. Figure 7.1 shows the distribution of cities of western Guatemala for 1893 and Figure 7.2 shows the same distribution for 1973. Both graphs show all cities of population 2000 or larger.[23] Administrative centers (the nine department capitals of the region, plus Coatepeque)[24] are identified and numbered with their population rank (as of 1973) on both graphs.

The regional distribution of city sizes for both time periods conforms to that for Guatemala as a whole. That is, the major cities appear to be too small vis-à-vis smaller towns, although somewhat less so now (1973) than before (1893). Quezaltenango in 1973 is less than half its expected size; in 1893 it was almost one-fifth its expected size. A good deal of reshuffling has taken place below Quezaltenango, most of it summarized by the rise of plantation-zone cities (Numbers 2, 3, and 4 in Figures 7.1 and 7.2) and the growth of administrative centers at the expense of nonadministrative centers (both these shifts were evident by 1950). Although administrative centers have grown over the 80 years since the first national census was completed, one would never guess from these graphs (of population size) that administrative centers were the only important towns in western Guatemala.

---

[23]I use 2000 population as the urban limit in this analysis, because, although somewhat arbitrary, it seems to be the size at which urban functions are typically added to towns. Smaller towns are no more than agglomerations of farmers.

[24]Coatepeque has a special kind of administrative status in western Guatemala. It is in the lowland, plantation area of Quezaltenango's department, while the town of Quezaltenango itself is in the highlands. In 1880 Coatepeque was a small, insignificant town (population 213), like most lowland towns that were not administrative centers. When the coffee economy developed, so did Coatepeque (population 1310 in 1893, 2517 in 1921, 6281 in 1950, and 15,979 in 1973). No other nonadministrative town grew as fast. As I see it, the reason for Coatepeque's development is that a number of Quezaltenango's administrative functions were shifted to Coatepeque for the convenience of plantation owners. In 1970 it had, for example, a national hospital, a national bank, a land registry office, and several public secondary schools—administrative functions found in no other town that was not a departmental capital. It also became the railhead for the only spur of the railroad to connect the highlands and lowlands (which led to Quezaltenango). Thus Coatepeque can be considered a special kind of high-level administrative center, one that serves the lowland portions of both Quezaltenango and San Marcos.

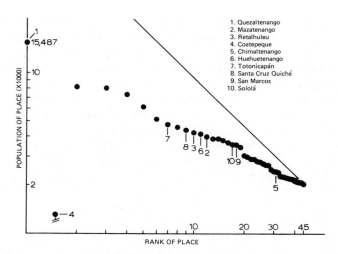

FIGURE 7.1   City-size distribution by rank of place and population: administrative centers, western Guatemala, 1893 (population threshold, 2000).

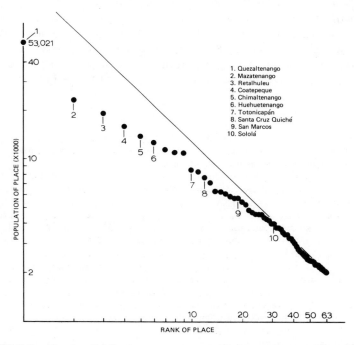

FIGURE 7.2   City-size distribution by rank of place and population: administrative centers, western Guatemala, 1973 (population threshold, 2000).

I now turn to the distribution of urban *functions* in the western region, looking for disparity between population and functions. The measure of urban functions I use is based on survey information I collected in 1970, when I undertook a complete census of business enterprises, commercial and industrial, in 162 towns of western Guatemala (Smith, 1972:27). I covered all the highland municipal centers and most of the larger lowland municipal centers. In 1974 Gene Paull (1976) gathered complementary information on all lowland municipalities, and I have integrated his information with mine in the following measures.[25] I undertook my census because I wanted the most precise instrument possible for measuring urban centrality. I did not expect the relationship between urban functions and population to be as weak as it turned out to be ($r^2 = .274$)—population size explaining less than one-third the variance in urban centrality. Nor did I expect it to show a very different picture of the region's urban hierarchy from the one I obtained by a close examination of urban population distribution, as it did.

My census counted fewer than 50 enterprises of fewer than 10 different types for the vast majority of places. Quezaltenango, the most-developed commercial center, had 76 distinct urban functions (of the 115 different kinds of urban functions found anywhere in the region) and more than 2000 permanent enterprises. The next-ranking center, Mazatenango, had only 51 different urban functions and many fewer enterprises. (Number of functions and number of enterprises are highly correlated at $r^2 = .88$.) Figure 7.3 graphs western Guatemala's urban centers by their rank on my count of urban establishments, using the same procedures I used in the charts of rank by population size (Figures 7.1 and 7.2). If urban centrality were correctly measured by urban population, Figure 7.3 should resemble Figure 7.2. It clearly does not. Instead of a concave distribution, with Quezaltenange much too small (250% smaller than predicted by the rank–size rule), we have a rank–size or log-normal distribution, with Quezaltenango a bit too large (50% larger than predicted by the rank–size rule).

Another way to show the distribution of urban functions in the region is to take a measure of urban establishments that gives appropriate weight to the *diversity* of functions as well as to the *number* of functions. A town with 20 bakeries, for example, would provide fewer urban commodities to the population it serves than a town with 5 bakeries, 3 general stores, 2 blacksmiths, and 1 doctor. (In fact, the number of establishments in a town

[25]Paull's measurement procedures are slightly different from mine, in that he accords administrative functions the same status as commercial functions; he also pays less attention to overall differentiation of urban functions, the feature of urban centrality to which I paid most attention. Our rankings of places therefore do not always agree. In using Paull's data, I tried to convert his measures into something closer to my own.

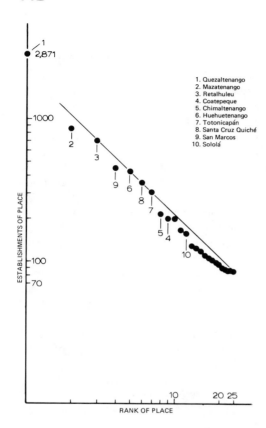

1. Quezaltenango
2. Mazatenango
3. Retalhuleu
4. Coatepeque
5. Chimaltenango
6. Huehuetenango
7. Totonicapán
8. Santa Cruz Quiché
9. San Marcos
10. Sololá

FIGURE 7.3   City-size distribution by rank of place and number of commercial establishments: administrative centers, western Guatemala, 1970 (establishment threshold, 70).

should in general be in proportion to its population size, whereas the diversity of establishments in a town should reflect the degree to which it is carrying out broader urban service functions.) Marshall (1969:85–89) describes a measure, termed a *centrality index,* designed specifically to weigh urban functional diversity. In this index, each urban function is assigned a score of 100 and each establishment performing that function is assigned the fraction of 100 it represents of the total number of such establishments in the region. Thus, if there are 50 blacksmiths in the region, each blacksmith garners 2 of the 100 points represented by blacksmithing as an urban function, and each town receives 2 points for each blacksmith it has. The only town in the region with a bank, however, receives the full 100 points for a single establishment.

The 115 different urban functions in western Guatemala yield 11,500 centrality points. The index constructed for each town from these points correlates highly with both number of urban establishments ($r^2 = .88$) and number of different types of urban functions ($r^2 = .88$); but because urban diversity is given more weight than size in this measure, it alters the positions of a number of places in the urban hierarchy. Santiago Atitlán, for example, drops from seventh place in population and seventeenth place in number of establishments, to thirty-fourth place in urban centrality. At the same time, Sololá (Number 10 on the charts) rises from thirty-first in population and twelfth in number of establishments to tenth in urban centrality.

Figure 7.4 shows how western Guatemala's towns line up by this centrality measure. Quezaltenango now displays considerable primacy, being seven times too large by the rank–size rule rather than two-and-one-half times too small. Quezaltenango is not the only city that stands apart. The nine other administrative centers of the region form a group separate from all nonadministrative centers—well above the line established by the smaller centers. Quezaltenango, with a score of 4347, has 36.9% of all centrality points in the region, and the 10 administrative centers of western Guatemala, whose cumulative score is 9463, have 82.3% of them. By these indicators, then, it would seem reasonable to conclude that the only truly "urban" places in western Guatemala are the 10 cities with important administrative functions. This is true despite the fact that my index is based solely on economic functions, gives no weight to administrative functions, and thus in some respects undervalues the urban functions of the 10 administrative centers.[26]

Lowland towns show the same basic pattern as highland towns. That is, major towns from both zones form one group, while nonadministrative towns from both zones form another. This indicates that the significant urban divide in the region is not between highland and lowland towns, but rather between places that house an administrative elite and places that do not. It is also indirect evidence that the lowland and highland towns of the region form an integrated urban system headed by Quezaltenango.[27]

---

[26]Many people, like Paull (1976), count all urban functions and add them together to obtain a functional index of urban centrality. I separated industrial, commercial, and administrative functions in order to see how closely they aligned with one another and compared each of these measures to population (see Smith, 1972:162–193). The index used here combines industrial and commercial functions. My study showed that industrial, commercial, and administrative functions were very closely aligned with one another, if not with population, when one separated out permanent commercial functions from periodic ones (functions carried out by periodic marketplaces). They were *more* closely aligned, in fact, than one would expect in a commercial as opposed to administrative central-place system.

[27]Commodity-flow analysis (Smith, 1972:57–134) also shows that lowland and highland towns of the region form an integrated urban system headed by Quezaltenango.

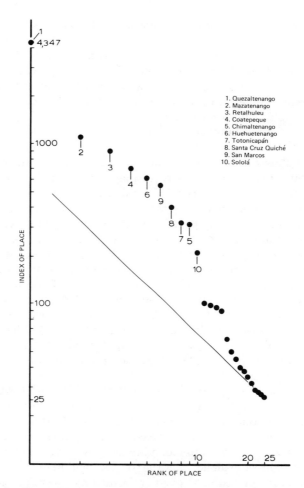

FIGURE 7.4   City-size distribution by rank of place and functional index: administrative centers, western Guatemala, 1970 (index threshold, 25).

   We cannot, of course, assume that a rank–size distribution of a weighted index of urban functions (Figure 7.4) means the same thing as a rank–size distribution of urban population (Figure 7.2). No studies have been made of the relationship between the two, nor do we know how the functional index graphs in developed countries with demonstrably well-developed, well-integrated commercial functions. On the other hand, we do have reason to expect number of urban establishments (Figure 7.3) to show the same pattern as number of urban peopoe.[28] On that basis, buttressed with the information shown in Figure 7.4, I make the following inferences about the urban structure of western Guatemala.

First, population size is *not* a good measure of urban functions, urban development, or even urban character. Sololá is much more urban than Santiago Atitlán, even though it has only one-third the population. Second, Quezaltenango seems to be developed enough to carry out fully the urban functions expected of a regional center, even though its population is small. Third, western Guatemala's administrative centers are clearly the most urban centers in the region—perhaps the only urban centers. They certainly appear to need little in the way of additional commercial and administrative infrastructure, precisely what they have a great deal of vis-à-vis smaller centers. Finally, and most important, it seems clear that commercial groups in administrative centers (the mercantile elite whose power base is political) have a monopoly hold over certain crucial urban services in the region and are excluding the population one would normally expect to be associated with a concentration of high-level urban functions. The policy implications of these findings, which I discuss below, are quite significant.

Further support for this interpretation can be found in Tables 7.3 and 7.4, which show that urban functions have become increasingly concentrated over time in western Guatemala—to a degree not adequately measured by urban population figures. Table 7.3 measures urban population concentration in several ways at three levels: the national level (all of Guatemala); the regional level (the nine westernmost departments of Guatemala, headed by Quezaltenango); and the local level (where the unit is a department, headed by a provincial capital, and the figures shown give an average of all departments in western Guatemala except for Quezaltenango, whose capital is the regional center).[29] Here we see that Guatemala City's population has grown from 4.5% of the national population to 13.6% while

---

[28]I have argued that log-normalcy in urban population (measured in my Figures 7.1 and 7.2) comes about only when there is a free and mobile wage labor force recruited primarily by cities; log-normalcy, then, should *not* be expected in western Guatemala, whose population consists mainly of a "tied" rural peasantry rather than free and mobile urban workers; and it should be rare for precapitalist urban systems in general. Log-normalcy in commercial establishments (my Figure 7.3), however, would require only freely mobile commercial establishments—which fits the situation in western Guatemala. Finally, log-normalcy of total urban infrastructure (measured in my Figure 7.4) would come about when political and economic services were dispersed in relation to population density and need; in Guatemala, of course, both political and commercial services are distributed in terms of power and wealth, which means they concentrate in administrative centers and fall off singificantly below that level.

[29]Local-level urban systems in Guatemala correspond to administrative units (departments) because of the commercial–distributional monopolies held by administrative towns. With

TABLE 7.3

Measures of Guatemala's Population Primacy by Area and Level, over Time[a]

	Guatemala (National level)[b]	Western region	
		Regional level[c]	Local level[d]
PRIMATE CITY POPULATION AS PERCENTAGE			
OF TOTAL POPULATION			
1893	4.5	2.2	6.7
1921	5.8	1.9	4.7
1950	10.2	2.2	6.1
1973	13.6	2.4	6.8
PRIMATE CITY POPULATION AS PERCENTAGE			
OF TOTAL URBAN POPULATION[e]			
1893	16.5	5.8	17.3
1921	26.5	8.6	21.3
1950	32.1	9.5	25.0
1973	37.3	10.8	29.9
PRIMACY INDEX (GINSBERG INDEX)			
1893	.662[f]	.397	.372
1921	.755[f]	.466	.408
1950	.841[f]	.499	.443
1973	.882[f]	.478	.454

[a] The italic figures in this table can be compared to the figures shown in Table 7.4.

[b] All cities and populations grouped.

[c] All cities and population in western Guatemala (nine westernmost departments) grouped.

[d] Departmental-system averages for the eight western departments, exclusive of Quezaltenango, are shown here. Thus on average each department had 6.7% of its population in a department capital in 1893, and 6.8% in 1973.

[e] All population in municipal centers (*cabeceras*) is considered urban.

[f] Significantly primate by this measure.

Quezaltenango has remained about the same percentage of its hinterland population, and local urban centers (department capitals) have also remained about the same. Provincial capitals and Quezaltenango have taken up an increasing share of the *urban* population, however, as has Guatemala City. This indicates that smaller (nonadministrative) centers have declined vis-à-vis larger (administrative) centers, even in western Guatemala, which does not have a primate distribution at either the regional or the local level.

---

few exceptions, towns within a department are supplied with imported goods from the *cabecera* (administrative center) of the department; the *cabecera* is, in turn, supplied with local (rural) goods mainly from its administrative district.

TABLE 7.4

Measures of Guatemala's Commercial Primacy by Area and Level, over Time [a]

	Guatemala (National level)	Western Region	
		Regional level	Local level
PRIMATE CITY ESTABLISHMENTS AS PERCENTAGE OF ALL URBAN ESTABLISHMENTS			
1893 [b]	30.8	22.8	49.3
ca. 1970 [c]	66.4	36.9	82.3
PRIMACY INDEX (GINSBERG INDEX) [c]			
1893 [c]	.541	.475	.446
ca. 1970 [d]	.806 [d]	.602 [d]	.650 [d]

[a] The units of comparison in this table are defined in Table 7.3. The figures in this table can be compared to the italic figures in Table 7.3.

[b] The figures for 1893 were derived from the 1893 census as follows. The occupational census lists three categories that can be considered a measure of urban commercial establishments: wholesale houses (*abastecedores*), barbers, and butchers. (Small shopkeepers, or *tienderos*, are mixed in with traveling salesmen, or *comerciantes*, and thus do not distinguish fixed from mobile establishments.) These figures were used as follows. The percentage in each of the three categories was calculated and then an average of the three was taken; this was done so the more numerous wholesale houses would not dominate the index. The figures on butcher shops in Totonicapán were not used for the regional-level and local-level measures because they seemed unusually high, probably reflecting the use of mobile rather than permanent establishments.

[c] Establishment data for Guatemala (the national level) in 1970 are taken from Guatemala's 1965 economic census: Volume 4 (1972) on industrial, Volume 3 (1971) on service, and Volume 6 (1972) on commercial establishments. Establishment data for the western region are taken from my economic census carried out in 1970, which counted all commercial and industrial establishments in the highland portion of western Guatemala and in one lowland department.

[d] Significantly primate by this measure.

[e] The Ginsberg Index can be used with an establishment count as well as with a population count.

Table 7.4 takes indirect measures of urban establishments for 1893[30] and direct measures of them for around 1970, and shows that the concentration of local urban functions in department capitals over the past 80 years is quite striking. Whereas slightly under 50% of all urban establishments were in department capitals before 1900, over 80% now are. Quezaltenango, which had slightly more than one-fifth of all urban establishments in the region in 1893, now holds more than one-third. Yet Table 7.3 shows that the population size of these places has held steady as a percentage of the region's total population.

[30] My indirect measure is simply a count of all the different occupations listed for 1893; most occupations listed are quite specific and thus indicate the commercial and industrial diversity of a town. In later censuses this method cannot be used because the occupational categories are taken from an industrial-society census model and are not locally meaningful.

The measures shown on Table 7.4 indicate that Guatemala City now has a much higher percentage of urban establishments than it did at the turn of the century. But it is not clear from this table whether this growth in urban functions is proportional to Guatemala City's growth in population relative to other cities. For this assessment I must use published figures on Guatemala's urban functions. The usable data, though spotty, are worth presenting because, when combined with the information presented above, they give a very different picture of Guatemala City's development than that indicated by population figures alone.

Table 7.5 sets forth a series of ratios (first-ranking to second-ranking city nationally and regionally) on a variety of urban functions and identifies the source and date of the information. At the national level Guatemala City is the first-ranking city and Quezaltenango the second-ranking city; at the regional level Quezaltenango is the first-ranking city and Mazatenango (a lowland town) the second-ranking city. On population, the ratios are 16:1 and 3:2—Guatemala City is 16 times larger than Quezaltenango, but Que-

TABLE 7.5

Comparisons of Guatemala's Urban Functions (as Ratios) by Level, circa 1970[a]

	National	Regional
1. Population	16:1	3:2
2. Lawyers[b]	15:1	5:1
3a. Number of industrial establishments[c]	8:1	3:1
3b. Employment in industry[c]	7:1	5:2
3c. Types of industrial establishments[d]	3:1	3:2
4a. Unlicensed service and commercial establishments (informal economy)[e]	11:1	1:1
4b. Unlicensed manufacturing establishments (informal economy)[f]	4:1	2:1

[a] The ratios in this table are based on the following comparisons: at the national level, Guatemala City's functions are compared to Quezaltenango; and at the regional level, Quezaltenango is compared to the region's second-ranking city, Mazatenango.

[b] Data are taken from Table 8–20 in Adams (1970:415–417).

[c] Data are taken from Guatemala's 1965 economic census, Volume 4 (1972). This volume considers only "major" (*con contabilidad*) industrial establishments. (This is the index used in Table 7.7.)

[d] Data for this index (used in Table 7.6) are also taken from Guatemala's 1965 economic census, Volume 4 (1972).

[e] Data on the informal economy are taken from Volumes 1 (small service establishments) and 2 (small commercial establishments) of Guatemala's 1965 economic census (published 1968). Data in these censuses are given by department, but virtually all such places are found only in department capitals. Figures for Quezaltenango have been adjusted downward slightly because Coatepeque, in Quezaltenango's department, is a substantial lowland town with a large number of such establishments.

[f] Data on the informal "production" economy are taken from Volume 5 of Guatemala's 1965 economic census (published in 1972). These, too, are small, unlicensed establishments, described in the census in the same way as unlicensed service establishments.

zaltenango is only 1½ times larger than Mazatenango. Population ratios will be the base-line for other comparisons.

It can be seen that the distribution of lawyers follows the population ratios closely, something that has been noted before (Adams, 1970:413–414). The only difference is that Quezaltenango has many more lawyers than one would guess from its population. Lawyers represent administrative concentration: they congregate where there is bureaucracy as well as wealth. There is no question about the concentration of political and bureaucratic power in Guatemala City. Apart from the national capital, virtually all legal action takes place in administrative centers, an area in which Quezaltenango is not especially privilged vis-à-vis other department capitals. Yet Quezaltenango does hold its own in its region.

The next group of measures (3a through 3c) are taken from Guatemala's 1965 economic census (Guatemala, 1968–1972). These show that Guatemala's commercial–industrial centrality may be half that indicated by its population figures.[31] Guatemala City is only seven times the size of Quezaltenango in industrial employment. Nor is the diversity of urban establishments in Guatemala City proportionally much greater than the diversity of Quezaltenango; whereas Guatemala City had three times as many different kinds of establishments as Quezaltenango, Quezaltenango had half again as many as Mazatenango. Guatemala City's economic centrality seems overrated by its population figures, as Quezaltenango's economic centrality is underrated by *its* population figures. Not that Guatemala City is economically or commercially log-normal, but its commercial centrality is out of line with its administrative and population primacy.

The fourth measure is a rough indicator of enterprises and employment in the informal economy, which Guatemala's 1965 economic census partially documents.[32] In taking the census it was found that the majority of enterprises in Guatemala City and elsewhere were very small, unlicensed affairs (and thus without internal statistics), which required special census coverage. Hence Guatemala's economic census divided enterprises into two groups, licensed (*con contabilidad*) and unlicensed (*sin contabilidad*). The characteristics of the unlicensed enterprises show them to fit very nicely into the *informal* category as defined above. More than half the informal service

[31]My measures are supported by W. D. Harris (1971:154). Using telephone directories, he observed that Guatemala City was much smaller in urban functions than one would expect by comparing its urban population to that of San Salvador. Guatemala City had twice the population but about the same number of urban functions as the capital of neighboring El Salvador.

[32]Guatemala's 1965 economic census includes only permanent establishments and thus leaves out the numerous hawkers, peddlers, and marketers of the cities; nor does it count the many thousands of household establishments that are producing commodities for sale.

establishments (72% of which purveyed food) sold less than $25 worth of goods per week. The average establishment employed 1.9 people, 62% of whom were women, less than half of them receiving a salary. People employed in this sector (whether by self or others) earned on average approximately $1 per day, or less than $25 per month. The informal commercial enterprises had many of the same characteristics: 80% were small food stores, 95% of their people were self-employed or unpaid family members, and the average return in these enterprises was $1.09 per person per day. These returns or earnings matched what unskilled plantation laborers earned per day at the time, the main difference being that plantation workers also obtained food for the day.

Guatemala City had nearly half the unlicensed establishments found in all of Guatemala (41% of the service establishments, 48% of the commercial establishments). It had more than 10 times the number found in Quezaltenango, which had about the same number found in Mazatenango. Guatemala City had as many people reportedly employed in the informal (unlicensed) sector as the formal sector. And the census clearly underreports informal employment, listing fewer than 10 shoeshine parlors (and 17 shoeshine boys) for all of Guatemala City.[33] It seems, then, that what Guatemala City has that no other place can match, other than just people (and lawyers), is the informal sector.

Table 7.6 presents similar measures on Guatemala's major towns for 1893. Quezaltenango was the second-ranking town in Guatemala in that year, as it was in 1973, but the second-ranking town in *western* Guatemala was by most measures (except occupational diversity) Totonicapán rather than Mazatenango. What Table 7.6 shows with rather striking clarity is that the most important urban shift that occurred in Guatemala between 1893 and 1973 was the simple movement of people (and with them, the informal economy) into Guatemala City, a movement that was not replicated in Quezaltenango. Bureaucracy also became more heavily concentrated in Guatemala City; but commercial, industrial, and occupational concentration (i.e., economic centrality) did not become that much more pronounced. Economic centrality did increase, of course, but not to the degree suggested by population growth. Table 7.6 also shows, even more clearly, that Quezaltenango's relative position in western Guatemala has not changed a great deal over time. It has always been somewhat small in population vis-à-vis other towns of the region; but it has remained three to four times more

---

[33]The degree to which the census undercounts the informal sector can be seen in these figures. If one were to add in the numerous "impermanent" establishments found in Guatemala City—a type that is much less evident in Quezaltenango and other provincial centers—one would have to double these figures (or more) for Guatemala City.

TABLE 7.6

Comparisons of Guatemala's Urban Functions (as Ratios) by Level, circa 1893[a]

	National	Regional
1. Population[b]	4:1	2:1
2. Lawyers[c]	6:1	6:1
3a. Wholesale houses[d]	5:1	3:1
3b. Employment in simple manufacture[e]	5:1	5:2
3c. Occupational diversity[f]	2:1	3:2
4. Servants[g]	7:2	4:1

[a] The ratios in this table are based on the following comparisons: at the national level, Guatemala City is compared to Quezaltenango; at the regional level, Quezaltenango is compared to the second-ranking city in the region on the measurement in question, excepting Retalhuleu, inflated in this census by its coincidence with the coffee harvest.

[b] Data for population and specific occupations are based on Guatemala's 1893 census.

[c] Guatemala City had 148 lawyers, Quezaltenango 24, Totonicapán 4; most department capitals had 3, a fair number of other places had 1; Retalhuleu had 7, but it is very likely that some had come down from the highlands for the coffee harvest.

[d] The count of wholesale houses is based on a commercial directory reprinted in Curtis *et al.* (1892:169-175), a publication of the Bureau of American Republics. Lowland places are excluded in the comparison because of their special commercial organization.

[e] Based on count of tailors and shoemakers, the most "developed" manufacturing of the day.

[f] Number of different occupations.

[g] Servants (including cooks) are the best measure available of the "informal" economy of 1893, although it is quite a different phenomenon in later years.

important—in economic, administrative, or wealth centrality—than any other place. What it seems to have lost over time is actual people, *and* the informal sector.

The census of 1893 does not yield a good measure of the informal economy. By today's standards, the entire urban economy at that time was informal. Few people worked in large industrial enterprises and urban establishments of all kinds employed mainly family members. Table 7.6 shows—in the same place the informal economy takes in Table 7.5—the ratios for servants found in the major cities of the time. Servants made up 9% of Guatemala City's employed population, 14% of Quezaltenango's, and 5% of Huehuetenango's. Servants, clearly not the same thing as people employed in the informal sector, although the informal sector includes many servants, are a measure of wealth in 1893, and Quezaltenango, by excluding the poor from its urban confines, had a greater proportion of wealthy people than even Guatemala City. As I argued earlier, excluding poor (and potentially competitive) rural migrants has always been Quezaltenango's urban policy, a policy that has kept the city small, exclusive, and tightly controlled by a local commercial elite that does not *allow* an informal economy like that in Guatemala City to flourish in its midst.

The local, regional, and national changes over the past 80 years in "basic" economic centrality are best described by Table 7.7. Economic centrality is measured by urban diversity, and this time the difference between western Guatemala as a whole and the western lowlands is shown. The diversity index for 1970 for most places is my count of the number of different types of urban functions found in a center; the figure for Guatemala City was calculated from Guatemala's 1965 economic census.[34] The measure of urban diversity for 1893 is number of different types of occupations found in a city (3c in Table 7.6); occupations are quite finely delineated in the 1893 census and correspond closely to types of urban establishments. All figures except for primate cities are averages.

TABLE 7.7

Average Commercial Centrality of Guatemala's Towns at Different Administrative Levels by Area, over Time, Compared to Population[a]

	Guatemala		Western region		Western highlands		Western lowlands	
1893								
Primate city	133	(62)	68	(15)	50	(4)[b]	50	(4)[b]
Department capital (average)	—	—	44	(4)	42	(4)	49	(4)
Municipal capital (average)	—	—	9	(1)	7	(1)	14	(1)
Largest nonadministrative centers[c] (average)	—	—	33	(5)	29	(5)	42	(3)
1970								
Primate city	240[d]	(890)	76	(53)	46	(13)[b]	51	(23)[b]
Department capital	—	—	43	(9)	43	(9)	50	(21)
Municipal capital	—	—	8	(2)	8	(2)	10	(2)
Largest nonadministrative centers[c]	—	—	21	(6)	23	(6)	17	(5)

[a] Population figures (rounded in thousands) are given in parentheses. The commercial centrality figures for 1893 are based on a count of the different occupations found in a place in that year. The centrality scores for 1970 are urban central functions, based on my census of all highland towns and Paull's information on the lowlands.

[b] The largest highland nonregional center in both 1893 and 1973 is Huehuetenango; and the largest lowland nonregional center in both years is Mazatenango.

[c] The largest nonadministrative centers are averages by department; the largest places in population are not necessarily the largest places in centrality.

[d] The centrality score for Guatemala City is based on Guatemala's 1965 economic census of major establishments (Volume 4, 1972). In this census Guatemala City has 131 different kinds of establishments to Quezaltenango's 42. I converted this ratio into a ratio comparable to my own urban-function scores so that lower-level centers could also be compared.

[34]Guatemala's 1965 economic census credits Guatemala City with 131 different types of manufacturing establishments to Quezaltenango's 42. I converted this ratio into a score for Guatemala City in order to compare Guatemala City to lower-level towns that are not noted in the 1965 census.

The stability of Guatemala's urban system as revealed by these measures is quite remarkable. Although the diversity of urban functions increased substantially throughout Guatemala between 1893 and 1970, the relative standing of different levels in the system hardly changed at all. Guatemala City did become more diverse vis-à-vis Quezaltenango, but not by a factor comparable to its growth in population. Even more remarkable, Quezaltenango has today the same position it had in the region in 1893 before the advent of plantation agriculture, wage labor, and motorized transport.

The data force me to conclude that Guatemala City is overlarge (primate) in population but not in infrastructure, whereas provincial cities in Guatemala are quite the opposite—overlarge in infrastructure and undersize in population. I have argued that the two conditions are related. People displaced by the transformations taking place in Guatemala's economy, the petty bourgeoisie as well as the peasantry, pour into the national capital not because it is the only attractive city in the country, but because they are barred from viable employment opportunity in most other places by a traditional mercantile elite attempting to safeguard its own livelihood by keeping out potential competitors.[35] This struggle between Guatemala's various local and national classes, then, is the underlying cause of Guatemala City's urban primacy. This kind of primacy, in population rather than infrastructure, is almost certainly transitional; but it is as likely transitional to another kind of primacy—infrastructural and thus relatively permanent—as it is to log-normalcy.

CONCLUSIONS AND POLICY IMPLICATIONS

As mentioned at the outset of this essay, most urban and regional planners agree on several basic principles of urban development: (1) log-normalcy is a desirable state of affairs for urban systems; (2) urban primacy, even if a sign of economic development or potential, exacerbates the pains of growth by promoting regional and social inequality and thus is a state to be curtailed, if not eliminated; (3) social equity is served by promoting urban growth poles in underdeveloped regions; and (4) social or cultural disruption wrought by urban planning is likely to be minor compared to other disruptions promoted in economic growth. The Guatemalan case, however, gives little support to these presuppositions. That is, the widely accepted "equitable solution" to Guatemala's urban growth pattern—a growth-pole strategy centered on Quezaltenango—would have more

---

[35]My informants in western Guatemala frequently discussed the difficulties of setting up their (informal) enterprises in places like Quezaltenango, where they would have preferred to live permanently, as opposed to Guatemala City.

negative than positive effects in Guatemala in precisely the area of equity, and little effect with respect to growth. The policy implications of this case, therefore, deserve specific notice.

Urban planners are already at work on Quezaltenango and several other secondary cities of Guatemala with ideas for industrial parks, more (government-supported) urban functions, and better (government-supported) urban services. The overall plan is to put more urban infrastructure in several of Guatemala's provincial towns at the cost of additional infrastructure in Guatemala City.[36] Yet these plans will precisely worsen the present situation. It will take infrastructure away from where it is most needed, Guatemala City, and put it where it is least needed, the underpopulated administrative towns of the provinces, making the per capita distribution of urban services more rather than less inequitable. Moreover, the plan will add to the economic power of administrative cities at the cost of smaller nonadministrative cities, which in western Guatemala are only now taking on important urban functions. The long-run effect might well be the failure of the only commercial competitors Guatemala's colonial towns, now provincial centers, have ever had. If this were to occur, the result of intervention could well be the underdevelopment rather than the development of the provincial economy. Apart from these risks is the problem of efficacy: there is no reason to expect that these changes will necessarily attract people away from the national capital to the smaller cities of Guatemala. For, if my argument is correct, rural people bypass Huehuetenango or Quezaltenango not because these towns lack urban amenities but because they lack free urban labor markets.

So far I have argued that the growth-pole strategy would not have the intended consequences in a place like Guatemala. But let us also consider what would happen to the economy if it *did* work, if Quezaltenango and selected secondary centers of Guatemala were to surge in population as well as in infrastructure. Would the outcome be log-normalcy? And, if so, would it provide any real economic benefit? Or would the infrastructural urban problems of Guatemala City simply be reiterated nationwide? To answer these questions I look briefly at the different contexts in which secondary-city growth has taken place recently in Latin America and consider some of its consequences.

Oaxaca, Mexico, and Puno, Peru, are small provincial cities in Latin

---

[36]Two other towns specifically targeted in Guatemala's plans are Escuintla and Puerto Barrios, Guatemala's third-ranking and fourth-ranking cities, respectively. Both are administrative centers and both dominate their respective hinterlands strongly in commercial as well as administrative functions.

America that are beginning to grow at a rapid rate.[37] These two cities are now clearly primate within their provincial regional systems, although before the turn of the century they were not at all primate. Earlier these cities headed immature urban systems, but today they head urban systems that are close to log-normal, though still primate. Both are towns that would have been chosen for enrichment by growth-pole stategists, yet both grew without planned intervention. Growth in neither town has been spurred by new industrial development or new state investment. Population growth, moreover, has run ahead of infrastructural growth, leading to large squatter settlements and an extremely high degree of "casual" employment.

In Puno, the rural migrants squatting in the town have played a major role in creating and manning a rural marketing system whose merchants are based in the provincial cities rather than in rural areas. In Oaxaca, the expanded urban marketplace as well as small artisanal and workshop enterprises provide new employment opportunity to many people. In both cases it appears that many urban functions now run by the new rural migrants were once monopolized by established urban groups that held guild-like monopoly privileges in the city. Yet in neither case does the growth of a *regional* primate city seem to auger well for the regional economy. While the life chances of the rural migrants to the regional primate cities may be improved over what they would have been in the countryside,[38] urban "growth" seems merely the obverse of rural collapse (Appleby's argument), not urban "development."

What is most interesting about these cases from the perspective of my thesis, however, is why collapse of these rural economies led to *regional* primate-city growth rather than *national* primate-city growth. Rural collapse, as I argued in Chapter 6, is an insufficient explanation for the selectivity of urban migration. My argument points to the existence of urban monopolies in provincial towns and the uneven emergence of a free urban labor market. My interpretation of the urbanization process in Oaxaca and Puno, then, is the following.[39] The various enterprises found in the small

---

[37]Neither town is now growing as fast as the national primate centers of Mexico and Lima, but their growth rates are accelerating while the growth rates of Mexico City and Lima are presently declining.

[38]Theresa Graedon (personal communication, 1982) has shown that the diet of the urban poor in Oaxaca (who are mostly migrants from rural areas) is much better (from the perspective of basic nutrition) than the diet of the rural people still living in the villages from which the migrants come.

[39]The analysis that follows rests primarily on personal communications with Gordon Appleby (for Puno), Theresa Graedon, and Alex Stepick (for Oaxaca). I cannot say that any of them would agree with my analysis completely.

towns and rural areas around Puno and Oaxaca continue to be based on various "tied" labor systems as opposed to free wage labor. Peasants, for example, utilize what they have in the way of family labor, whether surplus or short, and can do little to reallocate labor in a more rational fashion; in this manner, too, operate most small-town service enterprises.[40] But in the major towns of the Puno and Oaxaca regions, a competitive wage-labor market is emerging and drawing to it all the redundant (or merely "untied") labor in the economy. In the past this labor found no place in the provincial cities and went on to higher-level centers (e.g., Lima or Mexico City); but now it can find a place in the regional capital and does so.

What displaced the traditional mercantile elites in the provincial towns? An argument could be made that conditions became so overcrowded in the national or macroregional centers that pressure was finally put on provincial centers by the displaced rural populations. This seems unsatisfactory, however, because the national primate centers of Mexico City and Lima continue to grow. We need a plausible account for the failure or decline of the regional urban elites, which I can provide only for Puno.[41] The traditional merchants of Puno, who were closely connected with the wool export trade, seem to have left the provincial centers to newcomers because they, rather than the producers, were ruined by the failure of the wool market. The wool producers themselves—the peasant producers, anyway—did not "collapse" with the wool market; they merely shifted from producing wool to working as seasonal day laborers in the coastal areas. The result was that the wage-earning peasants now had more continuous cash incomes (and commodity needs) than they did earlier as wool producers, and thus were able to support a relatively dense rural marketing system run on cash payment where they once supported only provincial mercantile establishments run on debt. The growth of the rural marketing system, in turn,

---

[40]Both Puno and Oaxaca are regions made up predominantly of "freeholder" peasants who produce some of their own subsistence goods and some goods for the regional market, and who usually have some other means of supplementing their incomes. Though fully commercialized, these peasants are not yet free of the ties that bind them to a particular locale. Their land, for example, is more than a factor of production; it is part of their ethnic identity. Therefore, these peasants are not fully mobile nor free enough to move in response to wage levels. Partly proletarianized, they remain partly peasants.

[41]This account is not that given by Appleby (1978), but it is based on his account. Appleby argues that collapse of the rural economy caused peasants to migrate to the local cities; the enlargement of the local cities then caused expansion of the rural marketing system, which fueled the growth of informal sector employment in the growing cities. I find this argument weak in that it nowhere specifies the source of production on which the vast commercial expansion in the region is based. Appleby allows that many former wool producers now gain considerable income from seasonal work on coastal plantations, and this, I suggest, is the dynamic fueling the expansion of the system.

spurred the growth of Puno, still the commercial nerve center of the region.[42] But the commercialization of the region remained uneven and the proletarianization of the peasantry incomplete. Urban growth, therefore, was lopsided and informal (Appleby, 1978, terms it *involutionary*), as was commercial opportunity; and per capita incomes in most of Puno declined. The general process should, perhaps, be seen as the increased capitalist penetration of Puno, which nonetheless remains an economy based only partially on free and mobile wage labor (like western Guatemala).

In my view, then, the evolution of regional primacy in Oaxaca and Puno (the "natural" development of regional growth-poles) has ameliorated *national* primacy in Mexico and Peru very little and assisted even less the economic growth of Oaxaca and Puno. This interpretation gains support by the contrasting history of another region in Peru, one that developed a log-normal rather than a primate urban system, the Montaro Valley (Roberts, 1976, 1978). Roberts argues that this provincial region is developing economically thanks to the explosive growth of petty commodity production throughout the system, in small towns and large. The history of the urbanization process Roberts and his collaborators put together indicates that the two elements I have identified as crucial for relatively "even" urban (and economic) development—that is, transformation of the regional class structure and the creation of a regional labor market—took place in the Montaro Valley.[43]

In the early part of this century, the urban system of the Montaro Valley was both immature and primate. The administrative center of the region, Huancayo, dominated the system in urban functions if not in urban population, and the city's elite controlled the region politically and economically. The traditional commercial orientation of the region's towns changed when the local oligarchy, funded with outside capital, built a major textile mill in Huancayo in the 1940s, which then required large quantities of wage labor. The town drew in considerable numbers of people from the surrounding region to work in the mill and in the many new service enterprises that cropped up in order to feed and house the textile workers and move them between home and work. The textile mill eventually failed and with it perished the economic and political dominance of the region's traditional

---

[42]I oversimplify here somewhat, inasmuch as the region of Puno supports "dual" primacy: the administrative capital of Puno itself and a new commercial center, Juliaca. The two cities seem to share urban functions for the region.

[43]In his description of urbanization in the region, Roberts emphasizes the transformation of the region's class structure and the emergence of new forms of commercial enterprise (what he terms, variously, petty-commodity production and informal-sector enterprise). He does not document the emergence of a regional labor market, though he alludes to the responsiveness of both workers and enterepreneurs in the system to wage opportunities.

oligarchy, their commercial interests having been undermined by their industrial interests. But the former textile workers, rather than returning to their rural homes, stayed on to carry out many of the commercial functions of the town (and the region) once managed by the traditional oligarchy. The populace of the entire region, encouraged no doubt by the greater freedom of movement possible (both literally and figuratively) under this new regime, gradually moved into the production of various commodities for the growing urban market of Lima on a full-time commercial basis. Assisted by the creation of a regional labor market, the economy of the region diversified and became more productive at the same time that all the towns and cities of the region attracted rural people to them, fitting them into the new or expanding commercial–artisanal enterprises.[44]

Why the urban history of the Montaro Valley is so different from that of the Puno region is not entirely clear. It could simply be overall degree of commercialization at one point in time. But it does seem clear that the development of the well-integrated (and log-normal) urban system in the Montaro Valley rested upon the development of a relatively homogeneous regional class structure (dominated by a competitive petty bourgeoisie throughout), as well as a regional labor market. This is the kind of urban system I would envisage for western Guatemala if urban planning were designed to undermine rather than support the old colonial administrative towns (and their elites) in the region, so allowing the growth of the region's small nonadministrative towns—those places served by and serving rural (peasant) enterprise. The urban planners in Guatemala today, however, seem to be heading for quite a different outcome, one that at best would approximate Puno's situation. I conclude that development of a growth pole is no solution at all; it merely spreads the problems encountered in national-level urban primacy (of population rather than of infrastructure) to a regional level. To eliminate the problems of national urban primacy one needs more than competition from a regional primate center; one needs competition from the growth of an entire regional urban system.

A final lesson can be drawn from a case of permanent and infrastructural urban primacy in Latin America, that of Argentina. The lesson is that a free labor market does not necessarily eliminate political control or monopoly in an economy, nor does it necessarily eradicate urban primacy. Vapñarski (1975) showed that Argentina's urban system evinced primacy from the early part of the nineteenth century to the present. The primacy

---

[44]I should temper this rosy picture of economic expansion with the observation that most enterprise in the Montaro Valley is very small in scale and yields relatively little income. The people of this highland valley are relatively well off compared to other Peruvian highlanders, but that is not to say they are very well off.

of Buenos Aires was associated with a very immature national urban system in the nineteenth century, but with an increasingly log-normal urban system in the twentieth century. Vapñarski proposed that the growing log-normalcy of the urban system indicated growing commercial integration of the system as it matured. Primacy persisted, in his view, because of the continuing "openness" of the Argentine commercial system to external influences; that is, to its continuing "dependency." I agree with Vapñarski about the causes of log-normalcy, but I disagree with him about the causes of primacy. In my interpretation, Buenos Aires remains primate because of the persisting difference between the nationally dominant class and the provincial elites in economic aims and means.[45]

The immature urban system found in Argentina during the nineteenth century was linked to an economy made up of ranching haciendas and pre-capitalist systems of (tied) labor control. The mature (log-normal) urban system found in Argentina today is linked to an economy based on grain farming and free wage labor. Rural labor was quite scarce in nineteenth-century Argentina, population density was low, and provincial cities were very small. Even as wage labor became the means of allocating labor in the rural economy, the provinces absorbed relatively little of it because of the extensive nature of agrarian enterprises. Argentina, then, had little rural population to people its cities and Buenos Aires grew not from cast-off rural labor but from European immigrants, whose arrival coincided (not accidentally) with urban industrial growth in Buenos Aires. According to Balán (1976), the growth of Buenos Aires between 1895 and 1914 was dynamic (infrastructural) and due to the expansion of economic opportunities in the city rather than to the failure of agricultural enterprises or settlement policies. And according to Roberts (1978:51–53), lying behind the growth of Buenos Aires was the cohesion and strength of Argentina's national elite, formerly based in agrarian enterprise but quickly persuaded of the profitability of industrial enterprise. This dominant class lived in Buenos Aires and held political and economic power over the country throughout the entire period considered here. During the immature urban phase, regional commerce was poorly integrated, rural labor was immobilized, provincial urban functions were minimal. During the mature urban phase, regional commerce improved, as did provincial urban functions, but the interests of the petty bourgeoisie of the provincial towns had nothing in common, in either period, with those of the national bourgeoisie in the primate city.

Argentina's specific historical circumstances, then, produced permanent and infrastructural primacy in the nineteenth century that continued on

---

[45]My interpretation of class relations as well as the forces affecting urbanization in Argentina rests heavily on Roberts (1978) and Balán (1976).

through to the twentieth. This kind of primacy is commonplace in developed (core) countries of the modern world system (e.g., Japan, France), as well as underdeveloped (peripheral) countries (e.g., Argentina, Chile). To associate this kind of primacy with economic dependency, or openness, therefore makes little sense. Argentina's economy has certainly been an open one—as has Japan's, whose urban system seems as permanently and infrastructurally primate (Mera, 1973). Yet the core economies of both Germany and the United States, which are equally open and export-dependent, support classically log-normal urban systems that are *not* primate. Dependence on exports, or openness, therefore, cannot alone cause infrastructural primacy. I suggest, instead, that it is caused by various historical processes that produce a dominant elite who happen to be concentrated in a single city and who from there come to control most economic development.

The usual consequences of primacy, uneven development, and inequitable distribution of income and resources are even greater with infrastructural primacy (as in Argentina) than in the case of population primacy (as in Guatemala). But the inequity of an economy has little to do with its development potential. As both Mera (1973) and Hoch (1976) point out, infrastructural primacy has to become more pronounced than we now find anywhere before one can expect decentralization to come about from the workings of economic (as opposed to political) forces in a capitalist economy. It is foolish, therefore, to rail against the concentration of resources and power (and associated inequity) found in urban systems dominated by primate cities without recognizing that concentration, monopoly, and inequity are inherent in capitalist economies, whether organized into primate or log-normal urban systems. What is spatially apparent in Argentina—the gap between the privileged and underprivileged classes—exists in other forms in other capitalist economies. In this sense, then, the shape of the urban system is an epiphenomenon. It maps rather than causes class position in the system.

In emphasizing that the shape of an urban system is caused by class relations and class struggle in regional and national economies, I hope to have shown the error of reducing social processes to strictly material or economic processes—and urbanization is, after all, a social process. At the same time I would like to emphasize that my analysis does not directly contradict the various economic explanations for urban primacy that have been developed in the literature. Colonialism, export dependency, and agrarian transformation all affect class relations, inasmuch as these economic phenomena have helped mold particular regional and national classes as well as define some of the interests over which they have struggled. But the class relations theory can, in addition, account for those cases where the simple economic theories do not work; where, for example, colonialism or the development of export-oriented enterprises do not create the usual new class or class constellation conducive to the usual urban form. My point here is that a useful social analysis must attend both to the general material forces of history that produce certain generic results and to the historically particular—the unique constellation of events producing, for example, a region that refuses to bend to the dominion of capital. Concentrating on class relations permits one to do both.

8

URBAN PRIMACY AND INCORPORATION INTO THE WORLD-ECONOMY: THE CASE OF AUSTRALIA, 1850–1900

Roger Clark

INTRODUCTION

Planners in more and less developed countries alike have expressed concern about the future of their largest cities and about the impact of this future upon the populations for which they plan. The relative decline of previously preeminent cities like New York has generated one kind of interest; the apparent ascendancy of cities like Mexico City, another. These concerns have sparked a lively debate in the social sciences as well, a debate guided throughout much of its history by the proposition that the internal and external socioeconomic processes of a system are predictably related to the relative size of its largest cities. This essay focuses on two previously distinct lines of argument in this debate and attempts to show, through an account of urbanization within the Australian colonies during the latter half of the nineteenth century, how the two are at once complementary and somewhat misleading.

The lines of argument identify separate sets of variables linked with urban primacy, or the relative size and dominance of the largest city and/or cities in an urban system. The literature on urban primacy, which has been thoroughly reviewed by Walters (Chapter 5, this volume) and Smith (Chapter 6, this volume), is mentioned only briefly here. In particular, I stress that previous work has tended to emphasize either "internal development" or "international relations" in explaining urban primacy. This chapter looks to a case study, finding that these previous approaches are inadequate to an understanding of urban primacy in late nineteenth-century Australia.

Rather, it is necessary to consider the qualitative nature of internal development and how it is conditioned, in turn, by the nature of involvement of a region in the larger world-economy.

URBAN PRIMACY: INTERNAL DEVELOPMENT OR INTERNATIONAL RELATIONS?

For about 20 years after Mark Jefferson introduced the concept of the primate city in 1939, there was a fairly widespread presumption that primacy was somehow connected with low levels of national development. The presumption was ironic, since Jefferson himself believed the presence of a primate city reflected high levels of development,[1] but seemed reasonable in light of George Zipf's somewhat more persuasive suggestion, made 2 years later (1941), that the population of any city in a highly developed society would be an inverse function of its rank within the system.

Subsequent theorists saw that the original propositions of Jefferson and Zipf were inconsistent—that is, that it was impossible that development should lead simultaneously to both a single extraordinarily large city and a conformity with the rank–size rule among all cities. The belief developed that primacy was connected with low levels of development. It appeared, at first glance, that the Third World provided support for the notion that primate cities were *parasitic* in the sense that Bert Hoselitz (1955) used the word. Thus, the UNESCO Report of 1956 argued that primate cities inhibited the development of smaller urban places and drained the rest of the national economy.[2]

Toward the beginning of the 1960s, however, doubt was cast upon the idea that primacy inhibits economic growth. Cross-sectional analyses by Brian Berry (1961) and Surinder Mehta (1964) suggested that no relationship existed between the "type of city-size distribution and . . . relative economic growth" (Berry, 1961:587). The work of Berry and Mehta dealt a serious blow to the notion that primacy and internal socioeconomic development are related in a linear fashion, but the question of whether they were related in some other way remained.

El-Shakhs's argument (1972), discussed at length by Smith (Chapter 6, this volume) was based upon the theoretical work of modernization geog-

---

[1]Jefferson partially explained the absence of a well-defined primate city structure in the Soviet Union during the 1930s, for instance, as the result of low levels of "general education and easy communication" (Jefferson, 1939:232).
[2]UNESCO's sentiment was widely shared. See, for instance, Phillip Hauser (1957); Eric E. Lampard (1955:81–136); Norton S. Ginsberg (1955:455–462); Gist and Halberg (1956:68–71); Clyde Browning (1962); and Wolfgang Stolper (1955).

raphers like John Friedmann, Edward Soja, and Richard Tobin. These authors had posited that normal internal development entails a tension between core and peripheral areas within a regionally or nationally defined social system. During early stages, there is a tendency toward a polarization and an accentuation of differences between *core* regions, the "major centers of innovative change," and *peripheral* regions, or "all other areas within a given spatial system" (Friedmann, 1971:93). Soja and Tobin explained that this occurs, in part, because "crucial decisions are made during the early phases of development which establish a framework of locational advantages that tends to embed itself tenaciously" (Soja and Tobin, 1975:206).[3] Eventually, however, the ever-increasing tensions between core and periphery generate conflict over authority–dependency relations. The theory anticipates an eventual resolution of the conflicts between core and periphery in favor of the periphery, reflecting in part the likelihood that at advanced stages of development there is "sufficient surplus capital and geographically extensive organization structures available for the costly adjustment necessary to break the binds of core domination and move the spatial system towards a stable and integrated equilibrium" (Soja and Tobin, 1975: 208). El-Shakhs's cross-sectional test (75 countries) and longitudinal analysis (the United States and Great Britain) supported the curvilinear model.

I have shown that the positive relationship between primacy and development does not hold for less developed countries when primacy is measured as the ratio of the largest city to a national urban population (Clark, 1979). In fact, in cross-sectional and longitudinal analyses involving more than 100 nations in 1950, 1960, and 1970, I have found no relationship between this kind of primacy and development for less developed countries even while I did find the expected negative relationship for more developed ones. These findings raise the question, Why does the largest city of a developing region not necessarily gain in relation to the rest of its urban system the way El-Shakhs suggests it would? Before looking to the Australian case for an answer to this question, let us briefly consider explanations of primacy that emphasize international relations. (For a more thorough review of this literature, see Smith's discussion in Chapter 6, this volume, of colonialism and export dependency explanations of urban primacy.)

Changes in national city-size patterns have also been linked empirically to interdependencies among national systems. Export-oriented economies (e.g., Browning, 1962; Linsky, 1965; McGreevey, 1971), plantation systems geared toward foreign markets (Stewart, 1960), colonization (Fryer, 1953) and nationalist reactions against colonialism (Ginsberg, 1955, 1961; Linsky, 1965) have all been linked to urban primacy and shown to correlate with it

---

[3]Soja and Tobin's work was unpublished at the time El-Shakhs published his analysis.

in modest cross-sectional analyses. These earlier observations have been encapsulated and placed in an ecological framework by César A. Vapñarsky (1969).[4]

Vapñarsky's work is responsible for three notable advances in the literature on city-size distributions. The first is the application of the ecological concept of closure to the study of primacy. *Closure* refers to the degree to which the system is able to "maintain its ecological stability" independently of other systems (Vapñarsky, 1966:10), and it is conceived in terms of the intensity of interaction with the outside world. Vapñarsky stressed economic interaction, and examined meat and grain exports and manufactured imports in Argentina. The second advance entails the recognition that the size of the largest city and the distribution of all other cities in a system may vary independently.[5] In particular, a relatively heavy reliance on the outside world is likely to be associated with disproportionately large first cities because such cities, among other things, are avenues to this world and, therefore, function as part of some international system of cities. Third is the recognition that "national" systems can be artificial and imposed and that, in particular, subnational regions may, under certain circumstances, be more appropriate units of analysis than national ones.

However, in emphasizing the intensity of interactions rather than the nature of interactions with the outside world, Vapñarsky separates himself from much of the earlier work on Latin American economic development and urbanization that surely constituted a major context for his work. Much of this work proceeded from an institutional framework articulated by Latin American economists (e.g., Prebisch, 1950) and translated into the world-systems/dependency framework of current sociology (e.g., Frank, 1967; Galtung, 1971; Wallerstein, 1979). This perspective describes the economic conditions of many countries, most but not all of which are less developed: a specialized place in the world economic community that accords them peripheral positions with respect to the world-system's core. According to this view, many "internal" processes (such as urbanization) of a region are affected, not by the intensity of interaction with the outside world, but by the qualitative nature of that interaction.[6] The urbanization of developing

---

[4]Vapñarsky does not explicitly acknowledge these earlier studies, but his thesis is clearly consistent with them.

[5]Vapñarsky argues that the "creation of a national industry directed to the domestic market and the expansion of the tertiary sector" and "the development of new cultivated areas and of the railway system" (Vapñarsky, 1969:587–588) helped to enable ever closer fits of the distribution of all cities except the largest to the rank–size rule in Argentina.

[6]See the chapters by Chase-Dunn (12), Walters (5), and Smith (6) in this volume for theoretical treatments of the possible relationship between the world-system and regional primacy.

colonies of Australia during the latter half of the nineteenth century affords some insight into the usefulness of Vapñarsky's modification of this view.

Nineteenth–Century Australia

The prefederation (i.e., pre–twentieth-century) Australian colonies stand out as six relatively independent regions (Figure 8.1) that afford fairly reliable records about urbanization, socioeconomic development, and international relations during early development. One indicator of how independent the individual colonies were was the fact that even adjacent mainland colonies built railways of different gauges, making it difficult, as long as

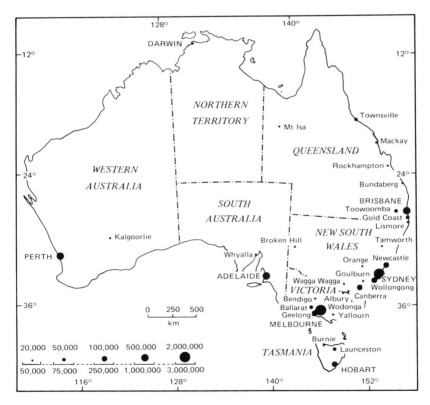

FIGURE 8.1   Australia and its urban centers with populations over 20,000:1971. Source: Neutze (1977). Printed with permission of Allen & Unwin Inc., Boston.

rail was an important means of transport, for urban centers to grow between two capitals and to draw support from more than one colony (see, e.g., Butlin, 1964:84–93). Fitzpatrick also describes the concern of both local and British leaders, as late as the 1890s, with the possibility of Australia's remaining a "juxtaposition of half a dozen similar communities, each with its own tariff and defence arrangements" (Fitzpatrick, 1969:259).

If the colonies were largely independent of one another, is there evidence that they were anything more than politically dependent upon Great Britain and hence appropriate subjects for a study of the effects of "closure"? One important example of the colonies' economic dependence is suggested by Fitzpatrick when he shows that the "wool industry, developed during three-quarters of a century after the 1830s, was, before the end of the nineteenth century, the principal single source of supply of the woollens manufacturers of the world" (Fitzpatrick, 1969:244). By the beginning of the twentieth century, Australia produced more wool than the next two producers (Russia and Argentina) combined and exported the largest part of its production. The wool went mainly to Britain, France, and Germany. The other side of this apparently enviable position was Australia's vulnerability to the steep decline of wool prices on international markets during the 1890s.

There are, of course, reasons for the cautious use of the Australian colonies as typical examples of developing areas, just as there would be in any particular cases. One is the fact of Australia's uniquely inhospitable interior. Another, the fact that most of the population growth during the period came from immigration, rather than natural increase. Such a note of caution has, in fact, been sounded by Arnold Rose (1966). Moreover, the British did choose Australia partly because of its sparse indigenous population and its resulting appropriateness for penal colonies. Finally, partly because all of the colonial capitals were excellent ports and ports-of-call (see Figure 8.1), most of Australia's early European residents spent at least some time in these cities. As a result, population moved outward from the several capitals into developing hinterlands, rather than from hinterland to city, the predominant mode in developing countries—clearly an unusual locational advantage for the capitals. Against such objections, however, stands the point that, even though a dependence upon immigration and an inhospitable interior may have contributed to the disproportionate growth of primate cities, as Rose suggests, the relative growth of such cities between 1851 and 1901 was inconsistent and actually showed occasional reversals.

In fact, although Table 8.1 presents data that support the generalization that the capital cities tended to grow at the expense of their surrounding hinterlands, it also shows that each of the capital cities experienced at least

TABLE 8.1

Capital City Population as a Percentage of Colonial Population, 1851–1901 [a]

City	1851	1861	1871	1881	1891	1901
Melbourne (Victoria)	38	23	26	31	41	40
Sydney (New South Wales)	28	27	27	30	35	37
Adelaide (South Australia)	28	28	27	33	37	39
Brisbane (Queensland)	—[b]	20	13	14	24	24
Perth (Western Australia)	—[b]	33	—[b]	30	32	33
Hobart (Tasmania)	—[b]	28	25	23	22	20

[a] Source: McCarty (1970:23). Adapted with permission of Sydney University Press.

[b] Not available.

one decade of relative decline.[7] Sydney's share of the colonial population of New South Wales did, in fact, grow from 28% in 1851 to 37% in 1901. Of the six capitals, only Hobart and Perth possessed equal or smaller shares of their colonial populations in 1901 than they did in the first year for which data are available, 1861. Nevertheless, in Victoria and New South Wales, the decade between 1851 and 1861 saw Melbourne's share of the population drop from 38 to 23% and Sydney's from 28 to 27%. In South Australia and Queensland, the decline occurred most dramatically between 1861 and 1871.

What caused these unusual declines in the face of overall increases? Was it that the colonies experienced declines in interaction with international markets? Was the subsequent upturn in the capital cities' relative fortunes due to increases in such interaction? Table 8.2 provides a useful starting point for addressing these questions. These data suggest that the capital cities grew rapidly, or at least that most of them grew rapidly most of the time, even though this growth was clearly outstripped by the cities' hinterlands during certain decades. Thus, for instance, Melbourne's population actually grew from 29,000 to 125,000 at a rate of 15.7% a year from 1851 to 1861, demonstrating that Melbourne's relative loss was due only to the rest of Victoria's explosive growth. During that period the population of

[7]Admittedly, the data in Table 8.1 do not provide ideal measures of urban primacy, since they are based on a comparison of the capital cities with the total populations of their colonies and not with the urban population alone. The data are used here because of the difficulty of obtaining comparable data on the urban populations of all the colonies before 1901 and because they broadly conform to more appropriate indicators where these exist. For instance, it is possible to construct indices involving the largest cities and the urban population for New South Wales, Victoria, and Queensland between 1861 and 1901, using data from Butlin (1964) and McCarty (1970), and the trends suggested in Table 8.1 are duplicated by these indices.

TABLE 8.2

Population of the Capital Cities, 1851–1911[a]

Year	Melbourne		Sydney		Adelaide		Brisbane		Perth		Hobart	
	I	II	I	II	I	II	I	II	I	II	I	II
1851	29	—[b]	54	—[b]	18	—[b]	3	—[b]	—[b]	—[b]	—[b]	—[b]
1861	125	15.7	96	5.9	35	6.9	6	7.2	5	—[b]	25	—[b]
1871	191	4.3	138	3.7	51	3.9	15	9.6	—[b]	—[b]	26	0.4
1881	268	3.4	225	5.0	92	6.1	31	7.6	9	2.8	27	0.4
1891	473	5.8	400	5.9	117	2.4	94	11.7	16	5.9	33	2.0
1901	478	0.1	496	2.2	141	1.9	119	2.4	61	14.3	40	1.3

[a] I, population in thousands; II, annual average percentage increase, by decades. Source: McCarty (1970:21). Adapted with permission of Sydney University Press.

[b] Not available.

Victoria grew from approximately 76,000 to approximately 543,000. Clearly both Victoria's and Melbourne's growth were extraordinary during the 1850s; just as clearly both must have depended upon at least one kind of interaction with the outside world—the social, more precisely demographic, interaction of immigration.

Victoria

But why this tremendous influx of people in the 1850s and later? In Victoria, it was the direct result of the discovery of gold in 1851 and the subsequent rushes. Compared to the wool-growing that was the mainstay of other colonies, alluvial gold mining created a large demand for labor at the point of production and favored the growth of country towns near the mining areas. It is estimated, for instance, that within 3 or 4 years of the discovery of gold, about 100,000 miners came to Victoria (Fitzpatrick, 1969:105). Many of the miners came from overseas but large numbers also came from other colonies where gold had not been found, primarily from South Australia and New Zealand.

The rushes had a decentralizing influence not only on the colony as a whole, but on its urban structure as well. Rather than reflecting a smaller than usual reliance upon British markets, this decentralization seems to have been correlated with a considerably greater reliance. In fact, the 7 years after 1851 saw the value of the Australian market as a whole to Great Britain increase by four-and-a-half times (Fitzpatrick, 1969:114). The bulk of this enlarged market was provided by Victoria. Fitzpatrick claims that "the colony's import trade had been less than three-quarters of a million pounds in 1850, and a little more than a million pounds, or £12 a head, in 1851; in 1853 it was nearly £16 million, or £29 a head, and in 1854 nearly £18 million, or £70 a head" (Fitzpatrick, 1969:114). Most of this import trade consisted of consumer goods, traded for the newly mined gold. The efficiency of this trade for extracting gold from the colony is indicated by Table 8.3. Making consumer goods accessible to miners provided the impetus for the growth of nonmetropolitan towns such as Bendigo, Ballarat, Eaglehawk, Stewell, St. Arnaud, Ararat, Clunes, Chiltern, and Buninyong (Butlin, 1964:186)—a growth that generally outstripped Melbourne's between 1851 and 1871.

From 1871 to 1891, the population of Melbourne made substantial absolute gains vis-à-vis the rest of the colony (see Table 8.1). These gains did not result from a substantially greater rate of growth than that experienced by the capital during the 1850s and 1860s, but simply from a relatively greater rate than that experienced by the rest of the colony during the same period. After 1870, most of the goldmining towns suffered losses, as avail-

TABLE 8.3

Gold Exports, Victoria and New South Wales: 1851–1865[a]

Year	Victoria (ounces)	New South Wales (ounces)
1851	145,146	144,120
1852	2,218,782	818,751
1853	2,676,345	548,052
1854	2,150,730	237,910
1855	2,751,535	64,384
1856	2,985,991	42,463
1857	2,762,460	253,564
1858	2,528,478	254,907
1859	2,280,950	435,995
1860	2,156,660	483,012
1861	1,967,420	488,293
1862	1,658,207	699,566
1863	1,626,872	605,722
1864	1,544,694	758,109
1865	1,543,801	682,521
	30,998,071	6,717,369

[a] Source: Fitzpatrick (1969:109). Adapted with permission of Macmillan Company of Australia.

able gold was mined and Victoria's internal economy reverted to its earlier reliance on pastoral and agricultural production, a reliance it shared with the other colonies and that was typically associated with relatively sparse concentrations of pastoralists and farmers. Partly because of this reversion and partly because the economies of New South Wales and Queensland developed more rapidly during this period, Victoria as a whole lost many young males to migration (Butlin, 1964:187). Toward the end of the 1870s and well into the 1880s, a combination of influences led to the relative expansion of Melbourne. Butlin provides a suggestive summary:

> No single explanation lay behind a growth as rapid and complex as Melbourne's and we can suggest only a few of the possible stimuli: the establishment of commercial and financial leadership in Australia, thanks to the influx of British capital through the medium of Melbourne's financial institutions, the growth of the centralised railway fan, by-passing other urban competitors and centralising the transactions of inland Victoria . . . in Melbourne, the enterprise and influx and structural change of population. At the same time, growth on this scale and at this speed produced its own internal dynamics. An increasing metropolitan population demanded enlarged services and public utilities which, in turn stimulated further expansion. (Butlin, 1964:187)

This passage alludes to the contribution made by a different kind of economic growth, based upon the "restoration of Victorian farming" and the growth of ancillary industrial enterprise, upon the relative growth of Melbourne. It also alludes to the contribution that foreign, especially British, capital made to that growth. The amounts of such capital, both public and private, entering the colony during the 1870s and 1880s grew dramatically, as suggested by Table 8.4. This table shows that the public debt of Victoria and New South Wales grew from negligible amounts in 1861 to quite substantial amounts by 1871 and later—growth that was paralleled in Queensland and South Australia between 1871 and 1881. Fitzpatrick suggests that this debt augmentation resulted from influxes of British capital in all cases (Fitzpatrick, 1969:162–163). These influxes were repaid by steady increases in the interest and dividends due from all the colonies until 1891 (see Table 8.5) or until the beginning of the 1890s' depression.

Melbourne's growth during the 1880s was to stall with the economic collapse of the 1890s, which came upon the heels of a worldwide depression. Butlin notes that "whereas 220,000 people were added to the city's population in the eighties, the metropolitan population increased by a mere 310 between 1891 and 1901" (Butlin, 1964:188). During the 1890s considerable overseas capital was withdrawn from Melbourne's banks, while a net emigration of 104,000 took place during the 7 years between 1891 and 1898 (Fitzpatrick, 1969:258). What urban expansion did occur during this period was in the country towns as people moved out of the depressed city in search of rural employment (Butlin, 1964:188). We are thus presented with the picture of a colony whose slumping economy, further weakened by the withdrawal of foreign capital and labor, put an end, temporarily, to the growth of its economic hub, the capital city of Melbourne.

Nonetheless, what we do not see in Victoria between 1851 and 1901 is a direct link between Melbourne's primacy and levels of Victoria's closure.

TABLE 8.4

Public Debt of the Six Australian Colonies: 1861, 1871, 1881, 1891 [a]

Colony	1861	1871	1881	1891
Victoria	6.3	11.99	22.4	43.63
New South Wales	4.0	10.60	16.9	52.95
Queensland	.07	4.00	13.2	29.46
South Australia	.87	2.20	11.2	20.35
Western Australia	.02	—[b]	.5	1.61
Tasmania	—[b]	1.32	2.0	7.11

[a] In millions of pounds. Source: Fitzpatrick (1969:161). Adapted with permission of Macmillan Company of Australia.

[b] Not available.

TABLE 8.5

Interest and Dividends Due Overseas from All Australia Colonies: 1861–1900[a]

Date	Private interest and dividends	Colonial government interest	Total interest and dividends
1861	0.34	0.26	0.60
1866	0.57	0.96	1.53
1871	0.85	1.37	2.22
1876	1.26	2.06	3.32
1881	1.87	2.99	4.86
1886	3.68	4.41	8.09
1891	5.98	5.87	11.85
1896	3.99	6.52	10.51
1900	3.66	6.88	10.54

[a] In millions of pounds. Source: Butlin (1962: 416).

The gold rushes of the 1850s and 1860s substantially opened up the colony to foreign imports, yet decentralization occurred in the urban system. The renewal of farming and sheep-rearing and the growth of ancillary enterprises and of a railway system centered on Melbourne led to a substantially greater reliance upon foreign capital, yet the predominant trend during the period was toward urban centralization. Surely, even the experience of the 1890s, when capital withdrawals and emigration accompanied a slight relative decline in Melbourne's share of the colony's population does not unequivocally support the hypothesis that increases in a region's interactions with the outside world lead to increases in urban primacy, even though the nature of those interactions is clearly very important.

The Other Colonies

The Victorian pattern was repeated in many of the other Australian colonies at one time or another. The mining of alluvial gold provided a substantial decentralizing influence in New South Wales in the late 1850s and the early 1860s, even though gold mining never attained the significance it did in Victoria. Mining of other sorts was one reason why Sydney's relative growth in New South Wales was not as great as Melbourne's in Victoria during the 1870s and 1880s. Copper mining in Cobar and coal mining in Newcastle, for instance, were important during this period. Gold exports were never as great from New South Wales as they were from Victoria (see Table 8.3), but coal production was always greatest in New South Wales, and "whereas in 1850 New South Wales had produced only 190,000 tons . . . in 1881 the colony was able to produce nearly 2 m. tons and export more than half of it" (Fitzpatrick, 1969:180). The 1870s and 1880s also marked the growth of regional market centers to serve the colony's thriving wheat and dairy industries (Butlin, 1964:190).

Once again the expansion of the railroad, depending as it did upon foreign capital (note the rapid growth of New South Wales debt between 1861 and 1871 in Table 8.4), eventually turned the balance in Sydney's favor. Fitzpatrick notes:

> Using the construction measure for New South Wales' economic advance
> . . . we find that when in the 'eighties the colony was borrowing £3m.–£4m. a
> year, it was adding 170 miles of new track each year to its railway system, com-
> pared with 51½ miles annual average in the 'seventies, when the rate of bor-
> rowing was only £600,000 a year. (Fitzpatrick, 1969:62).

The relative decline of both Brisbane and Adelaide during the 1860s in Queensland and South Australia can be similarly related, at least in part, to the comparative success of mining as a sustained industry, as can the continued decline of Hobart in Tasmania throughout the 50-year period and the relative stagnation of Perth during the 1870s. Once again, the railways built in South Australia and Queensland during the 1870s and 1880s depended upon British capital and contributed to Adelaide's and eventually Brisbane's dominance within those colonies.[8]

SUMMARY

The Australian cases offer some telling insights into the urbanization process in developing countries. On the one hand, they suggest a number of reasons why internal development need *not* always be associated with greater urban primacy, as suggested by Salah El-Shakhs. In the Australian colonies, for instance, development took on different forms at different times, as different types of commodity production became prominent. At one time, it involved the mining of natural resources; at another, agriculture, sheep-rearing, and manufacturing. Each of these types of commodity production affected the urban centralization of the colonies. Generally, agriculture, sheep-farming, and manufacturing tended to have a centralizing impact and to result in the disproportionate development of a colony's primate city. Mining seemed to have the opposite effect, causing decentralization within the urban system. Thus, it would seem that early development is often

[8]See, for instance, Max Neutze (1977:14ff.). In Tasmania, the area around Launceston, Hobart's main competitor, benefited from the mineral developments of the 1880s although its hinterland had generally more productive land than Hobart's southern counterpart. In Western Australia, which was by far the most economically and socially backward of the colonies studied here, Perth had a virtually stagnant hinterland until the gold discoveries of the 1890s.

founded upon few enough activities that one or another of these activities may easily become preeminent and, in turn, have a centralizing or decentralizing impact upon the urban system.

On the other hand, the Australian studies suggest a number of reasons for doubting that it is merely the intensity or level of interaction with the outside world that affects urban primacy, as suggested by César Vapñarsky. In each of the colonies, interactions with the outside world tended to increase between 1851 and 1901. From 1851 to 1871, for instance, there was an extraordinary rise in the number of immigrants and the amount of imported goods into Victoria, and from 1871 to 1891, a great rise in the investment of foreign capital in that colony. Yet these different kinds of inputs were associated with different kinds of urbanization. The import of processed goods to the mining sites, for instance, was associated with the rise of towns at those sites. The capital investment of the later period helped to finance sheep-farming and build the railway fans that focused upon the capital cities. All of this suggests that, contrary to Vapñarsky's thesis, the *nature* of Australia's interaction with the outside world was more formative for its urban system than was the *intensity* of those interactions; that, consistent with Walters' analysis (Chapter 5, this volume), Australia's place in the worldwide division of labor was more important than the monetary value of its interaction with the world economy.

It remains unclear whether the centralizing or decentralizing impact of different kinds of internal development dictate or are dictated by different kinds of external interactions. The general effects, however, of both particular kinds of development and external interactions did seem to augment each other in the Australian cases. Thus, when mining predominated inside Victoria, the importation of processed goods to mining sites tended to augment the decentralizing effect of that form of commodity production. When agriculture, sheep-farming, and manufacturing became predominant, the importation of investment capital tended to augment the centralizing impact of these forms.

The general effects of both internal development and international relations upon urban primacy do not seem to be as predictable as either El-Shakhs or Vapñarsky have suggested. The very simplicity of a developing area's economy is likely to make it particularly responsive to both centralizing and decentralizing influences from within and without. Moreover, the centralizing or decentralizing tendencies of these influences appear to be less a function of period of development or intensity of external interactions than of their forms.

9

THE POLITICAL ECONOMY OF CONTRASTING URBAN HIERARCHIES IN SOUTH KOREA AND THE PHILIPPINES*

Roger J. Nemeth and David A. Smith

INTRODUCTION

Comparative-historical research has begun to stress the inadequacies of homogenizing the experiences of urbanization and development in the Third World (Roberts, 1978a:9–13). While studies concerned with primacy have highlighted the "megacephalic growth" associated with this type of urbanization, recently there has been an emphasis on the substantial differences in the patterning and development of urban systems and the distribution of resources within them. Even among Third World nations within the same geographical region, significantly different patterns of urbanization are evident. In this regard, East Asia is an interesting and illuminating example.

In this study we contrast patterns and processes of city growth in two East Asian nations: South Korea and the Philippines. The Philippines offers a classic example of a primate city towering over its urban hierarchy and characterized by sprawling barrios and enormous social inequality. Korea, on the other hand, presents a contrasting configuration. While the capital, Seoul, is a major world city and is dominant functionally and culturally in many ways over other Korean cities, South Korea's overall urban pattern approximates a more even urban hierarchy.

*The authors' names are listed in alphabetical order. We thank Craig Calhoun, Gary Gereffi, Amos Hawley, Gerhard Lenski, Bruce London, Barbara Stenross, and Michael Timberlake for their helpful comments on earlier versions of this essay. Any remaining errors, of course, are the responsibility of the authors.

These divergent patterns of urban development are discussed in detail, alternative theoretical explanations of such variations are analyzed and evaluated, and an attempt is made to explain Korean–Philippine urban differences in terms of these theoretical considerations. The emphasis is on linking changes in Korean and Filipino urban patterns with the historical contexts in which the two nations experienced incorporation into the expanding world political and economic sytem. An effort is made to indicate the manner in which both external forces and indigenous elements affected the political and economic activity that shaped the configuration of urban development at these points and served to maintain these patterns through subsequent periods.

DIVERGENT URBAN HIERARCHIES

When compared with other major regions of the world, Southeast Asia's urban population is quite small (United Nations, 1980:Annex Tables 48, 50). This region, however, is characterized by the concentration of its urban population in a few very large cities and by an absence of a system of secondary urban centers (McGee, 1969). Thus, extremely high primacy ratios are distinguishing features of countries in this region. Over the past two decades, the degree of primacy (measured in this study by using the Standard Primacy Index; see Walters, Chapter 4, this volume) has generally increased in countries of this region. These characteristics, coupled with the observation that these countries share the distinction of having relatively low per capita incomes and economies dominated by large agricultural sectors, have prompted some researchers to describe Southeast Asian urban patterns as "lagging" in comparison with other regions (Hackenberg, 1980).

The population of the Philippines has grown an average of about 3% per year since 1960 (see United Nations, 1980:Annex Tables 48, 50). Furthermore, the majority of this increase has occurred in rural areas. Of the growth in urban populations, most has been concentrated in the national capital, Manila. While Manila has historically occupied a dominant position vis-à-vis other Filipino cities (as is documented below), this dominance has increased in recent years. Although, as of 1980, no other city had a population over 1 million,[1] the population of metropolitan Manila was ap-

---

[1]As of 1980 Manila's population was 5,664,000. When compared to the populations of the next three largest cities—Davao City (703,000), Cebu City (507,000), Zamboango City (318,000)—its primacy in demographic terms is evident (see United Nations, 1980). The increase in this primacy pattern is indicated by the changing SPI1 ratio: 1960, 26.24; 1970, 28.61.

proaching 6 million. Pernia (1976:28) has succintly summarized the Filipino urbanization pattern in the following passage:

> Thus, apart from the impact of large absolute increments to urban population overall, the phenomenal growth of metropolitan Manila has apparently created the illusion of rapid urbanization . . . it is clear that the problem to be coped with now in the Philippines (and most likely in other developing Asian countries as well) is not rapid urbanization but unbalanced urbanization.

Manila dominates the nation functionally as well as demographically (Wernstedt and Spencer, 1967:168–170). It is not only the national capital but is also the center of the nation's cultural, educational, and commercial activities. For instance, as of 1960 40% of all manufacturing establishments were located in metropolitan Manila (McGee, 1969:87). The degree of functional primacy is reflected in a study by the United Nations' Task Force on Human Settlements. In a ranking of provinces on four indicators of development (road kilometers, electrical consumption, number of establishments, and population density), Manila and Rijal Province (which covers a large part of the metropolitan area) consistently ranked highest on each item (Hollnsteiner and Lopez, 1976:71). Other studies of Manila have stressed the paramount political and administrative role Manila has played in national development (Laquian, 1966; McGee, 1969).

While Manila has undoubtedly shared disproportionately in the development of the Philippines, it is also abundantly clear that not all Manileños have benefited equally. One indicator of material inequality in the city is the distribution of housing. Nearly every study of the social and economic conditions in Manila comments on the size, density, and squalor of the squatter settlements. Estimates of the number of people living in these areas range from one-fourth to nearly one-half of the city's population (Hollnsteiner and Lopez, 1976; McGee, 1969).

It is clear that urbanization in the Philippines has been slow and uneven, with Manila the principal recipient of both migrants and economic development. It is also clear that within Manila there as been an uneven distribution of resources between a city elite and a massive underclass. Data for 1960 indicate that within the metropolitan area 37.5% of the total family income was shared by only 8.7% of the households (McGee, 1969:95).

The urbanization of South Korea, despite sharing some of the characteristics found in the Philippines, differs from the latter pattern in a number of important dimensions. For example, the South Korean population has grown at a relatively modest average of "only" 2.1% per year since 1970, and, in contrast to the Philippines, this growth has occurred predominantly in urban areas. Although much of this increase in urban population was centered in Seoul during the 1960s, a system of cities has developed in South Korea that is very different from that of the Philippines. This is reflected in both the relatively low Korean primacy ratio (5.29 in 1970) and in the fact that by 1980 seven cities had populations of over one-half million (United Nations, 1980:Annex Tables 48, 50). Mills and Song (1979:52) have commented on this even city growth that "shows no tendency to become still more primate. The size distribution of cities has shown remarkable stability during the last quarter of a century. Almost all Korean cities have grown rapidly, but there is no tendency for Seoul, or any other city, to become increasingly dominant."

This even hierarchy of cities is not a recent phenomenon; its origins are found deep in the nation's history, long before Korea had any contact with the West. Furthermore, this city-size distribution is associated with a system of functional interdependencies. There is no question that Seoul has long been and continues to be at the head of this urban hierarchy. Seoul, like Manila, is not only the national capital but is also the location of the Korean headquarters of most national and international corporations, the site of the national university, national museums, and other cultural centers, and the point of greatest travel contact with foreign countries (Meier, 1980: Chapter 2). The Korean urban hierarchy, however, differs from that found in the Philippines because other major urban centers, such as Pusan, Taegu, and Kwangchu, have become integrated into a system of specialized interdependencies. While Pusan, for example, has historically been Korea's most active port, it has also become the major national center for heavy industry and manufacturing (Mills and Song, 1979:53–54).

Beginning in the early 1960s and continuing up to today, South Korea has experienced tremendous economic growth (cf. World Bank, 1980). In contrast to other developing nations, however, South Korea has been able to maintain a relatively equal distribution of income during this period of rapidly rising production (for data on indices of inequality see Jain, 1975). This rapid and relatively equitable economic growth, which has been largely the result of labor intensive industrialization, served to (1) attract job-seeking migrants to the large industrial centers and (2) reduce the time needed to assimilate new migrants into the urban labor force. In this vein, Mills and Song (1979:26) argue that "In many developing countries, rapid urbanization has been accompanied by high unemployment rates among migrants and by long periods of transition into organized employment sectors in cities. Korea's rapid economic growth has enabled cities to absorb migrants into the urban labor force rapidly."

Estimates from the early 1970s indicate that illegal housing is on the decline in South Korea; about 8% of urban population nationwide, and perhaps up to 16% of Seoul's residents lived in illegal settlements in 1973 (Mills and Song, 1979:37).

In summary, South Korea has experienced much more rapid and balanced urbanization than the Philippines. While Seoul has been and continues to be at the top of its national urban hierarchy, it is clear that a relatively evenly distributed system of interdependent cities has developed in Korea, with some of the most rapid areas of growth occurring in regions far from Seoul (especially in the Southeast) (Mills and Song, 1979:53–54). Furthermore, urban growth in Korea has not been accompanied by the severe degree of inequality associated with Filipino urbanization.

DEPENDENT URBANIZATION: DEVELOPING A THEORETICAL PERSPECTIVE

Like other contributors to this volume, our research effort is grounded on the basic assumptions of the dependency–world-system perspective. Briefly put, we argue that the patterns and processes of urbanization are best understood as part of the expansion of the capitalist world-economy. Urban growth is shaped by the historical context of a region's initial incorporation into, and changing role within, this international system (Castells, 1977:44; Walton, 1977:12–13; Slater, 1978:27). Rather than rehashing the origins and major concepts of this world-system perspective on urbanization (see Timberlake, Chapter 1, this volume), we instead highlight the particular emphasis this research takes while working from that generic theoretical stance.

One concept that seems to be particularly useful is the notion of differential structural positions in the world-system (for a fuller discussion see Kentor, Chapter 2, this volume). While the general condition of dependency may have some very broad effect on urban patterns, it seems far more reasonable to expect somewhat different urban dynamics to be operating in the periphery and semiperiphery. We argue that our research provides further evidence of the value of distinguishing between these categories.

Another dimension that is very important is the articulation between the world-economy and international politics. It is hardly necessary to repeat the by-now-familiar critique directed against Wallerstein, Frank, and other world-system analysts. It is claimed that by focusing on the world market to explain other social structures, world-system explanations have framed economically reductionist arguments (Skocpol, 1977; Brenner, 1977). Cognizant of this critique, and aware of attempts by major world-system theorists to incorporate geopolitics into their analyses (Chase-Dunn, 1981), in this study attention is directed at geopolitical pressures and constraints that may not be direct derivations of world market positions. Particularly important, especially in an area like East Asia, are the effects of the strategems of the competing superpowers and their ramifications for spatial policies.

Another common criticism of the dependency–world-system perspective involves the overemphasis on external relations and inadequate attention to the internal dynamics of the areas labeled dependent (see Frank, 1978: Chapter 1; Portes, 1979:5–6). To remedy this problem we take cues from two theoretical traditions that, though appearing very different, share long-standing traditions as materialistic approaches to macrostructural change: human ecology and Marxist class analysis.

One of human ecology's major concerns has been the emergence of cities and urban systems, and a concern with urban dominance and primacy (see Timberlake, Chapter 1, this volume). A potentially useful emphasis in the human ecological approach is the critical effect that technology—and particular transportation and communication infrastructures—has in understanding spatial patterns of population distributions (Hawley, 1950, 1981). Unfortunately, despite its stress on dominance and hierarchical control, most human ecological analyses of concrete processes or urban growth show little appreciation for the manner in which the powerful in society shape processes such as infrastructural development. The tendency instead is to view urbanization as an aggregate adaptation to a material and social environment under a given level of technology. The political power of interest groups, elites, and various classes and class fractions has not been stressed. In an important recent article, Hawley (1984) argues that human ecological theory—with its stress on hierarchial control and dominance based on control of economic production—shares many of the concerns of Marxian theory. He acknowledges that many human ecological analyses have downplayed the power dimension and insists that there is a need for "a further development of the political economic implications" of this perspective (1984:16).

Mindful of the emphasis of human ecology on transportation and communications, we have tried to analyze the process of urbanization from such a political economy perspective (Walton, 1979b). Our strategy in this research has been to attempt to transcend the "external" versus "internal" causation problem by linking world exchanges to local modes of production and class structures (Cardoso and Faletto, 1979:xvi; Evans, 1979a:19). It is these explicitly political variables, closely linked to international class alignments and changes in the world-economy, that affect infrastructural change. Networks of transportation and communication are critical proximate causes shaping an urban system's growth. But roads, railroads, port facilities, and telegraph and telephone lines are constructed to facilitate the interest and needs of the powerful in various societies. Therefore, elite power and interests and class structures are critical determinants of urban structures.

In turn, we must stress that looking at internal politicoeconomic factors

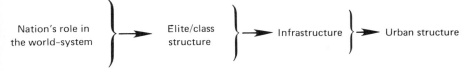

FIGURE 9.1   Urbanization in the world-system: model of how macrostructures set the parameters for urban development.

in isolation misses the crucial insight of the dependency–world-system approach. Class alignments and elite structure in dependent countries can only be understood as part of the expansion of the capitalist world-economy. Tracing the linkages backwards, our argument contends that urban configurations arise in response to infrastructural changes that are implemented to fulfill the needs of elite groups whose formation and interests are fully explicable only by understanding the historic relationship of a society to expanding capitalism (Figure 9.1). Therefore, a political economy approach to urbanization in Third World countries must adopt a "historical-structural" approach (see Cardoso and Faletto, 1979) sensitive to the changing dynamics of this process in the various phases of capitalist development. The following discussion focuses on the system of forces and relationships of the world-system that reinforce or retard certain patterns of urbanization. The analysis begins by centering on a crucial period in the histories of each nation—the era of their initial incorporation into the modern world-economy. This is followed by a brief discussion of the processes and events that worked to maintain or alter early urban patterns. To carry out a historical-structural analysis of urbanization, it is necessary to focus on the national political arenas of the two nations. Therefore, particular attention centers on the policy decisions of elite groups and their ramifications for the development of the Filipino and Korean urban systems. This approach is consistent with a trend toward "a more 'political' comparative urban sociology" in recent years (London, 1979:485). Throughout, the emphasis is on linking the external forces exerted by the world-economy and polity with the internal ramifications of city growth in the two East Asian countries.

ORIGINS AND HISTORICAL DEVELOPMENT

The Philippines

> The phenomenon of primacy . . . must be understood as the consequences of historical, demographic, and economic trends, engendered by the long tradition of interest in the metropolis and neglect elsewhere. (Pernia, 1976:29)

Prior to Spanish colonization there was no indigenous urban tradition anywhere in the Philippine Archipelago. In this regard, the Philippines differed from other Southeast Asian populations, where relatively large "sacred" and coastal city-states had long histories (McGee, 1969; Reed, 1972). When Magellan first landed in what is now the Philippines, he encountered an agrarian society that (1) lacked any large urban settlements or the division of labor needed to support them; (2) possessed a primitive mode of production, with only vaguely defined class boundaries; (3) had developed no unifing political or military force; and (4) possessed only relatively primitive transportation–communication technologies. This situation was to change very rapidly (at least in some areas). An analysis of the timing and manner of the Philippine's initial contact with and incorporation into the capitalist world-economy is critical to any understanding of the uneven pattern of urban development that evolved.

The fifteenth and sixteenth centuries witnessed the rise of mercantilism in Europe, with Spain at the early forefront. In a discussion of the Pacific galleon trade of this period, Wallerstein (1974) distinguishes between the types of colonization that Spain carried out in Latin America and in the Philippines. In America, Spain carried out a full-scale colonization effort involving the transformation of the entire economy and the deep penetration of capitalism into the countryside (Wallerstein, 1974:335). In the Philippines, Spanish contact took on more of the enclave form of imperialism, with the major mercantile efforts devoted to the establishment and maintenance of a Hispanic "trading post" in the archipelago (Wallerstein, 1974:335–336). Despite the initial implementation of an *economienda* system[2] and the continuing efforts of the Catholic church to convert the native population to Christianity (Constantino, 1975:Part I), the type and degree of the Hispanic penetration of the outlying areas was much less dramatic in the Philippines than the transformation of the Latin American hinterlands. Wallerstein (1974:336) explains this in terms of the greater rewards of colonizing America and the greater difficulties of colonizing Asia. Especially important was the tremendous distance between Spain and areas like the Philippines, especially given the primitive level of shipping technology (Wallerstein, 1974:338). No doubt the Spaniards' failure to discover a wealth of natural resources (see below) may also have lowered the rewards for such intensive internal colonization. Economically, the Spaniards showed little interest in areas far beyond the capital city for the first 200 years of their rule over the Philippines (Reed, 1967:174; Wernstedt and Spencer, 1967:181).

Manila became the capital city and permanent base for further Spanish

---

[2]Involving rights granted to Spanish soldiers and settlers to collect annual tribute from the native inhabitants of an area (see Constantino, 1975:43).

military conquests several years after the first Iberians arrived in the Philippines. In 1570 the Spaniards discovered a fairly large native village at the future site of the city. The area already had a reputation as a trade center and was surrounded by an area that appeared to be fertile and abundantly supplied with food (Wernstedt and Spencer, 1967:384). Coupled with a "sure harbor and port" (Reed, 1977:21), which provided for a measure of military security, the material wealth of the area made it an ideal site for the Hispanic capital. In 1571 Manila was formally declared a city and established as the base of Spanish operations in the archipelago (Reed, 1977:22; Wernstedt and Spender, 1967:384).

The Manila galleon trade was the vehicle of Spanish mercantile policy and was critical in shaping the uneven pattern of urbanization in the Philippines. From the founding of the city until 1815, Spanish ships plied the lonely, arduous, and dangerous Pacific route from Acapulco to Manila and back, each year one vessel traveling in each direction. To Spain, this commerce represented its mercantile ascendency over the Pacific (Reed, 1967: 101). To the colonists in the Philippines, the galleons constituted an essential but tenuous lifeline between the archipelago and its incredibly distant mother country (Reed, 1967:104).

Since the earliest voyages of discovery the Spaniards had coveted easy access to the spices of the East Indies and the fine silk of China. The Philippines and the port of Manila, through the galleon trade, came to represent the gateway to the Orient for Spain. Since early Spanish explorations of the islands turned up little in the way of either gold or spices (Schurz, 1939:44–45), the chief raison d'être for the Spanish settlement of the Philippines soon centered on the facilitation of the East–West trade of the Pacific galleons. Manila served as a major base and entrepôt from which the Spanish could (1) harbor and refurbish its galleons, (2) direct its Southeast Asian trade, and (3) administer, govern, and defend its territorial prerogatives.

After its initial selection as the capital and port of the colony, Manila grew rapidly. The city's key function was clearly the commercial role ordained by Spanish mercantile policy. The very life of the city and its people depended on the yearly voyages of the galleons (Schurz, 1939:38). Although it often proved to be a risky venture (Reed, 1967:107), the galleon trade paid off handsomely to the Manileños who acted as middlemen. Manila at the turn of the seventeenth century is described as a place of opulence and lavish consumption (Reed, 1967:39). Furthermore, wealthy traders, living a life of luxury in Manila, had scant incentive to invest in other productive enterprises. This lucrative trade had the additional effect of swelling Manila's population as settlers flooded in from Spain and the trade areas of Southeast Asia (Reed, 1967:110–112).

From a moderate-size village of 2000 persons in 1570, Manila grew to nearly 34,000 by 1591 (Reed, 1967:111), and topped 41,000 by 1620 (Reed, 1977:33). By the latter date it had established itself as a great world port.

Manila's dominance was reinforced in several ways. First, Manila was the administrative center and seat of the royal governor from its inception as a Spanish settlement (Reed, 1977:22). A second major administrative function, established soon after founding of the city, was that of the head-quarters of the Catholic prelate, the Archbishop of Manila (Reed, 1977:25). In 1583 an additional important role was bestowed upon the Philippine capital when the King of Spain established an *audiencia*[3] at the city (Reed, 1977).

Not only was Manila the obvious political, economic, and ecclesiastic center of the colony, but

> it is clear that Manila in 1622 was many times as populous, prosperous, and socially complex as the second and third ranked centers combined. Where Cavite had one hospital, Manila had four; where Cebu lacked risk capital to build a galleon, Manila had a relative abundance. While provincial settlements lacked trade or productive activity, Manilenos conspired to keep the China–Mexico exchange limited to the capital. Clearly the establishment of Manila's overwhelming functional and cultural predominance had a detrimental effect on the nascent provincial urban system. (Doeppers, 1972:778)

The above quotation clearly points to the obverse side of Manila's rapid growth and rise to urban dominance. The overwhelming importance of the Philippines' mercantile ties also had ramifications for the growth of other settlements: "Predictably the Manila galleon trade operated with the reverse effect upon smaller cities in the archipelago. Prevented from participation in international exchange, the provincial settlements stagnated commercially" (Reed, 1967:133). By the early years of the seventeenth century the shape of the urban structure in the Philippines had already solidified with Manila firmly entrenched as the dominant and primate city.

Throughout the 1600s and early 1700s the galleon trade remained the almost exclusive source of livelihood for the Spanish colony and Manila continued to maintain, and even strengthen, its position as the functionally dominant primate city (Reed, 1977:67).

As the years passed, however, Spain's hegemonic role in the world-economy began to change. Other European powers were on the ascent, particularly the Dutch and the British (Wallerstein, 1980). The rise of English naval power was evidenced in the Pacific by an increasing incidence of capture and harassment of the Manila galleons (see Schurz, 1939:15), and by the temporary capture of the Filipino capital itself in 1762 (Reed, 1967:176).

---

[3]The *audiencia* was the highest court of justice in the Hispanic Philippines and also served as a royal advisory board to the governor (Reed, 1967:208).

In addition to external threats, changes were also occurring within both Spain and her Pacific colony that would work against the continuity of a Filipino economy based on the galleon. In Spain there were growing doubts about the profitability of the trans-Pacific trade. Some ardent supporters of Spanish mercantilism saw the trade as dangerously depleting Spain's reserves of precious metals, which were being sent from Mexico to Manila and on to the Orient to pay for the spices and silk (Reed, 1967:122). More specific and concerted opposition to the galleon trade came from commercial and textile groups in Andulasion cities in Spain, whose economic well-being was being threatened by the flood of cheap but high-quality Chinese silks into the American markets they had previously controlled (Schurz, 1939:44). Even within the Philippines some advocates of the development of an indigenous expert economy were beginning to be heard by the end of the seventeenth century (Reed, 1967:175). All these pressures prompted the imposition of restrictions on the galleon trade, and led eventually to its demise in 1815 and to the beginnings of a reorientation of the Philippine economy toward export agriculture (Reed, 1967:118–123).

With the termination of the galleon trade the initial cause of Manila's primacy was removed. Why did the city remain overwhelmingly dominant in the Filipino urban hierarchy? An argument that attributes continued primacy to social inertia or initial advantage alone is unsatisfactory. Instead, we must look at the specific ways in which the elites, with their power concentrated in Manila, implemented policies (whether consciously or unconsciously) that furthered their own interests and affected spatial patterns.[4]

Two of the earliest developmental programs aimed at stimulating the export sector were the formation of the government tobacco monopoly and the Royal Company of the Philippines (Reed, 1967:177–179). However, both of these enterprises were under the direct control of Manila administrators and merchants. The profits flowed back to officials in the capital—many of whom received undue personal benefit through fraud and corruption (Reed, 1967; Constantino, 1975:130–131). Manila's rise as the undisputed center of Filipino manufacturing was given its original impetus when the tobacco monopoly established factories in Manila in the late eighteenth century and the production of cigars elsewhere was legally forbidden (Reed, 1967:195).

---

[4]Note an important difference between the Philippine situation in the nineteenth century and Smith's analysis (Chapter 7, this volume) of elite conflicts and urban primacy in Guatemala. Because of the overriding importance of the galleon trade and the Spaniards' economic neglect of the rest of the archipelago, Manila's elites enjoyed a tremendous degree of geographic hegemony. No power groups in the hinterland had developed that could successfully mount any serious challenges to the capital's elites.

Other trade and transportation policies in the late Spanish era also reflected the interests of the Manila elites and reinforced the capital's functional and demographic dominance. For example, despite the end of the galleon trade and the rise of commercial agriculture, Manila remained the only international port in the archipelago until 1855 (Reed, 1967:181). Prior to this date all exports from other islands had to be shipped first to Manila, incurring the trouble and expense fees for cabotage, unloading and reloading, and brokerage and wharfage (Reed, 1967:181). The Manila origin of all Philippine exports was undoubtedly due in part to the city's vastly better port facilities. The major reason that secondary ports did not develop international connections early on, however, was a matter of conscious policy designed by the Spanish authorities in Manila to restrict such trade (Reed, 1967:133). These regulations, while clearly not in the best interests of the entire colony's economic development, were kept in place largely due to the machinations of Manila elites (Doeppers, 1972:778).

The mid–eighteenth century also saw the penetration of non-Spanish financial and commercial interests into the Philippines. Foreign firms were located in the capital city in part to be close to the center of economic activity and to enjoy the urban amenities (Laquian, 1966:29). Their locations also were constrained by a variety of laws and executive edicts that prevented European trade in the provinces (Reed, 1967:180–181).

The end of the Spanish era also witnessed early efforts to bring modern transportation to the archipelago. Once again, these efforts, instead of leading to more balanced growth in the national urban system, served to exacerbate Manila's primacy. In 1830 Governor General Pascual Enrile launched a road-building program to smooth the economic transition the country was undergoing (Reed, 1967:188). Despite the relative primitiveness of these early roads, and the paucity of any thoroughfares elsewhere, they were "moderately functional" in intergrating Luzon Province with its immediate hinterlands (Reed, 1967:188). In 1875 the Philippines home government initiated a study aimed at developing railroads in Manila's hinterlands. In 1891 a rail line had been completed connecting Manila to its "rice basket," the fertile Central Plain of Luzon (Reed, 1967:188). By this time a fairly extensive set of tracks for a city street railway had already been laid inside Manila itself (Reed, 1967:190). Beyond central Luzon, though, the transportation sytem before the revolution remained extremely crude.

This developing transportation system, despite shortcomings, linked the city to its hinterland and served to extend Manila's political and military control while simultaneously opening up new areas for agricultural export production. These transportation policies seemed to reflect an underlying center-oriented strategy designed to enhance and consolidate the city's central political and economic dominance. Other authors note analogous phases of transportation system development in other underdeveloped countries (London, 1980:87–88; Taaffe, Morrill, and Gould, 1963:506).

Although the nineteenth century was a time of rapid economic change and rural transformation in the Philippines, Manila's position as the primate city was never challenged:

> All of the qualitative and quantitative agricultural alterations were merely physical expressions of political-economic policies which evolved in the Philippine cities. During the period of change Manila remained the primary innovational center from which emanated administrative decisions that determined the course of development. (Reed, 1967:190)

By the final years of the nineteenth century, Spain's already tenuous grasp on the Philippines was rapidly weakening as Spanish world power continued to wane. Meanwhile, the United States was rapidly becoming a major core power in the world-economy (Chirot, 1977:23) and was attempting to expand its influence in the Pacific. Concurrently, within the Philippines the transition to an export agriculture was breeding widespread discontent (Constantino, 1975:144–145; Agoncillo and Guerrero, 1973:123–124). The concatenation of these trends brought an end to Spanish rule in the Philippines and the beginning of the American era (Constantino, 1975:Chapters 10–13; Agoncillo and Guerrero, 1973:Part III).

The United States took control of the Philippines as a result of the treaty that ended the Spanish–American War in 1890 (Agoncillo and Guerrero, 1973:240–241). Although the Filipino people had been collaborating with the Americans fighting against Spain, it soon became clear that the United States intended to extend foreign domination and deny Filipino independence (Agoncillo and Guerrero, 1973:245–264). As a result, the target of the Philippine revolution switched from Spain to the United States (Laquain, 1969:31).

Because of the belligerency, the Americans established a highly centralized government apparatus and followed a policy of reconcentration around metropolitan Manila. The centralized nature of the early American occupation government was perpetuated under United States rule and continued during the Commonwealth period (1934–1946) and after formal independence (1946) (Laquain, 1969:23–43). The high degree of political centralism has meant that most of the crucial policy decisions at the national as well as the regional and local levels have been, and continue to be, made by national politicians in, and often from, Manila.

Other major sources of policy continuity during the initial years of the American period involve the directions that economic and infrastructural development took. For example, the United States administration put considerable effort and expense into transportation and communication improvement in the Philippines (Agoncillo and Guerrero, 1973:428). Railroad construction was continued and the existing road system was extended and improved. As under Spanish rule, however, transportation development was very uneven and focused primarily in the central Luzon area—an area of heavy population concentration and strong politicoeconomic demand (Wernstedt and Spencer, 1967:131). As a result of a transportation system that was growing more concentrated on the capital city, population movements to Manila accelerated during this period (Burley, 1973:244).

Export agriculture continued to be the primary focus of the Philippine economy for the first two decades of American control (Power and Sicat, 1971:13–16). Under a policy of free trade with the United States, Filipino exports rose to unprecedented levels (Agoncillo and Guerrero, 1973:427). Much of this increased flow of goods passed through Manila, where the enlargement and renovation of port facilities by the new American administration further stimulated the growth of commercial institutions (Wernstedt and Spencer, 1967:385).

In the late American period the orientation of the economy began to shift (Power and Sicat, 1971:16–19). Although primary-product exports remained important, a trend toward manufacturing, which has continued to the present, became evident. A fairly diversified group of industries developed in the period between the two world wars (Power and Sicat, 1971:Table 1.2:17). These products were produced for sale on the national market and exemplified an import substitution industrialization strategy that many less developed countries have attempted in the twentieth century (Cardoso and Faletto, 1977: Intruduction, 1–7). The expectation behind such a policy is that indigenous manufacturing of consumer goods would decrease dependency on foreign imports and help meet foreign-exchange and trade-deficit problems (Cardoso and Faletto, 1977:129).

This new economic direction for the nation required both the availability of a relatively highly trained and disciplined labor force and the existence of a sufficiently large consumer market. Roberts (1978a) claims that there has been a general drift in the Third World in recent years toward capital-intensive import substitution. This has ramifications for urbanization in these underdeveloped countries:

> The concentration of middle- and high-income populations in a few urban centers makes investments in capital-intensive consumer goods industries attractive. These industries are located in, or close to, the centers of population and contribute to the attraction of the large cities for rural migrants. Improvements in urban infrastructure such as roads, lighting, sanitation and housing are part of the dynamic of this industrialization. (Roberts, 1978a:81)

In fact the growth of import substitution industries and the infrastructure that accompanies this growth has been concentrated around metropolitan Manila. Consumer goods development as a national goal has resulted in the rapid growth of manufacturing establishments in and near the capital (Wernstedt and Spencer, 1967:279). The capital city and its outlying areas contained about two-thirds of all manufacturing in the country by 1960 (Burley, 1973:261).

Transportation infrastructure has developed in Manila's immediate hinterland to keep pace with its industrial development. In recent years Manila has continued to function as the major port of the nation. It receives and consumes, or transships, 85% of all Philippine imports (Wernstedt and Spencer, 1967:263) and possesses the latest technological innovations (Wernstedt and Spencer, 1967:261). In the 1960s, both road transportation and rail connections continued to be centered on central Luzon and Manila and were generally inadequate elsewhere (Wernstedt and Spencer, 1967:263–266; Burley, 1973:272).

In the most recent period of Filipino history, urban concentration in Manila and the growth of import substitution industrialization have been mutually reinforcing processes. The rise of capital-intensive consumer-oriented industry was aided by the historical processes that created the high degree of urban primacy that already existed in the early twentieth century. Conversely, this type of industrialization has reinforced the demographic, political, and economic dominance of the capital city.

In summary, prior to contact with the capitalist world-system the Philippines was essentially a hunting and gathering society with no urban tradition. Spanish interest in establishing a mercantile base for trade with the Orient, and their lack of interest in the rest of the archipelago, established Manila as the demographic and functional center of the colony. The capital's overwhelming urban primacy has been maintained over the years based on (1) Manila's continuing importance as a major port and (2) the implementation of policies affecting the spatial distribution of infrastructure and production facilities congruent with the needs and interests of an entrenched Manila elite.

South Korea

While Spain and the other European imperialist powers were consolidating their colonial dominion over Southeast Asia, Korea remained relatively remote and isolated. Perhaps Korea's location far north of the Eastern trade lines accounted for some disinterest on the part of Europeans, but geography alone does not adequately explain how Korea remained free of outside domination up to the twentieth century. Korea, unlike the Philippines, had developed an advanced agrarian society by the time of its incorporation into the world economy.[5] The country was ruled by a series of kingdoms, the first of which governed a unified peninsula in the early eighth century (Hatada, 1969:26–30; Henthorn, 1971:59). The development of a relatively strong central state capable of mobilizing and maintaining a large army is evidenced by Korea's ability, on several occasions, to repulse attacks from hostile neighbors (Hatada, 1969; Henthorn, 1971). The precolonial period in Korea also saw the emergence of a system of relatively large urban centers based on an incipient geographical division of labor and linked together by established regional trade routes (Henthorn, 1971:204–206). Although reliable estimates of precolonial city sizes are difficult to obtain, what data are available indicate that Korean cities contained populations close to those of the largest preindustrial cities in other societies (Henthorn, 1971).

The earliest reliable figures on urban populations are the Japanese counts taken soon after annexation. In 1920 only 3.2% of the nation's people lived in urban areas with populations over 20,000 (Renaud, 1974:26). There were eight cities of this size; Seoul was the largest with a population of about 250,000. Seoul was followed in size by Pusan (74,000), Pyeonayang (72,000), Taegu (45,000), Gaeseong (37,000), Incheon (36,000), Wonsan (28,000), and Jinnampo (21,000). These cities were either ports or colonial administrative centers and had served similar functions in the precolonial period (Renaud, 1974).

Thus, it is reasonably clear that when Korea was finally incorporated into the international economic system, its urban system already had a long history. After Japanese colonization, Korean cities experienced accelerated growth, but the cities all grew at rates commensurate with their earlier positions in the urban hierarchy (see Kwon *et al.,* 1975; Appendix, Table 1). Seoul did not become increasingly primate, and, in fact, the ratio actually declined slightly. What is perhaps even more remarkable is that after World War II, the liberation from Japan, the division of the country, the Korean War, and the industrial transformation, the major cities of South Korea continued to retain their 1920 rank order without a single alteration (Mills and Song, 1979:48).

As in the previous discussion of the Philippines, the persistence of this urban pattern may, to a degree, be a testimony to the momentum of institutionalized patterns of social organization. Elite groups acting in their own interest often find it advantageous to preserve the status quo. In this regard, the manner in which the urban structure was compatible with the changing needs of both the political and economic systems of the nation and its ruling elites are explored here. More specifically, the manner in which internal

---

[5]In this historical section, *Korea* refers to what is now North and South Korea.

policies have affected urban growth is examined in light of the changing role Korea has come to play in the world economic and political system.

Internationally, the period following 1870 was a period of renewed imperialism for most core and some semiperipheral nations. Stimulated by the belief that continual expansion and permanant security of raw material sources and markets were necessary for economic survival, these countries began to prepare for what they perceived to be the inevitable conflict over declining unclaimed peripheral areas (Chirot, 1977:48–54). As the core countries enlarged their militaries, the weaker semiperipheral nations (most notably Russia and Japan) struggled to keep pace in order to avoid being reduced to peripheral status (Chirot, 1977:50). It is in this international setting that Japan began its imperialistic expansion for raw materials and new markets. During this period, Taiwan, parts of China, and Korea became Japanese colonies.

Trade between Korea and Japan officially began in 1876 with the signing of the Kangwha Treaty. Pusan, in essence, became an open port, although after 1894 Japan was the only country involved in trade with Korea. In 1905 (following Japan's victory in the Russo–Japanese War) the Protectorate Treaty was signed between Korea and Japan, and in 1906 the Japanese inspector general was established to oversee all domestic administration and diplomatic activities. From 1910 to the end of World War II, the Korean political and economic systems were completely controlled by the Japanese colonial government. Not surprisingly, Japanese policies in Korea reflected almost entirely the needs of powerful groups in Japan. Therefore, any analysis of policies during this period "must be carried out with reference to the changing conditions of the Japanese economy during the period under review. Only in this way will the major factors that shaped the pattern of the Korean economy be made clear" (Suh, 1978:6).

During the initial period of colonization (1910–1930), Japan's major policy objectives were directed at developing Korea into a classic colony, with special emphasis placed on the export of agricultural produce. The Decree on Business Entities, which required the licensing of all business firms in Korea, enabled Japan to discourage development of modern manufacturing industries and "furthered their policy of making the Korean colony chiefly a supplier of grains and industrial raw materials to Japan and a market for Japanese manufactures" (Kim and Roemer, 1979:3).

This imperial "need" to transform the existing mode of production necessitated a more complete penetration of Korea by Japan. This was facilitated by further development of the transportation and communication systems. Although development of a transportation–communication network had begun long before incorporation, the road system connecting the major urban areas (while adequate for maintaining governmental administration between and within provinces) was inadequate for Japan's designs for the transformation of the Korean economy (Cumings, 1981; Hulbert, 1906; Reeve, 1963). Thus, in the early period, transportation development became a policy priority of the colonial government. Because of the opening of Pusan as a free port and the increased trade with Japan, a railway was built to connect Pusan with Seoul in 1896. By 1928 an entire system of railways and bridges linking Manchuria with Korea was finished (Reeve, 1963). The major north–south line connected Pusan with Siniuju on the Manchurian border with a linkage to the Manchurian rail lines. This north–south line included Pusan, Taegu, Seoul, and Pyongyang. Another major rail line connected Seoul and Wonsan, and yet another connected Taejon to the port city of Mokpo. In spite of the rugged terrain, nearly 4000 miles of rail line were completed by 1944 (Chang, 1971; Wood, 1977). The colonial government was also responsible for beginning construction of a highway and telecommunication network, along with improvements in maritime transportation. New ports (mostly on the eastern coast) were opened as trade with Japan increased during the colonial period (Suh, 1978; Cumings, 1981).

These advances in the transportation and communication systems served to maintain and strengthen the existing urban hierarchy by increasing the flow of interactions between cities. Lacking an adequate port and located on the western side of the peninsula (the region farthest from Japan), Seoul became dependent on intermediate rail and port cities for its trade with Japan. These intermediate cities were nodes in the trade system that developed, and, as such, became functionally important as junctions where freight from one transport system was shifted to another system. Thus, while massive investment in transportation and communication by Japan served to transform Korea into an export agricultural economy, it also strengthened an already existing urban hierarchy.

Between 1900 and 1929, Japan enjoyed a period of tremendous economic growth, with increases in GNP that far exceeded those of any core power (Kuznets, 1971:38–40). It was primarily during this period that Japan made the transition from semiperipheral to core status. In its effort to become an established power in the world political and economic system, however, Japan became heavily dependent on its export trade to finance the import of vital raw resources. With the world depression of the 1930s, protectionist policies pursued by the core powers resulted in the creation of tariffs to protect their domestic economies. Japan, more than any other core power, was vulnerable to the imposed trade restrictions (Chirot, 1977:103).

The military and large corporations, which by 1930 were in control of the Japanese economy and polity, directed Japan on a renewed policy of imperialism and heavy military industrialization (Chirot, 1977:103). Thus,

Korea was now needed for strategic as well as economic reasons. As early as annexation, Japan's expansionist policies drew attention to Korea as an avenue for continental penetration (this is partly the reason for the development of rail lines up to the Manchurian border).

In an attempt to reduce domestic economic competition, Japan in 1931 enacted the Law for Regulation of Major Industry, which controlled heavy industrial production within Japan (Kim and Roemer, 1979:5). The fact that industries in Korea were not subject to this law was very influential in the decisions of many Japanese firms to establish plants in Korea. In addition to this, Korea possessed a variety of mineral resources, an abundant supply of hydroelectric power, and a cheap supply of labor, all of which contributed to create a setting that offered cost advantages to heavy industries. Furthermore, with the taking of Manchuria in 1931, Korea was in a strategic location "wherein it became an important entrepôt for the trade between the two regions while expanding Japanese territory toward China" (Suh, 1978:13). Industrial diversification was also necessitated by domestic conditions. As a result of the agricultural depression experienced by Japan in the late 1920s, the initial plan for the agricultural development of Korea began to encounter difficulties (Suh, 1978:13). In an effort to avoid any further damage to its own domestic economy, Japan decided to discontinue expansion of Korean agricultural production.

As a result of these policy shifts, manufacturing output in Korea grew rapidly with heavy Japanese investment between 1930 and 1937. For the most part, this growth was entirely unrelated to Korean entrepreneurship, which was limited mainly to small industries.[6] With Japan's invasion of Manchuria, there began a conscious policy to expand heavy industries in Korea for military purposes (Suh, 1978). By 1941 the conversion to a wartime economy was complete.

The diversification of the Korean economy resulted in industries locating near the factors of production. Thus, regional specialization and interregional dependencies increased (Wood, 1977:32). This conscious policy of diversifing the Korean economy served to further develop urban areas in all regions of the country and to incorporate these cities in a system of interdependences.

With the end of World War II, Korea, while liberated from Japanese colonial rule, once again was dominated by foreign world powers. In the South, a United States military government was established, while in the

---

[6]It should be noted that a relatively small Korean bourgeoisie had developed by 1930. This group, for the most part, was so closely aligned with the Japanese that, for purposes of discussion, we can assume that their interests were nearly identical (see Cumings [1981:Chapter 1] for a fuller discussion of the origins and early development of capitalism in Korea).

North the Soviet Union was in control. The partitioning of Korea had a dramatic disorganizing effect on the economy and the functional relationships within the urban hierarchy. The South contained a greater population and the most productive agricultural land, while the North possessed most of the important mineral resources and the country's heavy industry and power plants (Hatada, 1969; Kim and Roemer, 1979). The cities in the two regions had developed a system of interdependencies that (given the removal of Japan and its restrictive growth policies) had the potential of developing much stronger complementary relationships. With the separation of the two regions, South Korea was forced to become heavily dependent on the United States to supply both manufactured goods and a large proportion of its food (Kim and Roemer, 1979). These shortages were further compounded as a result of the estimated 2.3 million Korean emigrants from Japan and North Korea entering South Korea between 1946 and 1948 (Kim and Roemer, 1979:25). Primarily as a result of this postwar migration, the proportion of the total population living in urban areas grew from 13 to 17% between 1944 and 1949. Furthermore, this growth was widely distributed, with 10 cities having growth rates of 8% or more (Mills and Song, 1979:70).

As a result of the near complete domination by the Japanese, there remained little of an elite class in Korea after World War II. This equalizing effect of the war was further enhanced by a series of successive land reforms initiated in 1947 by the United States military government. These reforms, which redistributed the land previously held by Japanese landlords, were apparently quite effective in equalizing income distribution (Kim and Roemer, 1979:164; Repetto, 1979). Perhaps even more important, however, the absence of a strong and unified elite class combined with the presence of an active foreign military government allowed for the beginning and continued growth of a "relatively autonomous" state apparatus (Koo, 1982). By this we do not mean to imply that the South Korean state was ever completely autonomous of either indigenous elite-class elements or from the constraints imposed by its structural position in the world-system. The state, while helping to fulfill the structural requirements of the world capitalist economy, was eventually able to transcend the individualized interests of specific capitalist class fractions.[7] For the purpose at hand, the relative strength of the Korean state was reflected in many policies that have both directly and indirectly reinforced the already existing urban system (Kim and Donaldson, 1980).

[7]The growth of the South Korean state can be viewed partly as a systemic property of countries undergoing "dependent development." In this regard, Evans (1979b) argues: "If classic dependence was associated with weak states, dependent development is associated with the strengthening of strong states in the 'semi-periphery.' The consolidation of state power may even be considered a prerequisite of dependent development."

The United States' interest in Korea was primarily, although not exclusively, geopolitical. Korea's strategic location vis-à-vis China, Japan, and the Soviet Union made it an important military position to the United States. Furthermore, Korea became a "quasi-experiment" for the testing of the dominate economic systems, capitalism and communism. Thus, the economic success of South Korea was of immense importance to the United States.

Despite the severe disruptions of World War II, industrial production began recovering by 1948, the year that the Republic of Korea was formally established. The economy continued to improve until the outbreak of the Korean War in 1950.

After the war, South Korea was more dependent on the United States than ever before. Massive foreign aid sustained South Korea during the reconstruction period following the war and has continued up to the present. Since 1945 South Korea has received nearly 6% of the total nonmilitary grants given by the United States (U.S. Bureau of the Census, 1980: 868–869). This continued assistance from the United States reflects the persisting strategic or geopolitical importance of South Korea. The extent of its strategic importance becomes clear when one considers that since 1970 South Korea also received nearly 3.5 billion dollars in United States military assistance, over three times that of any other East Asian country except Vietnam (U. S. Bureau of the Census, 1980:870).

Strategic considerations have always influenced South Korea's urban pattern. However, after the partitioning of the country (and especially since the Korean War), their importance greatly increased. The proximity of North Korea to Seoul poses an unusually strong threat to national security (Mills and Song, 1979:75).[8] It has been argued that, although cities were once important as fortresses for populations and economic functions, with changes in military technology large cities have become vulnerable and population spread to a number of centers is now strategically more desirable (Boulding, 1978). The rapid urban growth of the southeastern coastal region has, in part, been the result of a conscious policy to focus industrial growth away from North Korea (Mills and Song, 1979:53). During the 1970s, the growth rates of the major cities in the southeastern region have all been substantially higher than those for other cities, including Seoul.

Between 1953 and 1960 the South Korean economy grew slowly. Industry was characterized by production for the domestic market and a policy of import substitution was pursued (Kim and Roemer, 1979:153). Beginning in the early 1960s, however, South Korea began one of the most rapid and

---

[8]During the Korean War, Seoul suffered tremendous damage. So complete was the devastation that civilian movement to the city was severely restricted in the immediate postwar years and it was not until the late 1950s that Seoul recovered its political and economic functions.

sustained rates of growth ever recorded. This was largely the result of a shift to a policy of labor-intensive export manufacturing. This change was both the result of and a force acting to maintain the existing urban hierarchy.

South Korea's strong state and relatively even income distribution have been noted above. These factors, coupled with an even city-size distribution, have been influential in the shift to export manufacturing (Kim and Roemer, 1979:163–164). This type of industrialization operates most efficiently when plants locate close to the factors of production and are able to utilize regional resource advantages fully. In contrast, under a policy of import substitutional industrialization it is more advantageous to locate manufacturing close to a concentrated domestic market (as in the case of the Philippines). Export manufacturing industries need not consider this market element when making locational decisions (Roberts, 1978b:603–604). These locational decisions have been further influenced by the continued development of the transportation infrastructure that permits the relatively even spread of population and economic activity. All major cities are connected, not only be railroads, but also by an elaborate highway system similar to interstate routes in the United States (Hasan, 1976:30–35). Thus, the shift to export manufacturing has been made, in part, because of the strength of the South Korean state and the relative evenness of its income and urban structures. Once begun, this economic policy served to reinforce these existent structures.

In summary, there is evidence of an urban system existing even prior to Korean contact with the capitalist world-system. This historic urban pattern influenced the development of an urban hierarchy after Japanese colonization. The maintenance of a complex, fairly evenly distributed urban system up to the present is the result of (1) policies originating with the core powers, which have politically and economically dominated South Korea since the end of the nineteenth century, and (2) policies linked to the country's position within the world-economy and polity that, in turn, have been initiated from within South Korea. These policies have led to a remarkably even distribution of income and a successful economic policy of export manufacturing.

CONCLUSION

The major argument of this essay has been that an understanding of the historical context of urbanization—and especially key junctures in history such as the initial incorporation into the capitalist world-economy—is critical to explain adequately the shape of the present urban structures of South

Korea and the Philippines. We have tried to explain the way that the role the two countries played in the world economic and political system has had ramifications for internal economic and political policies, which in turn have shaped the patterns of urban growth and development. Our discussion has focused first on the effect that the nature and timing of the original contact with expanding capitalism had on urbanization in the two East Asian countries. The argument then shifted to a demonstration of the ways in which the urban patterns of each nation were maintained or reinforced as their roles in the world-system changed. A critical issue involves whether or not power is concentrated in the hands of urban elites who are able to influence policy decisions that have a bearing on infrastructural development or on the distribution of power and resources in the urban hierarchy.

A basic linkage that warrants attention is the relationship between the two countries' present structural positions in the world-economy and the functional roles their urban systems play. Although the concept of the *semiperiphery* is a slippery one, and it is not always clear exactly which countries belong in this category (Evans, 1979a:17), this notion may be useful in distinguishing South Korea from the Philippines. Wallerstein (1976:465) includes Korea as one of the "economically stronger countries" in Asia that fits into this intermediary status in the world-economy. In a very rapidly growing economy there will clearly be several advantages to population concentrations in large cities (Mills and Song, 1979:2–3). Furthermore, countries undergoing "dependent development" are also experiencing a reorientation of their economies away from the export of agricultural goods and mineral resources (Evans, 1979b:Chapter 1). The growth of manufacturing has promoted urbanization in nearly all nations where it has occurred (Mills and Song, 1979:10). But, as Roberts cogently argues, there are different types of *both* industrialization and urbanization in Third World countries (Roberts, 1978a). Perhaps the type of market that a nation's industries are oriented to as well as the diversity of the manufacturing performed are indicators of either peripheral or semiperipheral status. Similarities between South Korea, Brazil, and other semiperipheral countries suggest that this may be the case (Evans, 1979a). Primate patterns of urbanization may often be linked to import substitution industrialization and peripheral status in the contemporary world system in mutually reinforcing ways. Conversely, relatively nonprimate urban hierarchies, export manufacturing, and position in the semiperiphery may be positively related in reciprocal causal relationships.

Finally, we would like to propose a possible link or congruence between what at first glance would appear to be two very divergent theoretical perspectives: human ecology and dependency–world-system theory. As mentioned earlier, human ecology has long been concerned with urban dominance and hierarchy. This concern is perhaps most readily apparent in the later works of R. D. McKenzie (1927, 1934), who took an active interest in imperialism and the developing international system of the early twentieth century. McKenzie's 1927 article, "The Concepts of Dominance and World Organization," and his 1934 paper, "Industrial Expansion and the Inter-relationships of People," discuss dependency relations, international patterns of exploitation, and the expansion of the United States and Japanese economies into other countries and spheres of influence. The manner in which he addressed these issues (as well as the use of certain terms) reveals a remarkable congruence with contemporary world-system theorists formulations.

Both human ecology and dependency–world-system theory view divergent urban configurations not as consequences of different cultural orientations or value systems but as the outcomes of materially based conditions resulting from occupying particular positions within a hierarchically ordered system of relationships. The tendency of human ecologists, however, to view urbanization as an adaptation of a community to its environment clearly distinguishes it from how dependency–world-system theorists view the dynamics of the processes influencing urban formations. Communities do not adapt, but rather are the manifestations of the struggle between classes of conflicting interests. Technology is not simply used to enhance the ability of communities to sustain themselves, but rather to preserve and promote the interests of local, national, and international elites. Indeed, it is unfortunate that most human ecologists have chosen to neglect the role of politically and economically powerful groups in their analyses of the impact of transportation and communication technologies on urban patterns (Hawley, 1984). When policies concerning these technologies are viewed as reflections of class interests, they then can be used as indicators of how national and international elites, by pursuing their material interests, shape, direct, and redirect patterns of urbanization. Our research is an attempt to link the interests of national and international classes with infrastructural changes within two dependent countries, and to examine the effects these have had on their urban structures. In this manner, internal variables and processes are seen as operating within a given political and economic context, and reflect the material interests of powerful groups. Viewing infrastructural developments in this way facilitates understanding of why they are introduced into a society, how they are developed, and, ultimately, the effect they have in shaping urban structures.

10

THAI CITY–HINTERLAND RELATIONSHIPS IN AN INTERNATIONAL CONTEXT: DEVELOPMENT AS SOCIAL CONTROL IN NORTHERN THAILAND*

Bruce London

INTRODUCTION

The study of uneven development (or the persistence of severe regional–spatial inequalities) in Third World Nations is experiencing a dramatic paradigm shift. Fewer and fewer studies incorporate the traditional analysis, predominant through the 1960s, of the workings of impersonal, competitive market and institutional mechanisms in determining the relationships between city and hinterland. Increasingly, work in this area focuses on the role of intergroup power relationships in the urbanization and regional development processes. In other words, center–periphery relationships are studied in politicoeconomic terms, stressing especially the impact of the politics of public policymaking in creating and maintaining uneven development (cf. Cornelius, 1975; Portes and Walton, 1976).

Most of this more recent work has been applied to Latin America (Cornelius, 1975; Roberts, 1978a; Walton, 1975), to the relative neglect of Africa and, especially, Asia. One exception is my own (1977, 1979, 1980) work on Thailand. This work began as a study of primate city parasitism (1977). Urban primacy occurs when one overridingly large city dominates a nation functionally as well as in terms of size. Bangkok, for example, is not only the political, economic, and cultural center of Thailand, it was also 33.4

*Portions of this chapter are reprinted by permission of Westview Press from *Metropolis and Nation in Thailand: The Political Economy of Uneven Development,* by Bruce London. Copyright © 1980 by Westview Press, Boulder, Colorado.

times as large as the nation's second largest city, Chieng Mai, in 1970. The argument that such a city is parasitic suggests that primacy retards national development in general and results in uneven regional development in particular because the city somehow acts as an obstruction to the economic growth of its hinterland.

This essay elaborates upon my previous research on the political economy of urban primacy in Thailand. Unlike several other contributions to this volume (see Chapters 5, 7, 8, and 12), this chapter is about the *effects* (rather than the *causes*) of urban primacy. Why are primate cities often described as parasitic? My attempt to answer this question focuses on the idea that an understanding of intergroup power relationships (both within and between nations) is integral to explaining why urban primacy is associated with parasitism. In this regard, much of the material that follows may be more aptly described as political sociology or political history than as urban sociology. But, it is precisely the point of this essay that an understanding of political phenomena (i.e., intergroup power relationships) is a prerequisite to answering many questions about urbanization, including the one posed here: What is the effect of the primate city on its hinterland?

My attempts to understand the mechanisms involved in primate city parasitism—that is, the specific means by which such cities obstruct hinterland growth—led to a focus on internal colonialism (1979) and uneven development (1980) that stressed the parallels among these three concepts. In terms of their functional relationships with their hinterlands, primate cities are, first and foremost, *political* centers. The policies formulated in these centers by national elites have important implications in terms of the creation and perpetuation of regional *economic* inequalities. Therefore, center–periphery interactions are most fruitfully studied in politicoeconomic terms, with a main focus of concern being the role of power, group, or class interests, and public policymaking in creating and maintaining spatial inequalities (Cornelius, 1975:9–10).

Walton's (1974, 1975, 1976d) revision of the concept of internal colonialism is an important example of this emerging politicoeconomic approach to the analysis of the role of urbanization in the development process. His main reformulation of previous usages involves an attempt to specify the ways in which the internal structural conditions of Third World nations "articulate with influences from abroad" (1975:34):

> internal colonialism is defined as a process that produces certain intra-national forms of patterned socioeconomic inequality directly traceable to the exploitative practices through which national and international institutions are linked in the interests of surplus extraction and capital accumulation. . . . [The term] refers to those domestic structures of inequality whose origins lie in the interface between internal conditions and external influences stemming from metropolitan

economies . . . a process whose central characteristic is exploitation [or] the use
of power (as opposed to market or voluntaristic mechanisms) to [facilitate] capital accumulation . . . exploitation [must] be demonstrated as the causal basis
of the patterns of inequality. (pp. 34–35)

Walton (1975:36–48) proceeds to present a program for the study of internal colonialism. On an abstract, theoretical, or conceptual level, he ad-
umbrates the major forms of internal colonialism and suggests several ways
of measuring these. This discussion bears summarizing.

Internal colonialism is seen, at bottom, to be a hierarchical process of
surplus extraction caused by exploitative institutional practices and generating or perpetuating both social class and geographic inequalities. It is
manifest in a variety of practices of the state (e.g., foreign investment policies, infrastructural expenditures, fiscal policies, and social policies), the
agricultural sector (e.g., production for export, credit and land tenure policies, and the encouragement of agribusiness), the manufacturing sector
(e.g., the transnational corporation), and the trade and commerce sectors
(e.g., encouragement of monoculture and unilateral exchanges). And, to
the extent that these practices generate uneven development by being exploitative, internal colonialism is primate city parasitism.

Ultimately, then, my previous research on Thailand suggested that the
appropriate study of the urban bases of uneven development should revolve
around the core phenomena of exploitative and/or neglectful policymaking
(in the primate city or national capital), the intergroup power exchanges
behind policy decisions, and the role of extranational forces in determining
such intranational politics. To summarize a bit further, the study of primate
city–hinterland relationships should focus on the politics of national policymaking within an international or world-system (Wallerstein, 1974a) context. Both intra- and international causal processes must be understood. As
Timberlake argues in Chapter 1 (this volume), interpretations of socioeconomic changes within nations, including changing patterns of urbanization,
are incomplete without reference to "the many ways in which they articulate with the broader currents of the world-economy."

At this juncture, it is important to emphasize a key difference between
previous analyses of primate city parasitism and the present analysis. A
number of attempts have been made to measure the parasitic or generative
effects of primate cities (cf. Linsky, 1965; Mehta, 1969; Timberlake, 1979).
These efforts have been to no avail: inherent in any attempt to quantify
primate city parasitism by using standard demographic and socioeconomic
data is a reification of the concept of urban primacy. Cities do not act.
They cannot be parasitic. They cannot exploit. Exploitation—or the use of
power to gain profit (Walton, 1975:35)—is the province of power holders,
elites, hegemonic classes, decision- or policymakers. Any study of the effect

of a primate city on its hinterland must therefore focus on those individuals and groups that represent the primate city as they interact with those individuals and groups representing the hinterland. This is a matter of inter-group power relationships or the political economy of urban primacy. And, this is precisely the approach taken here.

With these general considerations as its foundation, my analysis of primate city–hinterland relationships in Thailand proceeded to stress the link between "development as an end" and "policy as a means" to that end (London, 1980:23–27). Of particular importance here is a consideration of both the motives that guide decision-makers in the choice of fiscal and/or development policies and, in turn, the relationship between these motives and parasitism (or colonialism or uneven development).

In terms of elite motives, a stated policy may be either rhetoric or reality. A development policy is *rhetoric* when a policymaker's motives are based more on hidden self-interest than on development as an ideal goal; a policy is *reality* when a policymaker's motives are based on the ideal of national development. Paradoxically, policies implemented may be parasitic—that is, they may generate or perpetuate uneven development—in both cases.

On the one hand, where development policy is purely rhetorical—that is, where talk of national development serves only a legitimating function— an exploitative sort of parasitism exists; elite policies serve narrow class interests rather than the public interest. On the other hand, even when the motives of decision-makers are not based on self-interest, the policies implemented may be parasitic in effect if not in intent. Such a result arises when the tension between goals and resources is insurmountable. A nation's decision-makers are then forced to neglect one sector of the economy or segment of the population in favor of another in the hope that the temporary concentration of limited resources in one area will lead to high productivity and a general "trickle-down" of resources to all areas in the future. In such a situation, development is a "prospective end" and certain inequities may well be expanded even while others are attenuated.

There is a third possibility that fits somewhere between the extremes of exploitative parasitism and development as a prospective end:

> One can conceive of a situation in which, after a lengthy history of exploitation and neglect, a nation's decision-makers find themselves in a position which forces them to implement "real" development policies, not because of any motive based upon development as an end in itself, but in order to maintain their elite status vis-à-vis other groups which have recently experienced an increase in their power or bargaining position. Given such circumstances, development policy is a means of *social control,* an instrument used by the decision-makers to serve their own interests by "buying off" potentially-disruptive ascendant groups. This type of behavior may be interpreted as parasitic by viewing it as a rather subtle form of exploitation, a manipulative blending of domination and legitimation via the

implemention of policies which may be easily retracted by the decision-makers if they perceive the bargaining position of their opponents to have diminished. (London, 1980:24)

The three types of primate city parasitism are illustrated in Figure 10.1. My essay, "Internal Colonialism in Thailand" (London, 1979), focused on one type of parasitism: development as a prospective end. The fact that Thailand's position in the world-system had a profound impact on national policy is most clearly illustrated here.

Beginning with Thailand's entry into sustained contact with the West in the 1850s and lasting until roughly the turn of the century, Thai policy-making in every administrative sector was constrained by an international context that presented national leaders with very real fears for Thailand's continued sovereignty. Decision-making focused on doing anything and everything necessary to maintain sovereignty (for a more detailed analysis of this period in Thai history, see London, 1979).

The survival of an independent Thailand in spite of British and French imperial aspirations was equated with modernization in the minds of Thai decision-makers. The types of modernization policies implemented were accorded priority in terms of the degree to which they served this end. For example, top priority was given to the administrative reform of the central and provincial governments in order to better mobilize national resources, extract surplus from the hinterland for expenses, and control a far-flung population. Without such reform, the defense of the kingdom would have been hopeless.

Such policy priorities of this era as fiscal conservatism, higher expendi-

		POLICY IMPACT	
		Negative	Positive
POLICYMAKERS' MOTIVES GUIDING	Development as rhetoric	Ideal-typical parasitism	Development as social control
DEVELOPMENT DECISIONS	Development as reality	Development as prospective end	Ideal-typical development

FIGURE 10.1 Schematic diagram of types (parasitic or developmental) of primate city-hinterland relationships. A *negative* policy impact occurs when a so-called development policy does not contribute to the redress of inter- or intranational inequities. A *positive* policy impact occurs when a so-called developmental policy does contribute to the redress of inter- or intranational inequities. A development policy is *rhetoric* when a policymaker's motives are based more on hidden self-interest than on development as an ideal goal. A development policy is *reality* when a policymaker's motives are based on the ideal of national development.

tures on transportation than on agriculture, low budgetary priorities for social services such as education, and a general "center-orientation" that saw Bangkok developed while the periphery was neglected may only be fully understood within an international context of challenge and response. The challenge of imperialism led to a response that may be called "conservative reform." Change in the status quo was a necessity. But the changes implemented were designed not to restructure the hierarchy of rewards and privileges, but to permit the hierarchy to exist in a minimally altered, yet strengthened, form. By design, nation-building policies focused on enhancing the position of Bangkok by "building on the best." Predictably, however, this exacerbated short-run regional inequalities, but always with the stated hopes of reducing them in the long run.

My paper on primate city parasitism (London, 1977) focused on the effects of national policy on Thailand's Northeast region. The priorities defined in the late nineteenth century led to decades of exploitation and neglect in Thailand's peripheral regions. In a very real sense, the initial policy of development as prospective end persisted for decades, and the inequalities set in motion became identified with entrenched, vested interests. As a result, the situation came to approximate closely that of exploitative parasitism. It was only in the post–World War II period (and especially since the 1960s), that the Northeastern situation began to resemble development as social control. Certain political and economic reversals, a fear of communist insurgency, and other intra- and international threats to elite ascendancy led to increased development or social overhead exenditures by the government in the Northeast. This sudden attenuation of neglect may be interpreted as an example of development as social control (London, 1977).

The same sequence of exploitation and neglect followed by an abrupt attenuation of neglect characterizes the center's relationship with Thailand's other peripheral regions. The present essay analyzes the interactions between Bangkok and Northern Thailand, emphasizing the recent emergence of fiscal policies that simultaneously serve development and social control functions.

This analysis is of more than descriptive interest in that the notion of "policy as social control" used here is very reminiscent of aspects of O'Connor's (1973) theory of the "fiscal crisis of the state" and of the emerging "social control theory of urban politics (cf. Boulay, 1979). This literature suggests that certain state budgetary expenditures primarily serve social control functions. O'Connor (1973:6–7), in particular, stresses that "State expenditures have a twofold character corresponding to the capitalist state's two basic functions" of accumulation and legitimization. The first type of expenditure, social capital, is "required for profitable private accumulation'' and is divided into two subtypes: social investment (projects and services such as state-financed industrial parks that increase the rate of profit by increasing the productivity of labor) and social consumption (projects and services such as education and social insurance spending that increase the rate of profit by lowering the reproduction costs of labor).

The second type of expenditure, social expenses, "consists of projects and services which are required to maintain social harmony—to fulfill the state's 'legitimization' function." Unlike social capital, social expenses are neither directly nor indirectly productive. O'Connor suggests that "the best example is the welfare system, which is designed chiefly to keep social peace among unemployed workers" (cf. Piven and Cloward, 1971).

It is the latter (social expenses), then, that serve primarily social control functions. Such social expenses become increasingly necessary when unrest among the urban poor threatens the "corporate-based interests upon which the urban economy rests" (Boulay, 1979:605). In other words, the formulation of fiscal–budgetary policy is a highly political phenomenon. Expenditures that appear to be serving the public interest (e.g., welfare) may actually be disproportionately serving the interests of elites.

At this point, O'Connor's notion of social expenses is very similar to the present concept of policy as social control. Both stress the need to analyze the motives guiding the formulation of fiscal–budgetary policy in order to discover who decides, who pays, and who benefits from the policies implemented. It is to just such an analysis of center–periphery relationships in Thailand that we now turn.

Bangkok–North Relationships

Using recent per capita income estimates as an initial summary indicator of level of development, the data reveal that only the Northeast has a lower per capita income than the North. Underlying and exacerbating this basic lack of integration with the center is the fact that the North is populated predominantly by groups having a unique regional–ethnic identity: hill tribes and a Northern Thai peasant minority. Consequently, any attempt to understand the problems of this region must be predicated upon an analysis of intergroup power relationships between the regionally dominant communal populations and the Central Thai (cf. Keyes, 1967; Van Roy, 1971; London, 1977).

As in the case of the Northeast, the history of the North is marked initially by isolation from the center and a high degree of local self-sufficiency. Isolation is followed by a period in which the region comes under central control and is subsequently exploited and neglected. Finally, there is a culmination in an era of changing central and peripheral bargaining positions engendering an attenuation of neglect.

The two major peripheral ethnolinguistic groups involved in center-periphery interaction are (1) the many non-Thai hill tribes inhabiting the higher elevations throughout the mountainous northern provinces; these people generally employ seminomadic agricultural techniques to produce their major cash crop, opium. And (2) the northern Thai lowlanders populating the valleys carved out of the rugged mountains by the major northern rivers; for the most part, they are engaged in a self-sufficient, settled, rice-growing type of economy. The hill tribes, whose combined population may total 400,000, dominated academic and governmental discussions of northern problems since 1955. This is largely because of the visibility of their cultural differences, their location in strategic border areas, their opium economy, and their sense of and allegiance to a cultural rather than a national identity. Moerman (1967:401–402), however, cautions observers not to permit a concern with tribal groups to blind them to the import of the far more numerous and equally strategically located Thai lowlanders.

Not unlike the cultural identity of the hill tribes, the lowlanders have a strong sense of regional identity. They refer to themselves as *khon muang,* "Northern Thai." This term is comparable to *isan* as used by Northeasterners (Manndorff, 1967:528). They speak a dialect called *caa muang,* "the Northern Thai language" (Chapman, 1973b:196), and they clearly distinguish *khon muang* from *khon doi,* "mountain men" or hill tribesmen (Manndorff, 1967:528). The latter distinction has important implications. The Thai villagers "ridicule and resent military and economic aid directed solely at the hill peoples, whom they generally regard as odd or foreign and whom they often think inferior" (Moerman, 1967:402).

The allegiance of both groups to a regional or ethnic rather than a national identity is worthy of additional emphasis. The concept of *nation-state* is completely unknown in the tribal world (Van Roy, 1971:182) and is only of marginal relevance among the *khon muang.* Indeed, Thai peasants know more about the history of the North than that of the nation and they "are better informed on their cultural heritage" than on the nature of the nation-state and their role within it (Van Roy, 1971:24). Moerman (1967:403) quotes a "sentiment" widely repeated in the North, one which serves as a reflection on peripheral loyalties: A villager remarked that his region was conquered by the Central Thai about 60 years earlier. The villagers offered the Central Thai signs of respect and loyalty, treating them as "officials" or "rulers," and, inevitably, paying them taxes. The villager then went on to speculate about the future:

> When the Communists come, they may conquer the Central Thai. Then we will offer them [respect and loyalty and call them rulers]. We will pay them taxes

and all will be as before. We are the common people; what happens to officials
does not concern us. . . . Whatever side wins, we will . . . call them our leaders.

One would not expect to hear such a statement in Central Thailand. It
emphasizes the physical and social distances that underlie Northern regionalism. An understanding of the contemporary implications of this regionalism requires an analysis of the historically changing relationships between
Northern Thai lowlanders and the hill tribe peoples, between the hill tribes
and the central government, and between the Northern Thai minorities and
the central government. In all this, the northern peoples' heritage of independence and the recency, suddenness, forcefulness, and completeness of
their inclusion into the Thai nation cannot be overemphasized because these
dramatic changes still have a negative impact on northern attitudes toward
the government (Moerman, 1967:405; Van Roy, 1971:29).

After political control was established in the early years of the twentieth
century, "the historical disinterest of the Central Thai in the uplands" (Van
Roy, 1971:197) reemerged as a fact of Thai political life. This appears to
be especially true of Bangkok's relationship with the hill tribes. There is
some debate over the precise nature of Bangkok's policy toward the tribal
peoples during this period. Manndorf (1967:529–530), for example, argues
that the tribes were, in effect, left entirely alone until the mid-1950s: "with
few exceptions there was no taxation, no conscription, no education, and
no legal registration. . . . Their legal position as residents or citizens of the
country was never clearly defined, and virtually no governmental administration was extended into the remote mountain areas."

Kunstadter (1967:377) notes, on the other hand, that hill tribesmen have
an ambiguous citizenship status. They are subject to taxes and to Thai crim-
inal law but, in practice, inaccessibility tends to mitigate these interactions.
Nonetheless, the "customary family patterns, inheritance laws, and property and religious customs . . . conflict at a number of points with Thai
law" (Kunstadter, 1967:377).

These policy ambiguities notwithstanding, it is clear that "distributive
inequalities maintained by the authorities in Bangkok between Thai and
upland tribal peoples" (Race, 1974:110) are the distinguishing characteristics of this particular "exchange." These inequalities range from a denial
of certain legal rights to forms of prejudice toward the tribal minority group.
In general, laws regarding minorities—for example, immigration and naturalization laws, restrictions on government employment, restrictions on
certain occupations, economic nationalism, property restrictions, and school
regulations—have been directed toward the Chinese (Kunstadter, 1967:375).
Particular policies have vacillated, and "variations in policy have been
clearly related to internal economic conditions (needs for labor; desires to
encourage Thai participation in, or control of, certain industries . . .) and

internal or external political conditions (use of antiminority-group action to promote national solidarity; response to threats from Japan during the Second World War, and from Communist China since the 1950s)" (Kunstadter, 1967:375).

In some cases, these laws and policies do have implications for the tribal minorities, especially in terms of the crucial definition of citizenship and the concomitant determination of legal status. In fact, tribal citizenship is not clearly defined (Kunstadter, 1967; Race, 1974). This renders the hill peoples subject to many of the same constraints as the Chinese. While there can be little control of tribal migration (migration in any direction across very remote and inaccessible borders is difficult to regulate), there is a most-evident exclusion of hill people from the Thai formal and informal political systems. They are not permitted to enter into government service (Race, 1974:89) and "only rarely do hill tribesmen occupy as high a position as commune headman" (Kunstadter, 1967:380). Nor do any tribesmen have the ability to establish entry into Thai entourages (as do some wealthy Chinese).

Of course, it is highly doubtful that many tribesmen seek government employment or active political participation to begin with. However, their lack of patronal representation has other implications. Some Thai officials, conversant with the workings of "the system," extort money from the hill tribes for minor infractions of rarely enforced laws (Race, 1974:89). More seriously, "the ordinary services (police, schools, public health, and medical care)" that ideally accrue to citizens or to those with patrons "have been brought into the hills only infrequently" (Kunstadter, 1967:379). Similarly, the question of tribal property rights is not at all clear and, since tribal peoples rarely receive the benefit of any doubt, they are left with no security of land ownership (Kunstadter, 1967:376–377). Further policies that hill people regard as arbitrarily repressive include laws against crossing national borders, suppression of opium production, limiting swidden areas, tribal relocation plans, and "Thai-ification"/acculturation efforts (Race, 1974:89; Van Roy, 1971:192).

Finally, "most lowlanders view the tribal people as fair game for exploitation" (Hanks, n.d.:4). In addition to being viewed as culturally inferior by lowlanders, "tribesmen are sometimes discriminated against in business dealings. This is especially true of the non–opium-growers . . . who do not have the benefit of possessing cash crops, and whose economic relationships with the lowlanders are on a less advantageous basis" (Manndorff, 1967:529). Even those uplanders who produce opium and other goods for the market are at the mercy of the lowlanders who set the conditions for trade. For example, lowland buyers are able to control prices because the tribesmen must transport their goods long distances to market and do not want to carry them back if unsold (Kunstadter, 1967:392).

Aside from this economic subordination in the market place, the interests of tribal groups are also invariably subordinated when any favored outside groups have interests in the resources of the areas occupied by the minority. "Restrictions have periodically been placed on swidden techniques and on the tribal use of local lumber resources ostensibly because such practices have a detrimental effect on the watersheds so vital to water supply and irrigation control in *the Central Plain,* but also . . . because the Royal Thai Government has granted forestry rights to large corporations" (Kunstadter, 1967:392). All in all, it appears safe to say that the hill tribes have been neglected, if not exploited, during recent Thai history.

The history of Bangkok's relationship with the *khon muang* differs perhaps in degree but not in kind. The northern peasants too find themselves "within the sphere of a superior political entity" and subject to "the imposition and enforcement of national policy primarily for the benefit of classes of the citizenry far removed from the Northern hills" (Van Roy, 1971:191).

Moerman (1967) and Van Roy (1971) both focus on the villagers' own perceptions of being exploited and neglected by the central government— a definition of the situation that is "real" in terms of both causes and consequences. The nature of villager–official contacts has historically been such that the former can hardly come to any other conclusion. To begin with, a sense of social distance between peasant and civil servant has been institutionalized and is perpetuated. Peasants perceive officials as high-ranking "untouchables," possessing a power they have no means of countering, people to be feared and avoided (Van Roy, 1971:192).

For their part, the officials rarely hide their contempt for the "inferior" villagers. It must be remembered that, until very recently, the North has been regarded by civil servants as a most undesirable posting that was to be terminated with a minimum of work and a maximum of dispatch. Conversely, it was also generally accepted that the least capable administrators were sent to the remoter regions.

The nature of the actual interactions between villager and official must be understood within this context. Moerman (1967:407) notes that "the farmer's main contacts with the government are the taxes and fees collected and the orders given." Thai peasants pay taxes to the central government both openly through direct levies and in the hidden form of government-controlled price ajustments (Van Roy, 1971:186). In either case, they fail to see any benefits derived from or "transfer payments" in return for these taxes. There are, in fact, "widespread local beliefs that taxation imposed at the center far exceeds services rendered to the region and that the regional terms of trade are kept purposely unfavorable" (Van Roy, 1971:31).

All in all, a picture emerges of exploitation and neglect of the Northern peasant, coupled with a very tangible popular awareness on the part of these peasants themselves of discriminatory treatment. Moerman (1967:407) notes that "most villagers are usually quite unaware of receiving any valuable services whatsoever from the government." He points out, further, that villagers tend to fear the police, and that they rarely use or receive postal, health, agricultural extension, and other services. Meanwhile, officials are able to demand labor and collect license fees for activities such as gambling, distilling, tree felling, and butchering. For their part, the villagers feel that the latter activities are legitimate, and they view official interference as simply a means to raise revenues: "Villagers assume that these fees and taxes, these exactions for which nothing is returned, become the officials' salaries. Since the Thai use reciprocity as the rhetoric for social relationships, it seems especially unjust for officials to harass and control while providing no palpable beneficial services" (Moerman, 1967:407–408).

Van Roy (1971:31) complements Moerman's description of exploitation and neglect by emphasizing that regional perceptions of being "discriminated against for the benefit of the Center" are not mere figments of local imaginations. "In all fairness it can only be admitted that Central Thai attitudes and central government actions appear to be not entirely free of a colonialist view of the North."

Changes similar to those taking place in the Northeast began to occur in the North in the 1950s. A series of internal and external events were making regional economic development a greater political priority than ever before. The deliberate process of government social overhead involvement in the North (as in the Northeast) was forthcoming only when certain problems demanded a new response. Among the most important of these were increasing international censure of opium production, deteriorating economic conditions, a sharply rising pressure of population on the land, and (somewhat later) fear of communist insurgency.

The first tangible evidence of government realization that it could no longer leave the North "entirely alone" (Manndorff, 1967:530) came with the inauguration of the Border Patrol Police (BPP) in 1955. BPP efforts were mainly directed towards the hill tribes. Various descriptions of its raison d'être emphasized that it was founded in order to actualize sovereignty in border areas (Race, 1974:90), that its primary missions are to ensure security and gather intelligence (Kunstadter, 1967:380), or that it was "assigned to provide for 'control and public safety in the remote hills and frontier regions' " (Manndorff, 1967:531). "In order to carry out its missions, the BPP has tried deliberately to befriend local populations" (Kunstadter,

1967:380). Although its efforts have been described as "extremely limited" (Race, 1974:90) through the early 1960s—a period of intensifying crisis— they did include such development measures as the establishment of schools and the distribution of some medical supplies and agricultural equipment to tribesmen (Manndorff, 1967:531). These efforts were augmented by certain social control or legitimating techniques. Village labor was enlisted for the construction of a large number of short take-off and landing airfields (Race, 1974:91), pictures of the king and queen were distributed, and political lectures were held (Kunstadter, 1967:382).

Although we cannot attribute the founding of the BPP directly to the fact that the hill tribes' economy is based upon the production of opium, it may well be closely related to pressures Thailand felt in the mid-1950s with the clamp down on international narcotics traffic by the United Nations (with support of the major Western powers) (Van Roy, 1971:198). At any rate, there are indications that government involvement in the North was intensified in 1959 (Manndorff, 1967:530), immediately following the enactment of Revolutionary Proclamation Number 37 by the Sarit government, prohibiting the sale and consumption of opium (Manndorff, 1967: 531; Van Roy, 1971:198). "This added urgency to the problem of dealing with the hill tribes. . . . Thus the opium problem became the reason for intensifying relations of the central government with hill tribe socities" (Manndorff, 1967:531).

Actually, the opium problem and increasing population pressures interacted in such a way as to compound the total situation. Geddes (1973:221) notes the extreme economic dependence of the hill tribes on opium production for cash: four-fifths of cultivated tribal land is used for opium and a full third of tribal households plant no rice at all. The poppy, however, depletes the soil, forcing a migratory way of life. Such a pattern can only remain viable either if there are unexploited areas to move to or if total population remains low enough to permit the eventual reexploitation of previously used land. It is at this juncture that recent demographic changes become crucial. Throughout the twentieth century, there has been a continuous southward migration of tribal groups from Burma and China into Thailand and, more recently, there has begun a flow of lowland Thai peasants northward from the increasingly crowded Central Plains (Hanks, n.d.:3; Van Roy, 1971:239).

Conditions, therefore, that would permit an opium economy to remain viable are disappearing as the Northern tribal and lowland populations increase (Geddes, 1973:223). The tribes' economic position is being progressively weakened by decreasing productivity (confined to a narrower area as more Thai peasants obtain title to formerly open lands or as other tribes compete for swidden sites, any given tribe may be forced to replant on land that would in the past have been abandoned). Not only are many tribesmen forced to seek employment as wage laborers (Van Roy, 1971) but they become increasingly hostile to the government and susceptible to communist propaganda.

The first antigovernment activities in the North date from 1960 to 1962 (Race, 1974:93–94). The government was "forced" to intervene more and more in upland economic affairs. And for their part, many tribesmen were forced to accept rice subsidies and other forms of "welfare" (Van Roy, 1971:239). However, the nature of this intervention has only served to exacerbate the situation by increasing tribal perceptions of prejudice and a hatred of the favored lowland civilization.

"The Ministry of the Interior assigned the Public Welfare Department to carry out certain research and development activities in the remote mountain regions" in 1959 (Manndorff, 1967:530). Among the earliest of these activities were plans to establish Land Settlement Projects for selected hill tribes. It was assumed that this would complement the government's anti-opium policy by encouraging tribes to migrate to settlement areas (*nikhom*) where they might replace opium with other cash crops (Geddes, 1973:244; Manndorff, 1967:531). Other land-use programs enacted at this time were to serve similar ends. Many areas were declared part of the public domain and restrictions were placed upon swidden agriculture—ostensibly because the deforestation concomitant with swiddening destroys watersheds, but more likely as an attempt to reduce opium cultivation (Van Roy, 1971:198). In this manner, the center's new policies in some cases "doubly preempted" tribal lands, both as public domain and as *nikhom* sites (Van Roy, 1971:224).

The whole problem was further compounded by the government's ambiguous policy of allowing hill tribes to continue growing their traditional opium crop until a replacement could be introduced. "Their persistence with an illegal crop at the same time as they are subjected to propaganda against it and interference with their trade outlets causes tension between the tribes and the government to the political disadvantage of the government" (Geddes, 1973:213).

At any rate, these early efforts were followed by other similarly motivated policies during the first half of the 1960s. Among these new programs was the inauguration in 1961–1962 of a "socio-economic survey of Northern hill tribes." Heretofore, the hill tribes had never been included in any census reports or district gazeteers compiled by the government. This research project (the Hill Tribe Project), sponsored by the newly created Hill Tribe Division within the Public Welfare Department of the Ministry of the Interior, "was the first government sponsored survey of the mountain peoples of Northern Thailand" (Manndorff, 1967:525–533). The tribes surveyed were "selected in accordance with the wishes of the government" and included only opium-growing tribes (Manndorff, 1967:534). This appears to be an excellent example of the link between potential insurgency problems and "academic" counterinsurgency research (cf. Chapman, 1973a:14; Coburn, 1971:99–100).

Another policy of the early 1960s was the expansion of BPP operations in the Tri-Province Area of Phetchabun, Phitsanulok, and Nan. This occurred in response to both trouble in Laos and persistent rumors of antigovernment organizational activities among the local hill tribes in this particularly strategic area, which divides the North from the Northeast and borders on Laos (Race, 1974:90). BPP teams would visit villages to give advice, bring in supplies, and so on, and in exchange they would seek information on hostile activities. Further evidence of this sort of cooptive exchange is provided by Race (1974:106):

> Because of the likely future importance of this area the BPP began its first school [here] . . . in 1961, and in cooperation with the Public Welfare Department a major development center. . . . [Also] considerable sums were devoted to expanding the number of schools in this area and to agricultural training for the tribal people. These efforts were accelerated when reports began to come in of a . . . group . . . propagandizing and training in the tri-province area.

Other new policies implemented between 1964 and 1966 included educational programs to promote the use of the Central Thai language and script (Kunstadter, 1967:383–385) and the establishment of a Tribal Research Center at Chiang Mai University. These served to increase contact between the government and the tribes. Predictably, however, they compounded the initial problems by diminishing the tribes' cherished independence and self-sufficiency, attacking their traditional ways, and subordinating their interests to central goals.

In short, the policies of 1955–1966, although they represent an attenuation of neglect, were more suppressive than developmental, more explicitly aimed at control than development. These very policies led to the eruption in 1967 of open warfare in Northern Thailand—a war that had remained just below the surface, but worsening, for the previous decade. After the outbreak of actual fighting, however, the center's priorities shifted, even more emphasis was placed on the Northern situation than before, and a very observable qualitative change in policy measures took place as development superseded suppression as a means of social control.

Race (1974) dates the outbreak of organized antigovernment violence in the North from February, 1967. Much more fighting was to follow, and Race attributes the escalation as much to the counterproductive nature of the government's initial military response as to the actual efforts of the communist insurgents. The entire situation seems to have been dominated by official fears that there was an increasingly serious threat of external subversion and insurgency in the North. The government has been facing similar threats in the Northeast since mid-1965 and had been legitimately stunned by the apparent ease with which the communists had recruited large numbers of guerillas. This "had produced a sense of crisis in Bangkok" (Race, 1974:98) and now the anxiety that communist successes in the Northeast could be duplicated in the North was stimulating an initial reactive response—the immediate military control of the situation.

Unfortunately, as soon as the army deployed to the upland areas the whole problem took a turn for the worse. The army began to create enemies where there had been none by such policies as the napalming of entire villages suspected of harboring enemies and the forced resettlement of whole villages to the valleys (Race, 1974:103). These acts were responses to what was initially only limited violence. Their result was the depopulation of large areas, the creation of many refugees, an increased cooperation of the people with the communists, and stablization of violence at a high level (Race, 1974:197–212; McCoy, 1971).

Eventually Bangkok realized the counterproductive nature of its efforts; even the king spoke out strongly against army policy (Race, 1974:105). The center's failure to achieve its goals with a suppressive policy was the ultimate catalyst in producing its decision to shift to another approach in the late 1960s; namely, "its now traditional recipe of stiffening an area's infrastructure" (Rimmer, 1971:125): "efforts have been made to reshape [old] policies into new ones which will have a net "constructive" effect—namely, to integrate the resident tribes into the nation" (Van Roy, 1971:199).

Starting in 1968, there was a spate of development programs aimed specifically at the North. These included agricultural diversification programs (designed to encourage the cultivation of "socially-desirable" and marketable crops) (Van Roy, 1971:199; Neher, 1974:76), transportation, and other infrastructure needs such as telecommunications, power, and irrigation (Rimmer, 1971:125; Van Roy, 1971:32). The Mobile Development Unit program was also extended to the North at this time (see London, 1977:64).

The new policies rest essentially on the assumption that they will renew villager support for the central government. Keeping with this goal, the government has also changed its policies toward the choice and placement of those central representatives who come into direct contact with the villagers, the local authorities. The recent "increase in insurgency and the emphasis on development programs in rural areas have caused the Ministry to post competent officers to more isolated districts" (Neher, 1974:35).

In the last analysis, then, there exists a situation that directly parallels that in the Northeastern case (London, 1977). The North was historically

exploited and neglected until "something happened" to change its bargaining position vis-à-vis the center. The elite felt threatened for the safety
of its borders (Hanks, n.d.:13; Manndorff, 1967:530–531; Van Roy,
1971:27), for its political security, or, ultimately, for its own position of
ascendancy. The source of this elite anxiety lay in a combination of indigenous regionalism and exogeneous communist expansionism during a period of economic reversals and widening gaps. Its response in the North is
another example of development as social control—an increased awareness
of and catering to peripheral needs, but only as a means to the end of maintaining central dominance. It appears that, in terms of the real actors or
groups involved, primate city–hinterland relationships throughout the past
century of Thai history have been epitomized by a dynamic of Bangkok's
political power elite's exploiting and neglecting peripheral groups until such
time as continued exploitation depends upon the attentuation of neglect.

THE MEANING OF PARASITISM

Clearly, the primate metropolis dominates the hinterland and hence the
nation. Just as clearly, however, a small elite dominates the metropolis. The
division of labor and concomitant stratification between urban and rural
areas is complemented by a parallel division of labor and stratification
within the metropolis. The members of a political elite are distinguished
from other nonagricultural specialists (artisans, laborers, etc.) who serve
them. Although the latter must share the surplus produced by the countryside, it is the elite that creates and appropriates not only the surplus but
the need for an urban service class that also must be fed by the surplus.
Thus the ultimate stratification pattern created by the division of labor is
not subsumed under a metropolis–hinterland dichotomy. It may be more
aptly described by the distinction between a primate city elite and all the
other urban and rural groups with which that elite interacts.

It is precisely that level of stratification that emphasizes urban elite control of the state, or the relationship between rulers and ruled—a phenomenon so crucial to the understanding of late development—that is ignored
in most previous analyses of the effect of the primate city upon its hinterland. The work of Keyfitz (1965) is an excellent case in point. The insights
yielded by his analysis may be sharply contrasted with those of the present
work. In so doing, it will be emphasized, first, that the two approaches
supplement each other and, second, that a group-level analysis reveals much
more of the detail and complexity of the meaning of parasitism.

Keyfitz (1965) begins by emphasizing that, while the metropolis has historically been the dominant in the regional community-stratification sys-

tem, the nature of the relationship between it and other communities within its sphere of influence may vary. He sees three logical types of relationships between city and nation (p. 265). The first is "economic domination in the ecological sense," characterized by a free-market exchange of goods between city and countryside. Second, "the city may dominate the surrounding territory largely by force and organization, by legitimate power." Finally, the countryside may use means such as agricultural price supports to effectively tax the city. Keyfitz (1965:265) suggests that the second situation characterizes preindustrial societies and that, "in them the flow of goods is on balance towards the city." Conversely, the first and third situations tend to occur "when industry has outpaced agriculture." "If this is true we may think of the cities at first exerting force on the countryside, and then in turn becoming the object of force, or at least of political pressure" (Keyfitz, 1965:265).

Keyfitz creates the typical dichotomy. He clearly implies here that primate cities in preindustrial societies are parasitic. They exert force on their hinterlands. But cities in industrial nations are generative since they are the object of force and the flow of goods between city and countryside is therefore no longer on balance toward the city.

The exercise and/or receipt of force appears to be a key defining characteristic of the parasitic–generative dichotomy yielded by an institutional analysis. The primate city historically coincides with the state, thus possessing a monopoly of the legitimate use of coercive force. This institutional or organizational power is the source of primate city dominance. It also defines the roles or functions that the metropolis must perform. As a result, it largely determines the organizational relationship between a primate city such as Bangkok and its subordinate cities and rural hinterlands.

The primate city must exercise social control within its national territory and must serve a defensive function vis-à-vis other states. If it fails to perform either of these functions it will lose its position of dominance to either internal or external competitors. The successful maintenance of social control and defense, in turn, requires resources, and these are acquired historically via various forms of redistribution of surplus from the producing periphery to the consuming center. Such techniques of surplus creation, control, and collection may easily be interpreted as parasitic (i.e., exploitative) in that they are means, based ultimately on the use of force, to the end of seeing that the needs of the "consumer city" (Weber, 1958) are met, regardless of the effect this may have on the producing hinterland.

The defining characteristic of the ideal-typical parasitic city seems, therefore, to be a forced, unreciprocated redistribution of surplus from periphery to center. In other words, the primate city–hinterland relationship is defined in terms of a particular type of exchange. The primate city is able to force the countryside to export its primary produce for urban consumption without receiving anything more tangible than political security in return. Unlike a generative division of labor based on the exchange of goods of equal value, this situation is interpreted as exploitative because it is maintained by the exercise of political domination—the use of power to generate a one-way flow of goods. The raison d'être for this relationship is seen to be the abstract, impersonal need of the city to feed its inhabitants. As long as this particular type of "exchange" persists, the national hinterland is placed in a subordinate role and remains underdeveloped.

Keyfitz's (1965) analysis may well describe the rural–urban division of labor in a primate urban structure. But this institutional focus tends to leave us with the impression that, because of its ascendant position in the community stratification hierarchy, the primate city itself is the impersonal agent of exploitation and neglect. I would argue that a much better understanding of the complex relationship between city and hinterland is to be gained by focusing, not on a stratified hierarchy of communities or places, but on the previously mentioned intergroup stratification patterns or intergroup power relationships within the community structure, especially as these are impinged upon by extranational forces. Indeed, I argue here that primate city dominance defined in terms of a focus on the use of central force to define and appropriate a surplus—that is, the main thrust of Keyfitz's work and the impetus for viewing such a relationship as parasitic—may well describe certain aspects of the situation in Thailand circa 1890–1900 (or earlier), but it does not explain more than the most superficial sources of what happened during this period. Furthermore, it is even less satisfactory as a heuristic device for the analysis of the events of subsequent decades.

THAI CENTER–PERIPHERY INTERACTION IN CHANGING SOCIOPOLITICAL AND INTERNATIONAL CONTEXTS

Throughout most of Thai history the balance between an asymmetrical exchange of goods and an inversely asymmetrical exchange of power between city and countryside was an unquestioned fact of life. This was especially true for the earliest periods reviewed. The Bangkok of 1850 was a very close empirical approximation of an ideal-typical parasitic primate city.

I would contend that this is largely due to the fact that, for all intents and purposes, there was no Thai nation in 1850. Bangkok existed as a monarchial city-state capable of extracting surplus from a surrounding countryside. However, its effectiveness in doing so diminshed quite rapidly as its ability to exercise power tangibly over the productive peasantry decreased with distance from the center.

Moreover, this city-state existed in preimperial isolation: it had little contact with, concern for, or fears of peoples beyond mainland Southeast Asia. Its monopoly of coercive force was used to tax the populace. There was no element of reciprocity. The only positive benefit for the masses was the minimal safety that was the unplanned, unintended by-product of the basic state functions of social control and defense. Such states served no positive welfare function. The very idea simply did not exist at the time. This fact, viewed from a contemporary normative context, is the basis for characterizing the relationship as parasitic.

Even at this point in time, however, it was the monarchial elite that defined the terms as well as the raison d'être of the city–hinterland exchange. That elite was the state; the city was the artifactual manifestation of elite interests, power, and hubris. Only on a most abstract level can the city be seen to be forcing the countryside to supply it with food. More concretely, the surplus resources (including labor and raw materials as well as food) exacted from the countryside were created by the elite for the elite. A large portion of these resources was used for the display of symbols of elite power (temples, palaces, courts, avenues, etc.), while other portions were set aside to feed the laborers and artisans who served the elite and to maintain the armies that tangibly defended elite interests against potentially competing city-states or reluctant tributaries. Still more of these resources were used to create an infrastructure (especially canals in the Central Plain—see Hafner, 1970, 1972; and Hubbard, n.d.) to facilitate the administration of the surplus-producing area, thus augmenting the total resources available to the elite.

Thus, in this early period the case is made for an interpretation of nearly pure parasitism. The premodern, monarchial elite operated in a position of virtually unopposed power. Within its very limited "national" territory, it had no need to legitimate its exploitative and neglectful use of power with promises of future development; the idea that the proper function of the state included the provision of welfare services simply did not exist. Internationally at this time, its autonomy was also unchallenged. Within its "national" borders, the elite was unhampered in the implementation of whatever redistributive policies served its own instrumental ends.

This situation was not to last much beyond midcentury. The introduction of Western powers as political interactors impinging upon the Thai elite began to alter the nature and intensity of center–periphery relationships. Ultimately, this presence changed the terms of the exchange between city and hinterland. The new relationship remained exploitative and neglectful, but there were certain significant qualitative differences.

The main defining characteristic of the parasitic relationship is the ability to use force with impunity: Bangkok of 1850 could do so, Bangkok of 1875 could not. Its days of isolated ascendancy were over with the coming of British and French imperial powers to Southeast Asia. Policies implemented by the elite could no longer be aimed simply at self-aggrandizement. An element of self-preservation became manifest as policies had to be found that would maintain sovereignty in the face of Western encroachments. This meant that larger and larger surpluses had to be generated and, in turn, that more places with more people had to come under Bangkok's effective and continuous control. To bring about these changes, the city-state had to become a nation and the simple use of power or force had to be augmented by efforts to gain legitimacy. In other words, a sharp escalation in the survival needs of the elite required it to find new and more efficient means of fulfilling these needs.

The administrative reconstruction that culminated in the reforms of 1892 may be interpreted in this context. In Keyfitz's (1965:276) terms, the Thai nation was "created" by Bangkok as "a projection of itself over a territory," largely because "the modern state is as much as anything else the institutional means by which the primate city wraps around itself, so to speak, a territory in which its food will be produced." But this exclusively institutional analysis leaves us with a partial picture. The creation of a nation in this case reflects needs transcending those of food. What has to be taken into account are the very concrete needs of the elite, not the abstract needs of the city.

For the elite to survive, to maintain its position of ascendancy under the newly imposed external conditions, it had to ensure national sovereignty. This, in turn, means that it had to control and utilize national resources more efficiently than ever before. Simply put, the premodern city-state had to transform itself into a modern nation in order to compete in an international context. It must be noted, however, that within a "modern" nation (defined in Western terms, because Western nations were the key external participants in this interaction), power is not its own justification. The role of the state includes the provision of welfare and this means the encouragement of both political and economic development. To augment its power with perceived legitimacy, the elite was obliged at the very least to extend the promise of future development to peripheral groups as one of the benefits to go along with the obligations of their new status as citizens.

All this implies a fundamental change in the ideal terms of the center–periphery exchange. Forced exploitation and neglect are no longer acceptable facts of life in a modern nation. In order to be viewed as legitimate in its new role, the center must reciprocate for the goods it extracts from the periphery. Initially, it is unable to reciprocate by performance—that is, by fulfillment of the promise of development. Instead, it does so by disseminating the symbols of nationalism. The producers are not coerced into giving up their surplus without adequate recompense. They choose to do so for "the good of the nation." They now exchange goods for legitimacy.

Yet very little has really changed. The elite at this time was indeed interested in or motivated by national development. As a minimum goal, they wanted to make the nation productive enough to compete in a hostile international environment. This, of course, was also in their own interest. But the very real tension between goals and resources has been documented, as has the need to establish priorities (which led to an emphasis on administrative reorganization), and the ultimate exploitation and neglect of peripheral regions in order to satisfy these priorities. The result was a form of parasitism that is analytically distinguishable from the ideal type. This parasitism was not based on the premodern use of force, but on the modern manipulation of the symbols and promises of legitimacy. The periphery remained exploited and neglected, but it was willing to enter into the asymmetrical exchange for the promise of future quid pro quo made by a legitimate national elite. I have called this type of parasitism *development as a prospective end;* the elite did appear to be motivated by development (of a sort) even though the tangible effect of elite policies on peripheral regions remained negative. That is, elite policies were clearly colonial in terms of their impact on the periphery; remote regions were definitely neglected in comparison with Bangkok and, as a result, social and spatial inequalities were generated and perpetuated.

Development as prospective end is clearly not the only form of parasitism that diverges from the ideal type. The next period of Thai history—the decades after the turn of the century when nationhood was established and secure and the bureaucratic elite replaced the monarchy—illustrates another possible parasitic interaction between center and periphery.

The period falling roughly between 1915 and 1960 is characterized by a very real change in the nature of ruler–ruled relationships. This change holds equally real implications for the primate city–hinterland relationship. It was at this time that a truly national power elite assumed its strongest position of unopposed ascendancy. In a relatively secure international context, it was able to turn the bulk of its attentions inward toward problems and policies of regional management. This juxtaposition of (1) near absolute power and (2) status as a national elite whose proper role is to be responsive to a citizenry defines the type of parasitism prevalent throughout this period of Thai history.

Analytically, this mid-twentieth century parasitic interaction is a much closer empirical approximation to the premodern ideal-type than had prevailed in the previous decades. This seeming regression is easily understandable. The power elite of this period, as had its monarchial predecessors, implemented without question those sorts of exploitative and neglectful policies that maintained center–periphery inequities. I argue, however, that there is a crucial difference between these earlier and later rulers. That difference lies in the fact that the former were motivated by a goal of development as a prospective end, whereas the latter merely used the promise of development as rhetoric to legitimate their pursuit of self-interest. I therefore label this type of parasitism *development as rhetoric*. The bureaucracy and the city and the state had become institutions of social class. They functioned to serve the interests of the power elite that controlled them.

The only real difference between development as rhetoric and premodern parasitism is that the former must operate within the context of the modern nation. In other words, the power of the decision-makers depends more on the use of legitimacy than of force. This is so because, in the modern nation (in an expanding world moral order), the ideal state no longer functions as institutions of social class but as one of welfare. Paying lip service to development as an ideal and an aim is a virtual must for a modern elite, whether or not it actually provides for such welfare. It is that case in which such normative ends serve the elite merely as legitimating rhetoric, without ever being seriously pursued in terms of policy, that most closely approximates an ideal-typical parasitism in modern contexts.

Paradoxically, however, in the Thai case it is precisely the fact that a modern elite must augment force with legitimating rhetoric—with promises of future development and public welfare—that paves the way for the appearance of yet another type of parasitism, development as social control.

The recent emergence of development as social control is, not unexpectedly, closely related to changes in the nature of ruler–ruled interaction. Beginning roughly in 1960, real signs of a shift in central and peripheral bargaining positions became evident. Groups that were formerly outsiders were becoming participants in the Thai polity as a minimal, yet unprecedented decentralization of power began. The sources of this fundamental shift may be traced, ultimately, to the dissemination for four or five decades of unfulfilled rhetorical promises of development. More immediately, it stems from popular internalization of conceptions of the state's new role perceived in the light of a worsening economic situation within Thailand and increasing threat from outside.

In an era bristling with palpable contradictions between elite rhetoric and everyday reality, the power elite found itself constrained by the very ideological rhetoric that had served its interests so well in the past. It was simply no longer possible to continue to exploit, neglect, and expand control in the peripheral regions while arguing that doing so was in the public interest and would lead to welfare and development in the long run.

Starting in the early 1960s in the troubled Northeast, and progressing to other peripheral regions only after their political and economic situations approached crisis proportions, a number of social overhead or welfare programs were in fact implemented. The crux of the present argument is that it is no mere coincidence that the fundamental policy shift followed perceived threats to the elite's position—threats that could no longer be suppressed either by force or by mere rhetorical appeal. Given this context, the actual development plans and policies that were implemented in Thailand's peripheral regions after 1960 must be understood as social control efforts on the part of the challenged decision-makers. They had no alternative. But the result was that for virtually the first time in Thai history national development was equated with elite self-interest.

11

CAPITAL MOBILITY AND LABOR MIGRATION: THEIR EXPRESSION IN CORE CITIES*

Saskia Sassen-Koob

INTRODUCTION

Technical developments and political struggles have ushered in a new phase of capital mobility. This process has received considerable attention in several of its specific outcomes, notably the outflow of capital from old industrial centers and the inflow of capital into newly industrializing countries. Considerable attention has also focused on the characteristics and development of the transnational corporation, one of the key agents in the restructuring of the economy associated with increased capital mobility.

But some important questions about the broader organization and control of the economic apparatus in this new phase of capital mobility have remained unasked and unexamined. Increased capital mobility does not only bring about changes in the organization of production, it also generates a demand for types of production needed to ensure the management, control, and servicing of this new organization of production: what I refer to as the *production of control capability*. The production of management, control, and service operations is concentrated largely in major urban centers at the core and a few in the semiperiphery. I refer to them as *global cities*. These have become the sites for this particular kind of production.

In reorganizing production, increased capital mobility also brings about

*This is derived from a larger project supported by the Center for Latin American and Caribbean Studies at New York University through grants from the Ford Foundation and the Tinker Foundation, and from a second project funded by the Research Foundation of the City University of New York. I am most grateful to Soon Kyoung Cho for her outstanding research assistance and for lively discussions.

a reorganization of the capital–labor relation. Again, this is a subject that has received considerable attention in some of its aspects: for example, the increased unemployment among well-paid workers and the weakening of their position vis-à-vis employers in locations losing capital, and the employment of young women from backgrounds that promote discipline and obedience in locations receiving capital.

But there are aspects of the capital–labor relation that have not been recognized as linked to economic restructuring. Notable among these are certain aspects of the new immigration to the United States, specifically its magnitude, timing, and main destinations. These aspects need to be examined in terms of the development of several key cities into the centers for the management, control, and servicing of the global economy. For a number of reasons to be discussed below, these new sites of production generate directly, and indirectly via agglomeration effects, a large supply of low-wage jobs that are a function of this restructuring, and hence are not marginal or a distortion of the normal pattern. In this context the politicization of supplies of native low-wage workers in many large cities since the 1960s is particularly threatening. This is not class struggle as usual. It is struggle in a moment of restructuring and in locations that are sites of key control and management operations in the new global economy. It is against this background that we need to examine the large new migrations to major core cities, particularly their continuation at ever-higher levels throughout the 1970s amid growing unemployment in the United States. Global cities can be seen as one location in the broader process of the reorganization of the capital–labor relation.

The purpose then is to focus on processes that operate at the global level and find one particular location in major core cities. The assumption is that, insofar as these processes are basic to the restructuring of the world-economy, they will throw light on key aspects of core urbanization in the current phase. The theoretical starting point lies in the propositions that cities cannot be taken as a given, that the urban "cannot be reified into a self-sufficient and analytically autonomous discourse" (Scott, 1980:4), and that space, in this case urban space, is a historically constituted social relation (Castells, 1977:vii). This essay elaborates these propositions theoretically and empirically. It also goes beyond these propositions by positing that major core cities have become sites for the production of control and management operations and highly specialized services, and that there is a contingency to this location due to the characteristics of production of such inputs and other constraints that can be grouped under the notion of agglomeration economies.

The next section briefly discusses basic issues of theory and conceptualization. The following section examines decentralizing trends in the organization of economic activity that have in turn fed the centralization of management and control operations, a centralization that is predicated on the development of global control capability. There follows an examination of the production of the new global control capability for which major core cities are the main sites of production. In the empirical elaboration of the issues I use data on the restructuring of economic activity and of labor demand, including my own research on New York City and Los Angeles. The focus running through this essay is on the conditions for, and the organization of, the *production* of the new global control capability. That is to say, this capability could, in principle, be discussed in terms of other dimensions, notably the technologies involved, governmental regulatory activities and research funding that facilitate the development of this new capability, or the socialization of the costs of developing this new capability.

CONCEPTUAL ISSUES

Capital mobility and labor migrations have been studied for the most part as unrelated processes. They appear as unrelated because they constitute different circuits within the accumulation process (Sassen-Koob, 1981). As social processes, each of these is highly specific, with components sufficiently distinct to have generated what are almost two separate discourses. The closest to a statement about systemic interdependence is the proposition that these represent options maximizing capital's locational opportunities: either capital or labor moves. The market model renders this in a more general form when it states that workers go where the jobs are or, if feasible, capital is moved where the labor supply is most adequate. These two kinds of statements indeed capture key aspects of the two processes and elaborate them in terms of factor mobility. But there are other aspects of the articulation between these two processes that are not captured in an analysis of factor mobility. These aspects concern the articulation between labor migrations and capital mobility as a constituent process in the reorganization of production on a world scale and correspondingly in the reorganization of the capital–labor relation.[1]

An elaboration of the concept of capital mobility allows me to posit an articulation between the major new labor migrations and the major components in the current phase of capital mobility. Of the three major new

[1]While there are some studies in the migration literature that begin to incorporate this articulation from the migration side (e.g., Bonilla and Campos, 1982; Grasmuck, 1983; Morales, 1983; Nash and Fernandez Kelly, 1983; Portes and Walton, 1981; Sassen-Koob, 1981, 1985b), I could find no such studies in the literature on capital mobility.

migratory flows that have developed since the mid-1960s, two are intra-periphery migrations: one to the oil-exporting countries and the other to industrial zones, most significantly export-processing zones (EPZs) and world-market factories. The third flow is the migration from Asia and the Caribbean Basin, directed mostly to major core cities: earlier London and more recently cities such as New York and Los Angeles. Each of these migrations is articulated with a specific moment in the circuits along which capital is mobilized and constituted as capital: (1) the redeployment of manufacturing plants and, increasingly, office work to periphery areas; (2) large-scale industrialization in OPEC members; and (3) the restructuring of economic activity in major core cities fed by the globalization of production and the technical transformation of the work process.

There are locations on the capital and labor circuits where the articulation between both processes assumes concrete forms rather than being a function of the accumulation process that can only be posited in theoretical terms. The first case is the migrations of women into the new industrial zones in the periphery (e.g., Lim, 1980).

Central to the current phase are the second and third cases. These are more highly mediated and require a prior theoretical elaboration of the concept of capital mobility (Sassen-Koob, 1982). The massive migrations into OPEC countries resulted from the shift of capital from core to periphery in the form of oil revenues. The transformation of such revenues into accelerated industrial development demanded large imports of foreign workers. The third case is that of global cities, the sites for the management and servicing of the globalized production process made possible by increased capital mobility. These activities have directly and indirectly generated a large supply of low-wage jobs for which immigrants are a desirable labor supply. Though in very different ways, both of these instances of capital mobility are articulated with the decentralization of manufacturing and of office work.

Studies on capital mobility have tended to focus on the decentralization of manufacturing, that is to say, they have tended to posit the spatial dimension of capital mobility.[2] A theoretical elaboration of the concept of capital mobility that takes it beyond a spatial and thus locational dimension allows for an incorporation of other capabilities besides what Storper and Walker (1982) have termed the "locational capability" of capital.

Such an elaboration must reckon with the reorganization of sources of surplus value, made possible by massive shifts of capital from one area of

---

[2]This emphasis on the spatial dimension occurs both in studies of capital mobility as a locational process and in those positing a new international division of labor. Considerations of technology are put in terms of spatial issues as well; for example, transportation technologies.

the world to another. Notable among these, but usually not recognized as such, is the transfer of money from core countries to OPEC members and to the energy industry via an increase in the international price of oil and the reinjection of oil revenues into the world-economy via the large-scale import of inputs for the massive development programs launched after 1973.[3]

And it must reckon with the capability of capital to manage and to service the global production process and to maintain control over it. While not evident on a spatial level, there is a connection between the decentralization of economic activity and the new or expanded role of major cities as producers of management and control functions. Briefly, the decentralization of various kinds of economic activity is one of the key processes feeding into the need for an increasingly centralized apparatus to manage and control the global production process and the global labor force.[4] Capital mobility is constituted not only in spatial terms but also in technical terms, both through the technologies that render capital mobile and through the capability of maintaining control over a vastly decentralized global production system. This is the subject of a later section.

Increased capital mobility has brought about a homogenization of economic space that conceivably could also have homogenized labor. On the

[3]Very briefly, my argument is as follows (see Sassen-Koob, 1982). The magnitude of the cumulative money flow from core oil-importing countries in the post-1973 period makes it qualitatively different from the pre-1973 period. This flow makes possible the launching of vast industrialization programs on a scale and at a pace that render it significant for the world-economy. The value of imported goods and services necessary for the realization of these programs eventually reached and surpassed the value of oil revenues in all OPEC countries except the Gulf states. From 1973 to 1978, oil revenues were $700 billion, compared with $80 billion in the decade preceding 1973. Imports increased by an average of 60% in the first few years after 1973. From 1973 to 1978, the cumulative value of imports was $530 billion, representing about 76% of oil revenues. In sum, accelerated industrialization in OPEC countries can be seen as a mechanism for the reinjection of oil revenues back into the world accumulation process. Indeed, most of those countries now have huge foreign debts. Luxury consumption in OPEC countries could not have generated this level of reinjection of oil revenues. Given a historically developed need for imported oil, the international price of oil operates as a mechanism generating forced savings and concentrating these diffuse expenditures in one massive flow of money directed to OPEC countries and to the international oil companies. I can think of few systems that would have been so effective in extracting additional surplus and concentrating it into a few highly select targets.

[4]Harvey (1982:140) observes that Marx seems to suggest there is some equilibrium organization of production that is consistent with capital accumulation and the law of value; he further seems to suggest this point would be struck, in theory at least, by the working out of tendencies toward centralization and decentralization. In *Capital I* and in the *Grundrisse,* Marx does discuss inducements for capital toward decentralization, notably subcontracting and the move into branches of production that are typically labor intensive and small scale.

one hand, there has been a worldwide standardization of consumer demands and decreasing differentiation among places in terms of cost quality and the availability of most inputs (Storper and Walker, 1983). On the other, the large size of firms has made it more profitable to internalize transaction and circulation costs, thereby reducing the barriers to capital circulation and raising capital's ability to equalize the profit rate. ''The centralization of capital may, therefore, improve rather than diminish the capacity to equalize profits'' (Harvey, 1982:145).

However, the decentralization of economic activity contributes to the reproduction of a structurally differentiated labor supply in this otherwise homogenized economic space. The spatial and social reorganization of production involved in decentralization permits access to peripheralized labor markets, whether abroad or at home, without undermining that peripheral condition, even when the jobs are in leading industries at the core. The historical tendency has been for workers employed by advanced sectors of capital such as the steel and auto industry to acquire considerable economic power; that is, to become a labor aristocracy. Under the organization of production prevalent today, even in a key industry such as electronics, labor needs can be met through a highly differentiated labor supply. This high level of differentiation is not eroded by the incorporation of workers into an advanced sector of capital. Certain forms of the capital–labor relation can be maintained even in the most advanced and technically developed sectors of capital; for example, sweatshops in electronics.

The decentralization of economic activity can then be seen as a tendency that ensures the reproduction of structurally differentiated labor supplies in a context of global-size firms, which by internalizing the functions of the market homogenize their space of operation. In this sense decentralization becomes a mechanism to prevent the generalized increase in the organic composition of capital or the tendency toward empowerment of workers in the advanced sectors of capital.

The incorporation of labor migrations in a discussion of capital mobility brings to the fore the greater spatial differentiation of labor compared with other factors in the production process.[5] This greater spatial differentiation of labor could generate rigidities for capital. Whether highly trained personnel or low-wage unskilled laborers, labor can become one of the key locational criteria; for example, the large-scale location of research and design components by high-technology firms in the Austin and San Diego areas, or the location of certain production components in Israel by major

[5]Storper and Walker (1983) note that neoclassic economics and location theorists have treated labor in the same terms as ''true'' commodity inputs and outputs and therefore have underestimated its importance in location decisions.

U.S. electronics firms in order to profit from the abundant supply of highly trained engineers, or the location of low-wage assembly plants in the periphery.

But there are a number of economic activities that do not lend themselves to such moves. Notable among these are the large array of service jobs that need to be performed in situ: hospitals, restaurants, and office buildings cannot be moved. The employment of immigrant workers, from highly trained personnel to unskilled laborers, is in this regard a sort of functional equivalent to the mobility of capital.

Finally, in the case of the production of control and management operations and highly specialized services there is a locational contingency that gives added meaning to the flexibility introduced by labor migrations. In this case, labor migrations can be conceived of as a component of, rather than alternative to, capital mobility insofar as this type of production is central to the globalization of economic activity—a subject I discuss in the final section.

The decentralization of economic activity that has contributed directly and indirectly to the large new migrations has also brought about new requirements for the control of the vast decentralized production system and labor force.[6] The decentralization of economic activity can be conceived of as a redeployment of growth poles. Thus, the development of EPZs represents a redeployment of manufacturing capacity from core to periphery areas. More indirectly, the oil-revenue-financed industrialization projects in OPEC members can also be conceived of as a redeployment of such growth poles (see footnote 3).

The worldwide redeployment of growth poles could, in principle, pose obstacles to the incorporation of such growth into surplus-generating processes for world capital. Though not necessarily with this particular purpose, various studies have focused on mechanisms for this incorporation; for example, studies on the development of multinational corporations, on direct foreign investment, on international subcontracting, and several other aspects that have together generated a voluminous literature. One mechanism that has not received this type of attention is what I refer to as global control capability.

---

[6]This has also introduced new elements in the relation between capital and the state in core countries, particularly in the case of transnational capital. In the earlier phase of monopoly capital, major growth poles were largely concentrated in core countries. What was good for General Motors was good for the state. Today this is much less the case. High growth in transnational sectors of capital does not necessarily translate into benefits for the state as was the case up to the immediate post–World War II period. This is one of the elements of the current restructuring at the core that I have sought to capture in the notion of peripheralization at the core (Sassen-Koob, 1982).

Global control capability is a key factor in the incorporation of decentralized growth poles into surplus-generating processes for world capital. In using this term I am seeking to displace the focus from the familiar issues of the concentration of control over the economy in large corporations, or the control of large corporations over governments, or the supracorporate concentration of power via interlocking directorates and organizations such as the Trilateral Commission.

I want to focus on what could be referred to as the *practice* of global control: the specialized activities involved in producing and reproducing the organization and management of the global production system and the global labor force. The focus here is not on power, as is typical in the literature on multinational corporations, but rather on the production of those inputs that constitute global control capability.

This focus on production brings to the fore the role of major core cities in the contemporary phase of the globalization of economic activity and the differences among core cities. A few core cities are the sites of production for the new global control capability that is a necessary factor in the decentralization of the economy while a large number of other core cities have lost their role as major world centers for the export of manufactures due to that decentralization (Sassen-Koob, 1982).

This global control capability cannot be taken for granted or simply subsumed under the structural aspects of the globalization of economic activity. It has a specificity that needs to be elaborated theoretically and empirically. The development, production, and reproduction of this capability need to be examined. This is the subject of the next two sections.

THE NEED FOR GLOBAL CONTROL CAPABILITY

Several trends have fed the need for and, in turn, are predicated upon, the development of global control capability: (1) the decentralization of manufacturing, (2) the decentralization of office work, (3) the move of large corporations into the consumer services market, (4) the increasing size and product diversification of large corporations. These trends have intensified the importance of planning, marketing, internal administration and distribution, control over a wide variety of types of information, and other activities that entail centralization of management, control, and highly specialized services.

Large corporations are a key agent for this intensified role of centralizing activities. The organization of production on a global scale with a large number of plants, offices, and service outlets requires the development of a vast centralized management and control operation. It has brought about the shift of various types of activities from plants, offices, and service outlets to headquarters and has generated a large demand for highly specialized services produced both within the corporation's headquarters and bought from outside firms. But the large corporation is by no means the only instance or location for this intensified role of management and control operations and highly specialized services. Governments too face an increasingly complex situation, from the production of specialized knowledge and a wide range of public services to the management of an immense regulatory apparatus.

In this section I examine the main trends that have fed the development of global control capability in economic activity. In the final section I examine the actual production of this capability.

Of all these trends it is the decentralization of manufacturing that has received most attention and become almost synonymous with the notion of capital mobility (see footnote 2). There is a vast and excellent literature ranging from studies on deindustrialization at the core to studies on direct foreign investment and the new international division of labor. The spatial reorganization of production has become the pivot around which these analyses move, it being one of the more distinct traits in the current phase and one that has brought the issue of capital mobility to the fore.

Different kinds of processes have fed this decentralization. On the one hand, the dismantling of the old industrial complex with its strong labor unions was an attempt to dismantle the capital–labor relation around which production had been organized. On the other hand, the decentralization of production in high-tech industries was a result of the introduction of new technologies where design separated low-wage, routine tasks from highly skilled tasks, thereby maximizing locational options. Moving rubber tire production to open shops in the Sunbelt or automobile assembly plants to Mexico represents the recomposition of old industries, while setting up low-wage semiconductor assembly plants in Southeast Asia represents the organization of a new industry. Both, however, entail an organization of the capital–labor relation that tends to maximize the use of low-wage labor and to minimize the effectiveness of mechanisms that empower labor vis-à-vis capital. Thus the term *decentralization,* while suggesting a spatial aspect, clearly involves a complex political and technical reorgnization of production as well.[7]

[7]The general direction of technological change has been mostly toward large scales of operation. This has given rise to a whole series of propositions linking profitability and productivity with large size. The current phase of economic development brings to the fore a new set of relationships. What is being produced and how it is being produced have created con-

There are several indicators of the magnitude of this transformation in the organization of production. Plant closings in old industrial centers and reopenings in open-shop regions, notably in the Sunbelt, are probably the most dramatic instances. Disinvestment, shrinking, attrition, lack of maintenance—all these represent mechanisms for deindustrialization that, while not as direct as plant closings, entail a severe erosion of the old industrial complex. From 1969 to 1976, shutdowns and long-distance relocations are estimated to have eliminated 22 million jobs in the United States (Bluestone and Harrison, 1982:29). This trend continues. It has been estimated that plant shutdowns led to an average loss of 900,000 jobs in manufacturing companies with 100 or more employees each year from 1978 to 1982 (Harris, 1983). During this same period, U.S. direct foreign investment in low-wage countries quadrupled, from $8.8 billion in 1966 to $42.4 billion in 1980 (Whichard, 1981), most of it for manufacturing and associated services.[8] A growing share of this investment is for production or assembly of components imported from the United States and exported back after processing. A partial indicator of this is the value of goods entered in the United States under Tariff Items 806.30 and 807, which had a threefold increase from 1966 to 1978. The value of products coming from less developed countries represented only 6.3% of the total in 1966 but 44% by 1978. These production units are distributed among over 80 EPZs and a large number of world-market factories.[9]

---

ditions that make small scales of operation highly profitable and productive. Important here is the fact that this is also happening in *leading* industries. At the same time, it is worth noting that decentralizing technologies emerged in certain key industries, notably plastics, already in the 1930s. "Up to the 1930s, observers of the industrial scene could be forgiven for having failed to foresee that what had been true of the past would not be true of the future" (Blair, 1972:95). What is different today is that the leading and technologically most developed sectors contain a new relationship to size from what was the case in leading sectors in an earlier phase.

[8]This investment, largely concentrated in a limited number of countries, has contributed to rather high growth rates in output and employment in manufacturing. Constant annual growth rates of manufacturing employment in less developed countries generally were 7% from 1968 to 1975 and 0.4 in developed market economies (UNIDO, 1979:223). Labor productivity gains for that same period were, respectively, 2 and 3.7%, hence unlikely to explain the full difference in growth rates. These differences in employment growth in manufacturing become even more marked if we look at particular industries and countries. For example, in Chemicals it was respectively 8.9 and 1%, and in Basic Metals, 14.4 and 0.5%. Looking at particular countries, overall growth rates in manufacturing employment for that same period ranged, for example, from 5 to 11% in countries like Colombia, Ecuador, and the Philippines, and from 15 to 20% in South Korea, Indonesia, and Hong Kong (UNIDO, 1979).

[9]The main immigrant-sending countries to the United States are among those with the largest number of EPZs, world-market factories, and generally labor-intensive direct foreign investment (see Sassen-Koob, 1985b). This raises a question in view of the long-held belief that

The concrete territorial and social organization of production underlying these figures is characterized by, first, a vast expansion in the spatial organization of production to incorporate, via relocation or first-time location, domestic and foreign areas with low-wage labor. Low-wage labor here may mean skilled and unskilled workers in the U.S. Sunbelt, unskilled workers in Southeast Asia, skilled workers in Ireland, or highly trained engineers in Israel. Second, there is a reorganization of the work process resulting from the new spatial organization of production as well as the expanded use of certain types of organization of the work process, such as small plants, sweatshops, industrial homework, and, generally, the fragmentation of production into multiple separate assembly and processing operations.

A major new pattern in the organization of work is the decentralization of office jobs. It involves the shipping or transmission of routine tasks to various foreign or domestic "offshore" locations, whether low-wage countries or suburban homes at the core.

Mechanical decentralization—the shipping out of work to be keypunched or put on discs and returned via air transport—started some 15 years ago. In many ways this form of decentralization limited the possibility of using offshore locations to very large data-entry jobs with no immediate deadlines. Today, the use of satellite transmission broadens the range of jobs that can be shipped abroad and minimizes the weight of distance in both time and cost. The work is typed into a computer in one location and transmitted via satellite to another. For example, Pacific Data Services, a Dallas company, recently opened a data-entry business in China that will have 96 computer terminals operated for three shifts a day. (*New York Times,* 1982, October 3). A crucial cost factor was that of earth stations and equipment. Once installed and given the growing market, the costs of transmission have declined. New developments, such as the word processor, are replacing traditional data-entry work as documents are being prepared directly in electronic form. In conjunction with the development of satellite transmission, this will broaden the range of possibilities.[10] For example, Satellite Data

---

significant levels of direct foreign investment should act as a deterrant to emigration insofar as such investment contributes to create jobs. This would seem to be particularly the case with foreign investment in export manufacturing, given its high labor intensity. However, in my study I found that labor-intensive investment in manufacturing and ancillary services has operated as a migration push factor because it has disrupted traditional waged and unwaged work structures. This is a complex and highly mediated process that I have discussed at length elsewhere (Sassen-Koob, 1985b).

[10]A development that may further speed this decentralization of office work is deregulation of the telecommunications industry. Until 1982 companies that needed satellite data-transmission facilities had to purchase these services from one of the international carriers,

Corporation of New York offers customers the work-processing and data-entry services of a facility in Barbados, charging 20–50% less than its land-locked competitors.

The cost of labor is clearly a key factor in this decentralization.[11] Currently Barbados and Jamaica are two desirable locations for overseas office work because of overall high literacy and English-speaking populations. And employees earn about $1.50 an hour for work that in the United States pays $4–12 dollars an hour. Within the United States, suburban clerical homework is growing and may also assume increasing importance for less routine tasks. The suburbs have large numbers of highly educated women who, because of family responsibilities, may find homework convenient. They also will tend to have the income to afford a computer, the equivalent of the working class woman's sewing machine.

Another factor that needs to be considered is that the international flow of these types of items fit into the expanding trade in services generally. No tariffs are levied against international flows of computer data. The U.S. government has for years tried to prevent other countries from levying such tariffs. There is great resistance to such tariffs at various levels, from U.S. congressional formulations regulating international trade in services to GATT (General Agreement on Tariffs and Trade) negotiations aimed at ensuring and maximizing the free flow of services (U.S. Senate, 1982). In this context it is interesting to note that services are the most rapidly growing U.S. export (DiLullo, 1981). The pressure by the U.S. government to ensure the free flow of services is also rooted in the fact that the United States has the world's most developed computer industry, which has meant that foreign companies often store data on computers based in the U.S. "The classic example is a Swedish fire department that uses a computer in Ohio" (Pollock, in the *New York Times,* October 3, 1982). On the other hand, it has also meant that, while for a time this advantage may have induced only factory relocations abroad and maintenance of computerized office work in the United States, now it also makes possible relocation of office work abroad.

---

such as ITT or AT&T. These are basically re-sellers of these services because the only one that can sell international satellite services in the case of the United States is Comstat, the U.S. representative in the Intelstat system. Comstat has a monopoly on international satellite services and until 1982 could sell those services only to the international communications companies. Since 1982, the FCC has ruled that companies can now purchase these services directly from Comstat, a fact that lowers the cost of acquisition and facilitates access. Now companies can develop their own transmission systems.

[11]Another form of this decentralization is the relocation of divisional offices in areas with a lower cost of living; for example, Citicorp's location of its credit center in Sioux Falls, South Dakota.

As happened with manufacturing plants, governments from various countries are trying to attract firms seeking offshore facilities for office work. These governments are providing subsidies to draw investors, including the training of workers for the facilities. For example, National Demographics, Ltd. of Denver has a data-entry plant in Barbados, whose government subsidized the training of employees. The facility is in a factory building, it is referred to as a factory, and it is run as a factory.

A third area that has contributed to the expansion of centralized management and control operations is the move by large corporations into the retailing of consumer services. The globalization of markets and production together with product diversification require the investment of greater resources in planning and marketing to reach the consumer. Advertising and consumer financing have become an increasingly important component in the final product or service.[12] It is the possibility of economies of scale on the delivery of such services and the expanding market for such services that have led large corporations to produce for the open market consumer services that used to be produced only by small entrepreneurs. This has brought about what Levitt (1976) has called the "industrialization of service."

Standardization and economies of scale in service production and delivery are predicated upon the shifting of certain components away from the actual service-delivery establishments and onto headquarters. These centralize planning, development, franchising, purchasing, and other such functions. The result has been a growth of large new firms or divisions within firms engaged in service delivery via multiple retail outlets and centralization of specialized functions. This fragmentation of the work process, parallel to that in manufacturing, is evident in hotels, restaurants, various kinds of repair services, movie theaters, car rentals, photo development, retail outlets for a broad range of consumer goods—from food to flowers—and a vast array of other service activities that used to be largely the domain of small, local entrepreneurs.

A fourth factor that has contributed to the expansion of central management and control operations and the producer services sector is the very size of corporations. The large national or transnational corporations have been key agents in the restructuring of economic activity.[13] The concentra-

---

[12]For example, the growing trend among nonfinancial firms to take over insurance companies. According to the 1978 edition of the *Directory of Corporate Affiliations* almost half of the Fortune 500 firms control either an insurance company or a consumer credit facility (Stanback, *et al.,* 1981:60–61).

[13]Though the data are inadequate and need to be related to variables such as market size and concentration, it is clear that large firms have increased in absolute size over time (Blair, 1972; Herman, 1981; Scherer, 1980). Large firms (defined as those with assets of $250 million

tion of capital in manufacturing and increasingly in consumer services has as its pivot the large corporation. The increasing size and product diversification of the large corporation in turn have intensified the importance of planning, marketing, internal administration and distribution, control over various kinds of information, and other such activities.[14] The organization of production on a global scale with a large number of plants or service outlets requires a vast expansion of the central and management apparatus.[15] This has generated a large demand for highly specialized services either produced within the corporation's headquarters or bought from outside firms.[16]

---

or over) controlled more than half of all assets in four major sectors: mining, manufacturing, transport and utilities, and banking and finance. These four sectors accounted for 45.6% of national income. Large firms controlled less than one-third of the assets in agriculture, construction, trade and services; together these accounted for 37.5% of national income. These figures are for 1975; that year there were 2 million firms, of which 1882 had assets of $250 million or over. Of these 448 were in manufacturing; these controlled 72.5% of all assets in manufacturing (Herman, 1981:188–190).

[14]Rapid new product development, product diversification and expansion into new markets generate a vast array of costs referred to as transaction and adjustment costs (for a detailed classification of these costs see Williamson, 1980). *Transaction costs* are those involved in bringing together the supply and demand side of a market; *adjustment costs* are those involved in increasing the supply of resources whose production demands time—for example, highly skilled labor, organization structures, technologically advanced machinery, and so forth. These costs, particularly transaction costs, involve a variety of services such as advertising, strategic planning, financial services, public relations, and other liaison activities, lobbying, research and forecasting, etc. These are specialized services produced for firms either in-house or on the market that have become basic inputs in a firm's operation. Case studies of particular corporations have found that these kinds of costs have become increasingly important with the growing size of firms and greater product diversification (Cohen *et al.,* 1980).

[15]The greater concentration of capital through mergers in combination with greater product diversification—Gulf and Western owns Wonder Bread and Coca-Cola owns Gallo wines— also shifts greater emphasis to centralized management and control operations. Similarly, the actual meaning of the Fortune 500, or top 100 for that matter, may be quite different from what it meant 20 years ago, given higher concentration and diversification. Thus the fact that today there is a smaller number of Fortune 500 companies in New York may nonetheless entail a greater control over the domestic and world economies. Thus, for example, Cohen (1981) found that in 1974 New York City-based Fortune 500 firms accounted for 40% of all export activity among the 500 firms even though that city had less than one-fifth of these firms.

[16]Chandler (1977:6) notes that the organization characteristic of today's large corporations "appeared for the first time in history when the volume of economic activities reached a level that made administrative coordination more efficient and more profitable than market coordination." There is a noteworthy dynamic here. Given the large size of firms it becomes more profitable for a firm to internalize transaction and circulation costs. At the same time

The decentralization of manufacturing and of office work, the move of large corporations into the retailing of consumer services, and the growing size and product diversification of large corporations have all intensified the role of management and control operations and of the producer services in economic activity generally. The technical transformation of the work process has made possible and in turn has been further induced by these developments.

In theory, the decentralization of production units can entail a decentralization in ownership. Subcontracting has expanded greatly, both domestically and internationally. There has been a significant growth of small, highly specialized firms in services and manufacturing associated with new technologies of production and new products. There even were predictions that the shift to a service economy would reduce the average size of firms and the influence of large firms over the economy (Fuchs, 1968). But ultimately it is a limited number of corporations that control a large share of production, and increasingly of service delivery as well. The decentralization of economic activity has not reduced centralized ownership and control, though it has created new requirements in terms of planning, organizing, distributing, marketing, and financing. The result is an expansion in the central apparatus needed for the control, management, and servicing of the decentralized production process and the global force. This operates at the microlevel of individual corporations. And it operates at the macrolevel of the system; that is, in the realm where the state intervenes to regulate and organize the increasingly complex system that has a local, national, and international arena of operation. All of these feed into the importance and expansion of centralized management and control operations.

The result has been a growing demand on the part of the various agents, from governments to corporations, for highly specialized services. These services have become a key input. Their development has further made possible these various trends, which in turn have generated a growing need for such inputs. The changing structure of production affects the demand and supply of various services (Caves, 1980), a fact that has not received sufficient attention in statements on the shift to a service economy. In the current phase, the need for a vast apparatus for control and management of the global politicoeconomic system has transformed the shape of the service sector. Once only a support structure, today the producer services have become something akin to a new basic industry.

---

this new expanded organizational structure generates a rapidly growing need for highly specialized services that, given their degree of specialization, are most profitably produced on an open market rather than internalized. This has given rise to a freestanding market of producer service firms.

Capital and Labor in the New Sites of Production

The trends discussed in the preceding sections may seem somewhat removed from issues of core urbanization. In fact they are central in explaining current developments in and differences among core cities. The worldwide reorganization of production and the redeployment of growth poles has generated a large demand for a range of inputs whose production tends to be concentrated in major core cities. These inputs consist basically of highly specialized services for producers and management and control operations. A focus on the production of these inputs brings to the fore the different roles of core cities in the current phase of capitalist development. Some of these cities are sites for the production of such inputs; others are not. Still others have lost their role as major manufacturing centers due to decentralization and now feed the boom in cities producing specialized inputs for export to the new growth areas. A focus on production also brings to the fore distinctions among core cities that are such sites of production in terms of their regional or global scope.

The production of inputs for the actual operations involved in the exercise of global control is clearly only one aspect of that capability. Under other rubrics and with other aims, several other aspects have been widely studied, notably the growth and size of the modern corporation, the weight of these corporations in domestic and international economic activity, and the increasing concentration of capital—technological developments that have made possible and further induced the transnationalization and global reach of corporations. This is, again, not the place to review these studies, many of which are well known. The focus here is on a particular level, that of production, that has received less attention and that formulates issues less in power terms than is characteristic of studies on the large corporation.

The evidence, though inadequate, is quite useful in documenting some of the issues of concern here. The evidence points to the growth and locational concentration of economic activities that generate key inputs for firms, particularly large corporations (Singelmann, 1978; Stanback and Noyelle, 1982; see Tables 11.1 and 11.2). The evidence also shows the pronounced growth in the export of such inputs, and how these exports are associated with the growth of an offshore manufacturing sector (DiLullo, 1981; Economic Consulting Services, 1981; U.S. Department of Commerce, 1980). There is also evidence showing that a few core cities produce such inputs for export to other domestic areas (Cohen, 1981; Conservation of Human Resources, 1977; Drennan, 1983; Stanback et al., 1981).

The concentration of these activities in major core cities and the corresponding internationalization in the economic base of such cities has brought about a pronounced reorganization in the capital–labor relation.

The manufacturing sector, once the economic base and key export sector in major core cities, no longer is the one shaping the organization of this relation. One indication of this reorganization is the increasing polarization in the occupational and earnings distribution of the labor force. The evidence shows a sharp expansion in a stratum of very-high-income workers, including as a key component what I call the *new cadres* in control, management and servicing operations (Sassen-Koob, 1984:167). Second, it shows a shrinking of middle-income workers, a function of the expulsion from the production process of a wide range of white- and blue-collar middle-income jobs. Finally, the evidence points to a vast expansion in the supply of low-wage jobs, a function not only of declining sectors, as is often believed, but primarily of growth sectors.

First I discuss the evidence pointing to the emergence of major core cities as sites for the production and export of producer services, management, and control operations. Then I discuss the evidence on the restructuring of the job supply and work process as an indicator of the reorganization of the capital–labor relation.

Capital: The Production of Global Control Capability

The industrial recomposition in the economic base of major core cities is not simply a function of the general shift from a manufacturing to a service economy. Thus, while all cities contain a core of service industries, location quotients for different size standard metropolitan statistical areas (SMSAs) clearly show the largest ones to have a disproportionate concentration of certain types of service industries, such as producer and distributive services.[17] These two account for 37% of the GNP and are, together with nonprofit services, the fastest-growing sector in the economy (Conservation of Human Resources, 1977; Ginzberg and Vojta, 1981; Stanback *et al.,* 1981). Also, the production of services for export to the world market is disproportionately concentrated in a few major cities (Cohen, 1981;

---

[17]Standard classifications of economic activities have become increasingly problematic with the technical transformation of the work process. Here I use the classification first developed by Browning and Singelmann (1978), further elaborated by Singelmann (1978:28–36) and Stanback *et al.* (1981). In this classification, *producer services* refer to industries that provide services mostly to producers of goods or property-related operations. They are then a type of intermediate output (Greenfield, 1966:11). They include banking, credit, and other financial services; insurance; real estate; engineering and architectural services; accounting and bookkeeping; miscellaneous business services; and legal services (Singelmann, 1978:31). Producer services represent the following SIC (Standard Industrial Classification) branches: 60 to 67, 73, 81, 83 (after 1974), 86 and 89.

Drennan, 1983; Sassen-Koob, 1984) at a time when services are the fastest-growing and the largest export in the United States (DiLullo, 1981).

Though inadequate, there are various types of information that can be used to document the new economic base in global cities and the fact that it is distinguishable from that in other core cities. I use evidence on the characteristics of production and locational patterns of various industries, particularly the producer services, a key input for the global control and management capability of capital. Then I discuss the evidence on the internationalization of the economic base in these cities, particularly in the service sector. This can be done using data on the export of services, the locational concentration of large corporations with high export activity, and the levels and locational concentration of foreign investment.

In a classification of the 140 largest SMSAs for 1976, Stanback and Noyelle (1982:20–26) found a distinct relationship between size and functional specialization. Of the 16 largest SMSAs (population over 2 million), 12 were centers for the production and export of producer and distributive services and the other 4 were government and educational centers. Of those 12, 4 were global centers and the remaining 8, regional.[18] Furthermore, controlling for type of service export, the authors found a direct relationship between size and type of service export. The larger the SMSA, the greater the weight of producer services compared with distributive services. It should be noted that the larger SMSAs were once predominantly centers for the production and export of manufacturing.

On the other hand, the group of smaller SMSAs (population under 1 million) had the highest single concentration of "production centers," mostly in manufacturing. Indeed, the authors found that comparing the location quotient of manufacturing in the smaller SMSAs for 1976 with 1959, the importance of manufacturing had increased.[19] This was sharpest in SMSAs with populations under 250,000, where the manufacturing quotient went from 92.8 in 1959 to 113.0 in 1976. In contrast, in the largest SMSAs this quotient went from 99.0 in 1959 to 90.5 in 1976. In terms of shares of employment, the share of manufacturing rises as the size of the SMSA declines. On the other hand, the share of the "corporate headquar-

[18]In this classification, New York, Los Angeles, Chicago, and San Francisco were the only truly global centers. Houston, though a recipient of many headquarters over the last few years, was found to be a regional center, a finding confirmed by Cohen's (1981) data showing the large headquarters that moved to Houston are continuing to use the advanced services produced by firms in New York and Chicago.

[19]These location quotients indicate the ratio of the average share of employment within a given industry group in a given size of SMSA to the share of total U.S. employment accounted for by that same industry.

ters complex" declines with size, ranging from 20% in the largest SMSAs to 8.7% in the smallest.

The ascendance of the producer services in economic activity generally and the development of the modern corporation make a distinction between local, regional, and global service firms increasingly important. Thus, the 8.7% employment share in the corporate headquarters complex in the smallest SMSAs most probably describes regional or local market firms. I find the term *corporate headquarters complex* (cf. Conservation of Human Resources, 1977) inadequate when dealing with such a wide range of sizes in the SMSAs. Any city has legal, accounting, and banking services. But some major service firms are global in their operations and make a significant share of their earnings from the export of their services. These firms are also the ones that handle the business for most of the large corporations, and regardless of the latter's location, they are the ones concentrated in global cities.

The locational concentration of these growth sectors is particularly significant if we consider that the overall share of services in the GNP has hardly grown, rising by only 4% from 1959 to 1977 (from 62 to 66%). Indeed, except for producer, nonprofit, and distributive services, all other service categories have declined in their shares of the GNP (Ginzberg and Vojta, 1981; Singelmann, 1978; Stanback *et al.,* 1981). In terms of employment shares, producer and nonprofit services doubled their shares of employment whereas consumer services declined. What emerges from this is that the share of services as final outputs (e.g., consumer services) is actually declining. What is increasing is the production of services as intermediate outputs; that is, producer and distributive services (Denison, 1979; Ginzberg and Vojta, 1981; Meyers, 1980; Singelmann, 1978; Stanback *et al.,* 1981). This shift from final to intermediate services is another indicator of the restructuring.[20]

Data on employment growth in various service industries throws some light on the different economic evolution of a manufacturing center like Detroit and the "new" global centers like New York City and Los Angeles whose economies were once also based on manufacturing. These data are inadequate as an index for industrial growth insofar as employment is an imprecise measure, particularly when dealing with highly capital-intensive industries like some of the producer services where employment figures un-

[20]It also points to a reorganization in the sources of surplus value, away from consumers and toward intermediate buyers. The import capability of OPEC members generated by the massive inflow of oil revenues and their transformation in accelerated development programs emerges as a new source for the realization of surplus value (Sassen-Koob, 1982). See also footnotes 3 and 21 on OPEC's imports of services and their weight on U.S. service industries earnings from international trading.

derestimate the weight of these in the economy. If we include the production of producer services in firms classified as goods producing, then the share of such services reaches almost a fourth of GNP (Ginzberg and Vojta, 1981:49). The ratio between employment share and GNP share varies considerably from one service industry to another. Based on the analysis of Stanback *et al.* (1981), it would seem that the ratio of employment share to GNP share is $\frac{1}{2}$ in the case of producer services, and almost the opposite in the case of consumer services. Some of these industries are producers both of final and intermediate outputs; for example, banking. Contextual characteristics will make for significant differences in the weight of each. Thus, while New York City and Los Angeles each has a large consumer banking sector because of the size of its population, the greater weight in economic terms comes from the banking industry as an intermediate producer. The reverse is the case in Detroit. But, these differences notwithstanding, the data show the employment growth in mostly producer service industries between 1977 and 1981 to be 11.8% in Detroit, 20.1% in New York City and 30.4% in Los Angeles. The share of all workers employed in producer service industries in these cities in 1981 was 12.6%, 30.7%, and 24.9%, respectively (Tables 11.1 and 11.2).

The locational concentration of producer services is in part explained by the characteristics of production of these services. These characteristics, in conjunction with the ascendance of such services in economic activity generally, both domestically and worldwide, are helpful in explaining the centralization of management and servicing functions that have fed the economic boom in global cities like New York and Los Angeles. Producer services, unlike other types of services, are mostly not dependent on vicinity to the buyers. Hence concentration of production in suitable locations and export, both domestically and abroad, are feasible. A factor inducing locational concentration in producer services is what has been called the *agglomeration effect* (Conservation of Human Resources, 1977). Production of these services benefits from proximity to other services, particularly when there is a wide array of specialized firms. Agglomeration economies occur to such firms when they locate close to others that are sellers of key inputs or are necessary for joint production of certain service offerings (Stanback and Noyelle, 1982:17–18). This would help explain why, while New York City continued to lose corporate headquarters throughout the decade, the number and employment of firms servicing such headquarters kept growing rapidly (Cohen, 1981; Conservation of Human Resources, 1977; Drennan, 1983). Another kind of agglomeration economy consists in the amenities and lifestyles that large urban centers can offer the high-income personnel employed in the producer services. In brief, the fact that producer services are relatively independent of proximity to the buyers, combined with the existence of agglomeration economies, makes possible both the concentra-

TABLE 11.1

Employment Growth Rates in Mostly Producer Service Industries: New York City, Los Angeles, and Detroit, 1977–1981 [a]

SIC [b]	Industry	New York City	Los Angeles	Detroit [c]
60	Banking	20.9	44.6	4.1
61	Credit agencies	29.1	16.0	13.3
62	Commodity brokers	34.1	14.5	− 1.4
63	Insurance carriers	8.4	5.7	− 7.3
64	Insurance agents	21.8	24.7	13.7
65	Real estate	1.1	43.9	− 3.6
66	Combined real estate and insurance	98.2	− 30.0	− 0.2
67	Holding, investment office	7.1	33.8	*
73	Business services	24.7	33.2	− 1.1
731	Advertising	17.3	12.6	− 17.8
737	Computer and data processing	65.4	41.2	88.2
81	Legal services	28.3	48.7	31.3
86	Membership organizations	− 0.1	13.8	4.7
89	Miscellaneous services	38.0	64.7	20.2
891	Engineering services	65.0	75.5	*
892	Research organizations	13.2	29.8	*
893	Accounting, auditing	17.8	51.3	*
Average Growth Rates		20.1	30.4	11.8

[a] Source: Saskia Sassen-Koob, "The New Labor Demand in Global Cities," pp. 152–157 in *Cities in Transformation* by Michael P. Smith (ed.). Copyright © 1984 by Sage Publications, Inc. Reprinted by permission of Sage Publications, Inc. Based on U.S. Bureau of the Census, *County Business Patterns California, 1977* (CBP-77-6); *County Business Patterns, California, 1980* (CBP-80-6); *County Business Patterns, California, 1981* (CBP-81-6); *County Business Patterns, Michigan, 1977* (CBP-77-24); *County Business Patterns, Michigan, 1980* (CBP-80-24); *County Business Patterns, Michigan, 1981* (CBP-81-24); *County Business Patterns, New York, 1977;* (CBP-77-34); *County Business Patterns, New York, 1980* (CBP-80-34); *County Business Patterns, New York, 1981* (CBP-81-34).

[b] Standard Industrial Classification.

[c] Asterisk indicates figure is insufficient to be captured in count.

tion of production in suitable locations and the export to other areas domestically and abroad. As a result we see the development of global centers—for example, New York and Los Angeles—and of regional centers—for example, Denver and Houston—for the production of such services.

Whether the production of these services is internalized by a firm or bought on the market depends on a number of factors. The available evidence shows that the freestanding producer services industry is growing fast and accounts for 19% of the GNP. Thus we know that a large share of these inputs are bought. In what has become a classic on the services industry, Stigler (1951) posited that the growing size of markets would increase both specialization and the realization of economies of scale on the production of such services. Stanback *et al.* (1981) note that Stigler failed

TABLE 11.2

Employment Share of Producer Services in All Industries: New York City, Los Angeles, and Detroit, 1977, 1981 [a]

	New York City	Los Angeles	Detroit
1977			
Employment share (%)	28.1	22.7	11.3
Employment in all			
industries (thousands)	3188	1367	490
1981			
Employment share (%)	30.7	24.9	12.6
Employment in all			
industries (thousands)	3340	1398	395

[a] Producer Services include SIC 60–67, 73, 81, 86, and 89. Sources: Based on U.S. Bureau of the Census, *County Business Patterns* (Various Issues); *Advance Estimates of Social, Economic and Housing Characteristics, California* (1983); *Advance Estimates of Social, Economic and Housing Characteristics, New York* (1983); *Advance Estimates of Social, Economic and Housing Characteristics—Michigan* (1983); City of Detroit, Planning Department, *Annual Overall Economic Development Program Report and Program Projection* (1983).

to see that specialization preceded the possibility of realizing economies of scale. The increasing specialization of service functions that arose first within the large firm indicated to entrepreneurs that there was a market for these services, whence we see the development of a specialized producer-services industry. Greenfield (1966) argues that specialization is the key factor pushing toward externalization. Eventually, a large demand reduces the price of such producer services and extends the market of such services to small firms that otherwise would have been unable to buy such services. This in turn further expands the specialized services industry largely concentrated in major cities. The development of such a market entails a specialization of inputs in the production of such services and a standardization of outputs; that is, these services can be sold to a large number of firms. The specialization of inputs explains why there is a freestanding market of such services with a large number of small firms. The standardization of outputs with its corresponding expansion of the market points to the possibility that large corporations may also move into this market, as they are doing with consumer services. This would entail a shift of highly specialized functions to headquarters and the downgrading of what are now producer-services firms to outlets for the sale of such services. But at the current stage, it is the high specialization of the inputs that explains the externalization of these types of production on the part of large corporations, a trend that is currently still in a growth phase.[21]

[21] Most of the remainder of this section and pages 259 and 262–263 is extracted from Saskia Sassen-Koob, "The New Labor Demand in Global Cities," pp. 152–157 in *Cities in Transformation* by Michael P. Smith (ed.). Copyright © 1984 by Sage Publications, Inc. Reprinted by permission of Sage Publications, Inc.

The same characteristics in the production of producer services that facilitate locational concentration also make possible their production for export. There has been a massive increase in the international trade of such services and in direct foreign investment in services—another form of the export of such services. The data illustrate major patterns. At the national level, the 1980 U.S. international trade balance recorded a $21 billion surplus in the service account. From 1970 to 1980, service exports increased at an average annual rate of 19% to $121 billion in 1980, making it "a decade of unprecedented expansion in these transactions" (DiLullo, 1981: 29; U.S. Senate, 1982). Direct foreign investment in services also has increased significantly, reaching 28.4% of all such investment by 1981 (Whichard, 1982). For example, the top 14 U.S. accounting firms had 746 affiliates in developing countries by 1978, besides 895 domestic outlets (Economic Consulting Services, Inc. 1981). It is important to distinguish among the various categories included in the account; for example, receipts of income on U.S. investment abroad increased at a faster rate than receipts for other services: they went from $8.2 billion in 1970 to $36.8 billion in 1980 (DiLullo, 1981:42). Though more slowly, many others, such as technical and consulting services have also grown as a result of the increase in U.S. direct foreign investment abroad (U.S. Department of Commerce, 1980).[22] Such investments are one component in the decentralization of manufacturing and ancillary services. The appropriation of the returns on these investments, on the other hand, contributes to activities feeding the centralization of global management and specialized servicing.

Another indicator of the sale of services abroad is provided by data on individual service industries. The earnings from such sales were found to be rather high for 10 major industries in a U.S. Department of Commerce Study (1980). For example, for the top 83 advertising firms in the United States, gross income from sales abroad represented 37.6% of their total income in 1980; for the top 10 this share was 51.7% (Economic Consulting Services, Inc., 1981:85). The top 8 accounting firms in the United States made 40% of their income from sales abroad in 1977, and in 1978 the two largest made over half their revenues from such sales (U.S. Department of Commerce, 1980:13–15).

Banking, a key service industry, has expanded its international operations at an accelerated pace over the past few years. From 1971 to 1981 foreign

---

[22]One could argue that yet another version of this increase in returns from direct foreign investment is the massive shift of money to OPEC members in the form of oil revenues. Suggestive here is the fact that one-third of oil revenues from 1973 to 1978 went for the import of services, including construction, engineering, consulting, and other technical services produced largely in core countries. Correspondingly, receipts in the service accounts of core countries increased significantly after 1973. OPEC members accounted for about one-third of U.S. worldwide receipts on contracts from 1972 to 1977 (Bach, 1978).

branch assets of U.S. banks had a sixfold increase, from $55.1 billion to $320 billion. A study by the United Nations Centre on Transnational Corporations (1981) found that six countries accounted for 76% of the assets of all transnational banks in 1978. United States banks account for 23% of such assets, and within the United States, New York City and Los Angeles are the two major financial centers.

It is interesting to note that, while within the national economy, New York and Los Angeles contain distinct trends of decline and growth associated with Frostbelt and Sunbelt configurations. What comes to the fore from the perspective of the global economy is, first, their role as centers for the corporate and financial complex. There are a variety of indicators that can be used to document the growth and weight of these activities in the economies of New York City and Los Angeles and, in turn, the weight of these two cities as centers for the production of such services and management functions in the U.S. economy generally. There were high rates of growth in employment in major service industries, with a good share of these jobs in high-income occupations (see Tables 11.1 and 11.2). Second, these two cities have been the leading recipients of the massive increase in the magnitude of financial assets and deposits in the United States. By 1980, the Los Angeles area, with $104 billion, was second only to the Greater New York Area, with $294 billion in total deposits and savings in financial institutions (Security Pacific National Bank, 1981).[23] Third, there was a sharp expansion in the numbers of foreign banks and branches and in the volume of foreign assets. New York and California are the two major international banking areas in the United States.[24] Fourth, there is a high concentration of world-market firms in a few major cities, which in turn have experienced a significant growth effect due to international demand.[25]

---

[23]The position once held by San Francisco seems to be shifting to Los Angeles. Eleven of the 12 largest U.S. banks headquartered outside California have their sole California office in Los Angeles.

[24]Assets of all foreign banks and branches increased by 42.6% in New York City from 1978 to 1980, reaching $112 billion. The numbers of foreign banks went from 47 in 1970 to 249 in 1981 (Drennan, 1983). The implementation of International Banking Facilities in 1981 will further add to this internationalization of the banking and financial system. Similar developments have taken place in Los Angeles. Of the 78 foreign agents of international banks in California, 57 are based in Los Angeles (Security Pacific National Bank, 1981).

[25]There is a significant growth effect associated with international demand. A taxonomy of economic activities in New York City that distinguishes economic activities responsive to international and national demand was developed as part of the Drennan Conservation of Human Resources econometric model and data base (Drennan, 1983). It shows trends in real value added (in 1972 dollars) for the five export-oriented groups of activities, the local groups, and the overall city's economy. From 1970 to 1975 there were generally declines in value added for all economic activities, with the exception of export consumer services. From 1975 to 1982, total value added in New York City grew by 1.9% a year. Disaggregating, we see

For example, while a large number of Fortune 500 firms moved their headquarters out of New York City, those that remained showed higher growth, especially in international activity and higher profits generally (Cohen, 1981).[26] Fifth, these major growth trends resulted in a sharp increase in construction activity, mostly of office buildings and secondarily of luxury residential high-rise buildings. For example, total construction activity in New York City was up 7.1% from 1980 to 1981, compared with 1.2% nationally (Port Authority, 1982:14).[27] In Los Angeles there was a 50% increase from 1972 to 1982 in high-rise office space, amounting to an addition of 30 million square feet (Security Pacific National Bank, 1981).

Labor: Economic Restructuring as Class Polarization

This structure of economic activity has brought about changes in the organization of work and in labor demand. They are reflected in a pronounced change in the job supply with a strong polarization in the income and occupational distribution. Decentralization and industrial decline have reduced the supply of middle-income jobs in major cities, while centralization activities have generated expansion of very-high-income and low-wage jobs.

It is the expansion in the supply of low-wage jobs as a function of growth sectors that is one of the key factors in the continuation at ever higher levels of the current immigration. Typically, immigrants are viewed as providing cheap labor for declining sectors of the economy in need of cheap labor for survival. The expansion of low-wage jobs as a function of growth trends entails a reorganization of the capital–labor relation. Two sets of analytic distinctions come to the fore: (1) the distinction between the characteristics

---

all local activities had declines and that the largest increase in value added was in export activities: the corporate services with a 4.8% increase per year, followed by its satellite, the corporate ancillary services with 3.5% per year.

[26]Profits of the 81 city-based firms in the list rose from 19% in 1978 of all Fortune 500 firms to 25% in 1980; in 1980, inflation-adjusted profits of city-based firms rose 12.6% compared with a 4.6% decline for Fortune 500 firms as a whole (City of New York, 1982:29). In the case of Los Angeles, by 1980 it had increased its number of Fortune 500 firms to 21, still far behind New York City's 81 but a significant concentration nonetheless (Erickson and Harris, 1982a).

[27]In 1981 awards for office construction in Manhattan amounted to over $600 million, in addition to $700 million in 1980. The demand for office space has been very strong in Manhattan: in 1981, for a third consecutive year, the amount of space that was pre-leased exceeded the current inventory of available space, a fact reflected in the 14% increase in the average rental price from 1981 to 1982 (Port Authority, 1982:15–16).

of jobs and the sectorial location of jobs—that is, low-wage dead-end jobs can be part of highly dynamic, technologically advanced growth sectors; and (2) the distinction between sectorial characteristics and growth patterns—that is, backward sectors such as the downgraded manufacturing sector, can be part of major growth trends in a highly industrialized economy. There is a strong tendency to assume backward jobs to be part of backward sectors and backward sectors to be part of decline trends. While there may have been a historical phase when this was prevalent, it is becoming increasingly less the case over the past decade.

The expansion of low-wage jobs is being fed generally by the shift from a manufacturing to a service economy. This shift has been well documented. More complex and indirect is the generation of low-wage jobs associated with the emergence of global and regional centers for the production of management and control functions and highly specialized services. For a number of reasons, some inherited from the past and others new, these major centers tend to contain rapidly expanding downgraded manufacturing sectors and a vast array of small service operations.

What is of interest here is that these major centers contain both the most dynamic sectors of the economy and the largest share of immigrants. The fact that about half of all immigrants live in the 10 largest cities in the United States, in contrast to only 11% of the total U.S. population, can partly be explained by the large concentration of low-wage jobs in major cities. The magnitude, timing, and destination of the current migration to the United States become more understandable when juxtaposed with these developments.[28] While changes in U.S. immigration legislation in 1965 and the existence of prior immigrant communities are important factors explaining immigration over the past decade and a half, they are not sufficient to explain the continuation of this flow at ever higher levels even during the late 1970s, a time of growing unemployment in the United States and rather high employment growth in countries of origin (see Table 11.3). Nor are they sufficient to explain the disproportionate concentration of immigrants in major cities. Thus, New York and Los Angeles have the largest Hispanic populations of all U.S. cities, respectively 2 million and 1.5 million, a size significantly larger than that of the next, Chicago and Miami,

---

[28]Entry levels over the last decade and a half are among the largest in U.S. immigration history. While annual legal entries numbered 265,000 in 1960, they reached half a million by the end of that decade, 700,000 during the second half of the 1970s (INS, 1978, 1981). Annual entry levels throughout the 1970s were higher than annual entries in the previous four decades. According to the 1980 census, the Asian population had the highest overall rate of increase, 100% between 1970 and 1980, a level surpassed by some of the Asian nationalities, e.g., the 412% increase of South Koreans. The Hispanic population increased by 62% (U.S. Bureau of the Census, 1981).

TABLE 11.3

Immigrants Admitted by Area: Caribbean, Latin America, and Asia, 1955–1979[a]

	West Indies	Central America	South America	Asia	Total
1955–1959	78,557	26,825	42,278	98,856	246,516
1960–1964	120,337	43,658	100,131	117,140	381,266
1965–1969	351,806	51,344	119,219	258,229	780,698
1970–1974	318,680	44,159	104,676	574,222	1,041,737
1975–1979	413,715	73,794	155,745	879,178	1,522,432
	1,283,095	239,780	522,049	1,927,625	3,972,549

[a] Data for Central America excludes Mexico. Source: INS (1981).

each with about 580,000 Hispanics (see Table 11.4). New York City and Los Angeles also contain, together with San Francisco, the largest concentrations of Asians. Finally, New York City is the major recipient of West Indians. The expansion in the supply of low-wage jobs, particularly pronounced in major cities, can then be seen as creating employment opportunities for immigrants even as middle-income blue- and white-collar native workers are experiencing high unemployment because their jobs are being either downgraded or expelled from the production process. Furthermore, a large immigrant population, especially if organized into fairly complex immigrant communities, generates its own demand for immigrant workers from professionals to unskilled laborers (Marshall, 1983; Wilson and Portes, 1980).

To evaluate the impact on the job supply resulting from the industrial shifts and locational concentrations discussed in the preceding sections, we can use data on the occupational and earnings distribution of industries in conjunction with the locational patterns of such industries. In view of the major shift to services, it is important to note that individual service industries vary greatly in terms of their occupational and earnings distribution.

First, the evidence shows that major growth industries are characterized by a much higher incidence of jobs at the high- and low-paying ends than was the case in what were once the major growth industries, notably manufacturing. Second, earnings vary not only according to occupation but also according to industry for a given occupation (U.S. Bureau of the Census, 1976). Third, the overall result of a different occupational mix and different earnings for occupations in different industries provides an earnings profile for each industry. Some industries, such as consumer and retailing, are low-paying industries: they have low average pay across occupations and a high

TABLE 11.4

Selected Characteristics of Population of Spanish–Hispanic Origin or Descent in SMSAs of 1,000,000 or More Population and 25,000 or More Hispanics, 1980[a]

SMSA	Hispanic median family income		Hispanics below the poverty level		Hispanics age 25+ with a high school degree		Persons who speak Spanish in the home as a % of Hispanics age 5+		Hispanics age 18+ who speak Spanish at home and speak English well or very well		Hispanic population size	
	Rank	Value ($)	Rank	Value (%)	Rank	Value (%)	Rank	Value (%)	Rank	Value (%)	Rank	Value
Los Angeles, Long Beach, CA	7	15,447	6	21.2	10	39.1	11	82.4	11	60.1	1	2,066,103
New York, NY–NJ	12	10,347	2	39.3	13	35.4	2	96.4	8	64.0	2	1,492,559
Chicago, IL	4	16,551	8	19.5	11	36.1	6	91.7	10	61.0	3	580,467
Miami, FL	5	16,133	10	15.9	5	53.3	1	101.4	12	57.8	4	580,427
San Antonio, TX	11	13,284	5	26.9	9	40.5	7	90.8	2	83.0	5	481,378
Houston, TX	3	17,185	9	18.1	8	44.9	3	93.1	7	73.5	6	424,957
Dallas, TX	6	15,754	7	20.1	12	35.8	5	91.8	6	74.4	7	247,937
Newark, NJ	8	14,596	4	30.1	7	45.2	8	90.1	9	62.0	8	131,655
Philadelphia, PA–NJ	10	13,287	3	33.4	4	56.8	9	88.9	4	80.1	9	116,869
Washington, D.C., MD–VA	1	22,834	13	10.6	1	74.5	1	101.4	3	82.9	10	93,686
Boston, MS	13	9,586	1	42.0	3	57.3	3	93.1	10	61.0	11	65,696
Fort Lauderdale, Hollywood, FL	2	19,174	12	12.2	2	62.5	4	92.7	5	78.2	12	40,345
Cleveland, OH	9	14,502	11	15.3	6	49.3	10	87.2	1	84.3	13	25,475

[a] Source: New York City Department of City Planning (unpublished table prepared for circulation by the Department of Population and Research Analysis.)

incidence of low-earning occupations. Distributive services and public administration, on the other hand, have few poorly paid jobs. Among producer and nonprofit services there is a polarization with concentrations in both well- and poorly paid jobs and occupations.

Stanback and Noyelle (1982) ranked the average annual earnings for each industry and occupational subgroup and found distributive services, manufacturing, and public administration to have the highest average rank. The producer services ranked somewhere in the middle, while consumer services and retailing were the worst. The data on earnings classes shows a very high incidence of the next-to-lowest earnings class in all services, except distributive services and public administration. Almost half of all workers in the producer services were in this earnings class, compared with 17% of manufacturing and 18.8% of construction workers. The other half of workers in producer services are in the two highest earnings classes. On the other hand, half of all construction and manufacturing workers are in the middle earnings class, compared with 2.8% of workers in the producer services. The highest single concentrations in the top earnings class are in wholesale and in corporate services.

A detailed empirical examination of the major service industries shows a significant subcategory of low-wage jobs: jobs with few if any skill and language requirements and no history of unionization—in brief, jobs that can conceivably be held by immigrant workers (Table 11.5). Using the data from the New York State Department of Labor (1979, 1980) occupational survey of major service industries, I identified the full array of this subtype of low-wage jobs in the major service industries in New York City.[29] These data have many limitations. Nonetheless, the results are suggestive. First, over 16% of jobs surveyed were low-wage unskilled or semi-skilled service jobs, lacking language proficiency requirements and mostly offering few if any advancement possibilities. Such jobs accounted for 10.8% of jobs in finance, insurance, and real estate; 23.9% in business services; and 18% in the remaining service industries. Second, the highest incidence of such jobs is found in the fastest-growing employment sector in the city (and in the nation as a whole), that is, business services.

The different occupational and earnings distributions of industries in conjunction with the changes in the industrial mix of the economy express

[29]Among the low-wage jobs included in the subsample are the following (as listed in the survey): maid, cleaner (light and heavy), janitor, porter, baggage porter, bellhop, kitchen helper, pantry, sandwich–coffee maker, food-service worker, room-service attendant, ticket taker, stock clerk (stock room, warehouse, storage yard), washer, machine washer, dry cleaner (hand), spotter (dry cleaning, washable materials), laundry presser, laundry folder, rug cleaner (hand and machine), shoe repairer, delivery and route worker, parking-lot attendant, exterminator, packager, and so forth.

TABLE 11.5

Low-Wage, Unskilled Jobs Likely to Employ Immigrants: Selected Service Industries, New York City, 1978[a]

| | Selected service industries | | | |
	Finance, insurance, real estate[b]	Business services[c]	Other service industries[d]	Total
Managers, professionals and technical	104,460	65,800	140,600	310,860
Services				
Low-wage jobs	30,520	52,430	40,900	123,850
Total	36,980	54,950	83,520	175,450
Maintenance				
Low-wage jobs	9,150	1,980	19,590	30,720
Total	12,700	15,880	45,510	74,090
Clerical				
Low-wage jobs	1,420	5,020	3,450	9,890
Total	201,630	102,140	80,710	384,480
Sales	23,890	10,180	4,490	38,560
Total all occupations	379,660	248,950	354,830	983,440
Total low-wage jobs[e] (N)	41,090	59,430	63,940	164,460
% of total	10.8	23.9	18.9	16.7

[a] This is derived from a survey by the New York State Department of Labor (1979, 1980). The sample was drawn from establishments (only those covered by New York State Unemployment Law) in select service industries. Excluded from the sample were the following service industries: educational services (SIC 82), private households (SIC 88), and the hospitals industry subgroup (SIC 806). Private households and hospitals contain significant numbers of low-wage jobs known to be held by immigrants. Excluded from the sample were establishments and activities that include significant numbers of low-wage jobs known to employ immigrants; notably, restaurants. Source: Sassen-Koob in Smith, 1984.

[b] SIC codes 61–65.

[c] SIC codes 73 and 81.

[d] SIC codes 70, 72, 75–80, 83, 84, 86, and 89.

[e] The jobs identified as low-wage are only a segment of all low-wage jobs. They are those that lack language proficiency requirements, are not part of a well-defined advancement ladder, and are not usually part of a highly unionized occupation. (For a partial listing, see footnote 29.)

themselves in a growing income polarization among workers over the past decade. Comparing the distribution of earnings for 1970 and 1980 using census data, I found a significant reduction in the two middle earnings classes (Table 11.6). The two highest earnings classes increased their share from 32 to 37%, the two middle classes reduced their share from 35.8 to 24.5%, and the two lowest earnings classes increased their share from 32 to 38.5%. When we control for sex, it becomes clear that jobs held by women account for a disproportionate share of the expansion of low-wage jobs. The expansion of low-wage jobs is taking the form of a feminization of the job *supply*.

The different earnings profiles of major industries need to be considered

TABLE 11.6

Distribution of Total U.S. Labor Force Among Earnings Classes, 1970 and 1980[a]

| Earnings classes[b] | Distribution of total U.S. labor force (%) | | | | | |
| | 1970 | | | 1980 | | |
	Total	Female	Male	Total	Female	Male
1.60 and above	11.3 ⎫ 32.2	7.5	9.4	12.9 ⎫ 37.0	4.8	11.0
1.59 to 1.30	20.9 ⎭	18.6	18.9	24.2 ⎭	14.5	20.7
1.29 to 1.00	18.9 ⎫ 35.8	21.5	23.1	12.8 ⎫ 24.5	12.8	15.6
.99 to .70	16.9 ⎭	10.5	14.3	11.7 ⎭	15.8	17.0
.69 to .40	22.8 ⎫ 32.0	13.5	15.4	25.2 ⎫ 38.5	16.7	11.8
.39 and below	9.2 ⎭	28.4	19.0	13.3 ⎭	35.4	23.9

[a] Civilian workers 14 years and over by total money earnings. Source: Based on U.S. Bureau of the Census, 1982. *Money Income of Households, Families and Persons in the United States: 1980.* (Current Population Reports: Series P-60, No. 132); and U.S. Bureau of the Census, 1972, *Money Income of Households, Families and Persons in the United States: 1970.*

[b] Earnings classes are derived from the application of 1975 average earnings for each major occupation within each industry group. A basic assumption is that the relative income at 1975 levels for each occupational-industrial subgroup is constant—in this case from 1970 to 1980. I followed the method used by Stanback and Noyelle (1982) in their comparison of 1960 and 1975 earnings for industry-occupational cells (see Chapter 3). The total earnings distribution obtained is then divided into sixtiles. The major industry groups are Manufacturing, Construction, Distributive Services, Retail, Producer Services, Consumer Services, Nonprofit Services (Health and Education), Public Administration. Not included are Agriculture, Fisheries and Mining. The major occupational groups are Professional, Technical, Manager, Office Clerical, Nonoffice Clerical, Sales, Craft Workers, Operatives, Service Workers, Laborers.

in combination with the different locational patterns of industries, notably the relation between a locality's size and industrial mix. The evidence discussed earlier shows the largest SMSAs to have a disproportionate concentration of producer and distributive services, an above-average concentration of consumer and nonprofit services, and a below average concentration of manufacturing and government. Thus, the largest SMSAs are experiencing an expansion in industries with concentrations of high- and poorly paid jobs and a shrinking in the share of industries with a heavy incidence of high- and medium-income jobs.

Polarization in global cities is further fed by several trends that contribute to an additional expansion in the supply of low-wage jobs. First, the existence of a critical mass of very-high-income workers has led to high-income residential and commercial gentrification of large areas of these cities. Such gentrification requires an army of low-wage workers: residential building attendants, dog walkers, housekeepers for the two-career family, workers in the gourmet restaurants and food shops, French hand laundries, and so on.[30] Part of the goods and services produced in the so-called informal sector that is emerging in major core cities circulate through the modern sector of the economy that caters to these high-income lifestyles: the preparation of specialty dishes for fine-food shops, the production of decorative items and luxury clothing and other personal goods, various kinds of services for cleaning, repair, errand running, and so forth. It would explain why such an informal sector is most developed in major urban cities experiencing very dynamic growth and not in cities like Detroit.

Second, there has been an expansion of low-wage jobs in the manufacturing sector as a result of (1) the social reorganization of the work process, notably the expansion of sweatshops and industrial homework; (2) the technical transformation of the work process that has induced a downgrading of a variety of jobs; and (3) the rapid growth of high-technology industries

---

[30]The fine, high-priced specialty item shop emerges as a key element in this new structure of consumption. It carries consequences for workers. This type of firm operates under constraints that differ from those of large department stores, that emerged as the central mechanism for the delivery of goods in the 1950s and 1960s. Lowering the cost of labor becomes very important; there is a considerable input on the part of owners, and an emphasis on distinct products addressed to a particular clientele rather than the mass middle-class market of department stores. There are strong inducements for subcontracting certain phases of production and servicing—from garments through decorative items to the preparation of food. Industrial homework and sweatshops become a possible way of organizing production, while it would have been cumbersome for the large department stores with huge orders of a given item and many different outlets all over a region or even the country. Furthermore, the possibility of lowering the cost of labor reflects significantly in the rate of profits. The rise of the boutique and the decline of the department store represents much more than a change in shopping patterns: they also stand for different forms of organizing production.

that are characterized by a large share of low-wage jobs in production. These three trends have resulted in what I call a *downgraded* manufacturing sector (Sassen-Koob, 1984:157).[31] The downgrading of the manufacturing sector entails a disenfranchisement of the working class via the restructuring of the job supply and the restructuring of the labor force. It is worth noting that the lowest levels of unionization tend to be in rapid-growth, high-tech industries (Wolff, 1984). Furthermore, the expansion of sweatshops and industrial homework has been greatest in major core cities, particularly Los Angeles and New York City, not only in garments (Abeles *et al.,* 1983; Waldinger, forthcoming) but also in footwear, furs, furniture, and electronics (New York State Department of Labor, 1982a, 1982b; Sassen-Koob, 1985b). Indicative of this recomposition is the drop in the average hourly wage in production in these two cities, which have at the same time experienced a boom in the financial and highly specialized services sector (Table 11.7).

This recomposition of the manufacturing sector would explain why two cities as diverse as New York City and Los Angeles both have experienced an expansion in the share of low-wage jobs in manufacturing and the rapid growth of sweatshops and industrial homework. Between 1970 and 1980, when New York City lost a third of a million manufacturing jobs, the Los Angeles region added 225,000. This represents, furthermore, a significant share of the total net addition in the country of 1 million manufacturing jobs from 1970 to 1980. Orange County alone, one of the highest growth

TABLE 11.7

Hourly Wages of Production Workers in Manufacturing
Industries: New York City, Los Angeles, U.S., 1970, 1982[a]

	1970	1982
U.S. average (A)	3.31	8.50
New York City (B)	3.35	7.45
B/A (%)	(101.2)	(87.6)
Los Angeles (C)	3.60	8.56
C/A (%)	(108.8)	(100.7)

[a] Source: U.S. Department of Labor (various issues).

[31] Here it is important to emphasize that employers do not simply seek low-wage labor, but labor that can be consumed under certain conditions of the organization of the work process. A focus on the different requirements in terms of control over labor associated with various types of organization of the labor process helps to explain differences between immigrant and minority workers, or other low-wage native workers and the varying weight of such differences (Sassen-Koob, 1981).

poles in the Los Angeles region, had reached a total manufacturing employment of 225,000 by 1980, a figure higher than Houston's for that same year (Erickson and Harris, 1982b). Again, unlike New York City, where total population and total employment declined in the decade from 1970 to 1980, in Los Angeles population grew by 1.3 million and employment by 1.3 million, which is twice Houston's net job addition of 685,900.

Furthermore, the particular content of the major growth sectors in manufacturing in Los Angeles—high-technology industries—could hardly contrast more with New York City's manufacturing base, the relentlessly backward garment industry. The aerospace and electronics industries, the high-tech core in the region, represent the largest such concentration in the country and perhaps in the world (Soja, Morales, and Wolff, 1983). In the decade of the 1970s this cluster grew by 50%. The growth in employment in high-tech industries has been larger than the total growth in manufacturing employment in Houston over the same decade. Total employment in electronics in the Los Angeles region is higher than in the other major high-tech center in the country, the so-called Silicon Valley in Santa Clara County. The Los Angeles region has increased its share of total U.S. employment in all these industries, except for aircraft and parts, where it declined from 22 to 19%.

When we disaggregate some of the economic data for these two cities, we find major growth sectors amid New York City's massive decline trends and major declines amid Los Angeles's massive growth trends. Less well-known than the scale of New York City's declines and losses is the scale of the growth trends. While overall employment and population in the city declined in absolute terms, there was a 17% increase in employment in the nine major service industries from 1977 to 1980 (U.S. Bureau of Labor Statistics, 1980, 1981). Similarly, while overall employment in manufacturing generally, and garments particularly, declined, there has in fact been a major expansion in manufacturing jobs, though mostly in forms of organization of work that do not get easily recorded in official figures, notably sweatshops and industrial homework, including homework in electronics (N.Y. State Department of Labor, 1982a, 1982b).

On the other hand, Los Angeles has experienced a massive decline in its older, established industries, notably automobile, once second only to Detroit, rubber tires, and a cluster of other industries associated with the automobile industry (Soja, Morales, and Wolff, 1983). But it also has had declines in aircrafts and parts. There has been an associated rapid decline in the share of unionized workers which had fallen to 19% by 1980 (Wolff, 1984). Interestingly, the sharpest decline, down to 13%, happened in Orange County, which also had the sharpest increase in high-tech industries. An examination of the job supply in high-tech industries shows a massive expansion in low-wage assembly-line jobs, mostly not unionized and held by immigrant or native minority women. Finally, well over a third of the net addition of jobs from 1970 to 1980, was in garments. Both in garments and electronics, sweatshops and industrial homework have expanded rapidly.

CONCLUSION

The emergence of massive new labor migrations in a period of increased capital mobility raises a number of theoretical and analytic questions concerning the relation between these two flows. It also raises questions about the role of immigration. This is particularly so because one of the central forms that the increased mobility of capital has assumed is the shift of jobs to low-wage areas. The possibility of moving a whole range of factory and office jobs to low-wage areas would seem to point to the partial obsolescence of labor migrations as a vehicle for supplying low-wage workers. It also suggests a reduction in the weight of pull factors and that labor migrations are increasingly a function of push factors in sending countries.

However, the evidence and analysis presented in this chapter show that new forms of capital mobility are directly and indirectly inducing new labor migrations. Major locations for this interaction between capital and labor mobility are (1) the newly industrializing countries that have received many of the redeployed manufacturing jobs and (2) large cities which centralize the management and new kinds of production needed for the operation of the world economic system.

This chapter focused mostly on the second type of location. The reorganization of the economic base brought about by these developments along with the technical transformation of the work process have also reorganized the capital–labor relation. Immigrant labor can be seen as having a distinct role in this reorganization, particularly in the context of a politicized native low-wage labor force. We can distinguish two situations here. One is the decline of certain traditional sectors intensified by the shift of plants to low-wage areas. Lowering costs of production becomes necessary to remain competitive with off-shore plants. Immigrants are clearly a suitable labor supply that facilitates competition with plants using low-wage labor in Third World locations. The other is the expansion of a range of low-wage jobs associated with major new growth sectors both in the sphere of production and consumption. Immigrants are, again, a suitable labor supply. It is then both the decline and the growth associated with the new phase in capital mobility that create conditions for the demand of immigrant workers. To the general conditions at work in most migration flows we need to add the specific conditions generated by the current phase in the world economic system. Global cities are one location where these specific conditions become evident.

PART IV
GLOBAL PATTERNS

12

THE SYSTEM OF WORLD CITIES, A.D. 800–1975*

Christopher K. Chase-Dunn

INTRODUCTION

City systems have most often been understood as existing within nation-states or economic regions. Functional differentiation of activities and structured hierarchies among cities and towns have long been studied at the regional level. This essay investigates the extent to which it is fruitful to view the cities of the capitalist world-economy as participating in a single interactive spatial system, albeit one that differs substantially from those most usually found within nation-states. Is there a system of world cities that exhibits regular tendencies of hierarchy and specialization analogous to those found in smaller areas? I argue that correct specification of the boundaries of the capitalist world-economy, and an understanding of its political and economic structures and processes can be used to explain the nature and varying features of the system of world cities.

CAPITALIST WORLD-SYSTEM

This discussion presumes a corpus of evidence and analysis about the nature of the capitalist world-system (much of which is yet controversial and tentative) in order to proceed with an explanation of patterns exhibited by the world city-size hierarchy. Following Immanuel Wallerstein (1974, 1979, 1980), Samir Amin (1980), and André Gunder Frank (1978, 1979), we can reinterpret the capitalist mode of production as an articulation be-

*This research was supported by National Science Foundation Grant SES7825071. I thank my colleagues in the Hopkins Urbanization Research Group and Professor Josef Gugler for their comments and for criticisms of this paper.

tween expanded reproduction in the core areas of the world-system and
primary accumulation in the peripheral areas. Thus imperialism is not a
stage of capitalism that emerged in the late nineteenth century but is rather
a reproduced relation of production necessary to the resolution of continually emerging contradictions between private accumulation of capital and
the political and economic opposition that the process of capitalist growth
produces. Labor in this system tends to become a commodity, but is not
always paid a wage, and there is a structural differential between the incomes of core and peripheral workers.

The political basis of the continued uneven expansion of capital and its
ability to adapt to opposition is the multicentric *interstate system* composed
of unequally powerful and competing nation-states. In Wallerstein's usage
both world-economies and world-empires have an integrated territorial economic network that links culturally separate societies, but *world-empires*
bring these under a single overarching state apparatus that can monopolize
the extraction of surplus product, while *world-economies* have a conflictive
interstate system that prevents long-run monopolies over the whole arena
of political and economic competition. The capitalist world-economy, thus
conceived, emerged in Europe and Spanish America during the long sixteenth century (1450–1640) and has since spread to encompass the whole
globe.[1]

System Boundaries

Analyses of urban systems usually assume that boundaries are constituted
by networks of exchange. Most usually a particular type of exchange is
shown to have differential densities that define regions. Our conceptualization of the capitalist world-economy as a qualitative type of socioeconomic system specifies boundaries in terms of both certain kinds of exchange

---

[1]This reconceptualization of capitalism differs from that of Marx in several ways. Marx's
(1967) most analytic model of capitalist development assumed a single caretaker state not
directly involved in production, a closed system, and two classes: labor and capital. Marx
also implied that primitive accumulation (the use of extraeconomic coercion to extract surplus
product and to create the institutional conditions for expanded reproduction) was but a tran-
sitory state that would eventually lead to the development of core-type capitalism in peripheral areas. International trade and colonial power relations, direct state action within core
economies, and the organizational products of class struggle were held to be "historical" or
exogenous to the main motors of capitalist accumulation.

Although the world-system perspective has not yet formulated an explicit theory of capitalist
development, such a theory would clearly include the processes of state formation, class formation, interstate competition, and primary accumulation as endogenous to the capitalist mode
of production.

(generalized commodity economy) and institutionalized power arrangements (production relations) that are either embedded in trade relations or constituted separately as property rights or political domination. These relations are not exactly continguous and take different forms depending on the previously existing modes of production in an area. Thus the empirical specification in time and space of the outer boundaries of the capitalist world-economy is subject to a certain amount of indeterminacy. Nevertheless, in order to study how cities function in the context of this system we must know which cities are "in" and which are "out" in a particular period. The research reported here is a first approximation to the problem of outer boundaries based on the suggestions of the Fernand Braudel Center (n.d.) and the work of Joan Sokolovsky (Chapter 3, this volume).

WORLD CITY SYSTEM

In order to understand what I mean by the world city system, imagine a map of the earth in 1900. The outer boundary problem is simplified at this point in time because nearly all areas of the earth have been incorporated into the system and we do not yet have to confront the sticky problem of the socialist states.[2] For the moment erase the national political boundaries that are drawn on the map and observe the cities, concentrations of human population in space. Now draw lines that indicate the commodity exchanges among the cities and towns of the world-system.

What can now be observed is an exchange network among cities that has differential densities within it indicating various national and regional subsystems, but that also exhibits a transnational structure similar in appearance to a familiar airline route map. Exchanges among the largest cities of the core are dense both within and across national boundaries, while peripheral cities exchange mostly with core cities and very little with one another. If we specified this network in terms of the types of commodities exchanged we would notice the familiar pattern of the core–periphery division of labor. Capital-intensive goods would circulate among core cities and flow to the periphery, while labor-intensive raw materials would flow from the periphery to the core.

If our map were differentiated into different economic functions we would discover that the "higher" functions of capital markets, insurance, international banking, and the headquarters of transnational corporations are located in a few world cities. In 1900 London, but also Paris, Berlin,

[2]I have argued elsewhere that the contemporary socialist states remain within the larger capitalist world-economy even though their internal structures may exhibit some of the features of socialism (Chase-Dunn, 1982a).

New York, and Amsterdam, were important centers of international commerce, commodity markets, banking, and economic decision-making, truly the centers of world capital. We would also observe a differentiation between large cities in terms of how international their links are. As Robert B. Cohen (1981) has found for the 1970s in the United States, some large cities are regional or national, while others specialize in international connections. This characteristic of the world-system (that it is composed of subregions with transnational connections) should not be analyzed in terms of the notions of "internal" and "external." This assumes much of what should be the focus of analysis—those processes that reproduce the boundaries of subsystems.

Now that we can clearly see the transnational links among cities in the world-economy we can redraw the boundaries of nation-states on our imaginary map. It would be foolhardy in any analysis of the dynamics of the capitalist system to ignore one of the most important types of competition that operates in the world-system: the geopolitical military competition among states. In our conception this is not an exogenous process, but rather is the structural basis of continued competitive commodity production for the world market. Capitalism is not only an "economic" system. It is also a system of structured power based on warfare, and the main organizers of both consensual and coercive power in the capitalist world-economy are not cities but nation-states (Chase-Dunn, 1981a).

If we add to our imaginary map not only the boundaries of nation-states but some representation of the military alliances and formal colonial ties that bind peripheral areas to core states we would discern (in 1900) a shifting set of alliances among core states. We could follow the convention of older cartographers in painting the British colonies all red, the French purple, and so forth. In 1985 the colonial empires have mostly been reorganized as formally sovereign peripheral "backyards" or "spheres of influence."

If we apply the notions of urban geography to the world-system, certain central place functions may be observed in the world cities. Like all complex social systems, the modern world-system has economic, political, cultural, and normative dimensions that are institutionally located in space. The capitalist world-system is not integrated primarily through cultural or normative institutions, although these are certainly important to its functioning. They remain, however, primarily structured at the national level. Rather, the dynamics of the capitalist world-system operate most powerfully in two specific institutional spheres: the world market and the geopolitical interstate system. The most important central place functions performed by world cities are as centers of capital accumulation and geopolitical power. In this they show great differentiation.

London was, in 1900, *the* hegemonic city of the world city system in both economic and political terms. But, unlike Rome in the Roman Empire,

London was never the *only* center of these central place functions. The organization of the world political system as a set of powerful core states prevents the emergence of a single center such as Rome.

In addition to the multicentric nature of the world city system, it is also differentiated according to function. Nation-states that are federations tend to separate their political capitals from their most economically important cities. Thus Amsterdam and The Hague, New York and Washington, D.C., and (since World War II) Berlin and Bonn are differentiated in this way. Paris, long the most important center of world culture and diplomacy, has never had the advantage of being located in a hegemonic core state.

The importance of Amsterdam in banking and commerce long outlasted the short-lived seventeenth-century hegemony of the United Provinces of the Netherlands, just as London has outlasted the nineteenth-century British hegemony. The world cities of hegemonic core powers lose first position, but they do not descend into the periphery.

Two recent articles on world cities have appeared that differ in some ways from the view presented here (Friedmann and Wolff, 1982; Cohen, 1981). Both articles present thoughtful discussions of the nature and functions of world cities, but they concentrate on the recent emergence of global functions and the so-called new international division of labor. While I do not deny that the world-system has changed in some ways since World War II, I do not see these changes as involving fundamental characteristics. Rather, certain trends that have been increasing for 500 years have continued to increase (the internationalization of capital, the increase in labor productivity), while several cycles that have long been operating (the rise and fall of hegemonic core powers, long waves of economic growth and stagnation) have continued to operate, and certain stable structural features (the interstate system, the core–periphery hierarchy) have been reproduced.

The system of world cities, as I have described it, did not appear in the 1950s, with cities having been "national" before that time. Rather cities have long been both national and international. Some authors demonstrate the autonomy of transnational corporations from the control of nation-states by pointing to recent developments in world finance, such as the Eurodollar market and such offshore banking centers as the Bahamas and Bahrein. This same autonomy of international capital has long been served by Zürich, a source of security and credit outside of the "normal" operations of the interstate system.

WORLD CITY-SIZE HIERARCHY

One indicator of the nature and integration of a city system is the city-size distribution. A large literature has been devoted to the study and interpretation of the distribution of population sizes of cities within regions.

Many authors have suggested that city systems tend toward a log-normal city-size distribution when forces of centralization and decentralization are approximately balanced. Theories of city-size distributions within regions attempt to explicate the causes of primate city systems in terms of central place functions or the concentration of power resources in central cities. A log-normal city-size distribution is one in which the largest city is twice as big as the second largest city, three times bigger than the third largest city, four times bigger than the fourth largest city, and so on. A primate distribution is one in which the largest city is much larger than would be predicated by the log-normal rank–size rule (see Chapter 5, this volume). It has been suggested that national city systems in the periphery may be expected to be primate due to the operation of the core–periphery division of labor that encourages the growth of middle-size industrial cities in the core but concentrates growth in the port cities of the periphery, which act as nodes connecting the raw material producing hinterland with the core countries.[3]

A city-size distribution is a surface-level empirical phenomenon only partially determined by functional and power hierarchies within any system. Many socially exogenous variables influence the relative growth rates of cities, and concentrations of population may be due to many factors not related to the economic and political relations among cities. In addition, the meaning and causation of urban primacy may differ from context to context and across different types of socioeconomic systems (Smith, 1982). Our interest here is to understand the urbanization process specific to the capitalist mode of production. This should be facilitated by comparison with other modes of production. It may also be the case that the meaning of urban primacy changes within a single mode of production at different historical periods due to major changes in transport costs, communications technology, or other important variables. This problem is considered below in our discussion of the cycles and trends of the world city-size distribution.

One of the basic premises of most studies of city systems is that an unintegrated or immature spatial economy will exhibit a convex or relatively unhierarchical size distribution (Rozman, 1976). Thus if we examine a region in which the towns are not participating in an integrated political economy we will expect to find a relatively flat (i.e., less hierarchical than the log-normal rule) city-size distribution.

Hierarchies emerge when political power is exercised over a region that concentrates resources in a central city, or when a commodity economy embraces an urban system such that central place functions (those most efficiently centralized) are performed for the entire region within one or a few large cities.

---

[3]A project is now underway to study the relationship over time (1800–1980) between the shape of national city-size distributions and the position of 131 nations in the core–periphery hierarchy of the world-economy (Chase-Dunn, 1982b).

Using the log-normal rule, we have constructed an index for estimating the deviations of a city-size distribution from the log-normal rule. This index (SPI: the Standardized Primacy Index) is zero when the city-size distribution conforms to the log-normal rule and takes positive values when the distribution is primate. It takes negative values when the distribution is less hierarchical than would be predicted by the log-normal rule (see Walters, Chapter 5, this volume).

UNHIERARCHICAL WORLD CITY-SIZE DISTRIBUTION

Calculating the SPI on the basis of the 10 largest cities of the capitalist world-system reveals that the city-size hierarchy of this system is always less hierarchical than the log-normal rule would predict. This finding might be interpreted as indicating that the notion of a world city system is mistaken. Instead it could be postulated from this fact that the globe is composed of many separate urban systems, and that comparing the sizes of the largest cities in this way combines things that ought to be analyzed separately. This hypothesis is discussed in detail below.

Figure 12.1 presents the distribution of population sizes of the 19 largest cities on Earth in 1900. It can be seen that, although there is a hierarchical distribution, this hierarchy is considerably flatter (has a milder slope) than the log-normal rule would predict. The straight line represents the slope predicted by the log-normal rule. It can be seen that the largest cities of the world in 1900 are located in the core states, with the exceptions of Peking, Calcutta, and Constantinople. These great cities in the periphery were located in areas of the globe that had highly developed civilizations prior to contact with the expanding capitalist world-economy. The large size of their cities partly reflects the vestiges of these great precapitalist world-empires.[4] Again, the outer boundaries of the system are important for studying the city-size hierarchy. Decisions about which cities to include in each period influence the outcome greatly. This is true because many cities in Asia were much larger than most cities in the European world-system until the beginning of the nineteenth-century. These large cities were produced by precapitalist world-empires in which political power was the main principle of centralization of resources and population. In order to study the distribution of cities within the capitalist world-economy we must determine when each large city was incorporated into the capitalist system of commodity production and/or came under the sway of the European interstate system.

Josef Gugler points out (personal communication, 1982) that there is a negative correlation between the size of a territory and the steepness of its

---

[4]Calcutta was founded by the British East India Company in the late seventeenth century and so is not a city built by a precapitalist world-empire. Moghul India at that time had two of the largest cities on Earth, Delhi and Ahmedadbad. The subsequent growth of large colonial cities in India must be partly attributed to its prior history of urban development.

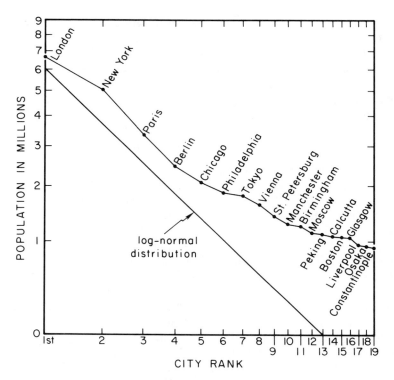

FIGURE 12.1   World city system in 1900.

city-size distribution. Thus small countries are more likely to have primate cities than are very large ones, and perhaps the very large size of the world-system accounts for its rather flat city-size distribution. This is undoubtedly an important consideration involving the way in which hierarchies are nested and how we bound them. The effects of size ought to be controlled in any comparative study of city-size distributions. We shall partially control the size effect here by studying changes over time in the city-size distribution of the world-system. Since the system gets larger over the period of our study, the size effect should result in a trend toward a flatter distribution.

CHANGES IN THE WORLD CITY HIERARCHY

The hypothesis that world cities do not really form a single integrated system can be further investigated by observing changes over time in the world city-size hierarchy. If it is true that the largest cities within the capitalist world-economy are parts of an immature or unintegrated set of separate regional systems, then we should observe a trend from an extremely flat distribution at an earlier time point toward the somewhat more hierarchical distribution shown in Figure 12.1 and then on to an even more hierarchical distribution as the twentieth century integration of the world-economy proceeds. This is based on the assumption that the unintegrated system is replaced over time with the more hierarchical distribution produced by the efficient location of central place functions in an integrated world commodity economy. Few would dispute the contention that the capitalist world-economy is more interdependent and integrated in 1980 than it was in 1800 or in the sixteenth century. If the hypothesis of central place theory holds for the world-economy, a more log-normal city-size hierarchy should emerge from the less integrated system of earlier centuries. However, if the size effect discussed above is the main determinant, the world city-size distribution should become flatter during periods when the system is expanding, and, since it never decreases its territory, the world-city system should never become more hierarchical.

Figure 12.2 plots the city-size distribution of, first, Europe from A.D. 800 to 1500, and then the expanding European world-economy from 1500 to 1975. It can be seen that, instead of the predicted secular trend from a

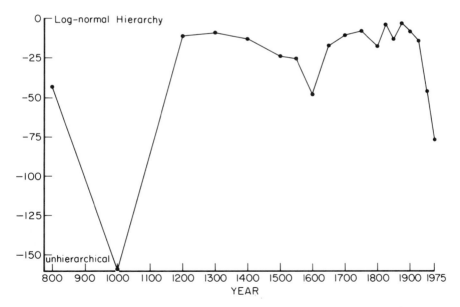

FIGURE 12.2   World city-size distribution, A.D. 800–1975. SPI computed from Table 12.1.

flatter to a more hierarchical distribution, the city-size hierarchy exhibits cyclical fluctuations that contradict the simple predictions made above.

WORLD CITIES AND THE INTERSTATE SYSTEM

Even though there are large variations in the degree of hierarchy over time shown in Figure 12.2, the city-size distribution of Europe and of the modern world-system is always flatter than the log-normal rule would predict. That is to say, the SPI always takes on negative values, but these vary from -3 in 1875 (closest to log-normal) to -159 for the completely decentralized cities of devolved European feudalism in the year 1000. I consider explanations for the variations below, but a prior question is why the world city system is, in general, less hierarchical than most national or regional city systems. As is pointed out below, the most common explanation for a flat distribution is that the area in question is not integrated into a single commodity economy. This undoubtedly accounts for the extreme flatness of the year 1000, but we have rejected this as an explanation of later decentralization because there is no secular trend toward greater hierarchy, although we know that the world-economy, especially in the twentieth century, becomes more economically integrated.

In addition to the size effect discussed above, what are the possible explanations for the fact that the world city system is generally flatter than national city systems? I suggest two features to explain this, and these are most relevant to the understanding of the system after the capitalist mode of production became dominant in the long sixteenth century.[5] The first is the structure of the interstate system. The multicentric polity that organizes the capitalist world-economy creates a long-run tendency to reproduce a certain level of decentralization in the system.

World-empires are much more likely to have hierarchical city-size distributions than are world-economies because they have a single political center. This generalization is supported by the archeological evidence on city systems assembled by Kowalewski (1982), although empires vary in their degree of urban primacy over time corresponding to changes in the centralization of power. A multicentric state system necessarily creates a number of world cities that compete with one another for power and central place functions within the larger system. This corresponds to another feature of the capitalist world-system; that is, it is composed of nested and overlapping subregions that are integrated into a single larger world net-

[5]The "long sixteenth century" is the period between 1450 and 1640 when, according to Immanuel Wallerstein (1974), agrarian capitalism became the dominant mode of production in the European world-economy.

TABLE 12.1

The World City-Size Hierarchy, A.D. 800–1975: Population[a]

FEUDAL EUROPE (EXCLUDES MOSLEM SPAIN)

	800		1000		1200		1300		1400
SPI =	**−43**	**SPI =**	**−159**	**SPI =**	**−10**	**SPI =**	**−8**	**SPI =**	**−14**
Rome	50	Ratisbon	40	Palermo	150	Paris	228	Paris	275
Naples	30	Amalfi[c]	35	Paris	110	Venice	110	Bruges	125
Verona	30	Rome	35	Venice	70	Milan	100	Milan	125
Metz	25	Pavia	30	Milan	60	Genoa	100	Venice	110
Paris	25	Mainz	30	Cologne	50	Seville	90	Genoa	100
Tours	20	Naples	30	London	40	Florence	60	Prague	95
Milan	25	Milan	30	Rouen	40	Cologne	54	Ghent	70
Reims	20	Laon (Fr.)	30	Bologna	35	Rouen	50	Seville	70
Pavia	15–20	London	25	Rome	35	Bruges	50	Rouen	70
Ratisbon[b]	15–20	Paris	20	Toledo	35	Valencia	44	Florence	61

CAPITALIST WORLD–ECONOMY

	1500		1550		1600		1650		1700
SPI =	**−24**	**SPI =**	**−25**	**SPI =**	**−48**	**SPI =**	**−17**	**SPI =**	**−11**
Paris	225	Paris	260	Naples	275	Paris	455	London	550
Naples	125	Naples	245	Paris	250	London	410	Paris	530
Venice	115	Venice	171	London	187	Naples	300	Naples	207
Milan	104	Lyon	108	Venice	151	Lisbon	170	Lisbon	188
Bruges	90	Granada	85	Potosi[d]	148	Venice	134	Amsterdam	172
Ghent	80	Seville	85	Seville	144	Potosí	130	Rome	149
Lyon	80	Milan	85	Milan	119	Palermo	128	Venice	143
Rouen	75	Lisbon	85	Lisbon	110	Rome	124	Milan	124
Florence	70	London	76	Granada	110	Amsterdam	110	Palermo	113
Granada	70	Antwerp	76	Rome	109	Lyon	109	Madrid	110

(*Continued*)

TABLE 12.1 (Continued)

CAPITALIST WORLD-ECONOMY

1750		1800		1825		1850		1875	
SPI = −9		SPI = −16		SPI = −4		SPI = −12		SPI = −3	
London	676	London	861	London	1,335	London	2,320	London	4,241
Paris	560	*Constantinople*	570	Paris	855	*Peking*	1,648	Paris	2,250
Naples	324	Paris	547	Constantinople	675	Paris	1,314	New York	1,900
Amsterdam	219	Naples	430	Naples	350	*Canton*	800	Peking	1,310
Lisbon	213	*Cairo*	263	St. Petersburg	324	Constantinople	785	Berlin	1,045
Vienna	169	Moscow	238	Bombay	300	*Hangchow*	700	Vienna	1,001
*Moscow*ᵉ	161	Lisbon	237	Vienna	288	New York	682	Canton	944
Venice	158	*Patna*	235	Patna	269	Bombay	575	Philadelphia	791
Rome	157	Vienna	231	Moscow	262	*Yedo*	567	Tokyo	780
St. Petersburg	138	St. Petersburg	220	Cairo	260	*Soochow*	550	St. Petersburg	764

1900ᶠ		1910		1920		1930		1940	
SPI = −10		SPI = −8		SPI = −15		SPI = −17		SPI = −29	
London	6,586	London	7,256	New York	8,490	New York	10,859	New York	11,660
New York	5,048	New York	7,049	London	7,488	London	8,216	London	8,700
Paris	3,330	Paris	2,888	Berlin	3,801	Tokyo	5,876	Tokyo	7,358
Berlin	2,424	Chicago	2,752	Chicago	3,521	Chicago	4,675	Paris	6,005
Chicago	2,092	Philadelphia	2,268	Tokyo	3,358	Berlin	4,243	Chicago	4,825
Philadelphia	1,892	Tokyo	2,186	Paris	2,907	Philadelphia	3,137	Berlin	4,332
Tokyo	1,818	Berlin	2,071	Philadelphia	2,714	Shanghai	3,124	Moscow	4,137
Vienna	1,675	Osaka	2,037	Osaka	1,961	Moscow	2,997	Buenos Aires	4,089
St. Petersburg	1,439	Vienna	2,031	Vienna	1,866	Osaka	2,990	Shanghai	3,595
Manchester	1,255	St. Petersburg	1,962	Buenos Aires	1,632	Paris	2,891	Calcutta	3,436

1950		1960		1970		1975	
SPI = −45		SPI = −63		SPI = −71		SPI = −86	
NY-NJ[g]	12,300	NY-NJ	15,422	NY-NJ	18,443	NY-NJ	19,800
London	10,400	London	10,727	Tokyo–Yokohama	14,865	Tokyo–Yokohama	17,700
Rhein–Ruhr	6,900	Tokyo–Yokohama	10,685	London	10,588	Osaka	13,770
Tokyo–Yokohama	6,700	Rhein–Ruhr	8,712	Shanghai	10,000	Mexico City	11,900
Paris	5,900	Osaka	8,122	Osaka	9,818	Shanghai	11,600
Shanghai	5,800	Shanghai	7,432	Los Angeles	9,530	Los Angeles	10,800
Buenos Aires	5,300	Paris	7,230	Rhein–Ruhr	9,337	São Paulo	10,700
Chicago	4,900	Los Angeles	7,109	Mexico City	8,997	London	10,400
Moscow	4,800	Buenos Aires	6,925	Paris	8,510	Rhein–Ruhr	9,300
Calcutta	4,800	Calcutta	6,522	Buenos Aires	8,469	Buenos Aires	9,300

[a] SPI, Standardized Primary Index. Population given in thousands. Sources: Chandler and Fox (1974); Mitchell (1976); Donald J. Bogue (1953); United Nations (1980); and additional sources for urban agglomerations.

[b] Regensburg, Bavaria.

[c] Near Naples.

[d] Bolivian boomtown.

[e] Cities shown in italics have been recently incorporated into the expanding capitalist world-economy.

[f] Figures for 1900–1940 are for municipalities and surrounding suburbs.

[g] New York–Northeastern New Jersey.

work. In other words, there are national and regional city systems that have a certain degree of boundedness due mostly to the operations of territorial state boundaries, but also due to geographic barriers to exchange, and these subregions are integrated into the larger network that is the world market. The closure or openness of national systems varies, of course, and it has been hypothesized that national closure increases during periods of overall economic stagnation as producers try to use political leverage to protect markets and incomes, while, during periods of world economic expansion, national systems become more open and world trade flows more in accord with market price considerations. This cycle of openness and closure to trade corresponds to changes in the structure of the interstate system. Periods of openness and economic expansion correspond to periods in which a single hegemonic core power holds clear sway in terms of productive advantage in a new lead core industry. Periods of closure and stagnation follow when other core powers become more economically competitive and eventually challenge the geopolitical dominance of the hegemone (Chase-Dunn, 1978). This cycle of core competition may be the main determinant of variation in the world city-size distribution, but before pursuing this line of thought let us look more closely at Figure 12.2 and Table 12.1.

HISTORICAL REVERSALS IN THE WORLD CITY-SIZE HIERARCHY

Inspection of Figure 12.2 reveals two and a half cycles in the city-size hierarchy since 800, with peaks of hierarchy in 800, 1300, 1875, and a small one in 1920. In this section I discuss the reasons for the changes in direction of the plotted SPI in the light of theories about city systems and information on the size of particular cities given in Table 12.1. A general overview of the reversals can be interpreted in terms of the demise of the Roman city system into European feudalism, the rise of the capitalist cities and administrative cities of the European nation-states, and then the cycle of core competition (the rise and fall of hegemonic core powers and their world cities).

DISINTEGRATION OF THE ROMAN CITY SYSTEM

In 800 the city-size hierarchy of Christian Europe reveals a somewhat less than log-normal but still hierarchical system that was the vestige of the Roman Empire. In A.D. 100 the Roman Empire had a city system that was more hierarchical than this, although not primate (see Table 12.2). Rome itself had 650,000 residents, while Alexandria, the second largest city in the empire, had 400,000. The political–military primacy of Rome created a log-

TABLE 12.2

The Roman World-Empire: City Populations[a]

	A.D. 100[b]		A.D. 361[c]
Rome	650	Constantinople	350
Alexandria	400	Rome	250
Ephesus	200	Alexandria	200
Antioch	150	Carthage	175[d]
Apamea	125	Antioch	150
Pergamum	120	Memphis	120[d]
Cadiz	100	Ephesus	100
Corinth	100	Milan	85[d]
Sardis	100	Edessa	
Memphis	95[d]	Corinth	
Carthage	90	Pergamum	
Edessa	85[d]		

[a] Population given in thousands. Source: Chandler and Fox (1974, p. 303).

[b] SPI $= -.5$, calculated on the eight largest cities.

[c] SPI $= -.17$, calculated on the eight largest cities.

[d] My interpolation.

normal city-size distribution at the level of the empire as a whole. The city-size hierarchy was not primate, partly because Roman expansion incorporated into the empire already very large cities of previous empires, such as Alexandria. If we exclude Alexandria from the hierarchy and look at the cities that grew as a result of the operation of the Roman world-empire itself,[6] the population primacy of Rome is much greater.

Roman primacy was built primarily on conquest and the imposition of a system of tribute that coordinated a territorial division of labor through a central state apparatus. The system had to expand in order to survive because of the need to replenish slave labor through warfare (Hopkins, 1978) and to pay the overhead costs of political integration. Political–military organization and technology eventually reached the point of zero returns from further effort, and the involution of the system began (Anderson, 1974a). By A.D. 361 the city system, now centered in Constantinople, had become much less hierarchical and the cities much smaller (see Table 12.2).

Looking at the size distribution within Christian Europe in A.D. 800 shows the vestigial hierarchy of the Roman cities. Table 12.1 shows the population sizes from which Figure 12.2 is calculated. In 800 the cities were smaller than during the empire, but trade and the urban system continued despite

[6] Norman J. G. Pounds (1969) maps and describes the establishment of Roman cities over the European region of the empire.

political fragmentation (Pirenne, 1980). By the year 1000 the city-size distribution had become almost completely flat and the size of cities decreased markedly. This extremely flat city-size distribution was the result of the involution of the spatial economy of Europe and the rise of the self-sufficient manorial economy. Long-distance and regional trade declined to a trickle and cities shrank to ecclesiastical centers or military strongholds. The obstacles to trade with Africa and the Levant posed by expansionist Islam reduced Europe to a prototypical feudalism of manorial isolation, political fragmentation, and urban decline.

CAPITALIST CITIES AND NATION-STATES

By A.D. 1200 a hierarchical city system was reemerging in Europe. This hierarchy was based on the growth of the political capitals of strong medieval states (Palermo and Paris) and the renaissance of the capitalist city states of Italy. This rank–size hierarchy reflected both the emergence of a spatial division of labor and uneven rates of growth due to localized causes. Capetian Paris, which emerged as the largest city by 1300, was a center of early French state-building, European trade, and cultural influence.

Russell's (1972:240) study, *Medieval Regions and Their Cities,* shows that 15 of the 18 regional city systems in feudal Europe were either log-normal or less hierarchical than log-normal. Most of Russell's regions are studied in the period from 1250 to 1348. Thus, in this period of urban growth in the "interstices" of fuedalism, a Europe-wide hierarchy emerged and regional city systems were most often not primate.

CONTENDING POWER CENTERS

From 1300 the emergence of competing centers turned the trend of the city system again toward less hierarchy as the Hundred Years War, Burgundian ascendance, and eventually the Hapsburg Empire challenged Parisian centrality. Somewhat surprising, at least to me, is the rapid growth of Naples. Whereas cities in Spain and Austria do not attain top rank, Naples, a conquered city used by the Spanish in their effort to dominate Italy, is the largest city in Europe in 1600. This well illustrates the point made above that population size and the location of control are not perfectly correlated. Another example of the same point is the rise and fall of Potosí, a South American silver boomtown, which was the fifth largest city in the capitalist world-economy in 1600. The concentration of coerced labor in this city high in the Andes to extract an entire mountain of silver for export to the core was certainly the consequence of core power, but was not an indication of the central location of Potosí in the world power structure.

By 1650 the continuing flatness of the European city system was due largely to the rapid growth of London, which surpassed Paris by 1700. E. A. Wrigley's (1978) discussion of the rapid growth of London deals with its importance for the development of the English economy, but not the causes of its growth. The world-system perspective does not emphasize the importance of international as opposed to intranational factors. Instead the point is that both "internal" and "external" processes operate in the context of the larger system. The interrelated processes of British state formation, continued commodification of agriculture, and success in both the Atlantic economy and the European interstate system combined to account for London's growth.

The long period of flatness of the European city system began with the downturn of Parisian prominence in 1300 and lasted until the arrival of a new hierarchy centered on London in 1825. This decline of one hierarchy and the rise of a new hierarchy, unlike the earlier dip between 800 and 1200, was not based on the disintegration of a space-economy, but rather on the fragmentation of political hegemony into a multicentric interstate system, and then the emergence of a new hegemonic core state, the United Kingdom of Great Britain. The world economy of market exchange continued to become more integrated over this period, albeit somewhat unevenly. What changed was the distribution of power among states, and indeed this is the period of the first formation of the European interstate system itself. As Frederic Lane (1973:241) put it, "the Italian state system was being expanded into a European state system" based on the institutions of diplomacy, shifting alliances, and periodic warfare. And this political–military matrix of competition among states was the fertile context for an emerging international market economy based partly on mercantile power and partly on competitive advantage in production.

Perry Anderson's (1974b) analysis of the rise of absolutism shows how different class structures and coalitions led to the emergence of the nation-states across Europe. Although Anderson downplays the importance of capitalist production and trade in his analysis of absolutism, his work may be reinterpreted in the context of the study of the role of cities in the emergence of the European world-economy. The commercial and landed classes of the Italian city states merged such that their political sovereignty, seen in the birth of the municipal communes, was unchallenged within their own polity. This created an early interpenetration of capitalist and state interests on a small scale (the city and its immediate hinterland). In Northern Europe the capitalist cities, growing in the interstices of the manorial economy, were not sufficiently powerful to dominate the feudal lords, although they did achieve significant and important autonomy within municipal boundaries. Their resources were important enough to allow kings to play the landed nobility and the urban patricians against one another, thus building larger nation-states. This created home markets of much greater size and allowed mercantilism abroad to be combined with integration of the national market at home, providing a fertile context for the continued expansion of capitalist production. The resulting international economy and interstate system that emerged in Europe was on a much greater scale, including the Baltic and the Atlantic with the older Mediterranean commodity economy.

The emergence of the Hapsburg Empire as the continental hegemone did not create a hierarchical city system in Europe. In part this was because the Hapsburg Empire did not have a single administrative center. Naples, an important center of Hapsburg power and of the regional trade that shifted south after the expulsion of the Moors, was the largest city in Europe in 1600, but it did not form a hierarchical city system. Paris and London soon outdistanced Naples as the long struggle between England and France for world hegemony began. The Dutch interlude did not have much impact on the European city system. Amsterdam appeared in the top 10 cities in 1650 just as the Dutch golden age was about to end (Barbour, 1963). Indeed Amsterdam's centrality improved as the Dutch hegemony in the maritime economy declined, a pattern repeated by London and New York in the later British and United States hegemonies. This may have been due to the shifting specialization of an economically hegemonic power from competitive advantage in production to the performance of central place services for the world economy such as commodity trading, international banking, and communications (Chase-Dunn, 1981b).

Table 12.1 italicizes the cities that were recently incorporated into the capitalist world-economy, usually into the periphery. These large cities, already discussed as the product of precapitalist systems, altered the city-size distribution to some extent. For example the incorporation of China, which we have designated as occurring between 1825 and 1850, brought 4 cities into the 10 largest cities of the capitalist world-economy. The very large size of Peking in 1850 temporarily caused the trend of the SPI to register a change in direction.[7] The continued rapid growth of London resulted in a

---

[7]This is the only part of the change in the world city-size distribution that can be attributed to the size effect mentioned above. Generally the territorial expansion of the system incorporated areas without large cities, although even small cities could be expected to flatten the overall distribution. Perhaps the fact that we are here studying only the very top of the city-size distribution hides the operation of the size effect. The study of changes in the distribution of all urban places in the world-system would probably reveal a correspondence between periods of expansion and increasing flatness of certain portions of the city-size distribution.

peak of the city-size hierarchy in 1875. This corresponded rather well with Great Britain's golden age of hegemony in the world-economy.

It is interesting to note that the *national* city-size hierarchy of Britain, which has been primate since Roman times, showed a trend toward less primacy, due to the rapid growth of the industrial cities between 1800 and 1850, but after that London's primacy began to increase again as British hegemony in core production declined with the rise of competitors in other core states. London's relatively greater growth rate in the last half of the nineteenth century (relative to the other cities within Britain) was due to the specialization of the economy in international central place functions, such as banking and insurance, as well as the location of world commodity and capital markets in the city (Hobsbawm, 1968), and the concentration of small batch processing and specialty manufacturing in the London area (Jones, n.d.).

By 1900 New York was catching up with London, but they were both so much larger than the other cities that the overall distribution remained hierarchical. New York passed London between 1910 and 1920 and achieved its own hierarchical peak in the 1920s and 1930s, corresponding to the hegemony in world material production of the United States. Since 1950 U.S. hegemony in world production was decreasing even while its golden age of political–military centrality had just arrived. Meyer *et al.* (1975:232) show that the U.S. GNP as a percentage of world product is 42% in 1950, 36% in 1960, and 30% in 1970.

The city-size distribution of the United States has always been less hierarchical than log-normal, due in part to the large geographic size of the country and the constitutional differentiation between political capitals and commercial cities. Thus Washington, D.C., and New York City divide functions that are located together in London and Westminster, and most of the single states of the U.S. federation have a similar differentation between the political capital and the largest commercial city.

Robert B. Cohen (1981) has shown that U.S. cities are also differentiated in the extent to which they are national, regional, or international cities. Studying the location of the headquarters of U.S.-based multinational corporations, he finds New York City and San Francisco to be the cities most oriented toward the international economy. The large size of the United States also makes it possible for the process of uneven development, which usually leads to the decline of hegemonic core states, to take place to a certain extent *within* the national boundaries. Thus the decline of the Northeastern cities is compensated by the rise of the cities of the Sunbelt. This has the result of prolonging and ameliorating, to a certain extent, the decline of U.S. hegemony in the world-economy (Chase-Dunn, 1981b).

One problem that now besets our study of world cities is the increasing difficulty of bounding cities in the twentieth century. From 1900 to 1940, I have used figures for municipalities and surrounding suburbs. After 1950 I use the figures for metropolitan agglomerations as defined by the United Nations. The formation of extensive conurbations in the core countries of the world makes it increasingly difficult to define what we mean by *city*, and thus the study of the city-size distributions becomes increasingly arbitrary, depending almost entirely on how we decide to combine metropoli into agglomerations.

In a sense this is a consequence of the process of urbanization itself. Many core countries have reached a situation in which nearly the entire population is urban and urban areas have interconnected so extensively that the definition of cities is extremely problematic.

Nevertheless, using the United Nations definitions of agglomerations, we can see a continuation of the trend toward a less hierarchical world city-size distribution which began in the 1920s. This may be due to the emergence of a new hegemonic world city (perhaps Tokyo) which will soon pass New York and establish a new hierarchy, thus continuing the cycles of hierarchy and flatness that have occurred in the past. Whether or not this happens depends on a number of political, economic, and technological variables that are very difficult to predict. It is possible, for example, to argue that the economics of location will no longer operate as strongly in the world-economy because of the rapid decline in transport costs and the explosion of communications technology. The location of any activity matters much less than it did in the past.

On the other hand, there is little reason to believe that the deep structural dynamics that have operated in the capitalist world-economy have undergone any fundamental change, and these will continue to have a great impact on the prosperity and growth rates of cities. World politics appears to be passing through another period of increasing interstate conflict and economic disorganization. This would lead us to predict a continuation of relative flatness in the world city-size hierarchy.

Another trend evident in Table 12.1 is the increasing presence of semiperipheral cities in the list of the world's largest metropolitan areas. In 1975 Mexico City ranked fourth, Shanghai fifth, and São Paulo seventh. These giant cities are truly semiperipheral in that they combine large "overurbanized" informal sectors with core-like industrial and service sectors dominated by large corporations. The kind of urbanization that has occurred in peripheral areas has been shown to differ greatly from that which occurred in core countries (Bairoch, 1975:Chapter 8; Kentor, 1981). For example, my study of Latin American national city systems shows that urban primacy emerged in the 1920s, 1930s, and 1940s. Before that some Latin American countries were primate and others were not. This was also the case with core countries: some, like Britain and France, were primate, while others (the United States and Germany) were not. Comparing 19 Latin American countries with 17 countries located in the core of the world-economy reveals that there was no significant difference in the level of urban primacy until the 1920s. By 1975 all Latin American countries with the exception of Colombia have primate urban systems, while core countries have begun to move toward less-hierarchical national-city systems (Chase-Dunn, 1982c).

One consequence of the rapid growth of great cities in the semiperiphery is to flatten further the world city-size distribution. Some contend that this is a symptom of a real shift of power and resources toward the periphery. It may be rather that some peripheral and semiperipheral areas are enjoying upward mobility in the core–periphery hierarchy at the same time that the hierarchy itself is being reproduced in new ways. The perspective that lends sense to this contention views the whole world-system as developing over time, such that commodification, proletarianization, and productivity are increasing in both the core and the periphery, but the relative gap between the two is reproduced or even extended. Thus peripheral urbanization and industrialization, rather than signaling the "modernization" of the periphery that is catching up with the "advanced" countries, are only the most recent forms in which the core–periphery hierarchy is institutionalized.

Urbanization in both the core and the periphery is subject to processes operating in an interdependent world, but core cities are much more likely to have access to relative dominance within this system, while peripheral cities are much more likely to be subjected to dependence. This does not discount the possibility of mobility up or down. The United States hegemony, like others before, is clearly waning, and some semiperipheral countries may really be gaining increased advantages in the world market and geopolitical system. The most difficult question is whether or not the structure itself is changing. Although I am not one who believes that inequality is inevitable, I do not presently see major structural reorganization taking place that will result in a decrease in the inequalities of the contemporary world-system.

SUMMARY AND CONCLUSION

Let us summarize the findings and interpretations presented above. First the empirical variations shown in Figure 12.1 in the city-size distribution of both Europe and the capitalist world-economy have different explanations at different points in time. The first decline in hierarchy (from A.D. 800 to 1000) is due to the involution of a space-economy and the disintegration of trade. Then, with the growth of the capitalist and administrative cities we have the reemergence of a trade network, which does not again dissolve during later declines in hierarchy. The main explanation for later declines in the city-size hierarchy is increased economic and political rivalry among core states of the capitalist world-economy. This corresponds to a slight "renationalization" of the international division of labor as controllers of production attempt to use political power to defend or expand their advantages, but the decline in hierarchy is due more to the growth of competing states and cities than to the decline in exchange among world cities. This contention is supported by the observation of the absolute city sizes. During the first flattening (A.D. 800–1000), not only does the shape of the distribution change but the sizes of cities also decline. After that city sizes always increase even though the distribution of sizes may be more or less hierarchical.

What, then is the explanation for the cycle of core competition that I am asserting explains the major changes in the world city-size distribution since the emergence of capitalism? Elsewhere (Chase-Dunn, 1981a) I have outlined an explanation that follows Amin (1980) and Wallerstein (1979). At the most general level the international set of alliances and coercive structures that constitute the world polity allow the expansion of the capitalist accumulation process until the consequences of that expansion create strains on existing political structures. Then follows a period of war and conflict among core states that reorganizes the interstate system and allows the continuation of the accumulation process.

As to why particular core powers succeed in attaining hegemony and then decline, we can refer to a familiar set of circumstances and processes that have been asserted to explain national development. I outline these social, geographical, political, and economic circumstances in my discussion of the current decline of the United States (Chase-Dunn, 1981b). One process relevant for our discussion of cities is the turnover time of fixed capital investment. Both public and private investments in fixed capital create constraints on future growth by sinking large amounts of resources in infrastructure—transport networks, and the built environment itself, including the stock of housing and commercial and public buildings.

Once a city is built or a transport system is created the country that has built it must operate with that system for some period of time. It is not economically possible to tear down and rebuild cities with every change in the technology of transport or construction, even though these changes may involve cost economies or spinoffs for productive activities. Thus the canals of Venice or Amsterdam were constructed on a certain scale that could not then easily be altered once built. The location of London on the Thames corresponds to a condition of navigability relative to a certain level of water transport technology, while New York's location on the Hudson allows the docking of much larger ships.

These locational decisions, as well as actual investment in fixed capital, create constraints that prevent the use of newer infrastructural technologies for a certain time period. Within that time period competing cities (either at home or abroad) may adopt the newer technologies and thus obtain a comparative advantage in production costs. This friction in the turnover time of fixed capital has long been understood to operate in the case of competition among firms, especially those with major investments in fixed capital, such as the steel industry. I am asserting that it may explain part of the cycle of core competition as well, and it may account for what appears to be a shortening of the period of alternation in the world city-size hierarchy. Figure 12.2 shows that the length of time between rises and falls in the world city-size hierarchy decreases as we approach the twentieth century. This may correspond in part to the increasing rate of change in infrastructural technology.

Other factors that may account for the cycle of core competition are the scale of social organization and the oppositional movements to private capital accumulation that the process of capitalist development generates. The size of firms is known to increase over the history of capitalist development, although this occurs unevenly. The British firms of the late nineteenth century were slower to adopt the expansionist reorganization that firms in the United States, Germany, and Japan pioneered. The U.S.-based multinational firms are showing similar reticence to go into partnership with the U.S. state, although competitors in most of the core have embraced this latest form of merger (Bergesen, 1982).

Similarly, one of the reasons why uneven development occurs is that increased claims by workers and citizens on the profits of accumulation in a successful core state encourage capital flight to areas where these claims are less effective. Wages and public expenditures rise as workers and other oppressed interest groups manage to gain access to the state. These movements are oriented toward their own territorial state, while capital can escape this opposition by moving across national boundaries to greener pastures. This too can explain the cycles of core competition bacause a mature hegemone tends to export capital, partly to avoid the claims of a mobilized working class and citizenry.

Will the cycle of core competition continue and will world cities continue to exhibit a changing hierarchical relationship to one another? The findings of this research clearly need to be improved by the use of data on the location of central place functions. Population size is not a good measure of centrality in the world-economy, although it may be a useful proxy. The confusion resulting from conurbations can be solved for recent years by studying the location of world firms, military decision-making, and central place functions such as banking and monetary institutions.

These improvements in data will not provide the answer to the above questions about the future, however. Here we need a good theory of constancy and change in the structure of the world-system itself, and this requires formalized theory construction and testing with research on the dynamics of the world-system. At this point we can merely speculate on the basis of past cycles and trends and present contradictions. The most likely scenario is for another period of violent conflict among core powers with the emergence of a new hegemone in the twenty-first century. If this holds true, the world city of the hegemone would undoubtedly attain centrality in the world city system. This extrapolation of the past, however, discounts the element of freedom and also the uniqueness of the present situation. Nuclear weapons make a military confrontation among core powers potentially devastating for the world-system, and indeed, for the human species. Alternatives to core war would seem to depend on the creation of a world federation that has the power to prevent international warfare. Few signs of movement toward this alternative are visible on the horizon, although a partial confrontation, or perhaps a middle-scale accident, could provide new political impetus toward a better integrated world-system.

13

CORE–PERIPHERY PATTERNS OF URBANIZATION*

Glenn Firebaugh

INTRODUCTION

In recent years comparative urban researchers have returned to a familiar theme: the relationship between spatial composition and economic structure and growth. This rekindled interest reflects developments in both urban research and comparative research. In urban research, the political economy perspective (e.g., Castells, 1976; Harvey, 1973) holds that cities should be the "focus," and not merely the "locus," of study (see Walton, 1976b: 302). This shift away from viewing cities as settings encourages, among other things, more attention to cities as actors, including the role they play in the world-economy. More important, in comparative research, dependency and world-system theories focus attention on nations and cities as parts of the larger world-economy. From this perspective, it has been argued that cities cannot be understood apart from the world-economy (Kentor, 1981b) and, conversely, that the world-econony cannot be understood apart from cities (Lojkine, 1976, among others).

This essay compares the broad patterns of spatial composition in the core and periphery of the world-system. The distinction between core nations and peripheral nations is important in discussions of national development. According to dependency theories, for example, the economic penetration of peripheral nations by richer core nations (penetration through such means as trade, aid, and investment) distorts the development of the peripheral nations. The result, as Frank (1966) describes it, is that peripheral nations are *under*developed, not *un*developed. This argument suggests nonparallel development patterns for core and peripheral nations.

*I thank Jack P. Gibbs for helpful comments on an earlier draft of this chapter.

In this essay I examine both historical and cross-sectional evidence in an attempt to detect such nonparallelism with respect to urbanization. The analysis reveals two important ways in which urbanization differs in the core and periphery:

1. High levels of urbanization of the *nonfarm* population are occurring much earlier in the periphery than one would expect from the Western experience.
2. For core nations, deconcentration technologies have perhaps severed the traditional link between urbanization and economic development. Using cross-national data for 1970, I find that GNP per capita has no effect on urbanization among core nations (but it does among peripheral nations).

COMPONENTS OF PROPORTION URBAN

Important core–periphery differences in urbanization can be seen by decomposing proportion urban in a certain way. Consider total population P, the sum of the agricultural and nonagricultural populations A and $\overline{A}$. The nonagricultural population A in turn consists of urban residents U and nonurban residents. If we assume that farmers do not live in urban areas (some can, of course, but there are practical limits to the distance of agricultural commuting), then U is a subset of $\overline{A}$, which is a subset of P. More formally:

$$U \subseteq \overline{A} \subseteq P \tag{1}$$

Proportion urban is of course U divided by P. Note that U/P increases when (1) U becomes a larger proportion of $\overline{A}$ (that is, $U/\overline{A}$ increases, $\overline{A}/P$ constant) or (2) $\overline{A}$ becomes a larger proportion of P (that is, $\overline{A}/P$ increases, $U/\overline{A}$ constant). Indeed, U/P is the product of $U/\overline{A}$ and $\overline{A}/P$:

$$U/P = U/\overline{A} \times \overline{A}/P \tag{2}$$

Equation (2) makes intuitive sense when we observe that $U/\overline{A}$ indicates the probability of city residence among those who are "eligible" (the nonfarmers). We multiply this by the proportion of the total population that is eligible ($\overline{A}/P$) to get the proportion of the total population who live in cities (U/P).

What insights are given by decomposing proportion urban in this manner? Note that an increase in $\overline{A}/P$ implies a sectorial shift in a nation's labor force (a shift out of agriculture) while an increase in $U/\overline{A}$ implies a residential shift (an increased inclination toward urban residence among those eligible). By decomposing U/P changes in this manner, then, we can locate the primary macrolevel force driving the urbanization: Is it driven by shifts out of agriculture, or by changing spatial patterns among non-farmers, or both?

Historical data for continental Western Europe (from Banks, 1971; Mitchell 1975) suggest that each has played a part in the urbanization of that region. The data indicate two distinct 40-year phases in Western Europe's urbanization. The first, from 1880 to 1920, was driven primarily by increased urbanization of the nonfarm population. During this period proportion urban (localities of 20,000+) increased from .159 to .311 as both $U/\overline{A}$ and $\overline{A}/P$ increased: $U/\overline{A}$ from .318 to .512, and $\overline{A}/P$ from .500 to .608 (Table 13.1). The change in proportion urban can be accounted for as follows:

$$.311/.159 = (.512/.318)(.608/.500), \qquad \text{or } 1.96 = (1.61)(1.22)$$

During this period, then, urbanization increased 96%, and this increase derived primarily from an increase in $U/\overline{A}$: the nonfarm population became 61% more urban, while the nonfarm population (as a proportion of the total) increased by only 22%.

A very different pattern emerges for 1920–1960 urbanization (Table 13.1). Farm outmigration was the primary urbanizing force in Western Europe during this period, while change in $U/\overline{A}$ was of relatively minor importance. Indeed, in 1960 the nonfarm people of Western Europe were only slightly more inclined to live in cities than were their 1920 counterparts ($U/\overline{A} = .561$ versus .512). By contrast, $\overline{A}/P$ increased by 28.6%—a rather

TABLE 13.1

Components of Urbanization: Western Europe, 1880–1960, and Peripheral Nations, 1920–1960[a]

Year	Western Europe[b]				Peripheral nations[c]		
	$U/\overline{A}$	$\overline{A}/P$	U/P		$U/\overline{A}$	$\overline{A}/P$	U/P
1880	.318	.500	.159				
1900	.453	.541	.245				
1920	.512	.608	.311		.299	.224	.067
1940	.541	.664	.359		.389[e]	.246[e]	.097
1960	.561	.782	.439		.570	.293	.167
	(.535)[d]				(.496)[d]		

[a] Source: Adapted from Firebaugh (1984; Tables 1 and 2). *Urban* refers to localities of 20,000 or more inhabitants.

[b] Belgium, Denmark, France, Germany, Italy, Netherlands, Norway, Portugal, Spain, Sweden, and Switzerland.

[c] "Developing countries with market economies" (see Bairoch, 1973).

[d] Adjusted for the presence of urban farmers (see Firebaugh [1984]).

[e] Interpolated, using 1930 and 1950 figures for $U/\overline{A}$ and $\overline{A}/P$, and the 1940 figure for U/P.

striking increase, given that this meant that the proportion of the population dependent on agriculture was almost halved (roughly, from .39 to .22; see Table 13.1). This 28.6% increase in $\overline{A}/P$ combined with a 9.6% increase in $U/\overline{A}$ to produce a 41% increase in percentage urban: $(1.096)(1.286) = 1.41$. The finding here—that farm outmigration was the primary urbanizing force during this period[1]—dovetails nicely with another result (below), based on cross-sectional analysis, that "percentage of labor force not engaged in agriculture" is the only significant predictor of urbanization for core nations in 1970.

What does this suggest about future urbanization in Western Europe? Briefly put, that urbanization will level off unless $U/\overline{A}$ begins to increase again. Note that the agricultural population of Western Europe had shrunk to about one-fifth of the total by 1960. The agricultural population is even a smaller minority now in the core. Thus, the potential future contribution of farm outmigration to urbanization in the core is limited. For example, in a region where the agricultural population constitutes 5% of the total (as in North America), halving this proportion would increase $\overline{A}/P$ only by 2.6% (from .95 to .975). Since percentage increase in proportion urban is a function of percentage increase in $\overline{A}/P$ and $U/\overline{A}$, the limited potential for increases in $\overline{A}/P$ means that further increases in proportion urban depend on increases in $U/\overline{A}$. Yet, if the Western European experience is any indication, rapid increases in $U/\overline{A}$ are unlikely. If $U/\overline{A}$ does indeed level off in the core, then urban growth there will slow to a crawl.

Urbanization prospects for the periphery are quite different. The farm population is still a majority—so (unlike the core) farm outmigration in the periphery can still significantly affect urbanization. In addition, the nonfarm population in the periphery appears to be more and more inclined toward urban residence. Based on Bairoch's (1973) estimates of labor force composition and proportion urban, I was able to calculate $U/\overline{A}$ for the periphery beginning with 1920. Between 1920 and 1960 it increased from .30 to .57 (Table 13.1). Even if we make generous allowances for measurement error, the upward trend in $U/\overline{A}$ is undeniable. Thus, unlike the 1920–1960 pattern for Western Europe, urbanization in the periphery was driven by significant increases in $U/\overline{A}$ as well as in $\overline{A}/P$. Using the com-

---

[1]To say that farm outmigration is the "primary urbanizing force" is not necessarily to say that it is the farm emigrants who are moving into cities (in the absence of individual-level data we cannot say who is moving into cities). If the farm emigrants are not moving into cities but are in effect "replacing" the nonfarm rural-to-urban migrants, then increases in $\overline{A}/P$ would retard the increase of $U/\overline{A}$. This may account in part for the modesty of the 1920–1960 increase in $U/\overline{A}$. If so, then as the farm exodus slows, $U/\overline{A}$ may once again show healthy gains (though, as I indicate below, I believe it is more likely that $U/\overline{A}$ in core nations will not increase much in the future).

ponents to calculate the percentage increase in U/P, we obtain: (1.906) (1.308) = 2.49, that is, a 91% increase in $U/\overline{A}$ (residential shift) and a 31% increase in $\overline{A}/P$ (sectorial shift) produced a 149% increase in proportion urban.

The significant feature of these core–periphery differences in 1920–1960 is *not* that proportion urban increased at a much faster rate for the periphery (149 versus 41% for Western Europe)—this is not unexpected, given the lower base for the periphery, and indeed Preston (1979) concludes that core nations experienced comparable rates of increase at a similar level of urbanization. Rather, what is significant is the *composition* of the urbanization. Note $U/\overline{A}$ in particular. Even though substantially different on proportion urban, Western Europe and the periphery are roughly equivalent with respect to $U/\overline{A}$. In 1960, for example, proportion urban was 2.5 times greater in Western Europe than in the periphery (.44 versus .17; Table 13.1), yet Western Europe and the periphery did not differ on $U/\overline{A}$ (.56 versus .57; Table 13.1). Similarly, we note (Table 13.1) that the urbanization of Western Europe in 1880 was roughly comparable to that of the periphery in 1960 (.16 versus .17), yet in Western Europe in 1880 only about one-third of the nonfarm population lived in urban places of 20,000 or more residents, while in the periphery in 1960 well over one-half did (.32 versus .57).

In short, peripheral regions are already reaching relatively high levels of urbanization of the nonfarm population, and this is occurring much earlier in the urbanization process than it did in Western Europe. If urbanization of the nonfarm population is taken as an indicator of the level of urbanization *among those who are eligible* ("eligible population urbanization," or EPU), then EPU in the periphery has apparently reached a level comparable to that of Western Europe. Put differently, if we standardize urbanization (like we do fertility rates) to take eligibility into account, then Western Europe and the periphery were roughly comparable on urbanization in 1960. This holds whether or not the estimates are adjusted for the presence of farmers in urban areas (the parenthesized numbers in Table 13.1; the adjustment procedure is discussed in Firebaugh, 1984).

Can these results be generalized? The Mitchell data set covers only Western Europe, and the labor force data end with 1960. Data for more recent years are available in other sources. However, I do not know how comparable these data are, and until comparability is established I hesitate to splice later data sets with earlier ones.

Nevertheless, broad patterns can be noted, using 1970 data collected for a cross-sectional regression analysis (described in more detail later). The 1970 data differ from the 1880–1960 data in that (1) *urban area* is defined more broadly (the minimum is often less than 20,000) and (2) six core nations are added to the analysis (Australia, Canada, England, Japan, the United States, and the Soviet Union). In addition, consistent with most cross-national regression analyses, unweighted country means are used (raw numbers were used for the calculations in Table 13.1, so the results there are weighted by country size). Using the 1970 data, the estimates for proportion urban and proportion nonfarm are: core, .681 and .877; periphery, .265 and .357. Since $U/\overline{A} = (U/P)/(\overline{A}/P)$, we calculate $U/\overline{A} = .78$ for the core and .74 for the periphery. In short, with an expanded sample and a more inclusive definition of urban area, the general pattern with respect to EPU is the same as earlier: the core and periphery are fairly similar on nonfarm urbanization $U/\overline{A}$, even though proportion urban is about 2.5 times greater in the core (.68 versus .27).

Moreover, EPU apparently is still increasing in the periphery (eventually it must level off, of course, since it cannot exceed 1.0). If we use the 1970 data source, and the same nations, to calculate $U/\overline{A}$ in 1960, the estimate is .700 (versus .742 for the 1970 estimate). If $U/\overline{A}$ continues its upward trend in the periphery and levels off or declines in the core, then in the long run the periphery could be both more agricultural (lower $\overline{A}/P$) *and* more urban (higher U/P) than the core.

CROSS-SECTIONAL ANALYSIS

Social scientists have long known that rich industrial nations are more highly urbanized than poor agricultural nations. Indeed, the cross-national correlation between urbanization and GNP per capita is quite large ($r = .70$ or greater in most studies), and the term *urban-industrial society* has become conventional in anthropology and sociology.

Many of the attempts to account for the cross-sectional relationship between urbanization and industrial–economic development reduce to reasons why individuals move to cities (for example, higher wages). Such "migration" analyses of urbanization do not explain why the cities are there and why they offer higher wages, nor do they explain how all of this relates to industrialization.

It is not difficult to compile a list of reasons why urbanization has accompanied industrialization over the past two centuries. During this period, industrialization and the technology of industrialization (1) increased farm productivity per worker, thereby enabling labor to move from the farm, (2) created the need for labor in central locations, and (3) with increased overall productivity, increased the need for centers of capital, consumption, and trade. The spatial concentration of population in turn permitted economies-of-scale and facilitated the movement of goods (transportation), symbols (communication), labor, and capital.

But such a list is not in itself a theory. Why should industrial–economic development in the nineteenth and twentieth centuries lead to a pattern of population distribution characterized by nodes of high-density settlements?

In one of the attempts to face this question squarely, Gibbs and Martin argued that "cities represent one way in which populations organize to obtain a greater quantity and variety of objects of consumption" (1958:268). According to Gibbs and Martin, technological advance and the concomitant changes in a nation's division of labor are prerequisites for urban growth. A "city depends on the acquisition of objects of consumption originating outside of its boundaries. However . . . it is only through the division of labor and an advanced technology that a population is able to bring material from great distances" (Gibbs and Martin, 1962:668). In addition to providing the basis for large-scale urbanization, technology and labor specialization stimulate it. Both lead to "the use of greater varieties and amounts of raw materials" and, on "a probability basis, this makes for a greater dispersion of objects of consumption" (1962:668). This dispersion leads to urbanization, as populations—"faced by the necessity of exchanging dispersed natural resources or bringing them together for combination into new objects of consumpton" (1958:268)—form nodes for exchange and processing, that is, they form cities.

The Gibbs–Martin articles provide the point of departure for the cross-sectional analysis. I chose the Gibbs–Martin model because it is well known, deductively based, and parsimonious, yet incorporates the three exogenous variables (economic–technological development, sectorial composition of labor force, and trade) that seem to appear most frequently in cross-national analyses of urbanization.

Nevertheless, one can question the relevance of traditional models of urbanization (such as the Gibbs–Martin model) to recent and future urbanization in the core. Traditional models detail how urbanization is inherent in the "logic" of industrialization. But core nations are moving into a postindustrial era, where the traditional arguments seem less applicable. Consider, for example, the nature of postindustrial technology. During industrialization, as Gibbs and Martin argue, new technologies increase a nation's capacity to process raw materials, thereby encouraging urbanization. But postindustrial technologies are not necessarily oriented toward the processing of raw materials; they are increasingly oriented toward the processing of information. Such technologies tend to be "deconcentration" technologies; that is, they reduce the cost of transporting goods, labor, and symbols and thus make dense population nodes less necessary.

In principle one could test the hypothesis that some types of technological change encourage urbanization while others permit alternatives to population concentration, but in practice technological changes are interrelated and difficult to separate. This analysis focuses on the overall effect of economic–technological development. If the above reasoning is correct, the overall effect represents the relative strengths of offsetting effects. It is difficult to specify at what level the deconcentration technologies substantially (or entirely) offset the concentration technologies, but this likely has already occurred in North America and much of Western Europe (Bourgeois-Pichat, 1981; Wardwell, 1980). Thus we expect traditional "industrialization" models of urbanization to fare better when applied to recent urbanization in the periphery than to recent urbanization in the core.

Measures

DEPENDENT VARIABLE   *Urbanization* as conventionally defined is proportion (or percentage) of population residing in "urban areas." The United Nations permits each country to employ its own criteria for urban area, so data typically are not strictly comparable across nations. In one U.N. publication (U.N., 1969:Chapter 2) localities with 20,000 or more inhabitants were defined as "agglomerates," but the United Nations subsequently abandoned this attempt to impose uniform criteria, arguing that "national statistical offices are in the best position to distinguish between urban and rural-type areas in their own country" (U.N., 1980b:9). Most nations choose a minimum smaller than 20,000.

This analysis uses World Bank data (IBRD, 1977) revised as necessary by updated census figures for 1970 urbanization (Bourgeois-Pichat, 1981: Table 2). These data use national definitions for urbanization. The 120 nations in the data set are classified by per capita GNP in 1970 (IBRD, 1977, Series IV). This classification forms the basis for the core–periphery scheme used here. Nations in the World Bank's bottom three categories (GNP of $375 or less per capita) are in the periphery ($N = 60$). The core consists of the 11 Western European nations in Table 13.1 plus Australia, Canada, England, Japan, the United States, and the Soviet Union.

INDEPENDENT VARIABLES   The indicator of economic–technological development is GNP per capita (in U.S. dollars). Cross-national studies of urbanization typically find that per capita GNP and percentage urban are highly correlated, and that the relationship persists after other variables are controlled for. However, we expect the relationship to differ for the core and periphery. In the technologically advanced core nations, transportation and communication technologies reduce the need for densely settled nodes.

Per capita GNP is highly skewed across nations. Separating the nations into core and periphery reduces the skewness considerably. Among the core nations it is trivial. Among the peripheral nations it is not, and logged values are used in the analysis.

The second independent variable, a population-weighted measure of trade, attempts to capture the Gibbs–Martin concept of "dispersion of objects of consumption." According to Gibbs and Martin, urbanization and dispersion are positively correlated: "a high degree of urbanization depends on widely scattered materials and represents the type of organization necessary for acquiring them" (1962:668). The acquisition of objects of consumption involves exchange; the greater the dispersion of these objects, the greater the need for nodes of collection and exchange, that is, cities.

The objects to be acquired can be within or without the nation's boundaries. The nation's participation in international trade (total value of trade as a percentage of total production) can be taken as a crude indicator of the latter (Gibbs and Martin [1962] weighted this by distance from trading partners, but I did not attempt this). Exchange within a nation's boundaries is more difficult to capture with readily available cross-national data. Here I used population as a proxy. It is well-known that larger nations tend to participate less in international trade (Kuznets, 1960), presumably because they exchange more within their boundaries. Thus, to estimate a nation's "total dispersion" I weight the trade measure by population. This measure is skewed markedly among the peripheral nations, so the logged form is used in analyzing the periphery.

The final independent variable is nonfarm labor force (expressed as a percentage of the total labor force). This corresponds to the $\overline{A}/P$ measure used in the historical analysis. We expect a positive effect for the nonfarm labor force measure: the larger the percentage of the labor force *not* engaged in farming, the greater the urbanization.[2]

Results

Table 13.2 reports the zero-order correlations among the variables. For the periphery, GNP and nonfarm labor force are both highly correlated with urbanization; for the core, only nonfarm labor force is substantially correlated with urbanization. Among the independent variables, the largest

---

[2]The careful reader will see that, while I relied heavily on Gibbs and Martin, I did not attempt an exact replication of their analysis (1962). Thus, my measures deviate from theirs (for example, they attempt to measure diversification of the labor force, and not merely its farm–nonfarm distribution). My goal here is an analysis that is representative of the field, and where possible I selected measures that are typical of the cross-national work in this area.

TABLE 13.2

Zero-Order Correlations among Variables: Core and Periphery[a]

Variable	A	B	C	D
A. % Urban (national definitions)		.43	.72	.41
B. GNP per capita	.80		.75	.08
C. Nonfarm labor force (as % of total)	.70	.57		.31
D. Trade × population	.24	.11	−.03	

[a] Core (shown above diagonal) includes 11 nations of continental Western Europe (see Table 13.1) plus Australia, Canada, England, Japan, the United States, and the Soviet Union. Periphery includes Afghanistan, Bangladesh, Benin, Burma, Burundi, Chad, Ethiopia, Indonesia, Lesotho, Malawi, Mali, Nepal, Niger, Rwanda, Somalia, Tanzania, Upper Volta, Zaire, Bolivia, Botswana, Cameroon, Gambia, Haiti, India, Kenya, Madagascar, Mauritania, Nigeria, Pakistan, Sierra Leone, Sri Lanka, Sudan, Swaziland, Thailand, Togo, Algeria, Colombia, Congo (People's Republic), Dominican Republic, Ecuador, Egypt, El Salvador, Ghana, Guatemala, Guyana, Honduras, Iraq, Ivory Coast, Jordan, Korea (Republic of), Liberia, Mauritius, Morocco, Papua New Guinea, Paraguay, Philippines, Senegal, Syria, Tunisia, Turkey.

relationship is that of GNP and nonfarm labor (r is .57 for the periphery and .75 for the core). Importantly, there are no extremely large correlations. This suggests that these measures are not redundant; they do measure conceptually and empirically distinguishable phenomena.

Table 13.3 reports the regression results for percentage urban, for the periphery and core. The results for the periphery are consistent with expectations. The indicators of economic development, labor force composition, and trade all have independent positive effects on percentage urban. Among peripheral nations, the richest, least agricultural, most active traders tend to have the highest levels of urbanization.

The core exhibits a quite different pattern. Nonfarm labor force has a statistically significant positive effect on urbanization. This is consistent with the earlier finding that recent urbanization in Western Europe has been driven primarily by farm outmigration. But the other coefficients are small and not statistically significant. Note in particular the difference between the core and periphery with respect to per capita GNP. Among peripheral nations the coefficient is positive and fairly large ($\beta = .55$); among core nations the coefficient is negative and not statistically significant.

Apparently city-inhibiting technologies offset city-promoting technologies in the core. Alternative explanations of the GNP result receive no empirical support. A scatterplot of the GNP–urbanization relationship (not shown) suggests that the results are due neither to outliers nor to a ceiling effect on urbanization. Nor can the GNP result be dismissed as an artifact of the ratio variables used. To be sure, the correlation of ratio variables with common terms is sometimes ill advised, since such correlations are particularly sensitive to measurement error (Long, 1979). In this case, however, measurement error would most likely bias the relationship in a positive direction.

TABLE 13.3

Determinants of Percentage Urban: Periphery and Core, 1970

Independent variable	Periphery		Core	
	b^a	β^b	b^a	β^b
GNP per capita	12.6**	.55	− .002	− .20
Nonfarm labor force (as % of total)	.33**	.39	1.5*	.82
Trade × population	2.6*	.19	.47	.17
R^2 (adjusted)	.74		.47	

[a] Metric regression coefficient. Since the GNP and trade variables are logged for the periphery but not for the core, the b's for core and periphery are not comparable for those variables.

[b] Standardized regression coefficient.

*Statistically significant at .05 level. **Statistically significant at .01 level.

The absence of a positive relationship between percentage urban and per capita GNP in the core, then, is not artifactual. For core nations, apparently, increasing urbanization is no longer an adjunct to increasing GNP.

CONCLUSION

Some cross-national studies of urbanization combine and analyze all nations with available data, without regard to a nation's position in the world-system. Other studies focus on a subset of nations (for example, Kentor's [1981b] study of 37 peripheral nations; Firebaugh's [1979] study of urbanization in Asia and Latin America). Few studies do both—that is, few analyze and compare urbanization in the important divisions of the world-system.

This essay separately analyzes urbanization in rich core nations and in poor peripheral nations. Significant differences are found. Among peripheral nations in 1970, GNP per capita, labor force composition, and trade all have independent effects on percentage of the population living in urban areas. Among core nations in 1970, only labor force composition has a statistically significant effect on percentage urban. Per capita GNP has no direct effect. Apparently, spatial contiguity is less tied to economic development in the core than in the periphery.

Historical patterns also differ for the core and periphery. Proportion urban (20,000+) in continental Western Europe increased from .31 to .44 during 1920–1960, an absolute increase of .13. During this period proportion urban (20,000+) also increased in peripheral nations, from .07 to .17. Hence in absolute terms the "urbanization gap" between Western Europe and the periphery increased slightly over this 40-year period.

But this focus on the "gap" in proportion urban obscures a significant point: by 1960 the periphery had substantially closed the gap with respect to urbanization of the *nonfarm* population $U/\overline{A}$. Indeed, by 1960 non-farmers in the periphery were no less likely than their Western European counterparts to live in urban places.

This result is consistent with the argument that deconcentration technologies make spatial concentration of the nonfarm population less important in the core. Even so, the *magnitude* of $U/\overline{A}$ in the periphery is a bit surprising; certainly, high $U/\overline{A}$ has occurred much earlier in the urbanization process than one would expect from the Western European experience. Moreover, the historical trends suggest that even the gap in proportion urban will soon narrow. The increased urbanization of Western Europe, 1920–1960, derived primarily from farm outmigration, a force that by now has about run its course in the core. Urbanization of the periphery, by contrast, was driven by an increase in $U/\overline{A}$, as well as by farm outmigration. These forces give no indication of abating soon in the periphery.

14

WOMEN AND URBANIZATION IN THE WORLD-SYSTEM*

Kathryn B. Ward

Introduction

Since the publication of Wallerstein's (1974) work on the world economic system, researchers have examined a variety of socioeconomic processes in the context of the world-system; for example, the growth of the tertiary labor force and overurbanization (see, for example, Evans and Timberlake, 1980; Fiala, 1983; Kentor, 1981b; Timberlake and Kentor, 1983; Timberlake and Lunday, Chapter 15, this volume). This research has established that under the influence of foreign investment and trade dependency, developing countries frequently experience the extraordinary growth of the service or tertiary labor force along with the stagnation of the industrial labor force. Further, investment and dependency are related to the rapid and somewhat skewed patterns of urbanization in developing countries.

These research efforts, however, have been notably gender-blind in the sense that the researchers have assumed that the processes of tertiary sector growth and overurbanization have affected women and men equally. In this chapter I argue that we can no longer ignore women's roles in and contributions to the processes of overurbanization and the growth of the tertiary labor force. Why? A large body of literature now documents how during economic development women, relative to men, had unequal access to the new economic resources and employment generated by the intrusion of the world-system and urbanization in both the rural and urban areas (Boserup, 1970; Papanek, 1976; Tinker, 1976; United Nations, 1980c). Little or no trickle down of these new resources has occurred from men to women (Pa-

*I wish to thank Seanza Prasai and Samuel Sifre for their assistance in coding and computer work.

panek, 1979a). First, because of gender differences in migration, determined in part by processes of investment and dependency, urban areas of
Africa and Latin America now have skewed sex ratios. Predominately male
towns exist in Africa, while heavily female towns exist in Latin America.
Second, the growth of the tertiary labor force has been shaped by women's
participation (Schmink, 1977). In the urban areas, women have been relegated to and compose most of the informal labor market (International
Center for Research on Women [ICRW], 1980b)—an important sector for
the functioning of the world economic system (Portes and Walton, 1981;
Portes, Chapter 4, this volume). Yet most treatments of the informal sector
relegate women to peripheral or negligible roles within this sector. For example, only men's roles in the informal sector are considered important;
women only have "little businesses."

Thus, in this chapter, I first examine the gender patterns of migration as
they vary by position of nations within the world-system and by geographic
region. Second, I examine the relationship between women's urban residence and access to economic resources in the context of changes introduced by the world economic system. Third, I analyze the patterns of
women's access to formal employment by reviewing cross-national employment statistics by position of nations within the world-system and by
geographic region. Finally I discuss briefly the consequences of these trends
in migration and the labor force for female-headed households and for
women who remain behind in the rural areas.

GENDER DIFFERENCES IN MIGRATION

The classic source on women's and men's patterns of migration is the
work of Boserup (1970), who noted that women, compared to men, had
four regional patterns of migration and labor force activity: Arab, Latin
American, Southeast Asian, and African–Indian. First, Arab and non-Arab
Muslim women tend to reside in rural areas. Their economic activities, in
both the rural and urban areas, are confined to the domestic realm or closely
related activiites (Boserup, 1970). When these women migrate with their
spouses, they may find limited job opportunities for women in urban areas.
If the women are educated, they may have opportunities for paid employment in education, medicine, or clerical work. Less well educated women
may find that traditional or rural forms of economic activities are unavail-
able to them. Traditional kin-support networks that have provided jobs and
social outlets also may be absent in urban areas. These lesser-educated
women may work within the home in cottage industries, for example, or
outside the home as domestic servants. Social sanctions against contact with

nonrelated men may further restrict women's economic opportunities in urban areas (Gulick and Gulick, 1978; Jahan, 1979; Papanek, 1971; Weiss, 1982; Youssef, 1971). These economic activities and sanctions, however, may vary by class, where middle- and upper-class married women may face more constraints on work than lower- or working-class women.

Second, in Latin America women are more likely to migrate than men. As a result, the urban areas in this region have a larger proportion of women relative to men (Boserup, 1970; Jelin, 1977; Youssef, 1974). This pattern has occurred as a consequence of the economic patterns of agriculture and dependency where women are less utilized in peasant and capital-intensive agriculture. Hence, young single women are released to migrate to the ur-ban areas in search of domestic and factory work, thereby providing the labor supply to fuel the extraordinary growth of the service and informal sectors. More highly educated women may find work in clerical and profes-sional occupations (Boserup, 1970). Over the life cycle, however, working women drop out of the formal labor force and comprise a large proportion of the informal sector, especially after marriage (Chaney and Schmink, 1980). Hence, Latin American women have high participation rates in only the urban areas. Their overall rates of participation remain low, however, owing to the low formal participation of women in the rural areas and the high dropout rate of married women who continue their economic partic-ipation through the informal sector. This form of informal economic par-ticipation, however, is rarely reflected in official labor force statistics.

Third, the Southeast Asian pattern of migration does not differ by sex; the urban areas have equal proportions of women and men. Women tend to migrate with their families since production in the rural and urban areas tends to take place in family forms via plantation agricultural production and peripheral industries. A number of researchers have noted the influx of young single educated women from the rural to urban areas in search of work with the multinational corporations (MNCs) (Cho and Koo, 1983; Grossman, 1978–1979; ICRW, 1980b; United Nations, 1980). Additionally, like their Latina counterparts, married women constitute a large part of the informal labor market (Cho and Koo, 1983; ICRW, 1980b). Still, Asian women have high and growing participation rates in both the urban and rural areas.

Fourth, the African–Indian pattern of migration reveals dramatic gender differences in migration. In the past, the urban areas in Africa have had a higher proportion of males as a result of the colonial and multinational officials' inducements and coercions for work in mines and urban areas (Hay, 1976; Seidman, 1981). As a consequence, women have been relegated largely to the subsistence agricultural sectors in the rural areas and to trad-ing and informal sectors in the urban areas. Here, capitalist and local patriarchal elites have assumed that women would provide their own means of subsistence for their families, while men were paid individual wages (Afonja, 1981; Mueller, 1977; Sudarkasa, 1977). Hence, such forms of migration and economic activity have meant that women have become more economically dependent on men for access to the cash economy (Van Allen, 1976). Meanwhile, women's subsistence production provides for the greater economic opportunities of men (Chaney and Schmink, 1980). Thus, under the African–Indian pattern, women have high rates of participation in rural areas and low rates of participation in urban areas.

Whatever the pattern of migration, however, most researchers have found that women are further disadvantaged relative to men in the urban areas because of patriarchal constraints, lower levels of education, and tight labor markets (Boserup, 1970; Lowe, 1976–1977; Sudarkasa, 1977; Youssef, 1976). First, husbands, as a result of local patriarchal patterns, have refused to allow their wives and/or daughters to associate with strange men. Second, since women have lesser access to educational institutions in developing countries (McGrath, 1976), they are at a disadvantage in the urban job market, given the high rates of male (and higher rates of female) unemployment and tight job market, even for educated men (Boserup, 1970; Standing, 1978; Todaro, 1981). Finally, women lose access to kin-support networks that were essential for economic subsistence and social support in the rural areas (Boserup, 1970; Van Allen, 1976).

Hence, the patterns of migration are related to the types of production engendered by the intrusion of the world-system and regional variations. As a result some areas are more highly female in the urban than other areas, although these differences are changing to parity over time. Data on mean

TABLE 14.1

Mean Levels of the Percentage of Women in Urban Areas by Geographic Region, 1960–1975[a]

Geographic region	1960	1965	1970	1975
Africa	49.6	47.4	48.2	48.7
	(8)	(6)	(10)	(8)
Latin America	52.2	52.3	51.7	51.8
	(20)	(11)	(11)	(13)
Asia	49.0	49.0	50.0	50.0
	(18)	(13)	(9)	(4)
Europe	52.4	52.1	52.1	51.4
	(21)	(15)	(17)	(12)
N	67	45	47	37

[a] Number of countries for each cell in parentheses. Source: United Nations Demographic Yearbook (various years).

TABLE 14.2

Mean Levels of the Percentage of Women in Urban Areas by World-System Position, 1960–1975[a]

Position	1960	1965	1970	1975
Core	52.0	51.5	51.9	51.3
	(15)	(12)	(12)	(10)
Semiperiphery	51.0	51.0	51.0	51.0
	(24)	(12)	(15)	(11)
Periphery	50.4	49.9	49.6	50.3
	(29)	(21)	(21)	(16)
N	68	45	48	37

[a] Number of countries in each cell in parentheses. Source: United Nations, *Demographic Yearbook* (various years).

levels of the proportion of females in urban areas over time for four regions are shown in Table 14.1. As previously noted, African towns are slightly more male, Latin American and European towns are more female, and Asian towns are more equal in the gender distribution. Then, the classification scheme of Timberlake and Lunday (Chapter 15, this volume) is used to arrange data by nations' position within the world-system. The core and semiperiphery areas become only slightly more female-populated over time, while the peripheral areas tend to be slightly more male-populated (see Table 14.2).

Thus, researchers examining urbanization in the context of the world economic system need to include some consideration of the gender differences in urban composition and migration in their research. These differences are related to the supply of female labor that is available for paid exploitation in the paid labor force as well as the supply of unpaid female labor that may subsidize the capitalist accumulation process through (1) unpaid domestic labor in the home or (2) the informal labor market. Thus, the structure of wages and the labor force may look very different in an urban area with a larger proportion of females compared to an area with a smaller proportion of females.

THE ECONOMIC STATUS OF WOMEN IN URBAN AREAS AND THE WORLD-SYSTEM

With development and urbanization, women in developed countries have gained increased access to educational and economic resources (Blake, 1974; Oppenheimer, 1970; Stolte-Heiskanen, 1977; Weiss *et al.,* 1976). At the same time, researchers have noted that in currently developing countries women have lost status during the process of development where women's status is defined as women's share of educational, economic, and political resources relative to men's (Blumberg, 1978; Ward, 1984a). Further, urbanization frequently has meant that women lose access to old and new types of economic subsistence and resources, such as autonomous means of income generation and kin or organizational networks (Boserup, 1970; ICRW, 1980b; Tinker and Bramsen, 1976; Van Allen, 1976). Like other phenomenon noted by world-system researchers, the effects of development and urbanization on women differ between developed and developing countries.

I have argued that women's loss of economic status during development is related to the intrusion of the world economic system and the pursuant effects on women's access to economic resources (Ward, 1983, 1984a). In developing countries, the intrusion of the world economic system via foreign investment and trade dependency has meant the introduction of new and valued economic resources into preexisting systems of production. In general, men had greater access to the new resources relative to women; women remained in the preexisting system(s) of production. For example, in agricultural production under trade dependency, men often had greater access to cash crops and the needed credit and technology for production, even when women had been the primary agricultural producers (Boserup, 1970; Mullings, 1976; Seidman, 1981; Tinker, 1976; UNECA, 1975; Wachtel, 1976). Meanwhile, women were relegated to subsistence agricultural production. Further, with the arrival of mechanized food-processing, women were displaced by the new technology (Jahan, 1979; ICRW, 1980b). For example, the introduction of rice rollers from Japan resulted in new jobs for men, thereby pushing women out of the paid labor force (Tinker, 1976).

For women's employment in urban areas, similar patterns have prevailed in trading, industry, service, and the informal sectors. In the following sections, I discuss the effects of the intrusion of the world-system on women's access to these resources, with special attention to the latest dimensions of women's employment in the world system: employment in labor-intensive MNCs in export processing and women's role in the informal sector. Then these patterns over time are examined empirically.

Women's Access to Commerce or Trading

In many regions of the world, women have had access to or control over major trading networks in precolonial economies. With the arrival of colonial officials in West Africa and in the Caribbean, women frequently were denied access to national and international trading routes and were left with local or regional routes. Men were given control over the more lucrative national and international routes. Furthermore, with the arrival of mechanized transport and modern refrigeration facilities, many women traders found that their roles and routes with the trading networks were disrupted (Boserup, 1970; Mintz, 1971; Robertson, 1976). Similar patterns led to the nearly total exclusion of women from commerce and trading in India (Jain *et al.*, 1979; Mazumdar, 1979). Only in Latin America have women gained increased access to paid employment in sales (Boserup, 1970).

Still other researchers have argued that women traders in these regions provide an important linkage between the subsistence sector of a developing country and the larger world-economy by cheaply facilitating the distribution of imported goods (Mintz, 1971; Simms and Dumor, 1976–1977; Sudarkasa, 1977). In this manner, the capitalist elements have a subsidized and cheap transportation and distribution infrastructure for goods. This trading enclave economy, dominated by women, thus has been a crucial element of the economic structure of peripheral and dependent nations.

At the same time, this pattern of economic subsistence has created economic uncertainty for women, because their economic fortunes now are tied to the economic health of the country, the world-economy, and local patriarchal attitudes toward women's economic roles. For example, women now need increasing amounts of capital to remain competitive with men in trading activities in many developing countries. A large number of women must borrow the capital from their husbands or others, thereby becoming dependent on other persons for their livelihood. (Some women, however, have remained competitive through forming women's economic associations). Further, women in trade have little mobility to other types of paid employment compared to men's mobility (Jules-Rosette, 1982; Mintz, 1971; Robertson, 1976; Simms and Dumor, 1976–1977). Hence, women's access to independent economic livelihood continues to be threatened by outside forces and competition from government-sanctioned supermarkets and other male competitors.

Women's Access to Industry

In general, with the intrusion of the world economic system and foreign investment, women's access to industrial employment has declined relative to men's employment. This decline has occurred even when factories displaced previously female cottage industries (Arizpe, 1977; Chinchilla, 1977; Jain *et al.*, 1979; Mazumdar, 1979; Miranda, 1977; United Nations, 1980c; Weiss, 1982). Men, instead of women, were drawn into the new factories and industries generated by development, foreign investment, and by contact with the world-system. In a more recent trend, MNCs have sought exclusively female labor for labor-intensive plants that are engaged in export processing. Why have these patterns of gender inequalities occurred?

The prior preference for male labor can be explained, first, by the nature of technology and factory investment in developing countries. Instead of the labor-intensive factories that were used in developed countries, developing countries frequently were given capital-intensive types of investment or the latest forms of technology from MNCs and developed countries (Chinchilla, 1977; Shapiro, 1980). With the high levels of unemployment in developing countries and the lower number of jobs created by capital-intensive investment compared to labor-intensive investment, men were given preference for employment (Boserup, 1970; Bossen, 1975; Miranda, 1977). Men, too, suffered from the limited number of industrial jobs, but they still had greater access to industrial employment than did women.

Differential patterns of employment generated by investment and dependency were reinforced by certain patriarchal attitudes imported from abroad and also found indigenously: women did not work, men's employment was more important than women's employment, or women should not be working under the direction of strange men (Boserup, 1970; Ward, 1984a). Concomitantly, men's greater access to economic resources introduced by the world-system via agriculture or industry resulted in men's gaining an external sphere of control over women (Sanday, 1974). This material sphere of control combined with patriarchal attitudes was strengthened with the advent of core–periphery relations (Saffioti, 1978; Ward, 1984a). The strength of these forces on women's employment can be seen in the effects of protective legislation on women's industrial employment. In Latin America, many industrial employers have chosen not to employ women to avoid paying increased maternity benefits or leaves. For example, after certain protective legislation was passed in Peru in the late 1950s, no more women were hired to industrial employment (Chaney and Schmink, 1980). Similar legislation proved ineffective in advancing working women's status in Colombia (Rosenberg, 1982).

Second, the preference for male labor and the demise of female cottage industries can be seen through the experience of women with the arrival of import substitution strategies. Many factories took over production that was previously conducted by women in cottage industries. Yet women were not hired in the new factories that replaced the home production. This process had devastating effects on women's industrial employment in India (Mazumdar, 1979) and Central America (Chinchilla, 1977; Arizpe, 1977).

Thus, in these manufacturing sectors, the capitalists and elites have chosen to pay higher wages to men working in these plants instead of hiring women at lower wages. At the same time, women have been denied access to paid employment generated by industrial employment, even though numerous women must support their households and families (Buvinic, Yous-sef, and Von Elm, 1978). More recently, however, women in Latin America and Asia have had access to a newer type of industrial employment in the global assembly line or the emerging international division of labor in the labor-intensive electronics, clothing, and other similar industries (Ehren-reich and Fuentes, 1981). Given the increasingly competitive nature of the global assembly line and the search for cheap labor and large profits, the labor of women may have become the new equilibrium mechanism for the world-system (Saffioti, 1978; Ward, 1984a).

Women and the Global Assembly Line

The trends of declining female industrial employment changed in parts of Central America and Southeast Asia with the arrival of the MNC in-vestment in production for export in the electronic, textile, and toy indus-tries (Cho and Koo, 1983; Grossman, 1978–1979; Lim, 1978; Safa, 1981). These plants specifically targeted educated female labor in Central America and Southeast Asia during the 1960s and 1970s. When the import substi-tution strategies did not bring about expected economic development, a number of developing countries sought a different strategy of processing for export. The MNC plants met these demands by moving their production from the more developed nations, first to Latin America in the 1960s and then on to Asia by the 1970s.

Developing countries and women employees were particularly in demand for this form of production as a result of lower wage levels and concessions by governments. In particular, MNCs sought women in developing coun-tries as employees because they were willing to accept wages 20–50% lower than men's (Elson and Pearson, 1981). Furthermore, the MNCs assumed that women would constitute a more docile, passive labor force than would men (Ehrenreich and Fuentes, 1981; Grossman, 1978–1979). As a conse-quence of the demand for female labor, up to 2 million women are now employed by multinational plants (Ehrenreich and Fuentes, 1981).

Still a number of problems remain, and the short-term increases in wom-en's industrial employment may not be maintained over time. The stabil-ity of MNC employment, wages, unionization, women's mobility, and benefits for the country all have consequences for women's economic status and future prospects. First, the export-oriented MNC employment has been relatively unstable over time because of the competitive nature of these in-dustries. For example, as a result of the international recessions, thousands of women workers have been laid off (Grossman, 1978–1979). If women workers become militant, form unions, or otherwise demand better wages, the MNCs move elsewhere. For example, plants have moved from South

Korea and Singapore to Malaysia, the Philippines, and Indonesia. Further, MNCs expect a high degree of worker turnover in the plants because of marriage, pregnancy, or women's inability to withstand the hazardous working conditions in the plants (Elson and Pearson, 1981; Grossman, 1978–1979). In some plants, for example, women peer through microscopes for 8 to 10 hours a day for several years. When their eyesight no longer conforms to the 20-20 vision required for employment, these women are fired (Grossman, 1978–1979). As a result of these employment conditions, over 9 million women have gone through the process of the global assembly line, according to some researchers' estimates (Ehrenreich and Fuentes, 1981).

Second, some MNC officials have argued that women's wages in the plants benefit both the women and the host country's development efforts. For example, women supposedly are able to purchase mopeds and other desired consumer items. The wage levels of women in these plants, however, only approach subsistence levels for the women's own country (see Grossman, 1978–1979 for comparison of wage levels and costs of living).

Third, if women have attempted to unionize for better wages and working conditions, the MNCs have responded by threats to move elsewhere or with physical repression, sometimes with government support, against strikers or organizers. In a number of countries, women's unionization attempts have brought them violence and death (Ehrenreich and Fuentes, 1981; Grossman, 1978–1979). Additionally, protective legislation frequently has disappeared when MNCs wanted to invest in a country (Elson and Pearson, 1981; Grossman, 1978–1979). As a result, women workers have found it difficult to organize or use existing legislation to protect their jobs and rights.

Fourth, in a number of developing countries, the proposed benefits of MNC investment, such as greater training and mobility of women workers along with new capital for development, have not been realized. Training in many of the MNC plants is not transferable to other types of production. If women are laid off, they are not trained for production in other factories (Grossman, 1978–1979). Additionally, the profits and capital generated by such forms of investment flow out of the country and/or go to elites within the peripheral nation (Siegel, 1978–1979). As a consequence, the only money generated that aids development has been these women's minimal wages in the plants.

Finally, the unemployment problem in developing countries has remained relatively unaffected by these forms of labor-intensive production. The MNCs have attracted a new category of worker into the labor force—young educated female workers—instead of the unemployed women and men whose jobs were displaced by capital-intensive investment. Hence, this form of labor-intensive investment, with its unstable employment and flow of capital and profits abroad, ultimately can contribute to the growth of the tertiary labor force problem in developing countries. For example, where do the women go from the MNC plants after being laid off? Some researchers have noted that prostitution provides one form of employment (Neumann, 1978–1979); still other women disappear into the tertiary and/or informal sectors.

Because of the capital-intensive trends in import substitution and unstable labor-intensive MNC employment in developing countries, I would argue that women's access to industrial employment in peripheral areas will remain tenuous, and might even decline over time. For example, I have reported that prior levels of foreign investment lowered women's share of industrial employment (Ward, 1984b). Further, I contend that in the long-run both women and men are affected negatively by this type of employment when capital continues to flow out of the country to core countries, the job market remains crowded, and women's unemployment in MNCs is unstable. Thus, for increases in women's employment, we must look to the one sector that has been expanding for peripheral nations: the service sector.

Women's Access to the Service Sector

Women's primary occupation within the service sector has been domestic service. The next most common areas are food preparation, sewing, small-scale production, and trading. This sector is also qualitatively diverse: women may work hawking single cigarettes or in fast-food establishments (Tinker, 1976). Jobs in this sector can be easily merged into the informal sector (discussed below), where jobs are either characterized by no wages, minimal wages, or no social security protection (Portes and Walton, 1981; Portes, Chapter 4, this volume).

Women's participation in the service sector is very strongly linked to women's unpaid labor in the home. Such a relationship derives first from the exportation of women's labor from within the home to the marketplace during economic development. Second, women's domestic labors within the home can be conveniently combined with similar forms of labor, but for pay—all within the confines of the home. For example, after marriage, a woman might take in washing or sewing for pay (Jelin, 1980). As Jelin (1977) notes, these two types of labor differ only because the latter type is paid.

At the same time, significant problems exist with domestic service and home-related types of service jobs as a means of raising women's economic status. First, young women generally perform domestic service until they marry. These women experience little in the way of mobility into other occupations (Jelin, 1977). Married women may work seasonally in rural areas or join the informal labor force in the urban areas (Deere and de Leal, 1981). Second, domestic service is a very marginal but accessible occupation that often involves little more compensation than room and board and low or nonexistent wages (especially for unpaid homemakers). For these reasons, domestic service is the predominant occupation among female migrants in Latin America and in other countries (Jelin, 1977; Shapiro, 1980). The ICRW (1980b:50) has estimated that 55–60% of all migrant women in urban areas are located in domestic work; similar patterns hold for the Philippines and India.

Other writers have argued that women's lower levels of education have limited access to well-paying jobs within the service sector. Although women have lower levels of education and literacy in developing countries, even women with secondary educations often have problems finding commensurate employment within the service sector, given an oversupply of educated male workers (Boserup, 1970; Chaney and Schmink, 1980; ICRW, 1980b; Matyepse, 1977; Standing, 1978; Tinker and Bramsen, 1976). Men also have often replaced women in service-sector jobs (Papanek, 1979b).

Women's Access to the Informal Sector

The informal sector has been estimated to constitute from "53 to 69 percent of *all* urban workers" (ICRW, 1980b:68). Contrary to the depictions in the development and world-system literature, women are the majority of workers in the informal sector in urban areas (Tinker and Bramsen, 1976). For example, the ICRW (1980b:68) has estimated that women provide between 46 and 70% of the informal sector in Latin America, in contrast to the smaller proportion of women in the formal labor force for these countries. In Southeast Asia, there are slightly lower proportions of women in the informal labor force.

Women's informal-sector participation, however, does not bode well for women's increased access to the new jobs generated by the world-system in urban areas. Women are less mobile than men out of the informal sector (Arizpe, 1977; Chaney and Schmink, 1980; ICRW, 1980b; Jules-Rosette, 1982; Schmink, 1977). In fact, even within the informal sector, men hold the upper-level jobs (ICRW, 1980b; Jules-Rosette, 1982; Papanek, 1979; Wachtel, 1976).

Many women migrants find that their only economic opportunities are in the informal sectors (Chaudhury, 1979; ICRW, 1980b; Koo and Smith, 1983, Latin American and Caribbean Women's Collective, 1977). Additionally, female-headed households are represented disproportionally in the informal sector (Buvinic *et al.,* 1978). Finally, women in the informal sector—in particular, women migrants—are much more likely than other workers to be in poverty. In the informal sector, women's wages, if they exist, average 40–50% less than men's (ICRW, 1980b).

Women's extensive informal-sector participation and their service-sector activity in developing countries demonstrate women's essential contribution to the operation of the capitalist world-economy at several different levels. If the informal sector has become essential to the process of capital accumulation, as Portes and Walton (1981) argue, then women's participation should become a central focus of our analyses. At the world-system level, Saffioti (1977:36) has noted that under conditions of unequal exchange in developing countries, there is a tendency toward the re-creation of precapitalist activities in the form of service or domestic work. In all countries, this work is performed by women, who have materially contributed to their societies through the reproduction of the labor force, use production within the home, and occasional exchange production. Now, in the context of the world-system, women are further contributing to capital accumulation through their informal-sector participation that has enabled the capitalist class to pay lower wages to family members employed outside the home (Deere, 1976; Jelin, 1977).

Alternatively, women traders in the enclave economies of West Africa and the Caribbean have provided essential, cheap linkages between precapitalist forms of production and the larger world-economy. Additionally, MNCs have promoted another use of female labor for unequal exchange by exploiting women's cheap labor in their plants or in the infrastructures of host countries (Neumann, 1978–1979). Finally, Schmink (1977) argues that the extraordinary growth of the tertiary sector observed for Latin America has been shaped predominately by women's participation in the service and informal sectors under dependent development—a phenomenon ignored by Portes and others (for an exception, see Timberlake and Kentor, 1983).

In these ways, the exploitation of women's labor within the home and the market has reached a new dimension in developing countries. This dimension, however, too rarely has been recognized by world-system and dependency theorists. For example, Boulding (1977) argues that women's unpaid labor and work within the informal sector constitutes a hidden prop for development efforts. If this prop is taken away, as it has been through development and government officials' ignorance of women's prior economic roles, as noted above, then the already disrupted economies could experience even greater problems in the near future. (See Boserup [1970] and Tinker [1976] for examples of how development and investment programs have been skewed toward men even though women have had equally important roles in production.) If we seek solutions to the problems of unequal exchange, women's roles must now form a central part of our analyses.

Empirical Indicators of Women's Economic Participation

Large-scale trends of women's economic participation are reflected by International Labour Organisation (1977) data on women's share of the labor force and economic sectors and by women's labor-force participation rates. The statistics in Table 14.3 are arranged by the position of nation's within the world-system and by geographic region. Further, these data provide an interesting contrast to the results of Timberlake and Lunday (Chapter 15, this volume).

An accurate picture of women's economic participation is difficult to acquire because of undernumeration of women's economic participation in many developing countries. For example, in some countries, women's economic activities are included in national accounts; in other countries, these activities are defined as women's unpaid labor within the home (Boserup, 1970; ICRW, 1980a; Nash, 1980; Newland, 1979). Furthermore, many researchers have argued that we must consider both women's paid and unpaid labor in calculating women's total economic contribution (Aguiar, 1983). Unfortunately, only data on women's overall formal participation are available to estimate women's participation in urban areas.

World-System and Cross-National Trends

Over time, women in core and semiperipheral areas have had access to a greater share of the labor force than women in peripheral areas (see Table 14.3). By 1975, women's share of the labor force relative to men's had increased several percentage points from the 1960 levels for both the core and semiperiphery (to 35 and 31%, respectively); women's share in the peripheral areas had increased only to 29%. Similar patterns are apparent for women's labor-force participation rates and women's share of agriculture, industry, and service relative to men's. What is notable about these statistics is the relative stagnation over time of women's share of economic resources at lower levels in the periphery than in either core countries or semiperiphery countries. For example, in the peripheral countries, women's participation in and share of the labor force has remained steady over the 15-year period. The only increase has been for women's share of the service sectors. Yet the levels of women's share of the service sector have remained below the levels of the other areas of the world-system.

Some might argue that these patterns merely reflect differences in levels

TABLE 14.3

Mean Percentage Levels of Women's Share of the Labor Force, Participation Rate, and Share of Agricultural, Industrial, and Service Sectors by Position within World-System, 1960 and 1975[a]

Position	N^b	PWLF 1960	PWLF 1975	WLFP 1960	WLFP 1975	PWAG 1960	PWAG 1975	PWIND 1960	PWIND 1975	PWSER 1960	PWSER 1975
Core	18	31	35	39	46	22	24	20	23	42	45
Semiperiphery	30	28	31	37	41	27	28	20	22	32	37
Periphery	78	28	29	40	40	26	26	17	19	27	30

[a] Definitions: PWLF: women's share of labor force relative to men's; WLFP: women's participation rate; PWAG, PWIND, PWSER: women's share of agricultural, industrial, and service sectors, respectively, relative to men's. The share variables are computed by dividing the female labor force aged 15–64 (total or by sector) by the overall labor force aged 15–64 or employment in each sector. The participation variable is computed by dividing the total female labor force by the total female population aged 15–64. Source: ILO (1977).

[b] Number of countries in each group.

of economic development. I argue, however, that the patterns represent the deleterious processes of the world economic system on the status of women. Women in the periphery are at a disadvantage relative to men in access to resources and also relative to other women and men in the hierarchial division of labor within the world-system (see also Safa, 1977). This argument is supported by data demonstrating that women's access to economic resources relative to men's is reduced by higher levels of foreign investment and trade dependency (Ward, 1983). Further, although one of the consequences of the world-system has been the extraordinary growth of the tertiary sector, we can see that women in peripheral areas have not increased dramatically their formal share of this sector. Obviously, the increased number of paid service-sector jobs has gone primarily to men. As noted above, women's economic participation has increased instead in the informal or unpaid sectors.

These negative effects on women's participation can be examined further by looking at the same labor statistics arranged by geographic region (see Table 14.4). Here European women have greater access to economic resources, relative to men, than do women in other regions. A substantial part of the stagnation in periphery women's access to resources has occurred in Africa, where women's share of the labor force has remained the same over time. African women's participation actually has declined. These patterns have occurred because the creation of employment opportunities has not kept pace with population growth under the processes of urbanization and the intrusion of the world-system (ICRW, 1980b; Safa, 1977; Todaro, 1981). Under these circumstances, preference has been given to hiring males. Nevertheless women have been expected to be economically

TABLE 14.4

Mean Percentage Levels of Women's Share of the Labor Force, Participation Rate, and Share of Agricultural, Manufacturing, and Service Sector by Geographic Region, 1960 and 1975[a]

Geographic region	N^b	PWLF		WLFP		PWAG		PWIND		PWSER	
		1960	1975	1960	1975	1960	1975	1960	1975	1960	1975
Africa	41	31	31	47	45	31	32	15	17	24	26
Americas	27	23	25	28	29	11	10	20	19	43	43
Asia	31	25	28	36	38	27	29	18	22	20	26
Europe	27	33	35	43	48	30	32	22	24	40	44
	126										

[a] Definitions: PWLF: women's share of labor force relative to men's; WLFP: women's participation rate; PWAG, PWIND, PWSER: women's share of agricultural, industrial, and service sectors, respectively, relative to men's. The share variables are computed by dividing the female labor force aged 15–64 (total or by sector) by the overall labor force aged 15–64 or employment in each sector. The participation variable is computed by dividing the total female labor force by the total female population aged 15–64. Source: ILO (1977).

[b] Number of countries in each group.

independent either as spouses or heads of households (Buvinic *et al.*, 1978; Van Allen, 1976).

In the Americas, women's share of industry has declined over time, while women's service-sector participation has remained constant at 43%. Thus, although the urban areas are more heavily female-populated and there are higher participation rates for women in the urban areas via the service sector, women still participate at lower rates when compared with women around the world. An exception to this pattern is in Arab and Muslim countries where women's participation is lower. In the Americas, this pattern of participation results from women's withdrawal from the labor force upon marriage and their increasing participation in the informal sector, where women's domestic duties can be more readily combined with paid work performed for nonfamily members (Chaney and Schmink, 1980; Youssef, 1971).

In Asia, increases in women's overall share of the industrial and service sectors have been magnified for women through multinational employment in labor-intensive plants and the pursuant infrastructure and service-sector growth that results (ICRW, 1980b; Papanek, 1976). As noted above, however, the labor force participation of these women has been tenuous, given the unstable, competitive nature of MNC export production.

Thus, women's share of economic resources has remained stagnant over time in the periphery. Some differences exist by region, in particular Africa, where women's access to employment has not kept pace with population growth. These patterns of gender inequality are significantly related to intrusion of the world-system and the disruptive effects of urbanization on women's access to the new resources and to the more traditional forms of subsistence employment. These dynamics also affect women who must support families.

FEMALE-HEADED HOUSEHOLDS

Over time the number of female-headed households has been increasing around the world. Such households, however, have been increasing most dramatically in Africa, Latin America, and Asia. In their landmark work, Buvinic *et al.* (1978:5) estimated that 25–33% of the households in the world are female headed. The mean percentage of potential female heads by geographic region ranges from 15% in South America to 22% in Africa south of the Sahara.

Migration and urbanization are viewed as major factors in the increase of female-headed households (Buvinic *et al.,* 1978). Both international and national migration have had an impact. For example, men in the Middle East, Turkey, and Morocco have been migrating to Europe and leaving women to work in subsistence agricultural production. In Africa, men have migrated to the mines and urban areas, leaving women in the rural areas. For example, almost 40% of the adult males of Lesotho work in the mines of South Africa (Mueller, 1977). Meanwhile, given the higher rates of female migration to the urban areas in Latin America, female-headed households are found predominately in the urban areas (ICRW, 1980b).

Likewise, in the urban areas, female-headed households are concentrated largely in the poverty population because of women's limited access to employment other than in the informal sector (Buvinic *et al.,* 1978; Mazumdar, 1978; Tinker, 1976). For example, in Brazil, 85% of the female heads of households who are in poverty are in the informal sector; only 25% of the male heads in poverty are similarly situated (Merrick and Schmink, 1983:257). Since female heads are more likely to be migrants in Latin America, Buvinic *et al.* (1978) argue that the urban areas create economic traps for women. Women are likely to perceive greater economic opportunities in the urban areas, yet opportunities are in fact very limited, especially for female heads of households. Further, although informal sector work can be combined with childcare more easily, it provides less subsistence or income than modern-sector employment (Blumberg, 1978; ICRW, 1980a).

Women Who Remain Behind in Rural Areas

As a consequence of the migration trends discussed above, many women are left with the double burden of running their households while providing the means of subsistence for their families. This is especially true if the males of the households are paid only individual wages as opposed to family wages (ICRW, 1980b). The MNCs and capitalists can pay lower wages if they assume that women will provide the bulk of subsistence for the household. This means that men may have very little money to send back to their families (Mueller, 1977). Then women who work primarily in agriculture must provide food for an ever-increasing number of persons, with only limited access to land, agricultural inputs, technology, and/or credit (Boserup, 1970; Hay, 1976; Seidman, 1981). A related problem has been discussed by Cho and Koo (1983), who note an increasing burden on older Korean women in agriculture as younger women migrate to urban areas to work in MNCs. As a consequence of these burdens on women, continued increases in food production, particularly in Africa, cannot be assured.

Summary and Conclusion

This brief description of women's economic roles in urban areas and the world-system demonstrates that women's roles need to be incorporated into our analyses for several reasons. First, we can no longer assume that patterns of migration to urban areas are similar for women and men. Boserup and other researchers have demonstrated that differential patterns of migration exist by sex. Second, these migration patterns have implications for the sex composition of urban areas and the availability of female labor for exploitation in the paid and unpaid sectors. Likewise, male wages and employment are affected by these patterns. With the greater presence of women in the urban areas, we would expect to find extraordinary large service and informal sectors in comparison to the industrial sector, because women are drawn into service and informal employment. Lower wages can be paid all workers, because the difference can be made up by using services and goods in the informal sector. At the same time, women are kept out of capital-intensive and better-paid employment. In towns marked by higher proportions of males, we find individual wage employment; women are expected to provide their own and their children's means of economic subsistence.

Third, the pattern of women's displacement from agricultural and industrial employment into the informal sector and the heightened demand for women's labor in MNC processing for export means that women are playing an increasingly important role in the operation of urban areas in developing countries and in the world-economy. Women provide the transitional and adaptive bridge between precapitalist sectors of the peripheral economies and the world-economy. When needed, women provide the cheap labor force necessary to maintain the competitive edge within the global assembly line.

Despite the importance of women's economic roles, many researchers and policymakers ignore the effects of development and the world-system on women's roles. This omission is a serious one on two counts. First, most women need access to paying jobs to support themselves and their families, even when they have employed spouses. With increasing population pressures, these women need additional laborers and other agricultural inputs to maintain current levels of food production. Second, if we seek remedies to the problems of unequal exchange and dependent development in the world-system, our remedies or solutions are apt to be ineffective or misguided without incorporation of women's economic and social roles. Further research and theoretical development are needed to incorporate fully *all* of the world's population into theories of urbanization and world-system.

15

LABOR FORCE STRUCTURE IN THE ZONES OF THE WORLD-ECONOMY, 1950-1970

Michael Timberlake and James Lunday

INTRODUCTION

The history of the progressive urbanization of the world's population in the modern global economy is fundamentally interwoven with the changing nature of its occupational requirements. The expansion of industrial production and the spread of market relations have produced an increasingly larger nonagricultural labor force, both in absolute numbers and in terms of the proportionate share of the labor force working in seemingly "modern" occupations. Of course global statements such as these mask many significant differences in the way in which men and women are employed around the world. It is the primary purpose of this chapter to describe in very broad terms differences in the labor force structure across zones of the world-system. It is shown that, in spite of the qualitatively limited data available on occupational distribution, there are discernible differences in employment patterns and these differences can be meaningfully interpreted from a world-system theoretical perspective.

It is in the cities of the world that one is confronted most directly with the diversity and contradictions of modern social life. Opulence is surrounded by stark poverty; recreation and leisure are enjoyed amid the intense hustle and bustle of activities through which people acquire the means of living; corporate executives and professionals walk streets crowded with petty vendors, prostitutes, beggars, and panhandlers. These incongruities, both intriguing and appalling to many observers, and identified with urban social problems of various kinds, have spread across the face of the globe.

From Calcutta to Nairobi to Lima to Baltimore, one finds this pattern of urban life reproduced in the face of considerable cultural and political variation.

The contradictions of urban life began to catch the attention of social scientists and development specialists in the 1950s, as urban poverty and unemployment seemed to spread inexorably rather than diminish with the spread of manufacturing and modern life styles. In the Third World the contrasts have been especially stark, and the questions for scholars of development have seemed correspondingly more urgent. These questions have included: (1) Why has urbanization progressed so rapidly in Third World countries? (2) Why is urban life marked by such contrasts and disparities as we observe? and (3) Are these phenomena a transitional aspect of progress toward better lives for Third World peoples, or just the reproduction of longstanding disparities of wealth and power in new forms? We address the second question in this chapter. But before doing so a comment on the level of our analysis is in order.

Urbanization and Changing Employment Patterns

The fact that this chapter like the others in this book deals with seemingly abstract and rather general social structures and processes should not obscure our assumption that these larger issues reflect aspects of reality that impinge fundamentally on the experiences of individuals, families, communities, and social classes. C. Wright Mills urged us to explore the connections between history, economy, and personal biography, and it is true that we do not focus on these connections per se in this volume. But that macro social structures and processes are examined in their own right should not be taken to indicate that we are unconcerned with how they relate to individuals. We assume that they do. Furthermore, we contend that analysis of the macroprocesses themselves is crucial to an understanding of fundamental aspects of social change that have too often been ignored in the literature on comparative development.

An example of a genre of conventional development studies indicates what social scientists often miss by ignoring these macroissues. There is a sizeable and growing body of literature that deals cross-nationally with social-status attainment (e.g., Hope, 1982; Koo and Smith, 1983; Tyree *et al.*, 1979), and extensions of this that, for example, assess the impact of rural-to-urban migration on changes in occupational mobility.

When done "correctly" on their own terms, these studies control for shifts in the occupational structure of the nation in question by statistically holding these shifts constant and asking how status-attainment patterns have changed independently of changes that are due to shifts of the occupational structure (e.g., increases in the proportion of skilled jobs). While this is the correct approach for answering the questions posed, it is one that ignores a set of questions that are central from our point of view: To what extent, how, and why does the structure of occupations vary across political regions of the world? The distribution of occupations is one crucial structural constraint that defines the context in which individuals in society "take new heart or go broke, peasants become workers, workers become unemployed," and, no doubt, sons and daughters occasionally exceed the social status attained by their fathers and mothers. For the comparative status-attainment research, expansion and contraction of the occupational system are taken into account only insofar as they need to be controlled—they are theoretically uninteresting. But from our point of view this is a crucial structural feature that, on the one hand, can be fairly concretely tied to processes of the world-system, and, on the other hand, is obviously important for individuals and the nature of class relations. It is the former set of relationships that we examine in this chapter.

In the past century the population of the world has become both increasingly urbanized and increasingly employed in nonagricultural occupations. In 1900 an estimated 28% of the world's labor force was engaged in nonagricultural occupations (Bairoch and Limbor, 1968) and 9% of the world's people lived in cities of 20,000 or more (Davis, 1955). By 1970, 50% of the labor force was employed in those kinds of occupations, and cities accounted for 28% of the world's people (Goldstein and Sly, 1975:43). Viewed historically these changes have been part of the expansion of capitalist market relations and industrialization, which created the conditions leading to the emergence and expanded reproduction of manufacturing and service occupations in the world-economy. Such statements, of course, mask a great deal of resistance and human suffering caused by these and any such large-scale social changes. The point is, nevertheless, that whether forced, cajoled, or attracted by the genuine advantages of city life a growing proportion of the world's population has become urban primarily because of expanding employment opportunities in cities.

These labor force changes have occurred quite unevenly in different parts of the world. Across nations the shifts from agricultural to nonagricultural employment have occurred at various times, at varying rates, and to varying degrees of completeness. Consequently, a major characteristic of the world labor force noted by many observers is that there is significant variation across nations in the distribution of the labor force into agricultural, manufacturing, and service occupations.

The differences in this regard between core and peripheral nations are striking. One widely noted difference is that the former have, for at least the past 30 years, had much less than one-fourth of their workers employed in agriculture (primary labor force sector),[1] while in the latter much more than half of the labor force has continued to be employed in those jobs. But, the more interesting labor force difference between the core nations and peripheral nations is that the latter have much larger service sectors than would be expected on the basis of the development histories of the core nations. In the core nations nonagricultural employment was concentrated more in manufacturing than in services until 1960 or 1970. Only in the post–World War II period has service sector employment surged ahead of employment in manufacturing. This shift to greater service sector employment is sometimes referred to as a *postindustrial* phase in national economic development (cf. Bell, 1973). The Third World has also experienced a rapid growth of service sector employment as agricultural populations have moved into the cities. But, unlike the presently industrialized nations, Third World nations have not had a leading phase of industrial employment growth. The service sectors of Third World economies thus appear to be premature, or overdeveloped.[2] This structural characteristic is referred to as "hypertrophy of the service sector" (Amin, 1976), the "pseudo tertiary" (Germani, 1973), the "overloaded" tertiary, and so on.

The observation that peripheral nations tend to have bloated tertiary employment sectors has been linked to inequalities of income and wealth (e.g., Evans and Timberlake, 1980; but also see Fiala [1983] for a different interpretation). This suggests that differences between conditions of employment in the manufacturing sector and the service sector may underlie the contrasts of urban life we have cited. However, the distinction between "service" jobs and "manufacturing" jobs often does not match another fundamental dichotomy among nonagricultural occupations. Within both secondary and tertiary labor sectors one finds jobs that are well paid and ill paid, high status and low status, safe and unsafe.

Another classification of labor force participation that has gained considerable attention in recent years seems to be more directly related to the observed contrasts of urban life with which we are concerned. Portes (Chapter 4, this volume) and others have suggested the crucial distinction between "formal" and "informal" economic activities. The utility of this distinction is supported by numerous case studies that have indicated that

---

[1]The primary sector is overwhelmingly agricultural, but also includes jobs in timber, quarrying, and, sometimes, mining.

[2]The notion that the service sector is overdeveloped is rooted in a particular theoretical perspective. Development specialists have typically supposed that nations follow a common path of economic development, and the development histories of the now-industrialized and wealthy nations are taken to be representative of this path.

peripheral national economies have much larger informal sectors than do core national economies.[3] The term *informal sector* refers to those economic activities that fall outside the purview of the state, require little start-up and operating capital, and operate on the basis of informal relationships (often family relationships) rather than formal bureaucratic rules (Merrick, 1977; Portes, Chapter 4, this volume; Senghass-Knoblock, 1977). This sector typically includes "marginal" and petty (frequently illegal) commercial and production activities. These include personal services, street vending, labor-intensive handicraft and artisan production, redundant government work, and a variety of other make-work jobs such as operating an automated elevator. Many of these jobs, as Portes points out, serve the important function of helping to reproduce formal sector labor at below market value, thus accounting for core–periphery differences in wages.

Our knowledge about informal employment is quite limited, but a growing number of case studies (e.g., Hart, 1973; Lobo, 1982; Perlman, 1976), allow us to proceed with research on the basis of hypotheses and informed suppositions. Moreover, we can make a few aggregate-level statements about these activities with some assurance. Generally speaking, it seems true that informal and formal sector economic activities are unevenly distributed between core and peripheral national economies, and informal sector economic activities are usually less remunerative than are formal sector activities (again, see Portes, Chapter 4, this volume). These assertions are explored, at least indirectly, in this chapter. Another interesting and important dimension of variation concerns gender differences in informal sector participation rates. A growing body of research indicates that women in many regions are more likely than men to be employed in informal, reproductive occupations (e.g., Boserup, 1970; Beneria and Sen, 1981; Youseff, 1974). While we do not explore gender variation in labor force status here, Ward (Chapter 14, this volume) does explicitly discuss female–male differences in the urbanization experience.

The general discussion of informal–formal sector employment patterns suggests that the differences between the two sectors in rates of employment and the numeric relationship between the two categories in a given city may underlie some of the contrasting features of urban life we so readily observe in Third World nations. This specific hypothesis has not been tested against cross-national data, and cannot be at present because of the lack of the

---

[3]The terms *traditional* and *modern* are often used in a similar way, usually in conjunction with the term *dual economy*. We prefer *formal* and *informal* because they are better grounded empirically and theoretically. On close inspection many "traditional" jobs did not exist, or at least did not exist in present form, prior to an area's involvement in the capitalist world-economy.

appropriate comparative data, but it specifies the direction in which the descriptive analysis reported here is aimed.

The World Labor Force, 1950-1970

The aim of the research reported here is limited. We wish simply to describe the structure of the labor force in the world as a whole and across the theoretically defined zones of the world-economy (see Kentor, Chapter 2, this volume). In spite of this modest goal, we face a number of obstacles, the most severe of which are the limited availability of data over time for large numbers of countries and the lack of detailed labor force data. Our theoretical discussion began by focusing on the importance of the large relative size of the tertiary labor sector in peripheral countries, but we concluded by agreeing with Portes that it is the large relative size of the informal labor sector that is the more theoretically relevant distinguishing feature of the periphery. While the two are likely to be correlated in the periphery, they are far from identical. Unfortunately, data are not normally available that classify workers into formal–informal categories. We are forced either to abandon any attempt to broadly describe labor force participation in the world-economy or to base it on the data that are available. We have chosen to do the latter, but we are well aware of the limitations this imposes on the inferences we make from our analysis.

Methodological Considerations

The descriptive analysis that follows employs two data sets published by the International Labour Organisation (ILO). The data on which we rely most heavily, because they are much more complete in terms of the number of countries covered, are those published in *Labour Force Estimates and Projections, 1950-2000* (ILO, 1977). More detailed data are available in ILO *Yearbooks* (various years), but these provide coverage for many fewer countries. The classification scheme used by the ILO includes occupations in agriculture as part of the primary sector of the labor force. The secondary sector includes manufacturing, construction, mining, and electrical and other utilities occupations, and the tertiary sector includes jobs in commerce, transportation and communications, and government, commercial, and personal services. We are concerned here with describing the labor force structure of the contemporary world-economy and recent changes therein. Accordingly we describe the broad labor force structure of the world-economy as a whole and we compare the labor force structure across hierarchical divisions (core, semiperiphery, and periphery) within this system. We can acknowledge that the broad categories of labor force participation that we examine are woefully general and yet reject the popular admonition that they are useless. These data should allow us to make some inferences concerning the distribution of informal and formal sector activities across areas of the world-economy. But these inferences are based on the assumed correlation between informal occupations and tertiary occupations, and it is only the latter that we directly observe. The data for secondary and tertiary subsectors (ILO *Yearbooks*) allow us to approximate even more closely the formal–informal sector dimension. Certain subcategories (e.g., banking and insurance) are less likely than others (e.g., personal services) to contain informal sector activities, and they can each be examined separately.

Another problem that we face with these data concerns the data collection procedure. Data on employment are gathered and reported by governments of nation-states. Because those governments collect and report statistics with considerably variable degrees of efficiency, detail, and thoroughness, and for varying social and political reasons, our numbers may contain distortions of reality. For example, since the more accurate data probably come from the developed countries, and from the "modern" sectors of less developed countries, we suspect that agricultural and certain service sector employments will be underreported in the country level data. However, the ILO has made every attempt to adjust for such biases in their *Labour Force Estimates and Projections.* In addition to examining the distribution of the labor force into the three major economic sectors, we also construct a ratio measure of tertiary sector employment to secondary sector employment. We refer to this as the *T/S ratio.* Recall from our discussion above that it is the seemingly large size of the tertiary labor sector compared to the size of the secondary sector in the periphery that has caught the attention of many observers of Third World cities. The T/S ratio measure will give us a way to document change in the "bloated tertiary" over time and to compare differences across zones in the world-economy. In constructing this measure we are not claiming that there is any known ideal ratio or any point at which distorted labor force development or "bloating" of the tertiary occurs. Nor do we wish to suggest that within-sector variability is insignificant. Rather, we examine this particular dimension of variability in nonagricultural employment because it has caught the attention of observers and may indicate more fundamental variation for which we do not now have comparative data.

Units of Analysis

For theoretical reasons we employ the world-system premise that the population of the world constitutes an effective global economy that is singular, geopolitically decentralized, and hierarchically coordinated (Wallerstein, 1974, 1979; Chase-Dunn and Rubinson, 1979; Kentor, Chapter 2, this volume; Sokolovsky, Chapter 3, this volume) as a basis for our comparative examination of the development of the sectoral distributions of employment from 1950 to 1970. We believe this conceptual premise provides a theoretical basis for explaining the cross-national labor force variations we observe, and for assessing their implications for the futures of Third World peoples. It should therefore serve our purposes to employ the conceptual categories of the world-system perspective in our comparative study of sectoral employment changes.

In this scheme two of the most important structural features of the world-economy are (1) the differentiation of the world's population into three unequal tiers or zones of economic and political power—the core, the semiperiphery, and the periphery— and (2) the organization of the world's peoples and territories into a global system of autonomous and competing states rather than into a single political system. We thus have three theoretically important units of analysis into which to organize our examination of the structure of the world labor force: the world-economy as a whole, the zones of the world-economy, and nations. We employ the former two here.

This is a departure from standard practice, and it raises empirical problems. One problem is that because there have been only a few attempts to analyze data in line with this theoretical perspective we do not have widely accepted methodological formulas for conducting our analysis. We have had to consider two interrelated problems: (1) empirically defining the boundaries of the world-economy and of the zones of the world division of labor, and (2) reaggregating the available data according to these newly defined units of analysis. The choices we have made may significantly affect our conclusions.

The problem of defining the boundaries of the world-economy is essentially the problem of how to decide whether a population involved in agricultural production is in or out of the system, since, in principle, such a population may be engaged in subsistence production. This cannot be the case for those working in the manufacturing or service sectors in which production is obviously for markets. Sokolovsky (Chapter 3, this volume) proposes that a population be regarded as "incorporated within the system when the structure of economic networks and power relations can be used to manipulate subsistence agriculture in response to global imperatives." This is a definition that we would like to use, but the necessary data collection is beyond the scope of this study. However, for two reasons we believe our inability to rigorously employ this definition is not a serious shortcoming.

First, the problem of defining the boundaries of the system as a whole is ameliorated by the fact that we are looking primarily at 1950 and later, and most world-system scholars would agree that by this time virtually all populations had been at least partially incorporated (e.g., Chase-Dunn,

Chapter 12, this volume). Second, although it is still possible that within peripheral countries there are significantly large populations that live in autonomous subsistence economies, it is likely that they function as labor reserves for the capitalist economy and/or are compelled to raise cash crops from time to time (cf. Sokolovsky, Chapter 3, this volume). We have concluded, therefore, that our data do not include sizable populations that are not part of the world-economy. However, to the extent that this is not the case we are likely to have an overestimate of the proportion of the labor force of the world-system engaged in agriculture, especially in the periphery. The reader will note that this bias works in a direction opposite to the collection and reporting biases discussed above. It is likely that it has been just those agricultural populations of autonomous subsistence producers that are likely to have been overlooked in national statistics.

The differentiation of the world's population into core, semiperipheral, and peripheral populations poses a more troublesome problem because there is not always direct correspondence between the conceptual boundaries of these zones and the boundaries of the units (usually nations) by which the data we use are aggregated. Conceptually, the zones are defined in terms of variable attributes of the relationships among the world's populations that constitute the hierarchically organized world division of labor. Allocating populations (and thereby geopolitical areas) to one or another zone is best done on the basis of examining those economic and political relationships that impart a hierarchical structure to the world division of labor and unevenly distribute control over world production to the world's peoples. But we must rely on national statistics that typically aggregate populations without regard to world market relations. Again, we cannot gather the data that would allow us to properly differentiate the world's population into core, semiperiphery, and periphery. Our working solution is to accept, in principle, the strategy employed by Kentor in Chapter 2 in classifying nations in the three zones. Since the world-system of states is a major structural component of the world division of labor, national statistics do capture some of the unequal distribution of control over world production. Kentor worked out some specific indicators of variation in control over world production that were used to designate national populations as primarily core, semiperipheral, or peripheral. Our classification is necessarily much more crude, and it is described in the appendix.

Data Analysis and Findings

For the purposes of our analysis we have calculated two sets of summary statistics. In Table 15.1 we present means for the distributions of national employment across employment sectors for each category of nations. For example, in 1950 the mean proportion of a national labor force engaged in

TABLE 15.1

Average National Percentage Distribution of Labor Force by Sector for Zones of the World-Economy, 1950, 1960, and 1970[a]

Year and labor force sector	World average (N = 130)	Core average (N = 16)	Semiperiphery average (N = 26)	Periphery average (N = 88)
1950				
Primary	62.3	26.4	48.7	72.8
Secondary	16.6	36.7	24.3	10.6
Tertiary	21.1	36.9	26.8	16.6
T/S ratio	1.58	1.01	1.12	1.82
1960				
Primary	56.7	18.4	40.9	68.3
Secondary	19.0	39.6	29.4	12.2
Tertiary	24.3	42.0	29.6	19.6
T/S ratio	1.54	1.08	1.03	1.77
1970				
Primary	50.2	11.3	32.6	62.4
Secondary	21.1	39.9	32.3	14.3
Tertiary	28.7	48.8	35.0	23.2
T/S ratio	1.58	1.25	1.12	1.78

[a] Hong Kong and Singapore are excluded from this analysis because they are essentially city-states and have virtually no agricultural sectors. They are included in the total labor force description in Table 15.2.

the primary sector was 62.3%. In the core zone of the world-economy the mean proportion was 26.4%. The figures in Table 15.2 represent the percentage distributions of the total world or zone labor forces into the employment categories. For example, in 1950, 64.3% of the world labor force was engaged in the primary sector. These two methods of aggregation produce a similar picture of the labor force structure of the world-economy. Differences that do appear are slight but are of interest. They are discussed where appropriate.

We begin with an examination of the labor force structure of the world-economy as a whole before going on to describe differences across zones of the system. Tables 15.1 and 15.2 indicate that, whether we look at national averages or total labor force, the basic discernible structure of the world labor force and changes therein are similar. About half of the world's labor force was employed in agricultural occupations in 1970 but this represents a substantial reduction in that percentage since 1950 (from 64%, Table 15.2). Because the world's population is overwhelmingly "less developed" it is not surprising that agricultural employment remains high. The 14% shift in relative employment opportunities out of the primary labor force was absorbed about equally into the two remaining labor force

TABLE 15.2

Percentage Distributions of World and Zone Labor Force by Sector, 1950, 1960, and 1970

Year and labor force sector	World	Core	Semiperiphery	Periphery
1950				
Primary	64.3	34.1	76.0	76.5
Secondary	16.3	31.7	11.2	8.4
Tertiary	19.4	34.2	12.7	15.1
T/S ratio	1.19	1.08	1.13	1.79
N (millions)	1099.2	309.8	519.4	270.4
% of world labor force	100.0	28.2	47.3	24.6
1960				
Primary	56.7	24.4	68.8	67.8
Secondary	20.6	35.4	16.8	12.0
Tertiary	22.7	40.2	14.4	20.2
T/S ratio	1.10	1.14	.85	1.69
N (millions)	1301.5	347.7	630.4	323.36
% of world labor force	100.0	26.7	48.4	24.8
1970				
Primary	49.6	14.5	62.2	60.2
Secondary	23.4	38.2	20.5	14.4
Tertiary	27.0	47.2	17.3	25.3
T/S ratio	1.16	1.24	.84	1.76
N (millions)	1520.3	386.6	729.6	404.1
% of world labor force	100.0	25.4	47.9	26.6

sectors over the 20-year-period, with each of these sectors increasing its representation in the total labor force by about 7%. This is reflected by the remarkable stability of the ratio of tertiary to secondary employment over the 20-year period. While the T/S ratio did decrease measurably from 1950 to 1960, it increased again almost to its 1950 level in 1970. The national averages (Table 15.1, Column 1) indicate more tertiary employment relative to secondary employment than does the total world labor force distribution (Table 15.2), but these national averages are even somewhat more stable over the 20-year period. There was a small, insignificant decrease from 1950 to 1960, but in 1970 the ratio returned to its 1950 level of 1.58.

This finding may call into question some of the recent observations regarding hypertrophication of the tertiary. When we look back to 1960 we see a secular "trend" in which tertiary sector employment is absorbing an increasing proportion of the nonagricultural labor force in comparison to the secondary. The 1950 T/S ratio, however, indicates that the sectoral distribution of urban employment may be a cyclical phenomenon (although it may certainly be changing in a secular fashion as well), shifting toward manufacturing in one period and back toward service sector employment in another. The T/S ratios for a sample of core countries for the period 1850 to 1970 (Table 15.3) would seem to corroborate this hypothesis. The ratio increases from 1850 to 1880, then falls in 1900 before increasing over the next 30-year period, and so on.

Shifting our attention to the hierarchical divisions of the world-system we find that there are significant differences between the percentage distributions given in Tables 15.1 and 15.2. These discrepancies occur in the semiperiphery category, and they are due to the fact that two extremely populous and highly agricultural countries—China and India—have been included in the semiperiphery. Including the workers of these countries in population totals for the zones of the world-economy (Table 15.2) has the effect of raising the percentage of the semiperipheral labor force in agriculture to the same level as that in the periphery because so many agricultural workers are added to the semiperiphery total. The averages for national labor forces (Table 15.1) standardize on populations, and so remove the population-size effects of India and China.[4] Even with this effect present in Table 15.2 it shows significant differences between the semiperiphery and the periphery. The relative numbers employed in secondary sector occupations is significantly higher in the semiperiphery and the T/S ratio is significantly lower there.

When the Chinese and Indian labor force data are excluded from our calculations, the numbers in Tables 15.1 and 15.2 become more similar. The proportions of semiperipheral workers in the primary sector are reduced to 52% for 1950, 41% for 1960, and 29% for 1970. These numbers are very close to those in Table 15.1. Similarly, the T/S ratios for the semiperiphery are changed by the exclusion of those workers. While the national labor force averages indicate that the ratio dropped from 1.12 in 1950 to 1.03 in 1960, and then rose to 1.12 in 1970, Table 15.2 does not show the increase in the second half of our period. With Indian and Chinese workers excluded, the ratios for each of the three decennial years become much closer to the national averages reported in Table 15.1, and the pattern of change (i.e., very little) in the ratio over the 20-year period is very similar

[4]This discrepancy highlights the problem we discussed above of using the national data. Not all of the agricultural workers in China and India belong in the semiperiphery category, even though the Chinese and Indian states are quite powerful domestically and internationally. Large numbers of Chinese and Indian agricultural workers are as economically and politically powerless as any in the world. On the other hand, both countries contain large (in comparison to other noncore countries) economically and politically powerful populations—people who control greater capital, technology, and military–political power than do others with whom they are associated economically.

TABLE 15.3

Tertiary/Secondary Ratios for Periphery and Core, 1850–1970[a]

Zone	1850	1880	1900	1920	1930	1950	1960	1970
Periphery	—	—	1.25	1.26	1.33	1.79	1.69	1.76
Core	.68	.87	.81	.92	1.09	1.08	1.14	1.24

[a] The 1850–1930 ratios are computed from data presented in Bairoch and Limbor (1968). The 1950–1970 figures are from Table 15.2. Computations for the periphery, based on the data of Bairoch and Limbor (1968) produced ratios of a somewhat smaller magnitude (1.67, 1.53, 1.62) than those shown here. This is probably due to the fact that their data are presented for "less developed countries" and are likely to include a few countries of the semiperiphery.

as well. Other figures are also brought into approximate correspondence by the exclusion of Chinese and Indian workers from Table 15.2.[5]

We focus on the distributions reported in Table 15.1 (nation averages) in discussing other labor force patterns in the world-economy. As expected, sectoral employment was unevenly distributed across zones of the world-economy during the 20-year period. Taking 1960 as a reference point, we find that the average peripheral country had about 68% of its labor force employed in primary sector activities, while the average core country had only about 18% of its labor force so employed. The typical semiperipheral nation had about 42% of its labor force employed in those occupations. This pattern of differences across zones is the same for all three time points.

Changes in the sectoral distributions of employment between 1950 and 1970 also varied across zones of the world-economy. In all three zones, average national primary sector employment as a proportion of total employment declined, but both the rate and magnitude of decline were smaller in the periphery than in the other two zones. The greatest decline occurred in the semiperiphery. This is not a surprising finding for two reasons. One is that the semiperiphery began the period with a much higher proportion of its labor force in the primary sector than did the core, so the amount of change possible in the core was more constrained. Second, the semiperiphery is perceived to be a very dynamic zone in the world-economy in which elites whose interest are tied to peripheral production vie for economic and political control with elites whose interests are tied to core production (Wallerstein, 1979). Such factors as foreign investment and state programs of import substitution are more likely to generate manufacturing growth in

[5] Part of the explanation for this is that China experienced rapid industrial labor-force growth during the period (from 8.1% in 1950 to 20.4% in 1970) and very slow tertiary sector growth (7.4 to 11.8%). On the other hand, Indian data have the opposite effect because the T/S ratio of that country was much higher (in 1960 India was 1.29 while China was .63), although still substantially lower than for the periphery.

that zone than in the periphery, especially during the upswing in a long cycle of world economic growth.

The rapid decline in primary sector employment in the semiperiphery is more striking than the percentage change indicates when it is realized that decline occurred during a period in which the absolute numbers of workers in the primary sector increased (as was also the case in the periphery). This was largely the result of high rates of natural population growth in those zones. (Were China and India not included in the semiperiphery, the absolute number of primary workers would register a decline from 1950 to 1970.)

Changes in secondary sector employment also varied across the zones of the world division of labor. Secondary employment in the core accounts for only a slightly larger percentage of the average core country's labor force in 1960 and 1970 than in 1950. Secondary sector employment increased only about 4 percentage points in the periphery but, because in 1950 the percentage of the labor force employed in secondary sector occupations in peripheral countries averaged around only 11%, the 3.7% increase to 1970 represents a very large proportionate increase over the 20-year period. Still, the 14.3% level of secondary sector employment for peripheral countries in 1970 indicates far less industrial activity than in either the semiperiphery or core. The average national share of the semiperipheral labor force in manufacturing and other secondary sector occupations increased substantially from around 24% in 1950 to more than 32% in 1970, thus closing the gap in this respect between these countries and those in the core.

Average tertiary sector employment substantially increased its share in each of the three zones of the world-economy over the 20-year period. Core employment in the tertiary increased from 37% to almost 50% in this time period, and the corresponding figures for the semiperiphery and periphery are 27 to 35% and 17 to 23%, respectively. Secondary and tertiary employment increased at about the same rates within both the semiperiphery and the periphery, but in the core secondary sector employment remains fairly constant over the 20-year period and the tertiary sector absorbed most of the almost 15% movement of labor out of the primary sector.

The increase in service sector employment in the core has been interpreted as an indication that these countries are moving into a postindustrial phase in which increasingly more people become involved in such fields as information processing, and in which industrial production becomes more automated, thus requiring fewer workers for given levels of output. But these changes are inseparable from the patterns of relations in the world-economy as a whole. For example, the expansion into the periphery and semiperiphery of core multinational corporation industrial activity occurs without a corresponding shift of associated services, such as top-level managerial functions and research and development activities. These remain in the core. The rapid increase in tertiary employment in peripheral economies cannot be interpreted in the same manner. This growth is not a response to industrial development; rather, the tertiary growth in petty services and the informal sector is in response to the low-wage nature of industrial employment coupled with increasing urban migration (Kentor, 1981).

This becomes clearer when we examine the size of the tertiary labor sector relative to that in the secondary labor sector, as shown by the T/S ratios in Table 15.1. The ratio was much higher for the periphery than either of the other two zones in 1950, and it decreased only insignificantly in 1960 and 1970. The difference between the ratios in the periphery and the core narrowed some between 1950 and 1970, but only because of the large "postindustrial" increase in tertiary employment in the core. The 1950 ratio in the semiperiphery drops from 1.12 to 1.03 in 1960, before increasing again to 1.12 in 1970. Actually, the only substantively significant change in the ratio for the three zones over the three time periods is the increase from 1.01 to 1.25 in the core from 1950 to 1970. The other ratios indicate virtually no change over time. The outstanding feature of the periphery in this respect, then, seems to be not that the size of the tertiary relative to the secondary labor force increases much over the three decennial periods, but rather that in 1950 it was already very high, and it was not significantly reduced by increases in industrial labor force participation.

The ILO data only allow us to examine the T/S ratios for a very short period, but data presented by Bairoch (1975, 1976b) and Bairoch and Limbor (1968) allow us to calculate ratios for six time points from 1900 to 1970 for several less developed countries and for more time points beginning in 1850 for several core countries. The ratios are given in Table 15.3. The figures indicate, somewhat surprisingly, that in the periphery the tertiary sector has been measurably larger than the secondary sector as far back as we have data, and the ratio increased steadily until 1950, after which it decreased somewhat then remained constant. The ratio of 1.25 for LDCs in 1900 is a level that is not achieved in the core until 1970. While the ratio has always been high in the periphery, it has increased significantly between 1900 and 1950, especially between 1930 and 1950, when the ratio jumped from 1.33 to 1.79. In the core in 1850 the tertiary sector employed significantly fewer people than the secondary sector, and it was not until 1920 that as many workers were employed in the latter as in the former in those countries. The patterns of change in the T/S ratios are graphically shown in Figure 15.1.

The secular increase in T/S ratio in the core may indeed reflect a postindustrial transformation of the occupational structure, but in the periphery the increases in already rather high ratios since 1900 cannot be interpreted

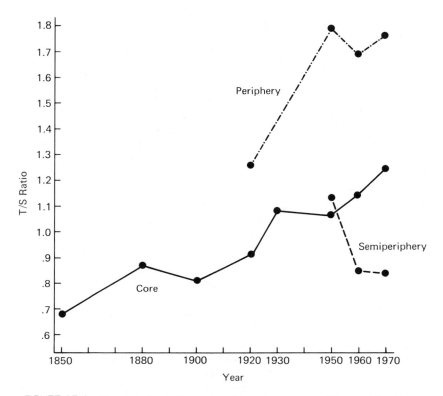

FIGURE 15.1   Trends in the tertiary/secondary ratio in zones of the world-system.

in the same manner. These countries have yet to achieve industrial status, so it makes little sense to think about applying postindustrial hypotheses to them.[6]

Again, we would like to be able to examine variation in the ratio of formal to informal sector employment across the zones of the world economy. However, the appropriate data are not available. We do have some cross-

[6]Bairoch and Limbor (1968:325–329) argue that the hypertrophication of the tertiary that characterizes their category of "developing countries" is due mainly to the weight of Latin American countries in this group. It is true that Latin American countries have larger tertiary sectors than other regions in the periphery, but one finds that they have also had more relative employment in secondary occupations. When the T/S ratio is computed from the figures presented by Bairoch and Limbor for Latin America and for their developing countries (which include Latin American countries), the T/S ratios are not much different. In fact, the ratio in 1960 for Latin America is somewhat lower (1.50) than for the entire group of developing countries (1.55).

national employment data that disaggregate sectoral employment into various subcategories. These categories do not necessarily correspond to the distinction between informal and formal activities, but the finer detail they provide offers a way to check some of the assumptions we have made regarding variation in patterns of urban employment. The more detailed figures on subcategories of employment are available only for a few countries and seldom for more than one relevant year. We are therefore able to present comparative data for the year 1960. They are presented in Table 15.4.

We have used these more detailed data to compute a ratio of service sector employment to manufacturing employment. This ratio is a little closer to our conceptual needs because it removes commercial and transportation workers from the tertiary sector and construction and utilities workers from the secondary sector. We think this statistic more closely approximates the notion of comparing the level of "nonproductive" to "productive" employment. We present this statistic for zones of the world economy as well as the percentage distributions for subsector employment in Table 15.4. The expected zonal differences are quite apparent. In 1960 the service–manufacturing ratio is only .81 for core countries, .86 for the semiperiphery, and 1.26 for the periphery. The ratio in the periphery is almost 50% larger than that of the core. Another way of describing this difference is to point out that these ratios indicate that in the core there are 4 jobs in the services for every 5 jobs in manufacturing, but in the periphery there are 6 service jobs for every 5 in manufacturing. Notice the ratios of residual tertiary employment to residual secondary employment are more similar across zones, indicating that it is the difference in the service–manufacturing ratio that accounts for most of the difference in the overall T/S ratios.[7]

In this section of our chapter we have examined the development of the labor force of the world-economy from 1950 to 1970 using the categories of primary, secondary, and tertiary sector employment. We compared the sectoral distributions of the laboring populations of the core, semiperiphery, and periphery and found, as expected, that those distributions were quite different and that they changed in different ways and at different rates. We found that the T/S ratio for peripheral countries has been comparatively high for as long as we have data. Furthermore, the ratio increases over this period of time. These findings are not entirely unexpected. In the next section we place these patterns within the theoretical framework that underlies the general approach to urbanization represented in this book.

---

[7]Similarly detailed 1970 data for a smaller number of countries showed similar patterns. The services–manufacturing ratios for the 15 core countries, 20 semiperipheral countries, and 30 peripheral countries were, respectively, .89, .88, and 1.70. The larger ratio in the periphery in 1970 than 1960 is probably due to a difference in the cases involved in the analysis.

TABLE 15.4

Percentage Distribution of World and Zone Labor Force by Subsector, 1960[a]

Sector and subsector	World	Core	Semiperiphery	Periphery
Primary				
Agriculture	49.3	12.2	61.4	66.9
Secondary	21.5	39.5	16.9	11.4
Manufacturing	16.0	29.2	13.0	8.1
Construction	3.9	7.6	2.6	2.3
Utilities	.5	1.1	.4	.2
Mining	1.1	1.6	.9	.8
Tertiary	27.3	46.4	20.3	19.1
Commerce	9.4	16.8	6.5	6.3
Transportation	3.5	5.9	2.6	2.6
Services	14.4	23.7	11.2	10.2
T/S ratio	1.27	1.17	1.20	1.68
Services/manufacturing	.90	.81	.86	1.26
Remainder tertiary/				
remainder secondary ratio	2.34	2.50	2.33	2.70
N (millions)	479.7	187.6	79.2	212.9
% of sample labor force	100.0	39.1	16.5	44.4

[a] Based on the distribution of workers in 69 countries (15 core, 11 semiperipheral, and 43 peripheral).

THEORETICAL CONSIDERATIONS

Our examination of variation in the sectoral distribution of employment across zones of the world-economy has been guided by a particular theoretical perspective. We view our findings in the preceding section as a contribution to the reconceptualization of a problem for empirical research as much as a contribution to the body of empirical knowledge. We do provide a more comprehensive view of world employment than is generally available, but our findings are not, with a few exceptions, unexpected. One obvious reason is that our conceptual distinction between zones of the world-economy is highly correlated with other conceptualizations of differences between nations (e.g., level of industrialization) that have been used to guide research on cross-national differences in employment patterns.

No doubt many of the differences we observe across zones of the world-economy can be attributed to what Colin Clark referred as "Petty's Law," after the seventeenth-century political economist (whom Marx called the father of political economy), who noted that "as Trades and Curious Arts increase, so the Trade of Husbandry will decrease" (cited in Clark, 1940: 176). But, that the proportion of the labor force in secondary and tertiary occupations grows in close association with levels of "advancement" (Clark,

1940:177) may be little more than a tautology, given the logic of the present world-economy. Certainly few would argue against the notion that industrialization has been the most important road to economic growth of countries. The distribution of the labor force can be seen as one indicator of the extent to which there has been access to this avenue of development, but this alone does not provide an adequate explanation of the global differences we have observed. What therefore must distinguish our study from others is the explanatory perspective our conceptual categories make operable. We develop that perspective here in order to hypothesize explanations for the patterns we have observed and to offer suggestions for future research.

Our discussion focuses on a phenomenon illustrated in our data and that has gained widespread attention—the alleged overdevelopment of the tertiary sector, which seems to accompany urbanization in the periphery. It is our argument that capital formation processes that are hypothesized to reproduce the hierarchical structure of the world division of labor are causally linked to the observed differences in sectoral employment patterns across the zones of the world-economy. The so-called bloated tertiary may thus be seen as a structural consequence of the "normal" development of the world-economy rather than as an aberration in that development.

The world-system perspective we employ involves a historical research tradition (both Marxist and non-Marxist) of imputing greater explanatory weight to economic processes than to other social processes. The production of goods and services is fundamental to all other human activities. Hence, our explanatory model links the uneven distribution of sectoral labor-force participation to the processes embedded in the social relations of production. Relations of production and socioeconomic processes have typically been studied using the nation as the unit of analysis. But, the theoretical innovation that defines the world-system perspective is the premise that the production of goods and services is realized on a global scale. Thus, the socioeconomic processes that are most important are global rather than national. By implication a nation is much more a geopolitical than an economic or social entity.

This premise has significant methodological implications for our problem. If there is a single world-economy, rather than a population of national economies, we are compelled to seek explanations for the phenomena we observe, whatever the units in which our observations are conceptualized, in those global relationships and processes that are basic to the production of goods and services. We have already asserted that a basic organizational dimension of the world-economy is the division of the world's population into zones of activities that constitute a hierarchical division of labor. We must, therefore, specify the relationships among those zones and the processes embedded in them that constitute them as a division of labor, and we must show why these relationships and processes will produce the observed labor force variation across those zones. Finally, we need to show why this model provides a more satisfactory explanation than models that view nations as relatively closed systems.

The contemporary world-economy is fundamentally capitalist. Its defining feature is a global class structure in which the ownership and control of capital and wealth are monopolized by a small number (relatively speaking) of very powerful people, while the actual work of producing wealth is carried out by the vast majority of people who neither control capital nor enjoy the wealth created by their labor. The former constitute a global capitalist class that is neither monolithic nor all powerful, but that does appear to be maintained and reproduced by a system of relationships among groups of capitalists that produce a global level of coordination of their economic decisions.[8] The latter constitute a global class of direct producers who are subjected to several different forms of labor control by capitalists and government officials who are the members of the global capitalist class (Wallerstein, 1979).

This view of the world-economy focuses our attention on a theoretically important characteristic. The world-economy is a dual system of production and exchange. On one level it produces useful goods and services, but on another level it produces and distributes social power. This appears in the abstract form of value. In the world-economy a system of value imputation to goods and services—the world market—is superimposed over and dominates our orientation to useful goods and services. Value, which appears in various forms but is ultimately converted into abstract forms such as money, titles of ownership, and so forth, is a socially enforced negation of the uniqueness of goods and services that makes possible the aggregation and dissaggregation of power over things (including the labor of people) in an extremely large range of combinations. This form of socially recognized and enforced power over things and people is capital.

This dual nature of the world-economy is theoretically important for our model because we hold that it is the basis for the global dominance of the capitalist class over the production of goods and services. It is thus seen as causally linked to the production and distribution of the material conditions

---

[8]To the extent those decisions are coordinated, it is accomplished either through shifts in the relative values imputed to goods and services in the market that alter calculations of profitability or through extramarket arrangements such as cartels and trade associations. However, since ownership and control are highly decentralized on a global scale, although they are frequently very concentrated at the national level, competitive struggles over shares of the value produced in the world-economy chronically undermine and periodically overwhelm coordination institutions.

of life, including the spatial and sectoral distributions of labor force participation in the world-economy.

From our perspective, then, the key global processes are (1) the production of capital in its various abstract forms, (2) the competitive accumulation of capital by various groups of capitalists, (3) the use of accumulated capital as social power over things and people, and (4) access to, and use of state power in a world-system of strong and weak states. The dependent-development literature has a great deal to say about how those processes are structured and about the cumulative consequences they produce. The key argument of the dependent-development school is that these processes are institutionalized in such a way that they produce a relatively uneven, and thus inequitable, distribution of productive effort and material well-being across the populations of the world-economy. They argue that those capitalists who command the greatest economic, political, and military powers by virtue of ownership of capital intentionally organize and sustain a structure of economic and political relationships between core and peripheral areas that tend to reproduce and expand the exploitation of the peripheral nations. Those relationships include trade, economic aid, and capital investment, the very relationships that constitute the world-division of labor.

The term *dependency* captures the essence of the situation of countries that are caught in the weaker roles in those relationships. National actors cannot pursue a course of material advancement without engaging in the production of commodities for exchange on the world market. Furthermore, since industrialization is perceived to be the most rapid and defensible route to material well-being, commodity exchanges with those nations that can provide inputs of technological knowledge and technically advanced equipment are deemed essential. But, capitalists and governments that already control capital and technology manipulate the structure of trade, aid, and investment relations facilitating these kinds of transfers in ways that actually institutionalize a long-run negative transfer of capital out of dependent nations. Dependence on economic relations with core capitalists and governments is thus the operational key to the exploitation of peripheral nations and peoples, and thus to the uneven distribution of sectoral employment across zones of the world-economy.

Of the various forms of dependency that are hypothesized to initiate and maintain the exploitation of peripheral nations, investment dependency is perhaps the most clearly linked to the socioeconomic outcomes in which we are interested, and those links have some empirical support. *Investment dependence* refers to a relationship between core and peripheral nations in which capitalists in one control the investment of capital in productive facilities in the other. This control appears in the form of financial relationships in which the transfer of capital is attended by the imposition of rules that bind the recipient nation to activities and relative prices that are beneficial to the providing nation (cf. Payer, 1974; Evans, 1979b). In other words, multinational corporations make investments in plants in the periphery, and core governments and core-controlled development agencies provide loans and grants of aid, with strings attached.

Several socioeconomic consequences of investment dependence that are relevant to our research problem are typically hypothesized. They include (1) a slowed rate of industrialization, (2) an excessively capital-intensive manufacturing sector, and (3) the disemployment and impoverishment of populations in agricultural areas through the reorganization of agricultural into more capital-intensive and land-consuming units (Perlman, 1976: Chapter 8).

These outcomes may be translated directly into changes in labor force participation and, in particular, into the hypertrophy of the service sectors in peripheral nations. Capital formation in a dependent nation, because it is controlled by core capitalists, is designed to initiate and sustain productive activities and trade relations that reinforce the capital accumulation positions of productive activities existing in the core nations. It is thus designed to minimize competition with core productive activities and to maximize the cost efficiency of core productive activities. Capital transfers from core nations therefore inhibit the replication of the development paths followed by those nations. By implication, we would not expect the sectoral distributions of core and peripheral labor forces to be the same. Furthermore, we would expect that those jobs that are less remunerative, more unsafe, harder and less pleasant, and that require fewer skills to be concentrated in peripheral nations. Finally, we agree with Portes's argument (Chapter 4, this volume) that the large informal sector in the periphery is a response to the conditions under which labor is employed in the *formal* sector there. Compared to the core, labor is underpaid and disadvantaged in other respects in this sector as well. This is one way dependent development exploits peripheral areas, and the services available in the informal sector make this possible by helping to reproduce formal sector labor at below market value. In short, we would expect informal sector jobs to be concentrated in the periphery.

There is some evidence in the literature to support the hypothesis that investment dependence contributes to the growth of service sector employment in peripheral countries. In a study of dependent development and income inequality, Evans and Timberlake (1980) found that investment dependence has a positive effect on service sector growth during the period from 1950 to 1960. Fiala (1983) replicated this finding in his critique of Evans and Timberlake's research, although effects of dependence on 1960–

1970 growth were not strong. Similarly, in a study of the relationship between investment dependence and urbanization, Kentor (1981) found that investment dependence has a positive effect on service sector growth of the period from 1950 to 1970. In addition, he found a negative effect on industrial sector employment growth. However, for the 10-year period from 1960 to 1970, he found no effect of investment dependence on sectorial labor force growth. Finally, Timberlake and Kentor (1983) found positive effects of investment dependence on change in the service–manufacturing ratio from 1967 to 1977 in a small number of less developed countries.

The findings in these studies are consistent with the theoretical argument that variation in labor force structures across the world-economy must, at least in part, be explained by the dependency-induced uneven development of the capitalist world-economy. However, these findings leave a great deal to be examined about the structure of the dependency effects on sectoral labor force growth. Of particular interest to us is the need to examine systematically subsector employment patterns and formal–informal employment distributions in the zones of the world-economy. We would like to be able to test the hypothesis that investment relations of dependency have their greatest effect on service sector growth in the periphery through a positive contribution to the expansion of informal service sector activities.

The corollary to this hypothesis is that the benefits of dominance that accrue to core nations induce the growth of formal rather than informal service sector activities. Many service activities are rather explicitly linked to the manufacturing sector. Hence, to the extent that the latter sector expands, we can expect services to expand. Second, and directly related to the nature of foreign investment, multinational firms tend to locate industrial activities in developing countries, while managerial, research, and development functions are retained in core. This geopolitical separation of functions would tend to have the effect of concentrating the growth of those services attached to ownership and control of manufacturing in the core nations—the "high technology," highly paid, safe, and interesting service occupations. Sassen-Koob (Chapter 11, this volume) shows that, while this statement seems true, it is only half the truth. There is also an expansion in certain key core cities of a low-wage, low-skilled tertiary subsector that services this high-tech sector. She refers to this process as "peripheralization at the core."

Again, although the dependency effect on sectoral labor force growth in the periphery can be theoretically reduced to its effect on the growth of informal activities, that relationship cannot now be statistically evaluated. Unfortunately, employment data disaggregated in terms of formal–informal activities are just not available. This suggests the direction future research should take. The next logical step is the collection and analysis of longitudinal cross-national employment data that disaggregate labor force participation into informal and formal activities as well as into the sectors now available. Such data would allow us to begin to evaluate a more tightly specified model of the relationship between dependent-development processes embedded in the core–periphery division of labor and variations in world urbanization. Equally important and perhaps more realistic are in-depth studies of specific cities in the Third World—studies that explore in qualitative and historical depth the nature of work in the informal sector.

APPENDIX: ASSIGNMENT OF COUNTRIES TO ZONES OF THE WORLD–SYSTEM

Proper classification of regions of the world into the three zones of the world-system is necessarily a complex matter. There have been several recent attempts to group countries into the three-tiered scheme (e.g., Gidengil, 1978; Snyder and Kick, 1979), and each has produced somewhat different assignments. The one feature that these efforts share is that they require rather detailed data on the economies of each country and/or data on economic exchanges among countries. Employing any one of these schemes would drastically limit the number of countries we would be able to classify because the data are not available to measure all the theoretically relevant dimensions that determine status in the world-system.

Instead we have chosen to classify countries mainly on the basis of only two pieces of information: total gross national product (GNP) and GNP per capita. We use 1965 data because that is near the midpoint of the three decennial years on which our labor force analysis is based and data coverage is best for this year. An unweighted index based on these two variables was constructed. We reasoned that countries high on these characteristics were likely to have strong states, large internal markets, and predominantly high-wage, capital-intensive production—all theoretically defining characteristics of core status. Countries with small economies and low GNP per capita are likely to have relatively weak states, small internal markets, and predominantly low-wage, labor-intensive production. The points at which we divided our list of 132 countries into the three zones were necessarily arbitrary, based on looking for "natural" breaks in the magnitude of the differences in index scores between consecutive countries on the cumulative index distribution. We tried also to use the classification efforts of others (mentioned above) to guide our decision on where to draw the lines.

We also found it necessary to use our limited historical and political knowledge to reclassify countries that came out "too high" or "too low" on the index. For example some of the oil-producing countries score very high on the index, but could hardly be described as core or even semiperipheral in the roles they played in the world-economy of 1965. We relegated these countries to the peripheral zone in our analysis. A few countries that had higher index values than some of our core countries were assigned to the semiperipheral zone. These included Luxembourg, Iceland, and New Zealand. We should also note that several countries that we classify as peripheral in 1965 would undoubtedly be considered semiperipheral now (e.g., Brazil and South Korea), and a few that were semiperipheral in 1965 would now likely fall in the periphery (e.g., Lebanon and Iran).

The list of countries falling into each zone in 1965 follows. Within zones, countries are listed alphabetically by region.

Core: Canada, United States, Japan, Belgium, Denmark, Finland, France, Federal Republic of Germany, Italy, Netherlands, Norway, Sweden, Switzerland, United Kingdom, Australia, and the Soviet Union.

Semiperiphery: South Africa, Mexico, Argentina, China, Cyprus, Hong Kong, India, Iran, Israel, Lebanon, Singapore, Turkey, Austria, Bulgaria, Czechoslovakia, German Democratic Republic, Greece, Hungary, Ireland, Luxembourg, Malta, Poland, Portugal, Rumania, Spain, Yugoslavia, New Zealand, and Iceland.

Periphery: Algeria, Angola, Benin, Botswana, Burundi, Cameroon, Central African Republic, Chad, Congo, Egypt, Ethiopia, Gabon, Gambia, Ghana, Guinea, Ivory Coast, Kenya, Lesotho, Liberia, Libya, Madagascar, Malawi, Mali, Mauritania, Mauritius, Morocco, Mozambique, Namibia, Niger, Nigeria, Rwanda, Senegal, Sierra Leone, Somalia, Sudan, Swaziland, Tanzania, Togo, Tunisia, Uganda, Upper Volta, Zaire, Zambia, Costa Rica, Cuba, Dominican Republic, El Salvador, Guatemala, Haiti, Honduras, Jamaica, Nicaragua, Panama, Puerto Rico, Trinidad and Tobago, Bolivia, Brazil, Chile, Colombia, Ecuador, Guyana, Paraguay, Peru, Surinam, Uruguay, Venezuela, Afghanistan, Burma, Cambodia, Sri Lanka, Indonesia, Iraq, Jordan, Republic of Korea, Democratic People's Republic of Korea, Kuwait, Laos, Malaysia, Mongolia, Nepal, Pakistan, Phillipines, Saudi Arabia, Syria, Thailand, Yemen, Albania, and Fiji.

REFERENCES

Abeles, Schwartz, Hackel, and Silverblatt, Inc.
1983   *The Chinatown Garmet Industry Study.* New York: Local 23–25 ILGWU and The New York Skirt and Sportswear Association.

Adams, Richard
1970   *Crucifixion by Power: Essays on Guatemalan National Social Structure, 1944–1966.* Austin: University of Texas Press.

Afonja, S.
1981   "Changing modes of production and the sexual division of labor among the Yoruba." *Signs* 7(2):299–313.

Agoncillo, T. and M. Guerrero
1973   *History of the Filipino People.* Quezon City, The Philippines: R. P. Garcia.

Aguiar, N.
1983   "Women in the labor force in Latin America: An introductory review." Paper presented at the Third World Women: Common Differences Conference. University of Illinois, Champaign-Urbana, April.

Alonso, William
1965   "Location theory." In J. Friedman and W. Alonso (eds.), *Regional Development and Planning.* Cambridge, Mass.: MIT Press.

Amin, Samir
1976   *Unequal Development: An Essay on the Social Formations of Peripheral Capitalism.* New York: Monthly Review Press.
1980   *Class and Nation, Historically and in the Current Crisis.* New York: Monthly Review Press.

Amsden, Alice
1976   "Trade in manufactures between developing countries." *The Economic Journal* 86:778–790.

Anderson, Perry
1974a   *Lineages of the Absolutist State.* London: Verso.
1974b   *Passages from Antiquity to Feudalism.* London: Verso.

Appleby, Gordon
1976   "Export monoculture and regional social structure in Puno, Peru." In C. A. Smith (ed.), *Regional Analysis: Vol. II. Social Systems.* New York: Academic Press.
1978   *Exportation and Its Aftermath: The Spatioeconomic Evolution of the Regional Marketing System in Highland Puno, Peru.* Unpublished Ph.D. Dissertation, Stanford University, Stanford, Calif.

Arizpe, L.
  1977   "Women in the informal labor sector: The case of Mexico City." *Signs* 3(1):25–
           37.
Arregui, Patricia
  1981   "Dependency and Primacy: Trends and Fluctuations in Peruvian Urban His-
           tory." Unpublished manuscript, Department of Social Relations, Johns Hop-
           kins University, Baltimore, Md.
Arrighi, G.
  1979   "Peripheralization of Southern Africa I: Changes in production processes." *Re-
           view* 3(2):161–192.
Bach, Christopher L.
  1978   "OPEC transactions in the United States International Accounts, 1972–1977."
           Survey of Current Business 58(4):21–32.
Bach, Robert
  1980   "On the holism of a world-systems perspective." In T. Hopkins and I. Wal-
           lerstein (eds.), *Processes of the World-System*. Beverly Hills, Calif.: Sage.
Bacha, Edmar
  1976   *Os Mitos de Uma Decada*. Rio de Janeiro: Paz e Terra.
Baer, Werner
  1975   "La reciente experiencia brasilena de desarrollo: Una interpretacion." *Revista
           Paraguaya de Sociologia* 34:7–39.
Bairoch, Paul
  1973   *Urban Unemployment in Developing Countries*. Geneva: International Labour
           Office.
  1975   *The Economic Development of the Third World Since 1900*. Berkeley: Univer-
           sity of California Press.
Bairoch, Paul and J. M. Limbor
  1968   "Changes in the industrial distribution of the world labor force by region, 1880–
           1960." *International Labour Review* 98(4):311–336.
Balán, Jorge
  1976   "Regional urbanization under primary sector expansion in neo-colonial socie-
           ties." In A. Portes and H. Browning, (eds.), *Current Perspectives in Latin
           American Urban Research*. Austin: University of Texas Press.
Banks, Arthur, S.
  1971   *Cross-Polity Time-Series Data*. Cambridge, Mass: MIT Press.
Barbour, Violet
  1963   *Capitalism in Amsterdam in the 17th Century*. Ann Arbor: University of Mich-
           igan Press.
Basu, Dilip
  1979   "The peripheralization of China: notes on the opium connection." In Goldfrank
           (ed.), *The World-System of Capitalism*. Beverly Hills, Calif.: Sage.
Bataillon, Claude and Lebot, Ivon
  1976   "Migracion interna y empleo agricola temporal en Guatemala." *Estudios So-
           ciales Centroamericanos* 13:35–67.
Bell, Daniel
  1973   *The Coming of Post-Industrial Society*. New York: Basic Books.
Benería, Lourdes and Gita Sen
  1981   "Accumulation, reproduction, and women's role in economic development:
           Boserup revisited." *Signs* 7(2):279–298.
Bergesen, Albert
  1980   *Studies of the Modern World-System*. New York: Academic Press.

1982   "Economic crisis and merger movements: 1880's Britain and 1980's United States." In Edward Friedman (ed.), *Ascent and Decline in the World-System*. Beverly Hills, Calif.: Sage.

Bergesen, Albert and Ronald Schoenberg
1978   "Long waves of colonial expansion and contraction, 1415-1969." In A. Bergesen (ed.), *Studies of the Modern World-System*. New York: Academic Press.

Berry, Brian J. L.
1961   "City size distributions and economic development." *Economic Development and Cultural Change* 9(4):573-588.
1965   "Cities as systems within systems of cities." In J. Friedman and W. Alonso (eds.), *Regional Development and Planning*. Cambridge, Mass.: MIT Press.
1966   *Essays on Commodity Flows and the Spatial Structure of the Indian Economy*. Chicago: University of Chicago, Department of Geography.
1970   *Geographic Perspectives on Urban Systems*. Englewood Cliffs, NJ: Prentice Hall.
1971   "City size and economic development." In L. Jakobson and V. Prakash (eds.), *Urbanization and National Development*. Beverly Hills, Calif.: Sage.
1973   *The Human Consequences of Urbanization*. New York: St. Martin's.

Berry, Brian J. L. and John K. Kasarda
1977   *Contemporary Urban Ecology*. New York: Macmillan Publishing Co., Inc.

Blair, John
1972   *Economic Concentration*. New York: Holt, Rinehart.

Blair, Thomas L. V.
1974   *The International Urban Crisis*. New York: Hill and Wang.

Blake, J.
1974   "The changing status of women in developed countries." *Scientific American* 231(Dec.):137-147.

Bluestone, Barry and Bennet Harrison
1980   *Capital and Communities*. Washington, D.C.: The Progressive Alliance.
1982   *The Deindustrialization of America*. New York City: Basic Books.

Bluestone, Barry, Bennett Harrison, and Luch Gorham
1984   "Storm clouds on the horizon: Labor market crisis and industrial policy." Boston: Economics Education Project.

Blumberg, R. L.
1976   "Fairy tales and facts: economy, family, fertility and the female." In I. Tinker and M. B. Bramsen (eds.), *Women and World Development*. Washington, D.C.: Overseas Development Council.
1978   *Stratficiation: Socioeconomic and Sexual Inequality*. Dubuque, Ia.: William Brown.

Bogue, Donald
1949   *The Structure of the Metropolitan Community: A Study of Dominance and Subdominance*. Ann Arbor: University of Michigan.
1953   *Population Growth in Standard Metropolitan Areas 1900-1950*. Washington, D.C.: Government Printing Office.

Bonilla, Frank and Ricardo Campos
1982   "Imperialist initiatives and the Puerto Rican worker: From Foraker to Reagan." In *The New Nomads: Immigration and Changes in the International Division of Labor*. Special Issue of *Contemporary Marxism* 5 (Summer):1-18.

Bornschier, Volker
1980   *Multinationale Konzerne, Wirtschaftspolitik and Nationale Entwicklung im Weltsystem*. Frankfurt: Campus Verlag.

Bornschier, Volker and T. Ballmer-Cao
  1979   "Income inequality: A cross national study of the relationships between MNC-penetration, dimensions of the power structure and income distribution." *American Sociological Review* 44:487–506.
Bornschier, Volker, Christopher Chase-Dunn, and Richard Rubinson
  1978   "Cross-national evidence of the effects of foreign investment and aid on economic growth and inequality: A survey of findings and a reanalysis." *American Journal of Sociology* 84:651–683.
Boserup, Ester
  1970   *Woman's Role in Economic Development.* New York: St. Martin's.
Bossen, L.
  1975   "Women in modernizing societies." *American Ethnologist* 2:587–601.
Boulay, H.
  1979   "Social control theories of urban politics." *Social Science Quarterly* 59(4):605–621
Boulding, Elise
  1977   *Women in the Twentieth Century World.* New York: Halstead Press.
Boulding, Kenneth
  1978   "The city as an element in the international system." In L. S. Bourne and J. W. Simmons (eds.), *Systems of Cities.* New York: Oxford University Press.
Bourgeois-Pichat, Jean
  1981   "Recent demographic change in Western Europe: An assessment." *Population and Development Review* 7(March):19–42.
Bourne, L. S. and J. W. Simmons
  1978a   "Introduction: The nature of urban systems." In L. S. Bourne and J. W. Simmons (eds.), *Systems of Cities.* New York: Oxford University Press.
  1978b   *Systems of Cities: Readings on Structure, Growth, and Policy.* New York: Oxford University Press.
Bousquet, N.
  1980   "From hegemony to competition: cycles of the core?" In T. Hopkins and I. Wallerstein (eds.), *Processes of the World System.* Beverly Hills, Calif.: Sage.
Breese, Gerald (ed.)
  1969   *The City in Newly Developing Countries.* Garden City, NJ: Prentice-Hall.
Brenner, R.
  1977   "The origins of capitalist development: A critique of neo-Smithian Marxism." *New Left Review* 104:25–92.
Bromley, R. D. F. and R. J. Bromley
  1975   "The debate on Sunday markets in nineteenth-century Ecuador." *Journal of Latin American Studies* 7:85–98.
Bromley, R. J. and Chris Gerry
  1979   "Who are the casual poor?" In R. J. Bromley and C. Gerry (eds.), *Casual Work and Poverty in Third World Cities.* New York: Wiley.
Brown, A. and J. P. Ford
  1975   *Brazil: Today's Business Opportunity.* London: Metra Counsulting Group in collaboration with International Joint Ventures.
Browning, Clyde E.
  1962   "Primate cities and related concepts." In F. R. Pitts (ed.), *Urban Systems and Economic Development.* Eugene: University of Oregon.
Browning, H. L.
  1958   "Recent trends in Latin American urbanization." *American Academy of Political and Social Science Annals* 316:111–120.

Browning, H. L. and J. Singelmann
1978   "The emergence of a service society and its sociological implications." *Politics and Society* 8(3 and 4): 481–509.

Bukharin, Nikolai
1973   *Imperialism and World Economy.* New York: Monthly Review Press.

Burgess, Ernest
1925   "The growth of the city: An introduction to a research project." In Robert Park, Ernest Burgess, and R. D. McKenzie (eds.), *The City.* Chicago: University of Chicago.

Burley, T.
1973   *The Philippines: An Economic and Social Geography.* London: G. Bell and Sons Ltd.

Butlin, N. G.
1962   *Australian Domestic Product, Investment and Foreign Borrowing, 1861–1938/39.* London: Cambridge University Press.
1964   *Investment in Australian Economic Development, 1861–1900.* London: Cambridge University Press.

Buvinic, M. and N. Youssef, with B. Von Elm
1978   *Women-Headed Household: The Ignored Factor in Development Planning.* Washington, D.C.: International Center for Research on Women.

Cardoso, C. F. S.
1973   "La formacion de la hacienda cafetalera en Costa Rica (Siglo XIX)." *Estudios Sociales Centroamericanos* 6:22–50.
1975   "Historia economica del cafe en Centroamerica." *Estudios Sociales Centroamericanos* 10:9–55.

Cardoso, Fernando H.
1972   "Dependency and development in Latin America." *The New Left Review* 74:83–95.

Cardoso, Fernando H. and Enzo Faletto
1971   *Dependencia y Desarrollo en America Latina.* Mexico: Siglo Veintiuno.

Cardoso, F. and E. Faletto
1979   *Dependency and Development in Latin America.* Berkeley: University of California Press.

Carmack, Robert M.
1979   *Historia Social de los Quiches* (Publication No. 38). Guatemala, Seminario de Integracion Social Guatemalteca.

Carroll, Glenn R.
1979   "National city-size distributions: What do we know after 65 years of research?" Unpublished manuscript, Sociology Department, Stanford University, Stanford, Calif.

Castells, Manuel
1976   "Urban sociology and urban politics: From a critique to new trends of research." In J. Walton and L. H. Masotti (eds.), *The City in Comparative Perspective: Cross-National Research and New Directions in Theory.* New York: Halstead Press.
1977   *The Urban Question: A Marxist Approach.* Cambridge, Mass.: MIT Press.

Caves, Richard
1980   "Industrial organization, corporate strategy, and structure." *Journal of Economic Literature* 28(1):64–92.

Chandler, Alfred
1977   *The Visible Hand: The Managerial Revolution in American Business.* Cambridge, Mass.: Harvard University Press.

Chandler, Tertius and Gerald Fox
1974   *Three Thousand Years of Urban Growth.* New York: Academic Press.
Chaney, E. and M. Schmink
1980   "Women and modernization: access to tools." In J. Nash and H. Safa (eds.),
        Sex and Class in Latin America. New York: Bergin.
Chang, Y.
1971   "Colonization as planned change: The Korean case." *Modern Asian Studies*
        5(2):161–186.
Chapman, E. C.
1973a   "Studies of contemporary Thailand: An introduction." In R. Ho and E. C.
        Chapman (eds.), *Studies of Contemporary Thailand* [Publication HB/8 (1973)].
        Canberra: Australian National University, Research School of Pacific Studies.
1973b   "Villagers as clients: A study of land development in Northern Thailand." In
        R. Ho and E. C. Chapman (eds.), *Studies of Contemporary Thailand* [Publi-
        cation HG/8 (1973)]. Canberra: Australian National University, Research School
        of Pacific Studies.
Chase-Dunn, Christopher
1975   "The effects of international economic dependence on development and ine-
        quality." *American Sociological Review* 40:720–739.
1978   "Core-periphery relations: The effects of core competition." In Barbara H. Kap-
        lan (ed.), *Social Change in the Capitalist World Economy.* Beverly Hills, Calif.:
        Sage.
1979a   "Comparative research on world-systems characteristics." *International Studies
        Quarterly* 23(4):601–623.
1979b   "World division of labor and the development of city systems: A longitudinal
        cross-national study." Proposal to the National Science Foundation.
1980   "Socialist states in the capitalist world-economy." *Social Problems* 27:505–526.
1980–   "Stages of dependency or cycles of world-system development?" *Humbolt Jour-
1981   nal of Social Relations* 8(1, Fall/Winter):1–24.
1981a   "International economic policy in a declining core state." In William Avery and
        David Rapkin (eds.), *America in a Changing Global Economy.* New York:
        Longman.
1981b   "Interstate system and capitalist world-economy: One logic or two?" *Interna-
        tional Studies Quarterly* 25(1):19–42.
1982a   "Socialist states in the capitalist world-economy." In C. Chase-Dunn (ed.), *So-
        cialist States in the World-System.* Beverly Hills, Calif.: Sage.
1982b   "World division of labor and the development of city systems: A longitudinal
        crossnational study." *Comparative Research* 9(3):3–9.
1983a   "Three approaches to the kernel of the capitalist world-economy." In William
        Thompson (ed.), *Contending Approaches to World-System Analysis.* Beverly
        Hills: Sage.
1983b   "Urbanization in the world-system: New directions for research." *Comparative
        Urban Research* 9(2):41–46.
Forth- "The coming of urban primacy in Latin America." *Comparative Urban Re-
coming search.*
Chase-Dunn, Christopher and Richard Rubinson
1977   "Toward a structural perspective on the world-system." *Politics and Society*
        7(4):454–476.
1979   "Cycles, trends and new departures in world-system development." In John
        Meyer and Michael Hannan (eds.), *National Development in the World-System.*
        Chicago: University of Chicago.
Chaudhury, R.

1979   "Marriage, urban women, and the labor force: The Bangladesh case." *Signs* 5(1):154–163.

Chilcote, Ronald E.
1974   "A critical synthesis of the dependency literature." *Latin American Perspectives* 1.

Chinchilla, N.
1977   "Industrialization, monopoly capitalism, and women's work in Guatemala." *Signs* 3(1):38–56.

Chirot, Daniel
1977   *Social Change in the Twentieth Century.* New York: Harcourt Brace Jovanovich.

Christaller, Walter
1966   *Central Places in Southern Germany.* Englewood Cliffs, NJ: Prentice-Hall.

Cho, U. and H. Koo
1983   "Capital accumulation, women's work, and informal economies in Korea" (Working Papers on Women in International Development No. 21). East Lansing: Michigan State University, Office of Women in International Development.

City of New York
1982   *Report on Economic Conditions in New York City: July–December 1981.* New York: Office of Management and Budget and Office of Economic Development.

Clark, Colin
1940   *The Conditions of Economic Progress.* London: Macmillan.
1945   "The economic functions of a city in relation to its size." *Econometrica* 13(April):97–113.

Clark, Roger
1979   *The Interrelations Among Urban Primacy, Development, and Trade Dependency.* Unpublished Ph.D. Dissertation, Brown University, Providence, RI.

Coburn, J.
1971   "Asian scholars and government: the chrysanthemum on the sword." In Friedman, E. and M. Selden (eds.), *America's Asia.* New York: Vintage.

Cohen, R. B.
1981   "The new international division of labor, multinational corporations and urban hierarchy." In Michael Dear and Allen Scott (eds.), *Urbanization and Urban Planning in Capitalist Society.* New York: Methuen.

Cohen, Steven M. and Saskia Sassen-Knoob
1982   *Survey of Six Immigrant Groups in Queens, New York City.* New York: Queens College, CUNY.

Collier, David
1976   *Squatters and Oligarchs, Authoritarian Rule and Policy Change in Peru.* Baltimore: Johns Hopkins University Press.

Compilation Group for the *"History of Modern China"* Series
1976   *The Opium War.* Peking: Foreign Languages Press.

Conservation of Human Resources Project
1977   *The Corporate Headquarters Complex in New York City.* New York: The Conservation of Human Resources Project, Columbia University.

Constantino, R.
1975   *A History of the Philippines.* New York: Monthly Review Press.

Cornelius, Wayne A.
1975   "Introduction." In W. A. Cornelius and F. M. Trueblood (eds.), *Urbanization and Inequality: The Political Economy of Urban and Rural Development in Latin America.* Beverly Hills, Calif.: Sage.

Cortes y Larraz, P.
1958   "Descripcion geografico-moral de la diocesis de Goathemala." Biblioteca "Go-
        athemala" (Vol. 20). Guatemala: Sociedad de Geografia e Historia de Guate-
        mala.
Cumings, B.
1981   *The Origins of the Korean War.* Princeton, N.J.: Princeton University Press.
Curtis, W. E.
1892   *Guatemala* (Bulletin No. 32). Washington, D.C.: Bureau of the American Re-
        publics.
Davis, Kingsley
1955   "The origin and growth of urbanization in the world." *American Journal of
        Sociology* 60:429–437.
1972   *World Urbanization 1950–1970, Volume II: Analysis of Trends, Relationships
        and Development* (Population Monograph Series, No. 9). Berkeley: University
        of California.
1976   *World Urbanization, 1950–1970. Volume I: Basic Data for Cities, Countries,
        and Regions* (rev. ed.). Berkeley: Institute of International Studies, University
        of California.
Davis, Kingsley and Hilda Golden
1954   "Urbanization and the development of preindustrial areas." *Economic Devel-
        opment and Cultural Change* 3(October):6–29.
Deere, C. D.
1976   "Rural women's subsistence production in the capitalist peripheries." *The Re-
        view of Radical Political Economics* 8(1):9–17.
Deere, C. and M. de Leal
1981   "Peasant production, proletarianization, and the sexual division of labor in the
        Andes." *Signs* 7(2):338–360.
Delacroix, J. and C. Ragin
1981   "Structural blockage: a cross-national study of economic dependency, state ef-
        ficacy and underdevelopment." *American Journal of Sociology* 86:1311–
        1347.
de Janvry, Alain
1976–   "Material determinants of the world food crisis." *Berkeley Journal of Sociology*
1977   21:3–26.
de Janvry, Alain and Carlos Garramon
1977   "The dynamics of rural poverty in Latin America." *Journal of Peasant Studies*
        4:206–216.
Denison, Edward
1979   *Accounting for Slower Economic Growth: The U.S. in the 1970s.* Washington,
        D.C.: Brookings Institution.
DiLullo, Anthony J.
1981   "Service transactions in the U.S. international accounts, 1970–1980." *Survey of
        Current Business* 61(11):29–46.
Dobb, Maurice
1963   *Studies in the Development of Capitalism.* New York: International Publishers.
Doeppers, D.
1972   "The development of Philippines cities before 1900." *Journal of Asian Studies*
        31:769–792.
Dolin, M. and B. Tomlin
1980   "First World-Third World linkages." *International Organization* 34:41–63.
Dolin, M., B. Tomlin, and H. Nichols
1980   "External linkages and economic growth and inequality in the Third World."

Paper presented at the Annual Meeting of the International Studies Association, Philadelphia, March.

Dos Santos, T.
1970 "The structure of dependence." *American Economic Review* 60:235–246.

Drennan, Matthew
1983 "Local economy and local revenues." In M. Hornton and C. Brecher (eds.), *Setting Municipal Priorities 1984*. New York: New York University Press.

Duncan, Otis Dudley and Leo Schnore
1959 "Cultural, behavioral, and ecological perspectives in the study of social organization." *The American Journal of Sociology* 65:132–146.

Duncan, Otis Dudley, W. R. Scott, Stanley Lieberson, Beverly Duncan, and Hal Winsborough
1960 *Metropolis and Region*. Baltimore: Johns Hopkins University Press.

Economic Consulting Services, Inc.
1981 *The International Operations of U.S. Service Industries: Current Data Collection and Analysis*. Washington, D.C.: Economic Consulting Services, Inc.

Edel, Matthew
1981 "Capitalism, accumulation and the explanation of urban phenomena." In Michael Dear and Allen Scott (eds.), *Urbanization and Urban Planning in Capitalist Society*. New York: Methuen.

Ehrenreich, B. and A. Fuentes
1981 "Life on the global assembly line." *Ms* 9(7):52–59, 71.

El-Shakhs, Salah
1972 "Development, primacy and systems of cities." *The Journal of Developing Areas* 7(October):11–36.

Elson, D. and R. Pearson
1981 " 'Nimble fingers make cheap workers': An analysis of women's employment in Third World export manufacturing." *Feminist Review* (Spring):87–107.

Elvin, M.
1973 *The Pattern of the Chinese Past*. Stanford, Calif.: Stanford University Press.

Emmanuel, Arghiri
1972 *Unequal Exchange: A Study of the Imperialism of Trade*. New York: Monthly Review Press.

Erickson, Charles E. and Michael Harris
1982a "California: Top 500 corporations." *California Business* (May):96–119.
1982b "Even in a recession there are 100 winners." *California Business* (September):81–93.

Evans, Peter B.
1979a "Beyond center and periphery: A comment on the world system approach to the study of development." *Sociological Inquiry* 49(4):15–20.
1979b *Dependent Development*. Princeton, N.J.: Princeton University Press.

Evans, Peter B. and Michael Timberlake
1980 "Dependence, inequality and the growth of the tertiary: A comparative analysis of less developed countries." *American Sociological Review* 45:531–552.

FAO Production Yearbook
1971 *Production Yearbook of the Food and Agricultural Organization of the United Nations*. Rome: Statistics Division, FAO.

Feldt, Alan G.
1965 "The metropolitan area concept: An evaluation of the 1950 SMA's." *Journal of the American Statistical Association* 60(June):617–636.

Fernand Braudel Center
n.d. "Spatio-temporal map of the world-economy." Unpublished manuscript. State University of New York, Binghamton.

Fiala, Robert
    1983   ''Inequality and the service sector in less developed countries: A reanalysis and respecification.'' *American Sociological Review* 48:421-428.

Firebaugh, Glenn
    1979   ''Structural determinants of urbanization in Asia and Latin America, 1950-1970.'' *American Sociological Review* 44:199-215.
    1984   ''Urbanization of the nonfarm population: A research note on the convergence of rich and poor nations.'' *Social Forces* 62(3):775-783.

Fitzpatrick, Brian
    1969   *The British Empire in Australia: An Economic History, 1834-1939.* Melbourne, Australia: Macmillan.

Fletcher, L., E. Graber, W. Merrill, and E. Thorbecke
    1970   *Guatemala's Economic Development: The Role of Agriculture.* Ames: Iowa State University Press.

Floyd, Troy
    1961   ''The Guatemala merchants, the government, and the provincianos, 1750-1800.'' *Hispanic American Historical Review* 41:90-110.

Fox, R. W.
    1975   *Urban Population Growth Trends in Latin America.* Washington, D.C.: Interamerican Development Bank.

Frank, Andre Gunder
    1966   ''The development of underdevelopment.'' *Monthly Review* (September).
    1967   *Capitalism and Underdevelopment in Latin America.* New York: Monthly Review Press.
    1969   *Latin America: Underdevelopment or Revolution.* New York: Monthly Review Press.
    1978a   *Dependent Accumulation and Underdevelopment.* New York: Monthly Review Press.
    1978b   *World Accumulation, 1492-1789.* New York: Monthly Review Press.
    1980   *The Contemporary World Crisis.* New York: Monthly Review Press.

Friedmann, John
    1964   ''Cities in Social Transformation.'' In J. Friedmann and W. Alonso (eds.), *Regional Development and Planning.* Cambridge, Mass.: MIT Press.
    1972   ''A general theory of polarized development.'' In N. Hansen (ed.), *Growth Centers in Regional Economic Development.* New York: Free Press.

Friedmann, John and William Alonso (eds.)
    1964   *Regional Development and Planning.* Cambridge, Mass.: MIT Press.

Friedmann, John and Flora Sullivan
    1974   ''The absorption of labor in the urban economy: The case of developing countries.'' *Economic Development and Cultural Change* 22:385-413.

Friedmann, John and Goetz Wolff
    1982   ''World city formation: An agenda for research and action.'' *International Journal of Urban and Regional Research* 6:309-44.

Friedmann, John and Goetz Wolff (eds.)
    Forth-   *World City Formation.* Special Issue of *Development and Change.*
    coming

Fryer, Donald
    1953   ''The million city in Southeast Asia.'' *Geographic Review* 43:474-494.

Fuchs, Victor
    1968   *The Services Economy.* New York: National Bureau of Economic Research and Columbia University Press.

Galtung, Johan
1971   "A structural theory of imperialism." *Journal of Peace Research* 2:88–111.
Geddes, W. R.
1973   "The opium problem in Northern Thailand." In R. Ho and E. C. Chapman (eds.), *Studies of Contemporary Thailand* (Publication HG/8 (1973):213–234). Canberra: Australian National University, Research School of Pacific Studies.
Germani, Gino
1973   "Urbanization, social change, and the great transformation." In G. Germani (ed.), *Modernization, Urbanization, and the Urban Crisis.* Boston: Little Brown.
Gibbs, Jack P. and Walter T. Martin
1958   "Urbanization and natural resources: A study in organizational ecology." *American Sociological Review* 23:266–277.
1962   "Urbanization, technology, and the division of labor: International patterns." *American Sociological Review* 27:667–677.
Gidengil, E.
1978   "Centers and peripheries: an empirical test of Galtung's theory of imperialism." *Journal of Peace Research* 15:51–66.
Ginsberg, Norton S.
1955   "The great city in Southeast Asia." *American Journal of Sociology* 60(March):455–462.
1961   *Atlas of Economic Development.* Chicago: University of Chicago Press.
Ginzberg, Eli and George J. Vojta
1981   "The service sector in the U.S. economy." *Scientific American* 244(3):48–55.
Gist, Noel P. and I. A. Halbert
1956   *Urban Society.* New York: Crowell.
Gobalet, J. and L. Diamond
1979   "Effects of investment dependence on economic growth: The role of internal structural characteristics and periods of the world economy." *International Studies Quarterly* 23:412–444.
Goldfrank, Walter (ed.)
1979   *The World-System of Capitalism: Past and Present.* Beverly Hills, Calif.: Sage.
Goldstein, Sidney and David Sly (eds.)
1977   *Patterns of Urbanization: Comparative Country Studies.* Belguim: International Union for the Scientific Study of Population.
Gordon, David
1978   "Capitalist development and the history of American cities." In William Tabb and Larry Sawers (eds.), *Marxism and the Metropolis.* New York: Oxford University Press.
Gras, N. S. B.
1922   *Introduction to Economic History.* New York: Harper.
Grasmuck, Sherri
1982   *The Impact of Emigration on National Development: Three Sending Communities in the Dominican Republic* (Occasional Papers, No. 34). New York: Center for Latin American and Caribbean Studies, New York University.
1983   "International stair-step migration: Dominican labor in the United States and Haitian labor in the Dominican Republic." In I. H. Simpson and R. L. Simpson (eds.), *Peripheral Workers: Research in the Sociology of Work.* Greenwich, Conn.: JAI Press.
Greenberg, M.
1951   *British Trade and the Opening of China.* Cambridge: Cambridge University Press.

Greenfield, H. I.
1966 *Manpower and the Growth of Producer Services.* New York: Columbia University Press.
Grossman, R.
1978– "Women's place in the integrated circuit." *Southeast Asia Chronicle 66—Pa-*
1979 *cific Research* 9:2–17.
Guatemala, Dirección General de Estadística
1882 *Censo General de la Republica de Guatemala, 1880.* Guatemala: Dirección General de Estadística.
1894 *Censo General, 1893.* Guatemala: Dirección General de Estadística.
1926 *Censo General de la Republica, 1921.* Guatemala: Dirección General de Estadística.
1957 *Sexto Censo de Poblacion, 1950.* Guatemala: Dirección General de Estadística.
1971 *Septimo Censo de Poblacion, 1964.* Guatemala: Dirección General de Estadística.
1968– *Censos Economicos, 1965, Vols. I–VI.* Guatemala: Dirección General de Estad-
1972 ística.
1975 *Octavo Censo de Poblacion, 1973. Serie III, Vol. I.* Guatemala: Dirección General de Estadística.
Gulick, J. and M. Gulick
1978 "The domestic social environment of women and girls in Isfahan Iran." In L. Beck and N. Keddie (eds.), *Women in the Muslim World.* Cambridge: Harvard University Press.
Hackenberg, R.
1980 "New patterns of urbanization in Southeast Asia: An assessment." *Population and Development Review* 6:391–419.
Hafner, J. A.
1970 *The Impact of Road Development in the Central Plain of Thailand.* Unpublished Ph.D. Thesis, University of Michigan, Ann Arbor.
1972 "Highway expansion and regional development in Central Thailand, 1917–1967." Paper presented at the 22nd International Geographical Congress, Commission Meetings, Toronto, Canada, July 25.
Hall, Peter
1966 *The World Cities.* New York: McGraw-Hill.
Hanks, J. R.
n.d. "National security in Northern Thailand." Mimeographed manuscript.
Hardoy, Jorge
1975 "Two thousand years of Latin American urbanization." In J. E. Hardoy (ed.), *Urbanization in Latin America.* Garden City, N.Y.: Anchor.
Harris, Candee S.
1983 "Plant closings: The magnitude of the problem." Working Paper No. 13, Business Microdata Project. Washington, D.C.: The Brookings Institution.
Harris, Chauncy
1970 *Cities of the Soviet Union.* Chicago: Rand McNally.
Harris, W. D.
1971 *The Growth of Latin American Cities.* Athens: Ohio University Press.
Hart, Keith
1973 "Informal income opportunities and urban employment in Ghana." *Journal of Modern African Studies* 11:61–89.
Hartigan, J. A.
1975 *Clustering Algorithms.* New York: Wiley and Sons.

Harvey, David
    1972   "Society, the city and the space-economy of urbanism" (Resource Paper No. 18, Commission in College Geography). Washington: Association of American Geographers.
    1973   *Social Justice and the City.* Baltimore: Johns Hopkins University.
 ▪ 1982   *The Limits to Capital.* Chicago: University of Chicago Press.
Hasan, P.
    1976   *Korea: Problems and Issues in a Rapidly Growing Economy.* Baltimore: Johns Hopkins University Press.
Hatada, T.
    1969   *A History of Korea.* Santa Barbara, Calif.: Clio Press.
Hauser, Phillip M.
    1957   "World and Asian urbanization in relation to economic development and social change." In Phillip M. Hauser (ed.), *Urbanization in Asia and the Far East.* Calcutta: UNESCO.
Hauser, Philip and Leo Schnore (eds.)
    1965   *The Study of Urbanization.* New York: Wiley.
Hawley, Amos
    1944   "Ecology and human ecology." *Social Forces* 22(May):398–405.
    1950   *Human Ecology: A Theory of Community Structure.* New York: Ronald Press.
    1968   "Human ecology." In the *International Encyclopedia of the Social Sciences.* New York: Macmillan.
    1981   *Urban Society: An Ecological Approach* (2nd ed.). New York: Ronald.
    1984   "Human ecological and Marxian theory." *American Journal of Sociology* 89(4):907–917.
Hay, M.
    1976   "Luo women and economic change during the colonial period." In N. Hafkin and E. Bay (eds.), *Women in Africa.* Stanford, Calif.: Stanford University Press.
Hay, Richard, Jr.
    1977   "Patterns of urbanization and socio-economic development in the Third World: An overview." In J. Abu-Lughod and R. Hay, Jr. (eds.), *Third World Urbanization.* Chicago: Maaroufa Press.
Henthorn, W.
    1971   *A History of Korea.* New York: The Free Press.
Herman, Edward
    1981   *Corporate Control, Corporate Power.* New York: Cambridge University Press.
Hill, Robert
    1974   "Urbanization and other dimensions of socioeconomic development: A cross-national longitudinal analysis." *Behavior Science Research* 9:211–245.
Hobsbawm, E. J.
    1968   *Industry and Empire.* Harmondsworth, Middlesex: Penguin.
Hoch, Irving
    1976   "City size effects, trends, and policies." *Science* 193:856–863.
Hollnsteiner, M. and M. E. Lopez
    1976   "Manila: The face of poverty." In Social Science Research Institute, International Christian University (ed.): *Asia Urbanizing: Population Growth & Concentration—& The Problems Thereof.* Tokyo: Simul Press.
Hope, Keith
    1982   "Vertical and nonvertical class mobility in three countries." *American Sociological Review* 47:1(February):99–113.

Hopkins, Keith
    1978a   *Conquerors and Slaves.* Cambridge: Cambridge University Press.
    1978b   "Economic growth and towns in classical antiquity." In Philip Abrams and E. A. Wrigley (eds.), *Towns in Societies: Essays in Economics and Historical Sociology.* New York: Cambridge University Press.
Hopkins, Terence
    1978   "World system analysis: Methodological issues." In Kaplan (ed.) *Social Change in the Capitalist World Economy.* Beverly Hills, Calif.: Sage.
Hoselitz, Bert
    1955   "Generative and parasitic cities." *Economic Development and Cultural Change* 3(April):278–294.
    1960   *Sociological Aspects of Economic Growth.* New York: Free Press.
Hoyt, Homer
    1939   *The Structure and Growth of Residential Neighborhoods in American Cities.* Washington, D.C.: Government Printing Office.
Hubbard, R. V.
    n.d.   *Canal Construction in Central Thailand. (Chao Phraya River System)* (Background Report No. 1). Applied Scientific Research Corporation of Thailand, Project 30.
Hulbert, H.
    1906   *The Passing of Korea.* New York: Doubleday, Page & Company.
Hurd, Richard
    1903   *Principles of City Land Values.* New York: The Record and Guide.
Immigration and Naturalization Service
    1981   Tabulation of Immigrants Admitted by Country of Birth, 1954–1979. Washington, D.C. Unpublished.
Ingersoll, Hazel
    1972   *The War of the Mountain: A Study of Reactionary Peasant Insurgency in Guatemala, 1837–1873.* Unpublished Ph.D. Dissertation, University of Maryland, College Park, MD.
Inkeles, Alex and David Smith
    1974   *Becoming Modern.* Cambridge, Mass.: Harvard University Press.
International Bank for Reconstruction and Development (IBRD)
    1977   *World Tables 1976.* Washington, D.C.: IBRD.
International Center for Research on Women
    1980a   *The Productivity of Women in Developing Countries: Measurement Issues and Recommendations* (AID/otr/C–1801). Washington, D.C.: Agency for International Development.
    1980b   *Keeping Women Out: A Structural Analysis of Women's Employment in Developing Countries.* Washington, D.C.: Agency for International Development.
International Labor Office
    1977   *Labour Force Estimates and Projections, 1950–2000.* Geneva: ILO.
    Various   *Yearbook of Labour Statistics.* Geneva: ILO.
      years
Jahan, R.
    1979   "Public policies, women and development: Reflections on a few structural problems." In R. Jahan and H. Papanek (eds.), *Women and Development.* Dacca: Bangladesh Institute of Law and International Affairs.
Jain, D., N. Singh, and M. Chand
    1979   "Women's work: methodological issues." In R. Jahan and H. Papanek (eds.),

Women and Development. Dacca: Bangladesh Institute of Law and International Affairs.

Jain, S.
1975   *Size Distribution of Income: A Compilation of Data.* Washington, D.C.: World Bank.

Jefferson, Mark
1939   "The law of the primate city." *Geographical Review* 29(April):226–232.

Jelin, E.
1977   "Migration and labor force participation of Latin American women: The domestic servants in the cities." *Signs* 3(1):129–141.
1980   "The Bahiana in the labor force in Salvador, Brazil." In J. Nash and H. Safa (eds.), *Sex and Class in Latin America.* New York: Bergin.

Johnson, E. A. J.
1970   *The Organization of Space in Developing Countries.* Cambridge, Mass.: Harvard University Press.

Johnson, Gregory
1980   "Rank size convexity and system integration: A view from archaeology." *Economic Geography* 56:234–247.

Jonas, Susanne
1974   "Guatemala: Land of eternal struggle." In R. Chileate and J. Edelstein (eds.), *Latin America: The Struggle with Dependency and Beyond.* New York: Wiley.

Jones, Chester L.
1940   *Guatemala, Past and Present.* Minneapolis: University of Minnesota Press.

Jones, Gareth Stedman
n.d.   *Outcaste London: A Study in the Relationship Between Classes in Victorian Society.* Harmondsworth, Middlesex: Penguin.

Jones, S. M. and P. Kuhn
1978   "Dynastic decline and roots of rebellion." In J. Fairbank (ed.), *The Cambridge History of China* (Vol. 10). Cambridge: Cambridge University Press.

Joseph, G.
1980   "Caribbean women: The impact of race, sex, and class." In B. Lindsay (ed.), *Comparative Perspectives of Third World Women.* New York: Praeger.

Juarros, Domingo
1823   *A Statistical and Community History of the Kingdom of Guatemala in Spanish America.* London: George Cowie.

Jules-Rosette, B.
1982   "Women's work in the informal sector: A Zambian case study" (Working Papers on Women in International Development No. 3). East Lansing: Michigan State University, Office of Women in International Development.

Kaplan, David
1965   "The Mexican marketplace: Then and now." *Proceedings of the American Ethnological Society.* Seattle: University of Washington Press.

Kentor, Jeffrey
1981a   "An examination of interaction effects in the world-economy." Manuscript submitted for publication.
1981b   "Structural determinants of peripheral urbanization: The effects of international dependence." *American Sociological Review* 46:201–211.

Keyes, C. F.
1967   *Isan: Regionalism in Northeast Thailand* (Data Paper No. 65). Ithaca, N.Y.: Cornell University Southeast Asia Program.

Keyfitz, N.
1965 "Political-economic aspects of urbanization in South and Southeast Asia." In P. M. Hauser and L. F. Schnore (eds.), *The Study of Urbanization.* New York: Wiley.
Kim, K. S. and M. Roemer
1979 *Growth and Structural Transformation.* Cambridge, Mass.: Harvard University Press.
Kim, S. and P. Donaldson
1980 "Seoul's population growth: Plans and implementation." In C. K. Park (ed.), *Human Resources and Social Development in Korea.* Seoul: Korean Development Institute.
Koo, Hagan
1982 "A conceptual framework for political economic analysis of dependent development: A preliminary analysis of South Korean and Taiwanese cases." Paper presented at the Annual Meeting of the American Sociological Association, San Francisco.
Koo, Hagan and Peter Smith
1983 "Migration, the urban informal sector, and earnings in the Philippines." *The Sociological Quarterly* 24(2):219–232.
Kowalewski, Stephen A.
1982 "The evolution of primate regional sytems." *Comparative Urban Research* 9(1):60–78.
Kunstadter, P.
1967 "Thailand: introduction." In P. Kunstadter (ed.), *Southeast Asian Tribes, Minorities, and Nations* (Two Volumes). Princeton, N.J.: Princeton University Press.
Kuznets, Simon
1960 "Economic growth of small nations." In E. A. G. Robinson (ed.), *Economic Consequences of the Size of Nations.* New York: St. Martin's.
1971 *Economic Growth of Nations: Total Output and Production Structure.* Cambridge, Mass.: The Belknap Press of Harvard University.
Kwon, T. H., H. Y. Lee, Y. Chang, and E. Y. Yu
1975 *The Population of Korea.* Seoul: Seoul National University.
Lampard, Eric E.
1955 "The history of cities in the economically advanced areas." *Economic Development and Cultural Change* 3(January):81–136.
Lane, Frederic C.
1973 *Venice: A Maritime Republic.* Baltimore: Johns Hopkins University Press.
Laquian, A.
1966 *The City in Nation-Building.* Manila: University of the Philippines.
Latin American and Caribbean Women's Collective
1977 *Slaves of Slaves: The Challenge of Latin American Women.* London: Zed.
Leeds, Anthony and Elizabeth Leeds
1969 "Brazil and the myths of urban rurality: Urban experience, work, and values in 'squatments' of Rio de Janeiro and Lima." In A. J. Field (ed.), *City and Country in the Third World.* Cambridge, Mass.: Schenckman.
Levitt, Theodore
1976 "The industrialization of service." *Harvard Business Review* 54(September):63–74.
Lim, L.
1978 "Workers in multinational corporations: The case of the electronics industry in

Malaysia and Singapore (No. 9)." Michigan Occasional Papers in Women's Studies.

1980   "Women workers in multinational corporations: The case of the electronics industry in Malaysia and Singapore." In K. Kumar (ed.), *Transnational Enterprises: Their Effects on Third World Societies and Cultures.* Boulder, CO: Westview Press.

Linsky, Arnold S.
1965   "Some generalizations concerning primate cities." *Annals of the Association of American Geographers* 55:506–513.

Lippit, V.
1978   "The development of underdevelopment in China." *Modern China* 4(3):251–328.

Lobo, Susan
1982   *A House of My Own: Social Organization in the Squatter Settlements of Lima, Peru.* Tucson: University of Arizona Press.

Lojkine, Jean
1976   "Contribution to a Marxist theory of capitalist urbanization." In C. G. Pickvance (ed.), *Urban Sociology: Critical Essays.* New York: St. Martin's.

Lomnitz, Larissa
1976   "Migration and network in Latin America." In Alejandro Portes and Harley L. Browning (eds.), *Current Perspectives in Latin American Urban Research.* Austin: University of Texas Press.

1977a   "Mechanisms of articulation between shantytown settlers and the urban system." Paper presented at the Symposium on "Shantytowns." The Wenner-Gren Foundation, Burg Wartenstein, Austria.

1977b   *Networks and Marginality, Life in a Mexican Shantytown.* New York: Academic Press.

London, Bruce
1977   "Is the primate city parasitic? The regional implications of national decision-making in Thailand." *The Journal of Developing Areas* 12(1):49–67.

1979   "Internal colonialism in Thailand: Primate city parasitism reconsidered." *Urban Affairs Quarterly* 14(4):485–514.

1980   *Metropolis and Nation in Thailand: The Political Economy of Uneven Development.* Boulder, Col.: Westview Press.

Long, Susan B.
1979   "The continuing debate over the use of ratio variables: Facts and fiction." In Karl F. Schuessler (ed.), *Sociological Methodology 1980.* San Francisco: Jossey-Bass.

Lösch, August
1954   *The Economics of Location.* New Haven, Conn.: Yale University Press.

1965   "The nature of economic regions." In J. Friedmann and W. Alonso, *Regional Development and Planning.* Cambridge, Mass.: MIT Press.

Lowe, L.
1976–   "The urban woman worker in Dar Es Salaam." *African Urban Notes* 2(3):
1977   11–19.

Luxemburg, Rosa
1968   *The Accumulation of Capital.* New York: Monthly Review Press.

Machlup, F.
1962   *The Production and Distribution of Knowledge in the United States.* Princeton, NJ: Princeton University Press.

MacLeod, Murdo J.
   1973   *Spanish Central America: A Socioeconomic History, 1520–1720.* Berkeley: University of California Press.
Magdoff, Harry
   1969   *The Age of Imperialism.* New York: Monthly Review Press.
Maizels, A.
   1963   *Industrial Growth and World Trade.* London: Cambridge University Press.
Mangin, William
   1967   "Latin American squatter settlements: A problem and a solution." *Latin American Research Review* 2:65–98.
Manndorff, H.
   1967   "The Hill Tribe program of the Public Welfare Department, Ministry of Interior, Thailand: Research and socio-economic development." In Kunstadter, P. (ed.), *Southeast Asian Tribes, Minorities, and Nations* (Two Volumes). Princeton, N.J.: Princeton University Press.
Marshall, Adriana
   1983   "Immigration in a surplus-worker labor market: The case of New York (Occasional Papers No. 39). New York: Center for Latin American and Caribbean Studies, New York University.
Marshall, John U.
   1969   *The Location of Service Towns: An Approach to the Analysis of Central Place Systems.* Toronto: University of Toronto Press.
Marx, Karl
   1967   *Capital* (Vol. 1). New York: International Publishers.
   1971   *The Grundrisse.* New York: Harper and Row.
   1977   *Capital* (Vol. 1). New York: Vintage Books.
Matyepse, I.
   1977   "Underdevelopment and African women." *Journal of Southern African Affairs* 21:6.
Mazumdar. V.
   1979   "Women, development and public policy." In R. Jahan and H. Papanek (eds.), *Women and Development.* Dacca: Bangladesh Institute of Law and International Affairs.
McCarty, J. W.
   1970   "Australian capital cities in the nineteenth century." In Schedvin and McCarty (eds.), *Urbanization in Australia: The Nineteenth Century.* Sydney, Australia: Sydney University Press.
McCoy, A.
   1971   "Subcontracting counterinsurgency." *Bulletin of the Committee of Concerned Asian Scholars* (Special Issue) February:56–70.
McDonald, A.
   1979   "Wallerstein's world economy." *Journal of Asian Studies* 38.3 (May):535–540.
McGee, T. G.
   1969   *The Southeast Asian City.* New York: Praeger.
   1973   *Hawkers in Hong Kong: A Study of Policy and Planning in a Third World City.* Hong Kong: University of Hong Kong, Centre of Asian Studies.
   1977   "Rural-urban mobility of South and Southeast Asia. Different formulations . . . Different answers." In J. Abu-Lughod and R. Hay, Jr. (eds.), *Third World Urbanization.* Chicago: Maarufa Press.

McGrath, P.
    1976   "The unfinished assignment: Equal education for women" (Worldwatch Paper
            No. 7). New York: Worldwatch Institute.
McGreevey, William Paul
    1971   "A statistical analysis of primacy and lognormality in the size distribution of
            Latin American cities, 1750–1920." In Richard M. Morse (ed.), *The Urban De-
            velopment of Latin America, 1750–1920*. Stanford, Calif.: Center for Latin
            American Studies, Stanford University.
McKenzie, Roderick
    1927   "The concept of dominance and world-organization." *American Journal of So-
            ciology* 33:28–42.
    1929   "Ecological succession in the Puget Sound region." *Publications of the Amer-
            ican Sociological Society* 23:60–80.
    1933   *The Metropolitan Community*. New York: McGraw-Hill.
    1934   "Industrial expansion and the interrelations of peoples." In E. P. Reuter (ed.)
            Race and Culture Contacts. New York: McGraw-Hill.
Mehta, Surinder K.
    1969   "Some demographic and economic correlates of primate cities: A case for reev-
            aluation." In G. Breese (ed.), *The City in Newly Developing Countries*. Garden
            City, NJ: Prentice-Hall, Inc.
Meier, R.
    1980   *Urban Futures Observed In The Asian Third World*. New York: Pergamon Press.
Meilink-Roelotsz, M. A. P.
    1962   *Asian Trade and European Influence*. The Hague: Martinus Nijhoff.
Meillassoux, C.
    1972   "From reproduction to production." *Economy and Society* 1:93–105.
Mera, Koichi
    1973   "On the urban agglomeration and economic efficiency." *Economic Develop-
            ment and Cultural Change* 21:309–324.
Merhav, Meir
    1969   *Technological Dependence, Monopoly, and Growth*. Oxford: Pergamon.
Merrick, Thomas W.
    1977   "Employment in the urban informal sector in Latin America." Paper presented
            at the seminar on Urbanization, Unemployment and Environmental Quality,
            Johns Hopkins University, Baltimore, March 7.
Merrick, T. and M. Schmink
    1983   "Households headed by women and urban poverty in Brazil." In M. Buvinic,
            M. Lycette, and W. McGreevy (eds.), *Women and Poverty in the Third World*.
            Baltimore: John Hopkins University Press.
Meyer, John W., John Boli-Bennett, and Christopher Chase-Dunn
    1975   "Convergence and divergence in development." *Annual Review of Sociology*
            (Vol. 1). Palo Alto, Calif.: Annual Reviews, Inc.
Meyers, John
    1980   "GNP: Perspectives on services." New York: Conservation of Human Re-
            sources Project, Columbia University.
Migdal, J.
    1974   *Peasants, Politics, and Revolution*. Princeton, N.J.: Princeton University Press.
Mills, E. and B. N. Song
    1979   *Studies in the Modernization of the Republic of Korea: 1945–1975: Urbanization
            and Urban Problems*. Cambridge: Harvard University Press.

Mintz, Sidney
   1971   "Men, women and trade." *Comparative Studies in Society and History* 13:247–269.
Miranda, G.
   1977   "Women's labor force participation in a developing society: The case of Brazil." *Signs* 3(1):261–274.
Mitchell, Brian R.
   1975   *European Historical Statistics, 1750–1970.* New York: Columbia University Press.
Moerman, M.
   1967   "A minority and its government: The Thai-Lue of Northern Thailand." In P. Kunstadter (ed.), *Southeast Asian Tribes, Minorities, and Nations* (Two Volumes). Princeton, N.J.: Princeton University Press.
Mollenkopf, John
   1978   "The postwar politics of urban development." In William Tabb and Larry Sawers (eds.), *Marxism and the Metropolis.* New York: Oxford University Press.
   1981   "Community and accumulation." In Michael Dear and Allen Scott (eds.), *Urbanization and Urban Planning in Capitalist Society.* New York: Methuen.
Moore, Barrington Jr.
   1966   *Social Origins of Dictatorship and Democracy.* Boston: Beacon Press.
Morales, Rebecca
   1983   "Undocumented workers in a changing automobile industry: Case studies in wheels, headers and batteries." Paper presented at the Conference on Contemporary Production: Capital Mobility and Labor Migration. San Diego: Center for U.S.–Mexican Studies, University of California.
Morse, Richard M.
   1971   "Latin American cities in the nineteenth century: Approaches and tentative generalizations." In R. Morse (ed.), *The Urban Development of Latin America, 1750–1920.* Stanford, Calif.: Stanford University, Center for Latin American Studies.
   1974   "Trends and patterns of Latin American urbanization, 1750–1920." *Comparative Studies in Society and History* 18:416–447.
Moulder, F.
   1977   *Japan, China and the Modern World Economy.* Cambridge: Cambridge University Press.
Mueller, M.
   1977   "Women and men, power and powerlessness in Lesotho." *Signs* 3(1):154–166.
Mullings, L.
   1976   "Women and economic change in Africa." In N. Hafkin and E. Bay (eds.), *Women in Africa.* Stanford, Calif.: Stanford University Press.
Murphy, R.
   1974   "The treaty ports and China's modernization." In Skinner (ed.), *The Chinese City Between Two Worlds.* Stanford, Calif.: Stanford University Press.
Nash, June
   1980   "A critique of social science roles in Latin America." In J. Nash and H. Safa (eds.), *Sex and Class in Latin America.* New York: Bergin.
Nash, June and Maria Patricia Fernandez Kelly (eds.)
   1983   *Women, Men and the New International Division of Labor.* Albany, N.Y.: SUNY Press.
Neher, C. C.
   1974   *The Dynamics of Politics and Administration in Rural Thailand* (Papers in In-

ternational Studies, Southeast Asia Series No. 30). Athens, Ohio: Ohio University Center for International Studies, Southeast Asia Program.

Neumann, L.
1978–   "Hospitality girls in the Phillippines." *Southeast Asia Chronicle 66—Pacific*
1979   *Research* 9:2–17.

New York State Department of Labor
1979   *Occupational Employment Statistics: Finance, Insurance and Real Estate, New York State, May–June 1978.* Albany: New York State Department of Labor.

1980   *Occupational Employment Statistics: Services, New York State, April–June 1978.* Albany: New York State Department of Labor.

1982a   *Report to the Governor and the Legislature on the Garment Manufacturing Industry and Industrial Homework.* New York: New York State Department of Labor.

1982b   *Study of State-Federal Employment Standards for Industrial Homeworkers in New York City.* Albany: New York State Department of Labor, Division of Labor Standards.

Neutze, Max
1977   *Urban Development in Australia: A Descriptive Analysis.* Sidney: George Allen and Unwin.

Newland, K.
1979   *The Sisterhood of Man.* New York: Norton.

O'Connor, James
1973   *The Fiscal Crisis of the State.* New York: St. Martin's

Oppenheimer, V.
1970   *The Female Labor Force in the United States* (Population Monograph No. 5). Berkeley: University of California Press.

Owen, Carol and Richard Witton
1973   "National division and mobilization: A reinterpretation of primacy." *Economic Development and Cultural Change* 21(January):325–337.

Papanek, H.
1971   "Purdah in Pakistan: Seclusion and modern occupations for women." *Journal of Marriage and the Family* 33(3):517–530.

1976   "Women in cities: Problems and perspectives." In I. Tinker and M. Bramsen (eds.), *Women and World Development.* Washington, D.C.: Overseas Development Council.

1979a   "Introduction." In R. Jahan and H. Papanek (eds.), *Women and Development.* Dacca: Bangladesh Institute of Law and International Affairs.

1979b   "Development planning for women: The implications of women's work." In R. Jahan and H. Papanek (eds.), *Women and Development.* Dacca: Bangladesh Institute of Law and International Affairs.

Paull, Gene
1976   *The Application of Central-place Theory to the Settlements of the Pacific Coast of Guatemala.* Unpublished Ph.D. Dissertation, University of Arizona, Phoenix.

Payer, Cheryl
1974   *The Debt Trap: The IMF and the Third World.* Harmondsworth, UK: Penguin.

Peattie, Lisa R.
1968   *The View from the Barrio.* Ann Arbor: University of Michigan Press.

Perlman, Janice
1976   *The Myth of Marginality: Urban Poverty and Politics in Rio de Janeiro.* Berkeley: University of California Press.

Pernia, E.
    1976   "Urbanization in the Philippines: Historical and comparative perspectives."
            (Papers of the East-West Population Institute Number 40, November). Manoa,
            Hawaii.
Pickvance, C. G.
    1978   "Competing paradigms in urban sociology: Some epistemological issues." *Com-
            parative Urban Research* 6(2,3):20–27.
    1983   "What is new about the new urban sociology." *Comparative Urban Research*
            9(2):19–23.
Pirenne, Henri
    1952   *Medieval Cities: Their Origins and the Revival of Trade.* Princeton, N.J.:
            Princeton University Press. (Original work published 1925)
    1980   *Mohammed and Charlemagne.* Totowa, N.J.: Barnes and Noble. (Original work
            published 1939)
Piven, Francis Fox, and Richard A. Cloward
    1971   *Regulating the Poor: The Functions of Public Welfare.* New York: Vintage.
Port Authority of New York and New Jersey
    1982   *Regional perspectives: The Regional Economy, 1981 Review, 1982 Outlook.* New
            York: Planning and Development Department, Regional Research Section.
Portes, Alejandro
    1976   "The economy and ecology of urban poverty." In A. Portes and J. Walton,
            Urban Latin America. Austin: University of Texas Press.
    1979   "Convergences between conflicting paradigms in national development." Paper
            presented at the Annual Meeting of the American Sociological Association, Bos-
            ton.
    1981   "Unequal exchange and the urban informal sector." In A. Portes and J. Walton
            (eds.), *Labor, Class, and the International System.* New York: Academic Press.
    1982   "The informal sector: Definition, controversy, and relations to national devel-
            opment." Unpublished manuscript, originally presented at the Third Seminar
            of the Working Group on Latin American Urbanization, Tepoztlan, Mexico.
Portes, Alejandro and John Walton
    1976   *Urban Latin America: The Political Condition from Above and Below.* Austin:
            University of Texas.
    1981   *Labor, Class and the International System.* New York: Academic Press.
Pounds, Norman J. G.
    1969   "The urbanization of the classical world." *Annals of the Association of Amer-
            ican Geographers* 59:135–157.
Power, J. and G. Sicat
    1971   *The Philippines: Industrialization and Trade Policies.* London: Oxford Univer-
            sity Press.
Prebisch, Raul
    1950   *The Economic Development of Latin America and Its Principal Problems.* New
            York: United Nations, Department of Economic Affairs, Economic Commis-
            sion for Latin America.
Preston, Samuel
    1979   "Urban growth in developing countries: A demographic reappraisal." *Popu-
            lation and Development Review* 5(June):195–216.
Procter, Ian
    1982   "Some political economies of urbanization and suggestions for a research
            framework." *International Journal of Urban and Regional Research* 6(11):
            83–97.

Pye, Lucian
    1969   "The political implications of urbanization and the development process." In
            Gerald Breese (ed.), *The City in Newly Developing Countries*. Englewood Cliffs,
            N.J.: Prentice-Hall.
Quijano, Anibal
    1974   "The marginal pole of the economy and the marginalized labor force." *Econ-
            omy and Society* 3:393–428.
    1975   "The urbanization of Latin American society." In J. Hardoy (ed.), *Urbanization
            in Latin America*. Garden City, N.Y.: Anchor.
Race, J.
    1974   "The war in Northern Thailand." *Modern Asian Studies* 8(1):85–112.
Ragin, Charles and Jacques Delacroix
    1979   "Comparative advantage, the world division of labor and underdevelopment:
            A cross national study." In R. Tomasson (ed.), *Comparative Studies in Soci-
            ology*. Greenwich, Conn.: JAI Press.
Redfield, Robert
    1955   *The Little Community*. Chicago: University of Chicago Press.
Reed, R.
    1967   *Hispanic Urbanism in the Philippines*. Manila: University of Manila.
    1977   *Colonial Manila*. Berkeley: University of California Press.
Reeve, W.
    1963   *The Republic of Korea: A Political and Economic Study*. New York: Oxford
            University Press.
Renaud, B.
    1974   "Evolution of the urban system in Korea 1910–1940: An economic interpreta-
            tion." *Bulletin of the Population and Development Studies Center* 3(26):
            Appendix Table.
Repetto, R.
    1979   *Economic Equality and Fertility in Developing Countries*. Baltimore: John Hop-
            kins University Press.
Rhodes, Robert I.
    1973   "Mexico—A model for capitalist development in Latin America?" In Charles
            K. Wilber (ed.), *The Political Economy of Development and Underdevelop-
            ment*. New York: Random House.
Richardson, Harry W.
    1973a   *The Economics of Urban Size*. Westmead, England: Saxon House, D.D. Heath
            Ltd.
    1973b   "Theory of the distribution of city sizes: Review and prospects." *Regional Stud-
            ies* 7:239–251.
Rimmer, P. J.
    1971   *Transport in Thailand: The Railway Decision* (Publication HG/6, 1971). Can-
            berra: Australian National University Press, Department of Human Geography.
Roberts, Bryan
    1973   *Organizing Strangers*. Austin: University of Texas Press.
    1976   "The provincial urban system and the process of dependency." In Alejandro
            Portes and Harley L. Browning (eds.), *Current Perspectives in Latin American
            Urban Research*. Austin: Institute of Latin American Studies and University of
            Texas Press.
    1978a   *Cities of Peasants*. Beverly Hills, Calif.: Sage Publications.
    1978b   "Comparative perspectives on urbanization." In David Street and Associates
            (eds.), *Handbook of Contemporary Urban Life*. San Francisco: Josey-Bass.

Robertson, C.
1976   "Ga women and socioeconomic change in Accra, Ghana." In N. Hafkin and
        E. Bay (eds.), *Women in Africa.* Stanford, Calif.: Stanford University Press.
Robson, Brian T.
1973   *Urban Growth: An Approach.* London: Methuen.
Rose, A. J.
1966   "Dissent from down-under: Metropolitan primacy as the normal state." *Pacific
        Viewpoint* 7:1-27.
Rosenberg, T. J.
1982   "Female industrial employment and protective labor legislation in Bogota, Col-
        ombia." *Journal of Interamerican Studies and World Affairs* 24(1):59-80.
Rozman, Gilbert
1976   *Urban Networks in Russia, 1750-1800, and Premodern Periodization.* Prince-
        ton, N.J.: Princeton University Press.
Russell, J. C.
1972   *Medieval Regions and Their Cities.* Bloomington: Indiana University Press.
Rubinson, Richard (ed.)
1981   *Dynamics of World Development.* Beverly Hills, Calif.: Sage.
Safa, Helen
1977   "The changing class composition of the female labor force in Latin America."
        Latin American Perspectives 4(Fall):126-136.
1981   "Runaway shops and female employment: the search for cheap labor." *Signs*
        7(2):418-433.
Saffioti, H.
1977   "Women, mode of production, and social formations." *Latin American Per-
        spectives* 4(Winter/Spring):27-37.
1978   *Women in Class Society.* New York: Monthly Review Press.
Sanday, P.
1974   "Female status in the public domain." In M. Rosaldo and L. Lamphere (eds.),
        Woman, Culture and Society. Stanford, Calif.: Stanford University Press.
Sassen-Koob, Saskia
1981   "Towards a conceptualization of immigrant labor." *Social Problems*
        29(October):65-85.
1982   "Recomposition and peripheralization at the core." *Contemporary Marxism*
        5(Summer):88-100.
1984   "The new labor demand in global cities." In Michael P. Smith (ed.), *Cities in
        Transformation.* Berkeley, Calif.: Sage.
1985a   *The Foreign Investment Connection: Rethinking Immigration.* London and New
        York: Cambridge University Press. (Forthcoming).
1985b   "The structuring of a new investment zone for the world market: Southern Cal-
        ifornia." San Diego: Center for U.S.-Mexican Studies, University of California.
Saul, S. B.
1960   *Studies in British Overseas Trade 1870-1914.* Liverpool: Liverpool University
        Press.
Scherer, F. M.
1980   *Industrial Market Structure and Economic Performance* (2nd ed.). Chicago:
        Rand McNally.
Schmink, M.
1977   "Dependent development and the division of labor by sex: Venezuela." *Latin
        American Perspectives* 4(1/2):153-179.
Schneider, J.
1977   "Was there a pre-capitalist world-system?" *Peasant Studies* 6(1):20-29.

Schnore, Leo
  1961   "The myth of human ecology." *Sociological Inquiry* 31(2):128–139.
Schurz, W.
  1939   *The Manila Galleon.* New York: E. P. Dutton & Company.
Scott, Allen J.
  1980   *The Urban Land Nexus and the State.* London: Pion.
Scott, J.
  1976   *The Moral Economy of the Peasant.* New Haven, Conn.: Yale University Press.
Security Pacific National Bank
  1981   *The Sixty Mile Circle: The Economy of the Greater Los Angeles Area* (Statistical
          Appendix). Los Angeles: Security Pacific National Bank, Public Affairs/
          Research Department.
Seidman, A.
  1981   "Women and the development of underdevelopment: The African experience
          (NAAS Selected Symposium No. 53). In R. Dauber and M. Cain (eds.), *Women
          and Technological Change in Developing Countries.* Boulder, Col.: West-
          view.
Senghaas-Knobloch, Eva
  1977   "Informal sector and peripheral capitalism: A critique of the prevailing concept
          of development." *Manpower and Unemployment Research* 10(2):3–34.
Shapiro, H.
  1980   "The many realities." *NACLA Report on the Americas* 14(5):2–13.
Siegel, L.
  1978–   "Orchestrating dependency." *Southeast Asia Chronicle 66—Pacific Research*
  1979   9:24–27.
Simkin, C. G. F.
  1968   *The Traditional Trade of Asia.* London: Oxford University Press.
Simms, R. and E. Dumor
  1976–   "Women in the urban economy of Ghana: Associational activity and the enclave
  1977   economy." *African Urban Notes* 2(3):43–64.
Singelmann, Joachim
  1978   *From Agriculture to Services: The Transformation of Industrial Employment.*
          Beverly Hills, Calif.: Sage.
Siverts, Henning
  1969   "Ethnic stability and boundary dynamics in southern Mexico. In F. Barth (ed.),
          Ethnic Groups and Boundaries. Boston: Little, Brown.
Skinner, G. William
  1971   "Chinese peasants and the closed community: An open and shut case." *Com-
          parative Studies in Society and History* 13:270–281.
  1977   "Regional urbanization in nineteenth-century China." In. G. W. Skinner
          (ed.), *The City in Late Imperial China.* Stanford, Calif.: Stanford University
          Press.
Skocpol, Theda
  1977   "Wallerstein's world capitalist system: A theoretical and historical critique."
          American Journal of Sociology 82:1075–1090.
Slater, David
  1978   "Towards a political economy of urbanization in peripheral capitalist societies."
          International Journal of Urban and Regional Research 2(1):26–52.
Smith, Carol A.
  1972   *The Domestic Marketing System in Western Guatemala: An Economic, Loca-
          tional, and Cultural Analysis.* Unpublished Ph.D. Dissertation, Stanford Uni-
          versity, Stanford, Calif.

1973 "La evolucion de los sistemas de marcado en el Occidente de Guatemala." *Estudios Sociales* (Guatemala) 10:38–71.
1975 "Examining stratification systems through peasant marketing arrangements." *Man* 10:95–122.
1976 "Regional economic systems: Linking geographical models and economic problems." In C. A. Smith (ed.), *Regional Analysis: Vol. 1. Economic Systems.* New York: Academic Press.
1978 "Beyond dependency theory: National and regional patterns of underdevelopment in Guatemala." *American Ethnologist* 5:574–617.
1982 "Modern and premodern urban primacy." *Current Urban Research* 9:79–96.
Smith, Michael P.
1984 *Cities in Transformation.* Berkeley, Calif.: Sage.
Smith, Waldemar
1977 *The Fiesta System and Economic Change.* New York: Columbia University Press.
Snyder, David and Edward Kick
1979 "Structural position in the world system and economic growth, 1955–1970: A multiple network analysis of transnational interaction." *American Journal of Sociology* 84:1097–1126.
Soares, Glaucio
1977 "The web of exploitation: State and peasants in Latin America." *Studies in Comparative International Development* 3:3–24.
Soja, Edward, Rebecca Morales, and Goetz Wolff
1983 "Urban restructuring: An analysis of social and spatial change in Los Angeles." *Economic Geography* 59(2):195–230.
Soja, Edward and Richard J. Tobin
1975 "The geography of modernization: Paths, patterns, and processes of spatial change in developing countries." In Brewer and Brunner (eds.), *Political Development and Change.* New York: Free Press.
Sokolovsky, J., J. Kentor, and P. Walters
1980 "Economic networks, political boundaries and city systems in the capitalist world-economy." Paper read at the Annual Meeting of the American Political Science Association, Washington, D.C.
Solorzano, F., Valentin
1963 *Historia de la evolucion economica de Guatemala.* Guatemala: Centro Editorial "José de Pineda Ibarra."
Stanback, Thomas M. Jr., Peter J. Bearse, Thierry J. Noyelle, and Robert Karasek
1981 *Services: The New Economy.* Montclair, N.J.: Allanheld, Osmun Publishers.
Stanback, Thomas M. Jr., and Thierry J. Noyelle
1982 *Cities in Transition: Changing Job Structures in Atlanta, Denver, Buffalo, Phoenix, Columbus (Ohio), Nashville, Charlotte.* Montclair, N.J.: Allanheld, Osmun Publishers.
Standing, G.
1978 *Labor Force Participation and Development.* Geneva: ILO.
Stavenhagen, Rodolfo
1969 *Social Classes in Agrarian Societies.* Garden City, N.Y.: Doubleday.
Stewart, C. T.
1960 "Migration as a function of population and distance." *American Sociological Review* 25:347–356.
Stigler, George
1951 "The division of labor is limited by the extent of the market." *Journal of Political Economy* 59(3):185–193.

Stolper, Wolfgang
  1955   "Spatial order and the economic growth of cities: A comment on Eric Lam-
            pard's paper." *Economic Development and Cultural Change* 3(January):137–
            146.
Stolte-Heiskanen, V.
  1977   "Fertility and women's employment outside the home in western Europe." In
            S. Kupinsky (ed.), *The Fertility of Working Women*. New York: Praeger.
Storper, Michael and David Walker
  1983   "The labor theory of location." *International Journal of Urban and Regional
            Research* 7(1):1–41.
Sudarkasa, N.
  1977   "Women and migration in contemporary West Africa." *Signs* 3(1):178–189.
Suh, S. C.
  1976   *Growth and Structural Changes in the Korean Economy, 1910–1940*. Cam-
            bridge, Mass.: Harvard University Press.
Sunkel, Osvaldo
  1973   "Transitional capitalism and national disintegration in Latin America." *Social
            and Economic Studies* 22:132–176.
Szalai, Alexander
  1965   "Cohesion indices for regional determination." *Papers of the Peace Research
            Society, Cracow Conference* 4:1–6.
Szymanski, Albert
  1981   *The Logic of Imperialism*. New York: Praeger.
Taaffe, E., R. Morrill, and P. Gould
  1963   "Transportation expansion in underdeveloped countries: A comparative anal-
            ysis." *Geographical Review* 53:503–529.
Timberlake, Michael
  1979   "The primate city and dependence." Paper presented at the Annual Meeting of
            the American Sociological Association, Boston.
Timberlake, Michael and Jeffrey Kentor
  1983   "Economic dependence, overurbanization and economic growth: A study of less
            developed countries." *The Sociological Quarterly* 24(4):489–507.
Tinker, I.
  1976   "The adverse impact of development on women." In I. Tinker and M. B. Bram-
            sen (eds.), *Women and World Development*. Washington D. C.: Overseas De-
            velopment Council.
Tinker, I. and M. Bramsen
  1976   *Women and World Development*. Washington, D.C.: Overseas Development
            Council.
Todaro, M.
  1981   *Economic Development in the Third World*. New York: Longman.
Torres Rivas, E.
  1971   *Interpretacion del Desarrollo Social Centroamericano*. San José: Educa.
Turner, John F. C.
  1968   "Uncontrolled urban settlement: problems and policies." *International Social
            Development Review* 1:107–130.
Tyree, Andrea, Moshe Semyonov, and Robert Hodge
  1979   "Gaps and glissandos: Inequality, economic development and social mobility in
            24 countries." *American Sociological Review* 44(3):410–424.
United Nations
  1960   *Demographic Yearbook*. New York: United Nations.

1968   *Demographic Yearbook.* New York: United Nations.

1969   *Growth of the World's Urban and Rural Population, 1920–2000* (Population Studies. No. 44). New York: U.N. Department of Economic and Social Affairs.

1970   *Demographic Yearbook.* New York: United Nations.

1973   *Demographic Yearbook.* New York: United Nations.

1977   *Demographic Yearbook.* New York: United Nations.

1980a   *Demographic Yearbook.* New York: United Nations.

1980b   *patterns of Urban and Rural Population Growth* (Population Studies #68). New York: U.N. Department of International Economic and Social Affairs.

1980c   "Review and evaluation of progress achieved in the implementation of the world plan of action: Employment." Paper prepared for the world conference of the United Nations Decade for Women. Copenhagen, Denmark, July 14–30. A/ CONF. 94/8.

1982   *Demographic Yearbook 1980.* New York: United Nations.

United Nations Centre on Transnational Corporations

1981   *Transnational Banks: Operations, Strategies, and Their Effects in Developing Countries.* New York: Centre on Transnational Corporations.

United Nations Economic Commission for Africa, Human Resources Development Division, African Training and Research Center for Women

1975   "Women and national development in African countries: Some profound contradictions." *African Studies Review* 18(3):47–70.

UNESCO

1956   *Report by the Director General on the Joint UN/UNESCO Seminar in Urbanization in the ECAFE Region.* Paris: UNESCO.

UNIDO (United Nations Industrial Development Organization)

1979   *World Industry Since 1960: Progress and Prospects.* Vienna: UNIDO, ID/ 229.

United States Bureau of the Census

1972   *Money Income of Households, Families and Persons in the United States, 1970.* Current Population Reports: Series P-60, No. 80. Washington, D.C.: U.S. Government Printing Office.

1976   *Survey of Income and Education, 1975.* Washington, D.C.: Government Printing Office.

1979   *"County Business Patterns, California, 1977* (CBP-77-6). Washington, D.C.: U.S. Government Printing Office.

1979   *County Business Patterns, Michigan, 1977* (CBP-77-24). Washington, D.C.: U.S. Government Printing Office.

1979   *County Business Patterns, New York, 1977* (CBP-77-24). Washington, D.C.: U.S. Government Printing Office.

1980   *Statistical Abstract of the United States.* Washington, D.C.: Government Printing Office.

1982   *County Business Patterns, California, 1980* (CBP-80-6). Washington, D.C.: U.S. Government Printing Office.

1982   *County Business Patterns, Michigan, 1980* (CBP-80-24). Washington, D.C.: U.S. Government Printing Office.

1982   *County Business Patterns, New York, 1980* (CBP-80-34). Washington, D.C.: U.S. Government Printing Office.

1982   *Money Income of Households, Families and Persons in the United States, 1980.* Current Population Reports: Series P-60, No. 132. Washington, D.C.: U.S. Government Printing Office.

1983   *Advance Estimates of Social, Economic and Housing Characteristics, California, 1980.* Part 6. Washington D.C.: U.S. Government Printing Office.

1983   *Advance Estimates of Social, Economic and Housing Characteristics, Michigan, 1980.* Part 24. Washington D.C.: U.S. Government Printing Office.

1983   *Advance Estimates of Social, Economic and Housing Characteristics, New York, 1980.* Part 34. Washington D.C.: U.S. Government Printing Office.

1983   *County Business Patterns, California, 1981* (CBP–81–6). Washington, D.C.: U.S. Government Printing Office.

1983   *County Business Patterns, Michigan, 1981* (CBP–81–24). Washington, D.C.: U.S. Government Printing Office.

1983   *County Business Patterns, New York, 1981* (CBP–81–34). Washington, D.C.: U.S. Government Printing Office.

United States Bureau of Labor Statistics

1980   *News* (various months). New York City: Middle Atlantic Region of the Bureau of Labor Statistics, U.S. Department of Labor. Washington D.C.: U.S. Government Printing Office.

1981   *News* (various months). New York City: Middle Atlantic Region of the Bureau of Labor Statistics, U.S. Department of Labor. Washington, D.C.: U.S. Government Printing Office.

United States Department of Commerce

1980   *Current Developments in U.S. International Services Industries.* Washington, D.C.: International Trade Administration.

United States Senate, Committee on Banking, Housing and Urban Affairs

1982   *Foreign Barriers to U.S. Trade: Service Exports.* U.S. Senate, 97th Congress, Hearing before the Subcommittee on International Finance and Monetary Policy of the Committee on Banking, Housing, and Urban Affairs. Washington, D.C.: U.S. Senate.

Uzzell, Douglas

1974   "The interaction of population and locality in the development of squatter settlements in Lima." In Wayne A. Cornelius and Felicity M. Trueblood (eds.), *Latin American Urban Research* (Vol. 4). Beverly Hills, Calif.: Sage.

Van Allen, J.

1976   "African women, 'modernization,' and national liberation." In L. Iglitzin and R. Ross (eds.), *Women in the World: A Comparative Study.* Santa Barbara, Calif.: Clio.

Van Roy, E.

1971   *Economic Systems of Northern Thailand: Structure and Change.* Ithaca, N.Y.: Cornell University Press.

Vapnarsky, Cesar A.

1966   *Rank-Size Distributions of Cities in Argentina.* Unpublished M.A. Thesis, Cornell University, Ithaca, N.Y.

1969   "On rank-size distributions of cities: An ecological approach." *Economic Development and Cultural Change* 17(July):584–595.

1975   "The Argentine system of cities: Primacy and rank-size rule." In J. Hardoy (ed.), *Urbanization in Latin America: Approaches and Issues.* Garden City, N.Y.: Anchor.

Vernon, Raymond

1977   *Storm over the Multinationals.* Cambridge, Mass.: Harvard University Press.

Wachtel, E.

1976   "Minding her own business: Women shopkeepers in Nakuru, Kenya." *African Urban Notes* 2(2):27–42.

Waldinger, Roger
  Forth-   "Immigration and Industrial Change in the New York Apparel Industry." In
  coming   George J. Borjas and Marta Tienda (eds.), *Hispanics in the U.S. Economy.* New
            York: Academic Press.
Wallerstein, Immanuel
  1974   *The Modern World-System I: Capitalist Agriculture and the Origins of the Eu-
            ropean World-Economy in the Sixteenth Century.* New York: Academic Press.
  1976   "Semi-peripheral countries and the contemporary world crisis." *Theory and So-
            ciety* 3:461–484.
  1977   "Rural economy in modern world society." *Studies in Comparative Interna-
            tional Development* 12:29–40.
  1978   "World-system analysis: Theoretical and interpretive issues." In Kaplan (ed.),
            Social Change in the Capitalist World Economy. Beverly Hills, Calif.: Sage.
  1979a   *The Capitalist World-Economy.* New York: Cambridge University Press.
  1979b   "The rise and future demise of the world capitalist system." In *The Capitalist
            World-Economy.* New York: Cambridge University Press.
  1980   *The Modern World-System II: Mercantilism and the Consolidation of the Eu-
            ropean World-Economy, 1600–1750.* New York: Academic Press.
Wallerstein, Immanuel and Terence Hopkins
  1977   "Patterns of development of the modern world-system." *Review* 1:111–145.
Wallerstein, I. and W. Martin
  1979   "Peripheralization of southern Africa II: Changes in household structure and
            labor-force formation." *Review* 3(2):193–210.
Walton, John
  1974   "Internal Colonialism: Problems of Definition and Measurement." Paper pre-
            sented to the Northwestern University Faculty Seminar on Comparative Urban
            Studies. Northwestern University, Evanston, Ill., November 6.
  1975   "Internal colonialism: Problems of definition and measurement." In W. A.
            Cornelius and F. M. Trueblood (eds.), *Urbanization and Inequality.* Beverly
            Hills, Calif.: Sage.
  1976a   "Elites and the politics of development: A comparative study of four cities."
            In Alejandro Portes and John Walton (eds.), *Urban Latin America: The Polit-
            ical Condition from Above and Below.* Austin: University of Texas.
  1976b   "Political economy of world urban systems: Directions for comparative re-
            search." In J. Walton and L. H. Masotti (eds.), *The City in Comparative Per-
            spective: Cross-National Research and New Directions in Theory.* New York:
            Halstead Press.
  1976c   "Structures of power in Latin American cities." In Portes and Walton, *Urban
            Latin America.* Austin: University of Texas Press.
  1976d   "Urban hierarchies and patterns of dependence in Latin America: Theoretical
            bases for a new research agenda." In Portes, A. and H. L. Browning (eds.),
            Current Perspectives on Latin American Urban Research. Austin: University of
            Texas Press.
  1977   "Accumulation and comparative urban systems: Theory and some tentative con-
            trasts of Latin America and Africa." *Comparative Urban Research* 5(1):5–18.
  1979a   "From cities to systems: Recent research on Latin American urbanization." *Latin
            American Research Review* 14:159–169.
  1979b   "Urban political economy: A new paradigm." *Comparative Urban Research*
            7(1):5–17.
  1981   "The new urban sociology." *International Social Science Journal* 33(2):374–
            390.

Ward, K.
1983   "The economic status of women in the world-system: A hidden crisis in development." In A. Bergesen (ed.), *Crises in the World-System*. Beverly Hills, Calif.: Sage.
1984a   *Women in the World-System*. New York: Praeger.
1984b   "The world economic system and the global assembly line: Some implications for women's economic status during development." Paper presented at the annual Meeting of the Midwest Sociological Society, Chicago, April.

Wardwell, John M.
1980   "Toward a theory of urban-rural migration in the developed world." In David L. Brown and John M. Wardwell (eds.), *New Directions in Urban-Rural Migration: The Population Turnaround in Rural America*. New York: Academic Press.

Warren, Bill
1980   *Imperialism: Pioneer of Capitalism*. London: Verso.

Weber, Adna
1967   *The Growth of Cities in the Nineteenth Century: A Study in Statistics*. Ithaca, N.Y.: Cornell University.

Weber, Max
1958   *The City*. New York: Free Press.

Weiss, A.
1982   "Women and factory work in Punjab, Pakistan." Paper presented at the Meetings of the American Sociological Association, San Francisco, September.

Weiss, J., F. Ramirez and T. Tracy
1976   "Female participation in the occupational system: A comparative institutional analysis." *Social Problems* 23:593–608.

Wernstedt, F., and J. Spencer
1967   *The Philippines Island World: A Physical, Cultural, and Regional Geography*. Berkeley: University of California Press.

Whetten, Nathan
1961   *Guatemala: The Land and the People*. New Haven, Conn.: Yale University Press.

Whichard, Obie G.
1981   "U.S. direct investment abroad in 1980." *Survey of Current Business* 61(8): 20–39.
1982   "U.S. direct investment abroad in 1981." *Survey of Current Business* 62(8): 11–29.

Williams, Kristen
1981   *The Relationships Between Wages and Development*. Unpublished doctoral dissertation, Department of Social Relations, Johns Hopkins University, Baltimore, Md.

Williamson, Oliver
1980   "Transaction costs economics: The governance of contractual relations." *Journal of Law and Economics* 22(2):233–261.

Wilson, Kenneth L. and Alejandro Portes
1980   "The immigrant enclave." *American Journal of Sociology* 86:295–319.

Winson, Anthony
1978   "Class structure and agrarian transition in Central America." *Latin American Perspectives* 5:27–48.

Wolff, Goetz
1984   *The Decline of Unionization and the Growth of Employment in the Los Angeles*

Region. Graduate School of Architecture and Urban Planning, University of California, Los Angeles.

World Bank
  1978   *Guatemala: Economic and Social Position and Prospects*. Washington, D.C.: World Bank.
  1980   *World Development Report*. Washington: IBRD.

Wood, L. E.
  1977   *South Korea: Geographic Change Through Planning*. Unpublished master's thesis, University of North Carolina, Chapel Hill.

Woodward, R. L.
  1966   *Class Privilege and Economic Development: The Consulado de Comercio of Guatemala, 1793–1871*. Chapel Hill: University of North Carolina Press.

Wrigley, E. A.
  1978   "A simple model of London's importance in changing English society and economy 1650–1750." In Philip Abrams and E. A. Wrigley (eds.), *Towns and Societies: Essays in Economic History and Historical Sociology*. New York: Cambridge University Press.

Yang, M.
  1945   *A Chinese Village*. New York: Columbia University Press.

Youssef, N.
  1971   "Social structure and the female labor force: The case of women workers in Muslim Middle Eastern countries." *Demography* 8(4):427–439.
  1974   *Women and Work in Developing Societies*. Berkeley: University of California Press.
  1976   "Women in development: Urban life and labor." In I. Tinker and M. Bramsen (eds.), *Women and World Development*. Washington, D.C.: Overseas Development Council.

Zarate, Alvan O.
  1967   "Principales patrones de migracion interna en Guatemala, 1964." *Estudios Centroamericanos* (No. 3). Guatemala: Seminario de Integracion Social.

Zipf, George K.
  1941   *National Unity and Disunity*. Bloomington, Ind.: Principia Press.
  1949   *Human Behavior and the Principle of Least Effort: An Introduction to Human Ecology*. Reading, Pa.: Addison-Wesley.

INDEX

STUDIES IN SOCIAL DISCONTINUITY
(Continued from page ii)